Societies after Slavery

Societies

after Slavery

*A Select Annotated Bibliography
of Printed Sources on Cuba, Brazil,
British Colonial Africa, South Africa,
and the British West Indies*

Rebecca J. Scott, Thomas C. Holt,
Frederick Cooper, and Aims McGuinness
EDITORS

UNIVERSITY OF PITTSBURGH PRESS

Published by the University of Pittsburgh Press, Pittsburgh, Pa., 15260

Copyright © 2002, Postemancipation Societies Project

Manufactured in the United States of America

Printed on acid-free paper

10 9 8 7 6 5 4 3 2 1

Library of Congress Cataloging-in-Publication Data

Societies after slavery : a select annotated bibliography of printed
sources on Cuba, Brazil, British colonial Africa, South Africa, and the
British West Indies.

     p.   cm. — (Pitt Latin American studies)

  ISBN 0-8229-4184-8 (cloth : alk. paper)

   1. Slaves—Emancipation—Bibliography. 2. Freedmen—Bibliography.
I. Pitt Latin American series.

  Z7164.S6 S64 2002

  [HT1037]

  016.326'8—dc21   2002000353

Societies after Slavery

Contents

Preface

In one society after another in the nineteenth century, slavery gave way in the face of attacks by abolitionists, changes in the world economy, wartime turmoil, and the initiatives of slaves themselves. Once slavery was gone, however, the struggle to determine what would replace it had just begun. Emancipation constituted, in effect, a historically privileged moment, one in which fundamental questions were raised and alternatives were explored. In the United States South, the Caribbean, Brazil, and Africa the meaning of "free labor" was contested not only among theoreticians and political economists but also among laborers and employers. The resolutions of their struggles—often contingent and provisional—cast a long shadow into the present, informing understandings of the meaning of freedom and citizenship and shaping the economic evolution of the societies in question.

Since the 1950s, the study of slavery has become one of the most productive fields within North American and Latin American history and, more recently, within African history as well. Much of the pioneering work of comparative history focused on slavery. With the maturation of slavery studies, however, scholars began to ask new questions about emancipation and the transition to freedom. It has become clear that the study of societies after slavery raises fundamental questions about worldwide economic changes, the international discussion of the meaning of free labor, the connections between national politics and global ideological currents, the evolution of systems of race relations, and the possibilities and constraints confronting former slaves and other rural workers.[1]

Enslavement, by its nature, took people across boundaries: slaves were those stripped of their social connections and therefore vulnerable to whatever uses captors or purchasers had in mind. The rise of the Atlantic system from the sixteenth century onward took this already familiar phenomenon to new dimensions, tying together three continents

1. For a detailed discussion of these issues, see Frederick Cooper, Thomas C. Holt, and Rebecca J. Scott, *Beyond Slavery: Explorations of Race, Labor, and Citizenship in Post-emancipation Societies* (Chapel Hill: University of North Carolina Press, 2000).

and shaping powerful networks and structures for the enslavement and transportation of people. The development of commercial agriculture and industrial capitalism in Europe, the enslavement of people in Africa, and the founding of large-scale units of agricultural production in the Americas linked distant parts of the world with unprecedented intensity.

The unraveling of this system was an equally international process. The abolitionists of the early nineteenth century posed the problem of slavery in terms of universal moral principles. In all the regions covered in this bibliography, debates about abolition hinged on the relationship of such a universalistic discourse to the particularities of regional politics and economic interests. All parties to these debates struggled over the power to frame moral issues and the power to act in the face of the conflicting wills of slaveowners, slaves, and others.

In the 1790s, the slaves of Saint Domingue seized an opening brought about by the struggles surrounding the French Revolution and by the possibility of turning a French discourse about the rights of man into a powerful claim for freedom for themselves. This was, in effect, the first emancipation, and other world powers did their best to contain the impact of the world's first society after slavery.[2] In the early nineteenth century, Great Britain, once the biggest slaving power of them all, became caught up in a debate about the political and moral viability of slavery. In the British West Indies, slaves were also actors in their own emancipation, and their collective actions in the early 1830s helped to turn an escalating political argument into an immediate necessity to act. By then, France, Spain, and Brazil were being confronted with the effects of international abolitionist movements as well.

From the Haitian Revolution onward, prior experiences of postemancipation society—as interpreted by opposing sides—became touchstones for evaluating the supposed capacity of former slaves to work for wages and emblems of the possibilities and dangers of broadening social and political participation by the descendants of slaves. The formal abolitions of slavery—1848 in the French colonies, the Civil War years in the southern United States, 1880–86 in Cuba, and 1888 in Brazil—were part of multifaceted struggles whose implications for economic, political, and social life would be played out in varied and interconnected ways. In each

2. Some slaves had been freed by general emancipation in a few New England states in the 1780s, following the American Revolution. But the number and circumstances were not comparable to those of Saint Domingue in the 1790s. See Ira Berlin, *Many Thousands Gone: The First Two Centuries of Slavery in North America* (Cambridge: Harvard University Press, 1998).

case, understanding the relationship of national politics, international pressure, and slave mobilization remains a complex historical problem.

By the end of the nineteenth century, European conquests of Africa were bringing to the fore a new set of issues. Colonizing powers had to decide what to do about indigenous forms of slavery, which in many places had been intensified in previous decades as the end of the European-led slave trade made slave labor more available and the rising demand in Europe for tropical products made slave production more attractive. But if the possibility of slave emancipation provided a rationale for colonization in Africa, actually implementing it would prove an ambiguous process, in which slaves would once again be important actors and whose course over the ensuing decades would lead in different directions.

This combination of diversity and interconnection makes the subject of this bibliography a difficult one to grasp. Since the pioneering work of W. E. B. Du Bois, C. L. R. James, and Eric Williams in the 1930s and 1940s, historians have been aware that slavery and emancipation were worldwide phenomena, impossible to understand from a single spatial location. From the 1940s to the present, the comparative study of slavery within the Atlantic system (and to a more limited extent beyond it) has been a rich field of scholarship. Ambitious attempts to reevaluate the dynamics of slavery across the entire Atlantic system have been made, but the process of emancipation has been much less studied in a comparative and integrated context. Even some of the most influential attempts to explain variations in patterns of race relations in contemporary societies preferred to find answers in the differences among slave systems rather than in the postemancipation decades that intervened.[3]

3. Crucial early works with a systematic approach include W. E. B. Du Bois, *Black Reconstruction: An Essay Toward a History of the Part which Black Folk Played in the Attempt to Reconstruct Democracy in America, 1860–1880* (Philadelphia: A. Saifer, 1935); C. L. R. James, *The Black Jacobins: Toussaint L'Ouverture and the San Domingo Revolution*, 2d ed. (New York, Vintage Books, 1963); and Eric Williams, *Capitalism and Slavery* (Chapel Hill: University of North Carolina Press, 1944). Influential and explicitly comparative works on slavery begin with Frank Tannenbaum, *Slave and Citizen: The Negro in the Americas* (New York: Vintage Books, 1946), and include Carl Degler, *Neither Black nor White: Slavery and Race Relations in Brazil and the United States* (New York: Macmillan, 1971); Peter Kolchin, *Unfree Labor: American Slavery and Russian Serfdom* (Cambridge: Belknap Press of Harvard University Press, 1987); and the works excerpted in Laura Foner and Eugene Genovese, *Slavery in the New World: A Reader in Comparative History* (Englewood Cliffs, N.J.: Prentice-Hall, 1969). Recent comparative and systematic works on emancipation include Eric Foner, *Nothing but Freedom: Eman-*

As the present editors have argued elsewhere, historians have had more difficulty confronting the diverse meanings of "freedom" than they have had in comparing different meanings of "slavery."[4] There are fine studies of the impact of the ending of slavery in particular contexts, most of them written within the past two decades, and we have cited as many as possible of these in the bibliography that follows. Explicitly comparative studies remain rare.

World history and comparative history are more easily invoked than done. Historical scholarship, for good reason, emphasizes the specifics of time and place and, above all, the finding of primary sources and their interpretation in the light of particular contexts. The entries in *Societies after Slavery* are designed to lower the barriers to undertaking comparative research and to make it possible for such comparison to employ primary documentation as well as secondary sources. They can also suggest new documentary sources for use in teaching, particularly for courses that undertake the ambitious challenge of an Atlantic Studies or other systemic approach to the history of Europe, Africa, and the Americas.[5]

The printed primary documentation is in fact rich, and it allows one to focus on comparable phenomena in different regions and at different historical moments: on work relations, social relations, and community in the aftermath of slavery. Our principal goal has been to identify primary material that can be found in major research libraries or can be accessed through interlibrary loan from any university library or public library participating in a research consortium. The primary printed

---

cipation and its Legacy (Baton Rouge: Louisiana State University Press, 1983); Robin Blackburn, *The Overthrow of Colonial Slavery, 1776–1848* (London: Verso Books, 1988); Seymour Drescher, *Capitalism and Antislavery: British Mobilization in Comparative Perspective* (New York: Oxford University Press, 1996), and *From Slavery to Freedom: Comparative Studies in the Rise and Fall of Atlantic Slavery* (New York: New York University Press, 1999); as well as the collection of essays edited by Drescher and Frank McGlynn, *The Meaning of Freedom: Economics, Politics, and Culture After Slavery* (Pittsburgh: University of Pittsburgh Press, 1992), and that edited by Mary Turner, *From Chattel Slaves to Wage Slaves: The Dynamics of Labour Bargaining in the Americas* (Bloomington, Ind.: Indiana University Press, 1995). See also *Slavery and Abolition* 21 (August 2000), a special issue entitled "After Slavery: Emancipation and its Discontents," with an introduction and edited by Howard Temperley.

4. Cooper, Holt, Scott, *Beyond Slavery*.

5. See the discussion stimulated by David Brion Davis in "Crossing Slavery's Boundaries," a forum with contributions by Davis, Peter Kolchin, Rebecca J. Scott, and Stanley L. Engerman in the *American Historical Review* 105 (April 2000): 451–84.

---

sources of the nineteenth and early twentieth centuries include parliamentary and congressional hearings and inquiries, reports of governmental and international agencies, missionary records, published census reports, correspondence published in the context of contemporary debates, personal memoirs, surveys, autobiographies, early sociological and ethnographic studies, and transcriptions of oral interviews.

Obviously, these bibliographies are not exhaustive—they cannot include every traveler who observed social relations in each corner of Brazil or Nigeria and cannot capture the diversity (and limitations) of archival resources. They nonetheless allow a student to begin a seminar paper or embark on a dissertation project with a good sense of the range of possibilities in published primary sources. We also hope that comparativists will use our references to extend research beyond areas most familiar to them, allowing them to gain an entrée into primary sources and get a feel for the differing points of view on the emancipation process in different historical contexts. The bibliography will allow scholars to investigate connections across regions, to look, for example, for echoes of the British West Indian emancipation struggles of the 1830s in the Spanish Caribbean in the 1880s or in the newly conquered colonies of British Africa in the 1890s.

With respect to the temporal coverage of the societies under consideration, we have been expansive, including not only sources that concern postemancipation developments but also items relating to the process of emancipation itself—especially when there was a period of apprenticeship or other intermediate status between the initial steps to end slavery and the completion of legal emancipation. The beginning date of each section is therefore particular to that section. At the same time, in order to capture the economic and social transformations that followed emancipation, the editors have extended the period of focus beyond the immediate postemancipation years, generally to around 1930. The bibliography thus covers a considerable span of emancipations, with the British occupying both the vanguard (after Haiti), in their West Indian colonies, and the rear, in Sierra Leone in 1927. (This range would, indeed, become even wider if one were to begin as one logically should, with Saint Domingue. But we have deferred on the task of assembling French-language sources to a team of Francophone colleagues, as we explain below.)

We have also been inclusive in our judgment as to those social groups whose experiences should be taken into account in the scholarly analysis of societies after slavery. The bibliography encompasses sources dealing not only with former slaves and former slaveowners but with other members of slaveholding societies whose lives were reshaped by emancipation. These include, for example, smallholders who were counted white, indentured laborers, people of color who had been free before the general emancipation, and immigrant workers. Our selection of sources comprises different aspects of the relationship of slavery to colonization and decolonization; it includes multiple crop production systems, including those on a plantation scale and those based on the extension of familial systems; and it includes a wide range of judicial systems and different forms of regulating marriage, land tenure, and inheritance.

Because slavery in the societies under consideration had been primarily a system of agricultural labor and because these societies remained predominantly agricultural for some time following emancipation, the bibliography concentrates on rural social transformations rather than urban developments. Sources that examine the interaction between rural and urban settings are included, but those sources that focus exclusively on urban life are generally not cited. This distinction, of course, is somewhat artificial, given the increased mobility that generally accompanied emancipation. But given our constraints of space, we have chosen to give preference to the rural over the urban. We hope that our colleagues carrying out innovative work on emancipation in cities, in places such as Brazil and the United States South, will excuse us.[6]

As one defines the problematic of postemancipation societies more and more broadly, the web of useful primary sources extends toward the infinite. And as this problematic attracts the attention of increasing numbers of researchers, the web of secondary sources also expands exponentially. In the last months before the text was submitted to the press, a half-dozen new books, articles, and review essays on Cuba came to hand, enabling us to provide a few new entries as of early 2001—but reminding us that key items will surely appear too late for inclusion. We can only hope that our compilation will please students and other scholars for the paths it opens up and that we will be forgiven for items overlooked or eliminated in the effort to remain concise. We are well aware, for example, that scholars in Brazil are uncovering sources and offering interpretations at an accelerating rate and that we have only captured a fraction of that production. But a glimpse of that fraction should stimulate scholars of other areas to pursue these leads vigorously and to be

6. See, for example, Sidney Chalhoub, *Visões da liberdade: uma história das últimas décadas da escravidão na Corte* (São Paulo: Companhia das Letras, 1990), and the work of Elsa Barkeley Brown on Richmond, Virginia, including her doctoral dissertation, "Uncle Ned's Children: Negotiating Community and Freedom in Postemancipation Richmond, Virginia" (Ph.D. diss., Kent State University, 1994).

alert to the excellent theses and essays emerging from such institutions as the State University at Campinas and the Federal University of Bahia in Salvador as well as the universities of Rio de Janeiro, Niterói, and São Paulo.

Nearly all of the printed primary sources cited in this volume have been annotated, and our annotations are designed to describe particular features and point the way to possible uses of the source. We do not attempt fully comprehensive annotations of sources encompassing large amounts of material, such as censuses. Instead, we focus on those aspects of the data that seem to us to be particularly promising for the study of societies after slavery. All of our annotations were composed by the editors or by advanced doctoral students, and they reflect our individual judgments on the potential value of different kinds of material.

The areas reviewed are ones for which a substantial printed primary and secondary literature exists in English, Spanish, or Portuguese, with occasional sources in French or German.[7] We have annotated the secondary sources written in languages other than English to encourage scholars to seek out these less-easily available works. In most of the sections, however, we did not fully annotate secondary sources published in English, given their relatively easy availability, although we often briefly note their geographical and chronological focus. Individual section editors have adjusted these guidelines to fit the particular needs of their sections, however, and describe in their introductions the conventions they have followed. In a few cases, for example, we have retained somewhat longer annotations that were prepared early in the compilation process, and in the one section whose sources were all in English—that on the British West Indies—some categories of relatively accessible primary sources were left unannotated.

The selection of geographical regions to be covered reflects both conscious choice and accidents of scholarly connections. Like all collaborative projects, this bibliography itself has a history. It began as a modest guide to sources for the students in a graduate seminar taught by Rebecca Scott and Thomas Holt at the University of Michigan in 1985. It expanded as Scott, Holt, and Frederick Cooper, with the collaboration

---

7. The coverage of Africa here is focused on the British colonies in part because the readily available *British Parliamentary Papers* constitute a rich base for departure. The comparable sources in the French case are in the archives in Dakar, but only a small portion of them are available on microfilm. A recent book by Martin Klein also provides comprehensive coverage and a valuable bibliography on French West Africa. See Martin A. Klein, *Slavery and Colonial Rule in French West Africa* (Cambridge: Cambridge University Press, 1998).

in the early years of Barbara J. Fields, constituted the University of Michigan Postemancipation Societies Project. Neil Foley and Barbara Ransby began to add sources and prepare annotations, and Leslie Rowland visited the project to develop a parallel section on the United States South. The seminar was offered in several subsequent years by Rebecca Scott and Frederick Cooper, and the geographical shape of a formal bibliography began to become clear. Ada Ferrer soon took on joint responsibility with Rebecca Scott for the Cuba section and developed many of the entries and annotations as she carried out her own doctoral research. Alejandra Bronfman and Kathleen Lopez added annotations, as did Aims McGuinness and Javier Morillo-Alicea. Melinda Campbell at the University of Chicago collaborated with Thomas Holt to seek out and annotate items on the British West Indies, as did Lisa Lindsay, Jill Dupont, and Tim Scarnecchia. Tim Scarnecchia and Lisa Lindsay also worked with Fred Cooper on the Africa sections, and Pamela Scully took on the compilation of a section on South Africa, later updated by Kerry Ward. Many of the entries on central Africa emerged from the research of César Solá-García, which began as a seminar paper and ended in the dissertation listed in the section on British Colonial Africa. The Brazil section, initiated by Rebecca Scott, was much enriched by the labors of João José Reis and Judith Allen, with further annotations by Lara Putnam, Aims McGuinness, and Karl Monsma. It also benefited from the helpful commentary of numerous colleagues in Brazil, including Sidney Chalhoub, Hebe Maria Mattos, Silvia Lara, Keila Grinberg, and Ana Maria Lugão Rios. We anticipate that an expanded version of the Brazil section will be published in Portuguese, perhaps under the auspices of colleagues at the Federal University of Bahia, the State University at Campinas, and the Universidade Federal Fluminense in Niterói.

Leslie Rowland, director of the Freedom History Project at the University of Maryland, took on the major responsibility for the bibliography on the United States South and also established many of the conventions and procedures for selection and annotation in *Societies after Slavery* as a whole. What began as the United States section of this work, however, has grown to constitute a large bibliographic compilation in itself, one that will be completed separately under Rowland's editorship. It has its own large supporting cast, whose work will be acknowledged in that volume.

All of the editors agreed on the importance of Haiti and the French West Indies, but we lacked the primary research experience necessary to assemble such a section. Myriam Cottias, Laurent Dubois, and Carlo

Celius took on this task and are preparing a bibliography on the Francophone Caribbean. That bibliography will also appear as a separate publication, in this case in French. Certain other geographic areas are not included in this volume, though they might be in an ideal bibliography. We hope that our efforts may stimulate new compilations by specialists on those regions.

The main contributors of annotations are indicated at the beginning of each section. Throughout the project, additional graduate students from the University of Michigan, including Michael Schroeder, Mark Patrick, Catherine Kaplan, Kerry Ward, and Kathleen Lopez helped locate sources and contributed annotations, as did Alejandra Bronfman from Princeton University and Hannah Rosen and Steve Essig from the University of Chicago. Many of the graduate student contributors now hold faculty positions, and we hope they will find that this work repays the effort they invested in it as students. We owe special thanks as well to the doctoral students who participated in various phases of the postemancipation seminar at the University of Michigan and in comparable seminars offered by Thomas Holt and Julie Saville at the University of Chicago. The Postemancipation Project itself was kept on track by a series of capable graduate assistants, beginning with Neil Foley, continuing with Ada Ferrer, Lisa Lindsay, and Javier Morillo-Alicea, and ending with Aims McGuinness.

In the final years of preparing the text for publication, Aims McGuinness became a fellow editor of the volume, writing numerous annotations for several of the sections, making difficult decisions about inclusions and exclusions, and exercising his scholarly judgment as he guided the manuscript through to completion. The other three editors are very much in his debt and are grateful for his willingness to devote time to this project as he was in the midst of completing a dissertation that dealt with questions of race and popular liberalism in areas entirely outside the scope of this bibliography.

Jeanette Diuble did yeoman work as a typist in the last stages. We also owe a special debt to the Interlibrary Loan Department of the University Library at the University of Michigan and particularly to Sharon Johnson, who did a remarkable job of tracking down hard-to-find sources located in libraries across the United States.

Work on this bibliography has been supported by the Kellogg Foundation, through a grant to the Presidential Initiatives Fund of the University of Michigan, and by the Rackham Graduate School, the Center for Afroamerican and African Studies (including grants to CAAS from the Ford Foundation), and the Office of the Vice President for Research of the University of Michigan. Work has also been made possible by grants to individual editors from the John D. and Catherine T. MacArthur Foundation and from the College of Literature, Science, and the Arts of the University of Michigan. We express our thanks to all of these organizations and particularly to the Center for Afroamerican and African Studies at Michigan for providing a home for this project for more than a decade. Directors Thomas Holt, Lemuel Johnson, Earl Lewis, Michael Awkward, Sharon Patton, and James Jackson, as well as Associate Director Evans Young and Program Administrator Gerry Brewer, have provided crucial moral, administrative, and financial support.

We dedicate this volume to students past and future, in recognition of the ways in which pedagogy and research have stimulated each other throughout this project.

I

British West Indies

EDITOR

Thomas C. Holt
University of Chicago

COMPILED BY

Thomas C. Holt

Melinda Campbell
Chadds Ford, Pennsylvania

Jill Dupont
University of North Texas

Steve Essig
Chicago, Illinois

Lisa Lindsay
University of North Carolina-Chapel Hill

Timothy Scarnecchia
Washington, D.C.

INTRODUCTION

Slave emancipation came to the British West Indies at a critical moment in the history of slavery in the Americas. The preeminent world power in the middle decades of the nineteenth century, Britain had intermittently exerted its influence to interdict the slave trade. Likewise, when it abolished slavery itself in the British colonies in 1833, Britain indirectly brought pressure on others to follow suit. In addition, British antislavery advocates influenced and supported abolitionists in other nations—most notably in the United States—and their eventual success encouraged renewed efforts elsewhere. They helped define abolition not simply as an issue of moral rectitude but as the dividing line between civilization and human progress, on one side, and the morally benighted and the socially backward, on the other. Such convictions not only produced a sense of emancipation as one of the great divides in the course of human history but also focused popular and governmental attention on the minutest details of its progress and on its consequences. Moreover, British emancipation involved an interim period of apprenticeship during which slaves freed de jure in 1833 would be prepared for complete emancipation de facto in 1838. All of this stimulated an intense examination of the evolution of free labor, of the evolution of free institutions, and of the fate of sugar cultivation.

Though the most intense period of this extraordinary attention was the 1830s and early 1840s, the story of slavery's destruction and its aftermath continued to unfold well into the twentieth century. One might well carry that story forward to colonial independence in 1962 or at least to the beginning of the process of decolonization in the 1940s. We have ended this bibliography in 1930, however, for the simple and pragmatic reason that the labor unrest and political contestation during the years of the Great Depression constitute an era deserving and requiring a bibliographic guide of their own.

For Anglophone readers, the British West Indian case is the most familiar of the emancipation stories in the Americas; the editorial decisions for this section reflect that judgment. Not only is there a large and constantly growing secondary literature, but there are several good bibliographies of primary and secondary sources, of particular societies and subjects, and even of other bibliographies. For one of our primary audiences—beginning doctoral and graduate seminar students—a quick entry into these resources (many of which are listed and annotated here) is essential for defining and refining research topics and locating the most easily accessible resources for conducting research. The bibliographic guides listed here provide access to an extensive listing of sources on almost any relevant topic down to the early 1980s. Our annotated list of secondary works in turn, although by no means comprehensive or complete, gives convenient access to sources on most topics and to historiographical debates about those topics as well. Students can thus learn of potentially interesting subjects to research and get more than a "good start" on relevant topics.

In the British West Indies section we have listed the most prominent and accessible printed primary sources, but we have not annotated them. The most voluminous and useful of these sources, perhaps, are journals, descriptive accounts by travelers, and the political pamphlets issued to protest or persuade contemporaries about various issues of the day. Often the very titles of the pamphlet literature convey a good sense of their content and point of view. By their very nature, journals and travelers' accounts—being episodic and impressionistic—are not well-served by brief synopses. A researcher is likely to turn to them less for an objective account of developments than for their chance observations, the revealing incident, or the striking personality the traveler encounters in his or her journey. A separate, comprehensive bibliography of travel literature for Latin America and the Caribbean, by Thomas Welch and Myriam Figueras, is listed in the bibliographies section below. Though not itself an annotated bibliography, it provides quotations and other descriptive material about its entries.

In our judgment the most important, and perhaps the most underutilized, printed primary sources for the West Indies are the *British Parliamentary Papers*, and we have concentrated our attention on annotating these. Although good finding aids exist for these documents, as noted below, this is a case where the titles of the documents often do not fully convey their content. Ostensibly generated to inform the legislative and oversight processes of Parliament, these papers consist of a variety of materials. At their most basic they are the exchange of correspondence between colonial governors and the Colonial Office, together with supporting documentation, like economic and population statistics, field reports of various government agents, and the letters, petitions, and testimony of planters, freedpeople, and other parties to disputes. Occasionally there are special reports, especially those by Royal Commissions, that provide an even greater abundance of systematic documentation on population, politics, labor and economics, and social life and conflicts. Given their importance, and their general accessibility, we have given extensive scope to the coverage and annotation of these documents. We believe that even advanced scholars will find this section helpful in developing their research agendas. The *British Parliamentary Papers* are available in printed or microform copies in many university libraries and through interlibrary loan. The Irish University Press has also issued a selected reprinting of the collection.

Thomas C. Holt

BIBLIOGRAPHIES, HISTORIOGRAPHICAL ESSAYS, AND INDEXES

1. Augier, F. R., and Shirley C. Gordon, comps. *Sources of West Indian History*. London: Longmans, 1962. 308 p.

   Consists of a collection of accounts selected from a variety of primary documents and is intended primarily "for use in the senior forms of secondary schools" to illustrate and inform about various aspects of Caribbean life and history. Includes sections on economic life, government and politics, religion and education before emancipation, slavery and its abolition, emancipation and apprenticeship, social conditions since emancipation, and attempts at unification, 1831–1958. Indexed.

2. Barbados Public Library. *Barbadiana: A List of Works Pertaining to the History of the Island of Barbados; Prepared in the Public Library to Mark the Attainment of Independence*. Bridgetown, Barbados: Barbados Public Library, 1966. 44 p.

   Organized by subject, including descriptive historical accounts and sections on government and politics, social and economic themes, and education. A mixture of both primary and secondary accounts with several entries pertaining to the postemancipation period listed among citations that precede and follow this period. Selected historical accounts are relevant for postemancipation issues, and various government reports dealing with early-twentieth-century economic issues are also included.

3. Blondel, Eaulin A., R. Annette Knight, and Margaret D. Rouse-Jones. *An Index to the Conference Papers of the Association of Caribbean Historians, 1969–1988*. St. Augustine, Trinidad: University of the West Indies, 1989. 90 p.

   This index begins with a "Historical Note on the Formation of the Association of Caribbean Historians," includes both an author and a subject index to conference papers, and concludes with a list of the published conference papers. The latter includes papers on "Social Groups and Institutions in the History of the Caribbean"; "Some Papers on Social, Political, and Economic Adjustments to the Ending of Slavery in the Caribbean"; and "Politics, Society, and Culture in the Caribbean."

4. Boomgaard, Peter, and Gert J. Oostindie. "Changing Sugar Technology and the Labour Nexus: The Caribbean, 1750–1900." *Nieuwe West-Indische Gids* 63 (1989): 3–22.

Boomgaard and Oostindie discuss two strains of historiographical literature in the Caribbean that address the connection between "technological development and changing labour relations in the Caribbean" and the revisions to these two historiographical traditions in recent decades. They note that this historiographical literature "is often embedded in a broader context, namely the debate on the profitability of slave labour as such" and cite the publication of Seymour Drescher's *Econocide* as marking a shift away from older economic arguments offered by Eric Williams and Lowell Ragatz. Boomgaard and Oostindie discuss various strategies and innovations sought by planters, the extent and quality of labor available to planters, and the relative merits of free as opposed to slave labor.

5. Brana-Shute, Rosemary, comp., ed. *A Bibliography of Caribbean Migration and Caribbean Immigrant Communities.* Gainesville, Fla.: Reference and Bibliographic Department, University of Florida Libraries, in cooperation with the Center for Latin American Studies, University of Florida, 1983. 339 p.

Arranged alphabetically by author and covers the entire Caribbean, including Belize, Guyana, Suriname, and French Guiana. Deals with groups who migrated into the Caribbean region, the process of acculturation, the migrants' influence on Caribbean societies, interregional migration, and migration outside of the region. The bibliography is multidisciplinary and includes literature in several languages.

6. Brereton, Bridget. "General Problems and Issues in Studying the History of Women." In *Gender in Caribbean Development,* edited by Patricia Mohammed and Catherine Shepherd. Mona, Jamaica: University of the West Indies Women and Development Studies Project, 1988. 123–141.

Brereton discusses the significance of gender as an analytical concept and the need for a conceptual approach incorporating gender into historical research on the British Caribbean. She outlines the experience of women during slavery and the documents left by them, approaches to family life and motherhood, the experience of female emigrants to the British West Indies, and their participation in the labor force.

7. Center for Research Libraries. *Latin American and Caribbean Research Material Available in Microform from the Latin American Microform Project and Center for Research Libraries.* Chicago: Center for Research Libraries, 1988. 23 p.

Listing of materials held at the Center for Research Libraries available to libraries belonging to LAMP and CRL. Listings for the British Caribbean include: *The Dominican* (1842–1907); the *Berbice Gazette* (1846, 1870–71); *Colonist* (Guyana; 1869–1870); *Demerara Daily Chronicle* (Nov. 5, 1881–1897); several Jamaican sources that run (respectively and discontinuously) from 1865 to 1956; records for the Wesleyan Methodist Missionary Society and Church Missionary Society; three newspaper holdings for Trinidad and Tobago that run from the mid-nineteenth to the early twentieth century; and other more recent holdings for the Caribbean as a whole.

8. Center for Research Libraries. *Latin American and Caribbean Official Gazettes Held at the Center for Research Libraries.* Chicago: Center for Research Libraries, 1991. 7 p.

This compilation includes holdings for gazettes from the Bahamas (1914–1921), Bermuda (July 1862–1864), Jamaica (1902, 1906–1907), and Trinidad (1895–1899 and 1914–1916), in addition to other Caribbean islands and Latin America. Some of these holdings are on microfilm, while others are originals.

9. Comitas, Lambros. *The Complete Caribbeana, 1900–1975: A Bibliographic Guide to the Scholarly Literature.* 4 vols. Millwood, N.Y.: KTO Press, 1977.

An expanded, updated, and improved version of the same author's *The Complete Caribbeana, 1900–1965,* published in 1968. The first three volumes are divided into sixty-three topical sections, while the fourth volume provides an author and geographical index. The first volume deals with "People," the second with "Institutions," and the third with "Resources." Several sections are relevant to the study of the postemancipation British Caribbean. Those of particular interest include: "Slavery and Emancipation" (ch. 6), "Population Segments: Afro-Caribbean" (ch. 11), "Population Segments: East Indian" (ch. 12), "Internal and External Migration" (ch. 17), "Plantation Economics and the Sugar Complex" (ch. 42), "Agricultural Economics" (ch. 43), and "Land Tenure" (ch. 44). There are also sections covering the general history and economics of the Caribbean, and an opening chapter on "Bibliographic and Archival Research." Many entries are cross-listed.

10. Craton, Michael. "The Transition from Slavery to Free Wage Labour in the Caribbean, 1790–1890: A Survey with Particular Reference to Recent Scholarship." *Slavery and Abolition* 13 (August 1992): 37–67.

Craton examines the transition from slavery to wage labor from the 1780s through 1886 and the emancipation of slaves in Cuba. He calls for greater integration between more localized studies of slave emancipation and broader transitions in the Atlantic world, with the goal of identifying commonalities and differences in the experience and structure of slavery and the transition to wage labor in the various Caribbean islands.

11. Cundall, Frank. *Political and Social Disturbances in the West Indies: A Brief Account and Bibliography*. Kingston, Jamaica: Educational Supply Company for the Institute of Jamaica, 1906. 35 p.

Chronological record of disturbances since emancipation, arranged by date and colony with brief overviews of the various disturbances and riots. Over four pages are devoted to the Morant Bay Rebellion, and two cover the 1903 Water Riot in Trinidad. The six-page bibliography includes folios, commission reports, and information contained in the *British Parliamentary Papers*.

12. Engerman, Stanley L. "Slavery and Emancipation in Comparative Perspective: A Look at Some Recent Debates." *Journal of Economic History* 46 (June 1986): 317–39.

Engerman outlines the general arguments offered to explain the onset of emancipation, including questions regarding the profitability of slavery and the extent to which slavery was on the decline in various slaveholding societies on the eve of emancipation. Engerman then discusses production outputs during the transition to free labor following emancipation, including consideration of the British colonies—Barbados and Antigua in particular—as well as the contemporary response to emancipation in the British West Indies generally.

13. Ferguson, Stephney. "Marcus Garvey: A Guide to Sources of Information at the National Library of Jamaica." *Jamaica Journal* 20 (August–October 1987): 93–99.

Bibliographical essay of works on and by Garvey, including bibliographies, his various writings, biographies, and works on the Garvey movement. More general works assessing Garvey in relationship to black nationalism are also mentioned. Brief mention is made of the religious aspects of Garveyism, newspaper and journal articles, pamphlets, unpublished theses, and audiovisual and other material. A bibliography of forty-six references is included at the end.

14. Fraser, Peter. "The Fictive Peasantry: Caribbean Rural Groups in the Nineteenth Century." In *Contemporary Caribbean: A Sociological Reader*, vol. 1, edited by Susan Craig. Port of Spain, Trinidad: Susan Craig (printed by Maracas, Trinidad and Tobago, West Indies: College Press), 1981.

Discusses rural groups in the nineteenth-century Caribbean, with particular focus on the British Caribbean. Fraser considers the economic importance of the Caribbean as a colonial area, particularly as it differed in both perception and function from other territories such as Australia. Also addresses theoretical frameworks employed by Immanuel Wallerstein, Karl Marx, and Don Robotham in exploring the nature and character of capitalism in the Caribbean. Discusses rural society prior to and following emancipation, particularly the "labour problem" after emancipation, the various choices and constraints facing rural groups, and the different relationships such groups had with the plantation. A selective bibliography of ninety-six references follows Fraser's essay.

15. Geggus, David, ed. *The Caribbean Collections at the University of Florida: A Brief Description*. Gainesville, Fla.: University of Florida Libraries, 1985. 26 p.

A listing of various manuscripts, microfilm collections, and maps available at the University of Florida and the Latin American Studies center located there. The "Bahamas Government Records" comprise fifty-five reels of microfilm covering the period from 1700 to 1860 and consist of deeds, mortgages, satisfactions and releases, crown grants, wills, House of Assembly records, chancery records, dowers, pleas, and slave emancipation papers (1831–45). The "Trinidad Papers" (1814–45) consist of "despatches" of the colonial governor, while the "Tobago Papers" cover the period from 1800 to 1880. Several newspapers of potential interest are also located here.

16. Goveia, Elsa V. *A Study on the Historiography of the British West Indies to the End of the Nineteenth Century*. Pan American Institute of Geography and History, no. 186. Mexico: Pan American Institute of Geography and History, 1956. 183 p.

Arranged chronologically, covering the period of discovery, seventeenth, eighteenth, and nineteenth centuries. Goveia discusses works covering the major developments and issues in the West Indies during this period, noting that the authors demonstrate some uniformity in both reflecting and refracting the intellectual currents of their day. Those writing in the eighteenth century displayed a concern for social order, crisis, and tension as the colonies were established, while those of the nineteenth century discussed slavery, abolition, political economy, and the potential problems of emancipation. Goveia concludes with a brief chapter summarizing some of the main themes as illustrated by particular authors, addressing in the process more general questions on the nature of historiography and historical objectivity.

17. Great Britain. Public Record Office. *List of Colonial Office Records Preserved in the Public Record Office.* London: His Majesty's Stationery Office, 1911. 337 p.

Arranged alphabetically by colony, including all British possessions. Incorporates original correspondence (Board of Trade and Secretary of State), entry books for commissions, sessional papers, government gazettes, newspapers, blue books, and miscellaneous categories of material. The record number, date, and a brief description is given for each entry. References date from the seventeenth to the late nineteenth century.

18. Green, William A. "Caribbean Historiography, 1600–1900: The Recent Tide." *Journal of Interdisciplinary History* 7 (winter 1977): 509–30.

Green emphasizes how West Indian historiography has always drawn upon other disciplines and that methodological and historiographical concerns are often intertwined. He sees Eric Williams's *Capitalism and Slavery* as "profoundly" influential in shaping the course of scholarly work on the British West Indies. Article proceeds chronologically from the slavery period, discussing such works as Richard Sheridan's *Sugar and Slavery,* Roger Anstey's *The Atlantic Slave Trade and British Abolition,* and Richard Dunn's *Sugar and Slaves.* J. Harry Bennett, Elsa Goveia, and Orlando Patterson are discussed in the section dealing with slavery studies, while studies of emancipation and postemancipation society begin with issues springing from Williams's work and continue with discussions of Philip Curtin's *Two Jamaicas,* Douglas Hall's *Free Jamaica,* Alan Adamson's *Sugar Without Slaves,* William Green's *British Slave Emancipation,* Donald Wood's *Trinidad in Transition,* and monographs on indentured labor by Judith Weller and Dwarka Nath.

19. Grieb, Kenneth J., ed. *Research Guide to Central America and the Caribbean.* Madison: University of Wisconsin Press, 1985. 431 p.

A broad introduction to the major research topics and archives in Central America and the Caribbean, including the non-British Caribbean. Topical essays of particular importance for research in the Caribbean include: Marianne D. Ramesar's "Migrant Groups in the Caribbean," Richard Sheridan's "Exploitative Systems: Slavery, Commerce, and Industry," and Franklin Knight's "Class, Race, and Religion in Caribbean Research." Describes archives in Jamaica, Trinidad and Tobago, Guyana, Barbados, the Bahamas, Bermuda, St. Vincent, the British Virgin Islands, and the rest of the eastern and western Caribbean.

20. Jordan, Alma, and Barbara Commissiong. *The English-Speaking Caribbean: A Bibliography of Bibliographies*. Boston: G. K. Hall, 1984. 411 p.

This bibliography is arranged alphabetically according to subject matter, and it covers "bibliographies produced up to April 1981 about the lands and peoples of the former British Caribbean territories," along with a listing of these territories. A name and subject index is included at the end, and locational symbols are given with each entry, many of which can be found only at collections housed in libraries and archives in particular West Indian countries. The sections include "Bibliography of Bibliographies," "Agriculture," "Economics," "Ethnic Groups," "History," "Industrial Relations," "Race Relations," and "Social and Economic Conditions." The "History" section includes a listing of guides to records and archives in the Caribbean, as well as unpublished bibliographies and typescripts held in various libraries in the West Indies. Some of these may have information relevant to the postemancipation period, including one on *The English-Speaking West Indies—Post Emancipation 1831–1865*, which lists holdings at the main library of the University of the West Indies. The section on "Law" covers various indexes to laws, court reports, decisions, and other primary legal materials, many of which fall within the postemancipation period.

21. Lent, John A., comp. "The Oldest Existing Newspapers in the Commonwealth Caribbean." *Caribbean Quarterly* 22 (December 1976): 90–106.

A comprehensive list of British West Indian newspapers founded between 1718 and 1969. Provides the name of paper, frequency of publication, and founding and, where available, ending date. List preceded by a brief commentary on the exigencies of West Indian newspaper publishing.

22. Marshall, Trevor G., comp. *A Bibliography of the Commonwealth Caribbean Peasantry, 1838–1974.* Cave Hill, Barbados: Institute of Social and Economic Research (Eastern Caribbean), University of the West Indies, 1975. 47 p.

Organized alphabetically by individual territories with an initial section on the Caribbean as a whole. Includes a listing of material available in the Institute of Social and Economic Research and the University of the West Indies in Cave Hill, as well as the St. Augustine library. Sections for each individual territory cover economic, sociological, and historical literature. Both postemancipation and more modern citations included. Orientation is toward more technical/economic/production-oriented contemporary accounts from agricultural journals such as *Timehri, Tropical Agriculture,* and *West India Bulletin.* Colonial Office reports covering the postemancipation period include reports from sugar commissions and economic circumstances generally, as well as reports on labor. Includes sections on Belize and British Honduras.

23. Moore, Brian L. "Walter Rodney: His Contribution to Guyanese Historiography." *Bulletin of Eastern Caribbean Affairs* 8 (1982): 23–29.

Moore discusses the integration of political and academic goals in the work of Walter Rodney, particularly as illustrated through his *A History of the Guyanese Working People,* finished shortly before his death.

24. Myers, Robert A., comp. *A Resource Guide to Dominica, 1493–1986.* 3 vols. New Haven, Conn.: Human Relations Area Files, 1987.

Divided into thirty-one topical sections. Opens with a discussion of the history of Dominica and a chapter on sources consulted, followed by chapters on such subjects as Amerindians, descriptive historical and travel literature, agriculture, British parliamentary materials and official records, and archives in Europe, Britain, the United States and the West Indies. Entries falling within the postemancipation period can be found in the History, Agriculture, and the British Parliamentary sections, including citations to pamphlets and speeches, reports on labor disturbances, reports on labor supply and agricultural conditions, and papers relating to apprenticeship. Not annotated. Includes a name and subject index, along with locational symbols for each entry.

25. National Library of Jamaica. *Marcus Mosiah Garvey, 1887–1940: An Annotated List of Materials in the National Library of Jamaica.* 3rd ed. Compiled by Debbie McGinnis. Edited by June Vernon. Kingston, Jamaica: National Library of Jamaica, 1987. 67 p.

Divided into ten sections, including bibliographies and catalogues, works by Garvey, major books on Garvey, other books and articles discussing Garvey, theses and dissertations, audio-visual materials, works relating Garvey to Rastafarianism, and various newspaper articles. Some entries have brief annotations.

26. Nodal, Roberto, comp. *An Annotated Bibliography of Historical Materials on Jamaica.* Milwaukee: Department of Afro-American Studies, University of Wisconsin-Milwaukee (Afro-American Studies Report no. 6), 1974. 42 p.

    Many citations cover or were published in the eighteenth and early nineteenth centuries, with a few references from the early twentieth century. Arranged alphabetically by author. Works related to emancipation and postemancipation studies include those of Martha Beckwith and Frank Cundall, John Bigelow's *Jamaica in 1850*, James A. Thome's *Emancipation in the West Indies*, William Finlanson's *The History of Jamaica*, Thomas Harvey's *Jamaica in 1866*, Sylvester Hovey's *Letters from the West Indies*, Mathew G. Lewis's *Journal of a Residence among the Negroes in the West Indies* (1845), the Rev. B. Luckock's *Jamaica: Enslaved and Free* (1846), and the Rev. James M. Phillipp's *Jamaica: Its Past and Present State.*

27. Pactor, Howard S., comp. *Colonial British Caribbean Newspapers: A Bibliography and Directory.* New York: Greenwood Press, 1990. 144 p.

    This bibliography begins with a brief overview of the nature and significance of British Caribbean newspapers, the survival and preservation of certain papers, and the social, political, and economic information that can be gleaned from such sources, particularly for the postemancipation period. Entries for this bibliography were taken primarily from the microfilmed collection and original holdings of the University of Florida's Latin American collection and cover the entire British Caribbean with the exception of Belize and British Guiana.

28. Rouse-Jones, Margaret D. "Recent Research in the History of Trinidad and Tobago: A Review of the Journal and Conference Literature, 1975–1985." In *Caribbean Collections: Recession Management Strategies for Libraries*, edited by Mina J. Grothey. Madison, Wis.: Seminar on the Acquisition of Latin American Library Materials (SALALM) Secretariat, Memorial Library, University of Wisconsin-Madison, 1988.

    Discussion of recent research on the preemancipation era, postemancipation, migration and East Indians, education, women's experiences, biography, and Tobago. A listing of conferences is included at the conclusion of her article, along with a bibliography of seventy-eight references to journal and conference literature.

29. Thomas, Timothy N. *Indians Overseas: A Guide to Source Materials in the India Office Records for the Study of Indian Emigration, 1830–1950.* London: British Library, 1985. 97 p.

Deals with Indian emigration to and settlement in the British Commonwealth and other territories from 1830 to 1950. Primary concern is with the indentured labor system and related social, political, and economic issues as they unfolded in areas where Indians settled. Part 1 includes a general historical background, information on the primary areas of Indian settlement, and a select bibliography. Part 2 gives a description and listing of the various holdings and records in the India Office, which include industry, economic, judicial, private files, and private papers including correspondence and committee records. An appendix lists other holdings in overseas archives, including some for Jamaica. Some individual entries pertain to Trinidad, British Guiana, and Jamaica.

30. Travis, Carol, ed. *A Guide to Latin American and Caribbean Census Material: A Bibliography and Union List.* Boston: G. K. Hall, 1990. 739 p.

A bibliographical guide to published census material for each country in Latin America and the Caribbean up to 1979, providing a listing of the libraries (with location, address, and telephone number) that hold the material and a library code for each entry. The editor notes that some of the older censuses were more broadly defined than contemporary censuses and include missionary reports and conversions, baptismal, and burial records as well as lists of merchants' and travelers' accounts. Each country is listed alphabetically, and there is also a section covering the Commonwealth Caribbean. The majority of the entries for Barbados, Belize (British Honduras), Guyana (British Guiana), the Leeward Islands, and Trinidad and Tobago were published prior to 1946. Nine of the entries for Jamaica were published prior to 1943. Several entries would be of interest to researchers of the postemancipation era in the British West Indies, including an 1845 census "of the population in each of the British Islands . . . with information re. numbers of emancipated negroes who have become freeholders."

31. Trouillot, Michel-Rolph. "Labour and Emancipation in Dominica: Contribution to a Debate." *Caribbean Quarterly* 30 (September–December 1984): 73–84.

Addresses both theoretically and historiographically the "flight" debate and labor shortage issues following emancipation as discussed by historians such as Douglas Hall and Emanuel Rivière. Uses material from three Dominican parishes, from the beginning of emancipation to November of 1838, to discuss both the underlying assumptions guiding previous work and to examine the complex relationships between notions of freedom and choice and structural factors, including estate size and working conditions.

32. Welch, Thomas L., and Myriam Figueras, comps. *Travel Accounts and Descriptions of Latin America and the Caribbean, 1800–1920; A Selected Bibliography*. Washington, D.C.: Columbus Memorial Library, Organization of American States, 1982. 293 p.

Includes the non-British West Indies, Central America, Mexico, and South America. Arranged alphabetically by country. Not annotated, though some citations carry quotations from the sources. Includes work focused on particular social and economic issues, including emancipation and postemancipation society such as William Sewell's *The Ordeal of Free Labour in the British West Indies,* Joseph Sturge's *The West Indies in 1837,* James A. Thome's *Emancipation in the West Indies,* as well as more general historical and descriptive accounts covering topography, climate, natural history, and travel literature. The section on British Guiana consists of several entries dealing with various ethnic groups.

33. Williams, Eric. *British Historians and the West Indies.* 1964. Reprint. New York: Africana Publishing Corporation, 1972. 238 p.

Covers historical writing on the British West Indies from the slavery period to the era following World War II. Included in this chronology is coverage of the years between 1830 and 1880, between 1880 and 1914, and the period between the two World Wars. Three chapters are devoted to the Morant Bay Rebellion of 1865 and various interpretations of that event. Williams sketches the political, social, intellectual, economic, and colonial contexts and assumptions that informed the work of British historians. This includes a discussion of how the ideas of Adam Smith and Jeremy Bentham informed some work, as well as how racial ideas were intertwined with labor issues and problems in Britain. Williams discusses, among others, the work of Thomas Carlyle, Anthony Trollope, and William Sewell. Frank Tannenbaum, W. L. Burn, and Williams are among those discussed in the chapter dealing with the period following World War II, when some writing was influenced by the burgeoning independence movements.

34. Anderson, William Wemyss. *Jamaica and the Americans.* New York: Stanford and Swords, 1851. 30 p.

35. Anonymous. *Jamaica Under the Apprenticeship System.* London: J. Andrews, 1838. 2 p.

36. Anti-Slavery Society. *Negro Apprenticeship in the British Colonies.* London: Office of the Anti-Slavery Society, 1838. 32 p.

37. August, Eugene R., ed. *Thomas Carlyle The Nigger Question, John Stuart Mill The Negro Question.* New York: Crofts Classics, 1971. 59 p.

38. Barclay, Alexander. *Remarks on Emigration to Jamaica: Addressed to the Coloured Class of the United States.* New York: James van Norden, 1840. 16 p.

39. Barron, T. and K. J. Cable. "The Diary of James Stephen, 1846." *Historical Studies* 13 (April 1969): 503–19.

40. Barton, Premium. *Eight years in British Guiana; being the journal of a residence in that province, from 1840 to 1848, inclusive. With anecdotes and incidents illustrating the social condition of its inhabitants; and of the opinions of the writer on the state and prospects of our sugar colonies generally.* London: Longman, Brown, Green, and Longmans, 1850. 305 p.

41. Beckles, W. *The Barbados Disturbances 1937: Reproduction of the Evidence, and Report of the Commission.* Bridgetown, Barbados : Advocate, 1937. 282 p.

42. Bell, Kenneth N., and W. P. Morrell, eds. *Select Documents on British Colonial Policy, 1830–1860.* Oxford: Clarendon Press, 1928. 610 p.

43. Bernau, John Henry. *Missionary Labours in British Guiana: with Remarks on the Manners, Customs, and Superstitious Rites of the Aborigines.* London: J. F. Shaw, 1847. 242 p.

44. Bigelow, John. *Jamaica in 1850, or, the effects of sixteen years of freedom in a slave colony.* New York: G. P. Putnam, 1851. 214 p.

45. Bleby, Henry. *Death Struggles of Slavery.* London: W. Nichols, 1868. 332 p.

46. Bourne, S. *The British West Indian Colonies in Connection with Slavery and Emancipation.* London: T. Bosworth, 1853.

47. Breen, Henry H. *St. Lucia, Historical, Statistical and Descriptive.* 1844. Reprint. London: Thomas Cass, 1970. 423 p.

48. Bronkhurst, H. V. P. *The Colony of British Guyana and its Labouring Population.* London: T. Woolmer, 1883. 479 p.

49. Brumell, John. *Demerara after Fifteen Years of Freedom.* London: T. Bosworth, 1853. 117 p.

50. Burnley, W. H. *Observations on the present condition of the island of Trinidad and the actual state of the experiment of negro emancipation.* London: Longman, Brown, Green, and Longmans, 1842. 177 p.

51. Cameron, N. E. *The Evolution of the Negro.* 2 vols. 1929–1934. Reprint. Westport, Conn.: Negro Universities Press and Greenwood Press, 1970.

52. Campbell, Persia Crawford. *Chinese Coolie Emigration to Countries within the British Empire.* London: P. S. King and Son, 1923. 240 p.

53. Capadose, Henry. *Sixteen Years in the West Indies.* 2 vols. London: T. C. Newby, 1845.

54. Carmichael, Mrs. A. C. *Domestic Manners and Social Conditions of the White, Coloured, and Negro Population of the West Indies.* 2 vols. London: Whittaker, Treacher, 1833.

55. Charles, Jay. *Observations on the Present State and Future Prospects of the West Indies, Considered as National, Commercial, and Financial Questions.* London: E. Wilson, 1847. 37 p.

56. Clementi, Cecil. *The Chinese in British Guiana.* Georgetown: Argosy, 1915. 416 p.

57. Comins, D. W. D. *Notes on Emigration from India to British Guiana.* Georgetown, Demerara: Baldwin and Co, 1894. 100 p.

58. Craton, Michael, James Walvin, and David Wright. *Slavery, Abolition, and Emancipation: Black Slaves and the British Empire: A Thematic Documentary.* London: Longman, 1976. 347 p.

59. Crookall, Lawrence. *British Guiana: or Work and Wanderings among the Creoles and Coolies, the Africans and Indians of the Wild Country.* London: T. Fisher Unwin, 1898. 247 p.

60. Cust, Sir Edward. *Reflections on West India Affairs, After a Recent Visit to the Colonies. Addressed to the Consideration of the Colonial Office.* London: J. Hatchard, 1839. 88 p.

61. Day, Charles William. *Five Years' Residence in the West Indies.* 2 vols. London: Colburn, 1852.

62. De Lisser, H. G. *Twentieth Century Jamaica.* Kingston, Jamaica: Jamaica Times, 1913. 208 p.

63. de Montagnac, Noel. *Negro Nobodies. Being a Series of Sketches of Peasant Life in Jamaica.* London: T. F. Unwin, 1899. 212 p.

64. Derby, Edward Henry Stanley. *Claims and Resources of the West Indian Colonies. A Letter to the Rt. Hon. W. E. Gladstone. . . . By the Hon. E. Stanley, M.P.* London: T. and W. Boone, 1850. 11 p.

65. Des Voeux, George W. *My colonial service in British Guiana, St. Lucia, Trinidad, Fiji, Australia, Newfoundland, and Hong Kong, with interludes.* 2 vols. London: J. Murray, 1903.

66. De Verteuil, Louis Antoine Aime Gaston. *Trinidad: Its Geography, Natural Resources, Administration, Present Condition, and Prospects.* London: Ward and Lock, 1858. 508 p.

67. Emery, Robert. *About Jamaica: Its Past, Its Present, and its Future.* London: J. Evans, 1859. 32 p.

68. Finlason, W. F. *The History of the Jamaica Case.* 1869. Reprint. London: Frank Cass, 1972.

69. Froude, James Anthony. "England and Her Colonies." *Fraser's Magazine.* New Series 1 (January 1870): 1–16.

70. Froude, James Anthony. *The English in the West Indies, Or, The Bow of Ulysses.* New York: Charles Scribner's Sons, 1888. 373 p.

71. Gordon, Shirley C. *Reports and Repercussions in West Indian Education, 1835–1933.* London: Ginn, 1968. 190 p.

72. Gore, Montague. *Reflections on the Present State and Prospects of the British West Indies.* London: Ridgway, 1848. 40 p.

73. Gurney, Joseph John. *Familiar Letters to Henry Clay of Kentucky Describing a Winter in the West Indies.* New York: Mahlon Day, 1840. 203 p.

74. Halliday, Sir Andrew. *The West Indies: the natural and physical history of the Windward and Leeward colonies, with some account of the moral, social, and political condition of their inhabitants, immediately before and after the abolition of negro slavery.* London: J. W. Parker, 1837. 408 p.

75. Hancock, Thomas. *Are the West India colonies to be preserved? A few plain facts; showing the necessity of immigration into British Guiana and the West Indies, and the utter futility of all efforts towards the abolition of slavery and the slave trade which do not include this. Addressed more particularly to the legislature.* London: W. E. Painter, Strand, Printer, 1840. 16 p.

76. Hart, Daniel. *Trinidad and the Other West Indian Islands and Colonies.* Port-of-Spain, Trinidad: Chronicle, 1866. 250 p.

77. Harvey, Thomas, and William Brewin. *Jamaica in 1866. A narrative of a tour through the island, with remarks on its social, educational, and industrial condition.* London: A. W. Bennett, 1867. 126 p.

78. Henny, Thomas, and Raynes W. Smith, W. F. Whitehouse, W. A. Clements, James Sullivan, and G. W. Gordon. *Eight Practical Treatises on the Cultivation of the Sugar Cane. Written in Consequence of His Excellency the Earl of Elgin's Offer of a Prize of One Hundred Pounds in the Latter Part of 1842.* Jamaica: Jordan and Osborn, 1843.

79. Higman, B. W., ed. "The Jamaican Censuses of 1844 and 1861. A New Edition, Derived from the Manuscript and Printed Schedules in the Jamaica Archives." Mona, Jamaica: Social History Project, Department of History, University of the West Indies, 1980. 58 p.

80. Hildreth, Richard. *The 'Ruin' of Jamaica.* New York: American Anti-Slavery Society, 1855. 12 p.

81. Hodgson, Capt. Studholm. *Truths from the West Indies, Including a Sketch of Maderia in 1833.* London: W. Ball, 1838. 372 p.

82. Hovey, Sylvester. *Letters from the West Indies, Relating Especially to the Danish Island, St. Croix, and to the British Islands, Antigua, Barbadoes, and Jamaica.* New York: Gould and Newman, 1838. 212 p.

83. *The Jamaica Question: Papers Relative to the Condition of the Labouring Population of the West Indies.* Lindfield: W. Eade, 1839. 28 p.

84. Jenkins, Edward. *The Coolie; His Rights and Wrongs.* London: Strahan, 1871. 446 p.

85. Johnston, Sir Harry. *The Negro in the New World.* 1910. Reprint. New York: Johnson Reprint Corporation, 1969. 499 p.

86. Kaye, John William, ed. *Selections from the Papers of Lord Metcalfe.* London: Smith, Elder, 1855. 476 p.

87. King, David. *The State and Prospects of Jamaica.* London: Johnstone and Hunter, 1850. 235 p.

88. Kumar Mahabir, Noor, comp. *The Still Cry: Personal Accounts of East Indians in Trinidad and Tobago During Indentureship, 1845–1917.* Tacarigua, Trinidad: Calaloux Publications, 1985. 191 p.

89. Lamont, Norman. *Problems of the Antilles: A Collection of Speeches and Writings on West Indian Questions.* Glasgow: Johns Smith and Son, 1912. 178 p.

90. Lanaghan, Mrs. *Antigua and Antiguans: A Full Account of the Colony and its Inhabitants.* 2 vols. 1844. Reprint. London: Macmillan, 1991.

91. Lewis, Matthew Gregory. *Journal of a West India Proprietors, Kept During a Residence in the Island of Jamaica.* London: J. Murray, 1834. 408 p.

92. Lloyd, William. *Letters from the West Indies, during a visit in the autumn of 1836, and the spring of 1837.* London: Darton and Harvey, 1839. 263 p.

93. Madden, R. R. *A Twelvemonth's Residence in the West Indies, During the Transition from Slavery to Apprenticeship, With Incidental Notices of the State of Society, Prospects, and Natural Resources of Jamaica and Other Islands.* 2 vols. Philadelphia: Carey, Lea, and Blanchard, 1835.

94. M'Mahon, Benjamin. *Jamaica Plantership.* London: E. Wilson, 1839. 300 p.

95. Marshall, Woodville K., ed. *The Colthurst Journal: Journal of a Special Magistrate in the Islands of Barbados and St. Vincent, July 1835–September 1838.* Millwood, N.Y.: кто Press, 1977. 255 p.

96. Maxwell, James, ed. *Remarks on the Present State of Jamaica, with a Proposal of Measures for the Resuscitation of our West India Colonies.* London: Smith, Elder, 1848. 51 p.

97. McLarty, R. W. *Jamaica: Our Present Condition and Crisis.* Kingston, Jamaica, 1919. 43 p.

98. Menezes, Mary Noel, ed. *The Amerindians in Guyana, 1803–1873: A Documentary History.* London: Cass, 1979. 314 p.

99. Milner, Thomas Hughes. *The Present and Future State of Jamaica Considered.* London: H. Hooper, 1839. 96 p.

100. Moister, William. *The West Indies, enslaved and free: a concise account of the islands and colonies: their history and geography.* London: T. Woolmer, 1883. 394 p.

101. Moore, Richard B. *Richard B. Moore, Caribbean Militant in Harlem: Collected Writings,* 1920–1972. Edited by W. Burghardt Turner and Joyce Moore Turner. Bloomington: Indiana University Press, 1988. 324 p.

102. Morson, Henry. *The present condition of the British West Indies; their wants, and the remedy for these with some practical hints, shewing the policy of a new system, as a means to their future regeneration.* London: Smith, Elder, 1841. 63 p.

103. National Association for the Protection of British Industry and Capital. Colonial Sub-Committee. *The case of the free-labour British colonies, submitted to the British legislature and British nation for an impartial re-hearing.* London: J. Madden, 1852. 155 p.

104. Olivier, Lord [Sydney Haldane]. *Jamaica, the Blessed Island.* London: Faber & Faber, 1936. 466 p.

105. Olivier, Sydney. "Progress of a Negro Peasantry." *Edinburgh Review* 249 (1929): 105–16.

106. Olivier, Sydney. "The Improvement of Negro Agriculture." *Journal of the Royal Society of Arts* 77 (1929): 396–419.

107. Olivier, Sydney. *Letters and Selected Writings.* Edited by Margaret Olivier. New York: Macmillan, 1948. 252 p.

108. Orderson, J. W. *Creoleana: Or Social and Domestic Scenes and Incidents in Barbados in Days of Yore.* London: Saunders and Otley, 1842. 246 p.

109. Phillippo, James Mursell. *Jamaica: its Past and Present State.* London: J. Snow, 1843. 487 p.

110. Pim, Bedford Clapperton Trevelyan. *The Negro and Jamaica.* 1866. Reprint. Freeport, N.Y.: Books for Libraries Press, 1971. 72 p.

111. Pringle, J. W. *Remarks on the state and prospects of the West Indian colonies. By Captain J. W. Pringle, employed on a mission of inquiry into the state of the prisons of these colonies, in the year* 1837–1838. London: Ridgway, 1839. 20 p.

112. Pullen-Burry, Bessie. *Ethiopia in Exile: Jamaica Revisited.* 1905. Reprint. Freeport, N.Y.: Books for Libraries Press, 1971. 200 p.

113. Pullen-Burry, Bessie. *Jamaica as it is, 1903*. London: T. F. Unwin, 1903. 240 p.

114. Rodney, Walter, ed. *Guyanese Sugar Plantations in the Late Nineteenth Century*. Georgetown: Release Publishers, 1979. 97 p.

115. Root, John William. *The British West Indies and the Sugar Industry*. Liverpool: J. W. Root, 1899. 159 p.

116. Rutter, Owen. *If Crab No Walk: A Traveller in the West Indies*. London: Hutchinson, 1933. 288 p.

117. Salmon, C. W. *Depression in the West Indies. Free Trade the Only Remedy*. London: Cassell, 1884. 31 p.

118. Salmon, Charles Spencer. *The Caribbean Confederation. A Plan for the Union of the Fifteen British West Indian Colonies, Preceded by an Account of the Past and Present Condition of the Europeans and the African Races Inhabiting Them, with a True Explanation of the Haytian Mystery, in which is Embodied a Refutation of the Chief Statements Made by Mr. Froude in his Recent Work, "The English in the West Indies."* London: Cassell, 1888. 175 p.

119. Schomburgk, Sir Robert Hermann. *A description of British Guiana, geographical and statistical: exhibiting its resources and capabilities, together with the present and future condition and prospects of the colony.* 1840. Reprint. New York: A. M. Kelly, 1970. 155 p.

120. Schomburgk, Sir Robert Hermann. *The History of Barbados. Comprising a Geographical and Statistical Description of the Islands; a Sketch of the Historical Events since the Settlement; and an Account of its Geology and Natural Productions.* London: Longman, Brown, Green and Longmans, 1848.

121. Senior, Bernard Martin. *Jamaica as It Was, as It Is, and as It May Be. Comprising Interesting Topics for Absent Proprietors, Merchants and C., and Valuable Hints to Persons Intending to Emigrate to the Island. Also an Authentic Narrative of the Negro Insurrection in 1831, with a Faithful Detail of the Manners, Customs and Habits of the Colonists, and a Description of the Country, Climate, Production and C., including an Abridgement of the Slave Law.* London: T. Hurst, 1835. 313 p.

122. Sewell, Wm. G. *The Ordeal of Free Labor in the British West Indies*. New York: Harper, 1861. 325 p.

123. Smith, Keithlyn B. and Fernando C. Smith. *To Shoot Hard Labour: The Life and Times of Samuel Smith, an Antiguan Workingman, 1877–1982.* Scarborough, Ontario: Edan's, 1986. 172 p.

124. Spackman, Ann, comp. *Constitutional Development of the West Indies, 1922–1968: A Selection from the Major Documents.* St. Lawrence, Barbados: Caribbean Universities Press in Association with the Bowker Publishing, 1975. 619 p.

125. Spedding, James. *Reviews and Discussions: Literary, Political, and Historical, Not Relating to Bacon.* London: C. Kegan Paul, 1879. 419 p.

126. Spinner, Alice. *A Study in Colour.* London: T. F. Unwin, 1894. 214 p.

127. St. Johnston, Sir Reginald. *From a Colonial Governor's Notebook.* 1936. Reprint. Westport, Conn.: Negro Universities Press, 1970. 285 p.

128. Starkey, Otis Paul. *The Economic Geography of Barbados; a Study of the Relationships between Environmental Variations and Economic Development.* New York: Columbia University Press, 1939. 228 p.

129. *Statement of facts, illustrating the administration of the abolition law, and the sufferings of the negro apprentices, in the island of Jamaica.* London: W. Ball, 1837.

130. Stephen, James. *The Right Honourable Sir James Stephen: Letters with Biographical Notes.* Edited by Caroline Emelia Stephen. Gloucester: J. Bellows, 1906. 298 p.

131. Sterne, Henry. *A statement of facts . . . with an exposure of the present system of Jamaica apprenticeship.* London: J. C. Chappell, 1837. 282 p.

132. Stuart, Charles. *The West India Question. Immediation Emancipation Would Be Safe for the Masters; Profitable for the Masters; Happy for the Slaves; Right in the Government; Advantageous to the Nation; Would Interfere with No Feelings but Such as are Disgraceful and Destructive; Cannot be Postponed Without Continually Increasing Danger. An Outline for Immediate Emancipation; and Remarks on Compensation.* New Haven: Hezekiah Howe, 1833. 43 p.

133. Sturge, Joseph. *The present condition of the negro population in the British colonies; particularly in relation to the working of the apprenticeship system established under the "Act for the Abolition of Slavery"* London: Johnston & Barrett, 1837.

134. Sturge, Joseph, and Thomas Harvey. *The West Indies in 1837: being the Journal of a visit to Antigua, Montserrat, Dominica, St. Lucia, Barbados, and Jamaica; undertaken for the purpose of ascertaining the actual condition of the negro population of those islands.* 2d ed. London: Hamilton, Adams, 1838. 476 p.

135. Taylor, Henry. *Autobiography of Henry Taylor, 1800–1875.* 2 vols. London: Longmans, 1885.

136. Taylor, Henry. *Correspondence of Henry Taylor.* Edited by Edward Dowden. London: Longmans, 1888. 421 p.

137. Thome, James A., and J. Horace Kimball. *Emancipation in the West Indies: A Six Months' Tour in Antigua, Barbadoes, and Jamaica, in the Year 1837.* New York: American Anti-Slavery Society, 1838. 128 p.

138. Trollope, Anthony. *The West Indies and the Spanish Main.* 1860. Reprint. London: Cass, 1968. 395 p.

139. Underhill, Edward B. *The Tragedy of Morant Bay.* 1895. Reprint. Freeport, N.Y.: Books for Libraries Press, 1971. 219 p.

140. Underhill, Edward Bean. *The West Indies: Their Social and Religious Condition.* London: Jackson, Walford, and Hodder, 1862. 493 p.

141. Wells, Carveth. *Bermuda in Three Colors.* New York: R. M. McBride, 1935. 271 p.

142. Williams, Eric, comp. *Documents on British West Indian History, 1807–1833.* Port-of-Spain, Trinidad: Trinidad, 1952. 406 p.

143. Williams, James. *A Narrative of Events Since the First of August, 1834. By James Williams, An Apprenticed Labourer in Jamaica.* London: W. Ball, 1837.

144. Wilmot, Swithin R., ed. *Adjustments to Emancipation in Jamaica.* Mona, Jamaica: Social History Project, Dept. of History, University of the West Indies, 1988. 40 p.

BRITISH PARLIAMENTARY PAPERS

145. Great Britain. Parliament. House of Commons. "Protest of the West India Merchants, Transmitted to Viscount Goderich on the 6th of April 1832." *Parliamentary Papers* 1831–32 (382), vol. 31. 2 p.

These merchants protested against and claimed compensation for the losses resulting from the Order of the King in Council of 2 November 1831 regarding the Crown colonies. They also protested actions by the Crown toward the legislative colonies in the British West Indies, arguing that "the intention of His Majesty's Ministers to propose to Parliament to adopt Fiscal Regulations for the purpose of coercing the Legislative Colonies" was "cruelly oppressive" given the "commercial distress to which they have been reduced." They also argued that given "the present dangerous and excited state of the Colonies, it is calculated to produce no other effect than the ruin and destruction of the Property of the Colonists, and ultimately the degradation and barbarism of the Negro Population." They also resented what they characterized as "arbitrary interference with private Property without first providing a Parliamentary Fund for compensation."

146. Great Britain. Parliament. House of Commons. "Report from the Select Committee on the Extinction of Slavery throughout the British Dominions: with Minutes and Evidence, Appendix and Index." *Parliamentary Papers* 1831–32 (721), vol. 20.

Materials of the 1823 Select Committee were primarily confined to Jamaica, including an investigation of "the fair and equitable consideration of the Interests of Private Property," in connection with the upcoming emancipation. Contains 560 pages of oral evidence, carefully indexed, from Jamaican religious leaders, colonial administrators, estate owners, and others. Testimonies give a detailed description of slave plantation political economy, as well as assessments of "willingness to work" on the part of the future "free black population." Population statistics for twelve estates (1817–29) include African and Creole population. Also contains commentary by the "Protector of Slaves" for British Guiana.

147. Great Britain. Parliament. House of Commons. "Papers in Explanation of Measures Adopted for Giving Effect to the Act for the Abolition of Slavery throughout the British Colonies, Part I: Jamaica." *Parliamentary Papers*. 1833–35, 1835 (177), vol. 50. 130 p.

Collection begins with Secretary of State Stanley's dispatches to British West India Governors asking for their cooperation in improving the lot of ex-slaves and asking for information on how best to proceed. Includes Stanley's original resolution for the Abolition of Colonial Slavery (14 May 1833) and the text of Jamaica's Slavery Abolition Act and Proclamation (March and April 1834). The legislative debates and Governor Musgrave's speeches concerning the act are included, as well as information related to Governor Sligo's subsequent difficulties with an intransigent House of Assembly. Also includes descriptions of early "acts of violence" related to the transition from slavery, including resistance by ex-slaves at Belvedere estate led by a woman, seventy-year-old Christian Mowatt. Evidence includes interviews with estate managers, proprietors, and special magistrates relating to the performance of apprentices, wages, and work conditions.

148. Great Britain. Parliament. House of Commons. "Papers Relating to the Abolition of Slavery (Jamaica, Barbadoes, British Guiana, and Mauritius)." *Parliamentary Papers* 1835 (278-I), vol. 50. 391 p.

This large collection of papers concerns the transition from slavery to apprenticeship. For Jamaica, collection includes Governor Sligo's advice to newly apprenticed ex-slaves, explaining work hours and rights as workers (August 1834). Also includes reports by Special Magistrates in a number of parishes on how ex-slaves reacted to wage labor and the apprenticeship system. A discussion of measures to establish minimum conditions for work hours, wages, and rations is included. Similar materials are found for British Guiana, including debate over "scales of task work" for day laborers, Sunday markets, and a new police force. Includes special judicial reports for 1834, which relay complaints from planters and evidence of resistance to the new system by workers, including the transcript of the "Trial of Damon," an ex-slave sentenced to death for "riotous behaviour" in Demerara. Evidence of violence on Grenada at the commencement of the apprentice system is also included. Appendices contain legislative acts and proclamations relative to the transformation from slavery to apprenticeship, including Jamaica's Act for the Abolition of Slavery (12 December 1833).

149. Great Britain. Parliament. House of Commons. "Papers Relating to the Abolition of Slavery (Antigua, Montserrat, St. Christopher, Nevis, Virgin Islands, Dominica, St. Vincent, Grenada, Tobago, Trinidad, St. Lucie, Honduras, Bahamas, Grand Caymanas, Bermuda, Cape of Good Hope)." *Parliamentary Papers* 1835 (278-II), vol. 50.

Similar in nature to (278-I), described above, this item includes numerous proclamations and ordinances for the establishment of new judicial and police districts. Description of work stoppages in Trinidad and the government's response (August 1834) are included. Speeches and proclamations by Governors for most colonies addressing the newly apprenticed ex-slave population reveal a great deal about colonial expectations of a smooth and rational transformation to wage labor. The speech of newly arrived Governor Young at St. Lucia to ex-slaves is indicative of this discourse.

150. Great Britain. Parliament. House of Commons. "Order in Council, Declaring that Satisfactory Provision Has Been Made in Various Colonies for Abolition of Slavery." *Parliamentary Papers* 1835 (514), vol. 51. 3 p.

151. Great Britain. Parliament. House of Commons. "Papers in Explanation of Proceedings of the Legislature of Jamaica in reference to the amendment of their original Act for Giving Effect to the Act of Parliament for Abolition of Slavery." *Parliamentary Papers* 1836 (0.44), vol. 48. 33 p.

Contains revision of original Act of Abolition by House of Assembly and the subsequent debate between the "Imperial and Colonial Legislatures." Lord Glenelg threatens to deny access to compensation loan money (act-in-aid) if the Jamaican legislature continues to be intransigent. This should be read with the collection of letters which follow in the same volume [1835 (174), vol. 480] from William Burge of the Jamaican Assembly to Lord Glenelg complaining of Governor Sligo's role in implementing abolition. These debates reveal much about the interests of planters and their control of the legislature.

152. Great Britain. Parliament. House of Commons. "Papers Relating to the Abolition of Slavery in the West India Colonies." *Parliamentary Papers* 1836 (166-I) (166-II), vol. 48–49.

Important aspects of the transition to apprenticeship are introduced in this item. The debate over valuation of apprentices is investigated in response to accusations that some planters and special magistrates are setting values too high in order to keep apprentices on plantations, particularly women apprentices. Statistics and individual cases for valuations for Jamaica are included. Special magistrates' reports are included for 1835 in Jamaica, including inspections of "native grounds" explaining living conditions and provisions for 987 estates. Reports describe employer complaints and worker resistance to new work schedules, as well as women's protests about working conditions. Also discusses initial investigations of corporal punishments of women in work houses, including the testimonies of women concerning such treatment. Part I concerns Jamaica, and part II the rest of British West India, including special magistrate's reports for British Guiana.

153. Great Britain. Parliament. House of Commons. "Report from the Select Committee on Negro Apprenticeship in the Colonies; together

with the Minutes of Evidence, Appendix and Index." *Parliamentary Papers* 1836 (560), vol. 15.

Extensive investigation into labor conditions in Jamaica following a Jamaican legislative attempt to change terms of apprenticeship against the advice of the Colonial Office. The contested issues included hours of work, use of "work houses" as punishment, using chains on women prisoners, marriage law provisions, and inadequate education. Oral evidence from a group of prominent Jamaican politicians, planters, and labor agents is included. Appendices are rich in material for British Guiana and Jamaica, as well as acts and ordinances from smaller colonies. There are replies to a questionnaire in Jamaica concerning the treatment of prisoners in eighteen parishes. Summarizes special magistrates' reports concerning the "industry and conduct" of the apprentices and conduct of masters (1835–36). Also has summaries by special magistrates of living conditions in and near plantations, wages, and valuation tables. Captain Oldrey comments on Jamaica's abolition acts, including their effects on Creoles, Maroons, and skilled "free" labor.

154. Great Britain. Parliament. House of Commons. "Papers in Explanation of Measures Adopted by Her Majesty's Government for giving effect to the Act for the Abolition of Slavery throughout the British Colonies; Part IV—(1) Jamaica, Barbados, British Guiana." *Parliamentary Papers* 1837 (521-I), vol. 53. 585 p. plus appendix.

Details production before and after abolition in Jamaica, including a general return of exports over a fifty-three-year period (1772–1836) as well as special magistrates' accounts of relative progress of apprentice system, testimony of apprentice laborers on "abuses and irregularities" existing in the House of Correction in St. John's and St. Mary's Parishes, and testimonies from St. Thomas-in-the-Vale concerning disputes between men and women apprentices over domestic work. Other items include stories of runaway apprentices, statistics on fines paid by overseers, and valuation returns. Barbados evidence includes prison investigations, lists of assaults, classification problems of apprentices, and useful monthly reports of special magistrates on the state of apprenticed labor (1836–37). British Guiana material is similar in content, including summaries of monthly reports of fifteen special magistrates for 1836. Also relates complaints lodged from Antigua and Montserrat that British Guiana was drawing away their laborers. Appendix contains a good collection in one place of acts and ordinances regulating lives of ex-slaves between 1836 and 1837, for example, masters and servants ordinances, Sunday markets proclamations, and criminal justice acts.

155. Great Britain. Parliament. House of Commons. "Report from C. J. Latrobe on Negro Education in Jamaica, with Correspondence Relating Thereto." *Parliamentary Papers* 1837–38 (113), vol. 48. 96 p.

Latrobe went to Jamaica in April 1837 to investigate how British money for Negro education had been utilized. His report (19 October 1837) related how he found numerous obstacles impeding the creation of schools. Missionaries complained that landowners were not cooperating in giving up land for the purpose, while others blamed missionaries for moving too slowly. Comparisons of various mission societies are provided as well as statistics on schools, attendance, and type of instruction for all parishes and major towns.

156. Great Britain. Parliament. House of Commons. "Papers Relative to the Abolition of Slavery: Part V—1: Jamaica." *Parliamentary Papers* 1837–38 (154-I), vol. 49.

Collection of papers relating to the public exposure in Britain of the severity of work and punishment in Jamaica. Includes the text of eighteen-year-old apprentice James William's "A Narrative of Events since the 1st August 1834," which describes the abuses of the workhouse and the treadmill. Popularized by the Anti-Slavery Society in Britain, William's narrative prompted an investigation of St. Ann Parish which produced further testimonies, including twenty-one by women and men describing "acts of severity and cruelty" experienced in the workhouse. Also contains special magistrates' reports, including comparisons of slavery and apprenticeship and correspondence between Governor Smith and Lord Glenelg (1837) on the failure to implement the nine-hour work day for apprentices. Includes apprentice valuation tables for all parishes for the years 1836 and 1837.

157. Great Britain. Parliament. House of Commons. "Papers Relative to the Abolition of Slavery throughout the British Colonies: Part V: Barbados and British Guiana." *Parliamentary Papers* 1837–38 (154-II), vol. 49.

Correspondence covers the period just prior to the abolition of the apprentice system, with reports by special magistrates and others on the crisis created over the apprentice classification system and valuations. Barbados material also discusses apprenticeship of children, valuations, classifications, statistics on punishments, and a reply by planters to accusations in the press that the apprentice system was equivalent to slavery. Similar materials included for British Guiana, such as responses to a Mr. Scoble, of the British Anti-Slavery Society, who wrote critically on the apprenticeship system. Includes Governor Young's reply to Scoble's descriptions of women apprentices being "condemned to the treadmill." Governor Young charges Scoble with spreading alarming rumors in St. Patrick Parish concerning a murdered laborer. Testimonies by other workers around the case are enclosed as well as examples of the inflated valuations of men and women apprentices, which made it more difficult for apprentices to buy out their contracts.

158. Great Britain. Parliament. House of Commons. "Orders in Council and Colonial Ordinances for the Better Regulation and Enforcement of the Relative Duties of Masters and Employers and Articled Servants, Tradesmen, and Labourers in the Colony of British Guiana, and of Correspondence Thereon." *Parliamentary Papers* 1837–38 (180)(232), vol. 52. 11 p.

Collection covers important negotiations between British Guiana and labor recruiters in Calcutta concerning East Indian emigration. John Gladstone of British Guiana expressed the opinion that "Negro Apprentices" were not likely to continue working on estates in the same manner after apprenticeship. Condition of Indian laborers is discussed, including charges of abuses of "Hill Coolies" in Demerara, comparison of treatment of Black and Indian laborers, and the ratio of men and women immigrants. Describes origin of term "Hill Coolies" and relates new masters and servants ordinances regarding the treatment of Indian workers.

159. Great Britain. Parliament. House of Commons. "Report from C. J. Latrobe to Lord Glenelg, on Negro Education in the Windward and Leeward Islands [also, Schedule Showing the Appropriation of the Sum of £30,000 Voted by Parliament in 1837, for the Promotion of Negro Education; also, Report of Trustees of Lady Mico's Charity]." *Parliamentary Papers* 1837–38 (520), vol. 48.

Latrobe visited a number of Islands in April 1838, collecting comparative evidence from the propertied classes about their views on "Negro Education." This report, similar to the report on Jamaica, contains schedules giving detailed information on each school and the missions running such schools. Contains general demographic material, including statistics on apprentice populations on various islands. Also contains data on how the monies appropriated for the "Promotion of Negro Education" were spent between 1837 and 1838, by Colony and Parish. The 1838 report of the Trustees of Lady Mico's Charity, established to help provide education for ex-slaves, is also included.

160. Great Britain. Parliament. House of Commons. "Papers Relating to the Measures Adopted by the Legislatures of Barbados, Montserrat, Nevis, Virgin Islands, St. Christopher, and St. Vincent, for the Abolition of the System of Apprenticeship of 1 August 1838." *Parliamentary Papers* 1837–38 (535), vol. 48. 35 p.

Concerns the views of the governors and special magistrates regarding the decision to end apprenticeships for both classes of apprentices in 1838—two years earlier than originally stipulated for the "praedial" class. Includes accounts of Privy Council meetings on Barbados, as well as an account of initial opposition in the Virgin Islands, which gave way to subsequent celebrations after President Isaacs attained approval of the measure. Includes texts of the acts for each island.

161. Great Britain. Parliament. House of Commons. "Papers Relating to Measures Adopted by the Legislatures of Jamaica, British Guiana, Dominica, Grenada, and Tobago, for the Abolition of the System of Apprenticeship on the 1st August 1838." *Parliamentary Papers* 1837–38 (727), vol. 48. 19 p.

Contains Jamaican Governor Smith's address to special session of the Assembly called to discuss the ending of apprenticeships for both praedial and nonpraedial classes. Address by Col. M'Turk in British Guiana to the Court Of Policy in favor of abolition is included, as are extracts from legislative councils on Dominica and Grenada on that topic. There is also a letter of opposition to the move from Tobago planters.

162. Great Britain. Parliament. House of Commons. "Papers Relative to the West Indies: Part I: Circular Instructions, Jamaica and British Guiana." *Parliamentary Papers* 1839 (107-I), vol. 35. 337 p.

Covering the period June 1838 to February 1839, this collection of correspondence covers the debate over the early ending of the apprenticeship system. Dispatches from Lord Glenelg recommend keeping special magistrates in place to help with a smooth transition and queries to colonial governors on the implementation of new legal protections for "free laborers." Responses from Jamaican Governor Smith contain texts of new acts, along with extensive reports from special magistrates on the problems incurred during the transition. Also contains "letters of thanks" to Governor Smith from "Freedmen," and the governor's proclamation to the freedmen telling them of their new responsibilities, particularly concerning rents. Reports on celebrations on the day of abolition and of threats of violence in Trelawny Parish led by "two black women." Includes numerous special magistrate reports on difficulties over wages and rents as well as Governor Smith's pessimistic report (December 1838) on the general failure of laborers and planters to come to agreement. Also includes petitions from "Emancipated Peasantry" (three thousand persons) complaining of lack of enfranchisement in St. Mary's Parish as well as rich material on British Guiana, with details of the day of abolition and reports by special magistrates on the immediate performance of free laborers.

163. Great Britain. Parliament. House of Commons. "Papers Relative to the West Indies, 1839: Part II, the Windward Islands' Government, Comprising Barbados, St. Vincent, Grenada, Tobago, Trinidad, St. Lucia." *Parliamentary Papers* 1839 (107-IV), vol. 36; (107-VI), vol. 37. 280 p.

This collection contains the text of each colony's Act for Abolishing Apprenticeships (1 August 1838). Contains various governors' speeches to apprenticed laborers prior to abolition; subsequent bills and acts to regulate free labor contracts, vagrancy, poor relief, and landlord and tenant relations. Gives evidence of each colony's response to abolition, such as increasing police powers and scope in rural areas. Also has accounts of disputes between proprietors and workers, special magistrates' records of cases heard after 1 August, and reports of violence in places such as Grenada, where ex-apprentices protected property, which they alleged had been "given to them by the Queen." Useful survey of responses related to the "Free system" in Barbados, as well as detailed reports from other Windward Islands about the performance of ex-apprentices.

164. Great Britain. Parliament. House of Commons. "Papers Relative to the West Indies, 1839: Part III., the Leeward Islands, Comprising Antigua, Montserrat, St. Christopher, Nevis, Virgin Islands, Dominica." *Parliamentary Papers* 1839 (107-V), vol. 37. 477 p.

Provides extensive material on the transition from apprenticeship to the "free labour" system, including accounts from special magistrates regarding the many problems encountered by such officials, who were often accused of favoritism towards workers. Questionnaires from the Colonial Office ask special magistrates about topics including labor conditions, health, education, living conditions, marriage, and old age. Details of prisons, police, and punishment are included, as are the changes in laws concerning masters and servants and vagrancy and trespassing. Specific statistics included on apprentice populations, giving wages, work hours, and disputes between workers and employers.

165. Great Britain. Parliament. House of Commons. "Report from C. J. Latrobe on Negro Education in British Guiana and Trinidad." *Parliamentary Papers* 1839 (35), vol. 34. 89 p.

166. Great Britain. Parliament. House of Commons. "Correspondence Relative to the Condition of the Hill Coolies, and of Other Labourers Who Have Been Introduced into British Guiana." *Parliamentary Papers* 1839 (463), vol. 39. 127 p.

Includes extensive census data of all recorded indentured laborers in British Guiana, covering the fifteen special magistrate districts. Includes name, place of origin, monthly wages, employment type, clothing inventory, health status, and comments related to "general behaviour." Census data for May 1838 gives idea of number of apprentices three months prior to the abolition of apprenticeship on 1 August 1838. Includes data on 1,877 males and 522 females of Indian, African, and European origin. Also includes an overview on the status of ex-apprentices, and their ability to redress injustices. Comments on intermarriage between Indians and Africans. Lengthy description of treatment of laborers on two plantations, "Bellevue" and "Vreed-en-Hoop," regarding mistreatment of "Hill Coolies."

167. Great Britain. Parliament. House of Commons. "Papers Relative to the West Indies, 1839: Part I—(5), Jamaica, British Guiana." *Parliamentary Papers* 1839 (523), vol. 36. 306 p.

Collection provides coverage of disputes both in government and on the plantations in the year following the end of apprenticeships. Includes accusations regarding special magistrates' role in mediating disputes over wages, rents, and working conditions for new wage workers. Other materials include: special magistrates' reports, court proceedings, school inspections, correspondence from landowners' associations, and newspaper reports. Includes accusations that Baptist missionaries were inciting laborers against landowners and transcripts of meetings. Nonpayment of rent by laborers in first year triggers Governor Smith's proclamation (25 May 1839) declaring that workers' belief that they owned houses and land was "totally erroneous." Includes workers' protest petitions and letters concerning accusations of "increased profligacy and immorality" of African women after end of apprenticeship. British Guiana materials include Governor Light's address on the effects of emancipation of indentured laborers (19 February 1839), returns from special magistrates for 1839 recording the complaints of laborers and employers, and protest petitions from "Free Labourers" to the Governor complaining of "ill-treatment, overwork, and underpay."

168. Great Britain. Parliament. House of Commons. "Papers Relative to the West Indies, 1840: Part I. Jamaica." *Parliamentary Papers* 1840 (212), vol. 35. 90 p.

Correspondence between colonial governors of Jamaica, Smith and Metcalfe, and the Marquis of Normanby and Lord John Russell on problems with the transition from an apprentice to a wage labor system. Descriptions of disturbances in St. George Parish, where magistrates were "pelted with stones" by women over issues of rents and evictions. Includes special magistrates' reports on conditions of agriculture, a resolution from peasantry in Vere Parish making claims to their houses and gardens, and statistics on land under cultivation for all parishes. Also contains reports from Westmoreland Parish on an insurrection allegedly begun by rumors originating from a black woman, Sara Oliphant, of the impending murder of all black men by the white and brown men, and the re-enslavement of black women. Also contains papers on the transition from Governor Smith to Governor Metcalfe, with reports of threats on Smith's life and Metcalfe's report on the state of the island (16 October 1939).

169. Great Britain. Parliament. House of Commons. "Despatch of Lord Glenelg, May 1838, Prohibiting the Further Apprenticeship of Liberated Africans in the West Indies. . . ." *Parliamentary Papers* 1840 (224), vol. 34. 5 p.

Contains orders to the governors of the West Indies Colonies from Lord Glenelg (15 May 1839) to stop the practice of indenturing Africans sent to these islands after having been freed from slave ships. A subsequent despatch gives special magistrates the responsibility for seeing that such freed Africans are assisted in finding employment and accommodation. (See *PP* 1841 Sess. II [346], vol. 3 for a detailed example of this process recorded by a special magistrate in British Guiana.)

170. Great Britain. Parliament. House of Commons. "Reports from, or Despatches to, the Governor of British Guiana, Respecting the Hill Coolies Introduced into that Colony." *Parliamentary Papers* 1840 (77), vol. 34. 55 p.

Contains reports of conditions of Indian laborers based on investigation of complaints on various plantations. Includes monthly special magistrate reports for 1839 covering six districts with answers to survey on treatment of Indian workers and reference to relations between Indians and Africans. Also includes detailed statistical return for 257 Indians apprenticed to Demerara and Berbice, including names, place of origin in India, caste, and the name of proprietor to whom they were contracted.

171. Great Britain. Parliament. House of Commons. "Papers Relative to the West Indies, 1840: Part II: Barbados." *Parliamentary Papers* 1841 (282), vol. 35. 255 p.

Correspondence between Governor MacGregor and the Marquis of Normanby and Lord Russell from February 1839 to May 1840. Primary topic is court reforms, including changes in judicial offices, the Court of Appeals, marriage laws, and an act "to prevent the clandestine deportation of young persons." Reports from police magistrates on the working of the "free labor system," with comparisons made to the performance of labor during apprenticeships. Also includes information on prisons, punishments, and laws to help keep laborers on the island. Records of an experimental "Court of Reconciliation" give testimony of workers, including cases involving women, domestic violence, and land disputes.

172. Great Britain. Parliament. House of Commons. "Papers Relative to the West Indies: British Guiana." *Parliamentary Papers* 1841 (321), vol. 16; 1842 (376), vol. 29.

Concerns the attempt by Governor Light and landowners to revive immigration of Indians to the colony, including monthly reports on the status of the "Hill Coolies," production statistics, ordinances on establishment of police, abolition of Sunday markets, and poor relief. Special magistrates' records of complaints (monthly, 1839–41) are included. Collection is a good source on the progress made by ex-slaves and apprentices in purchasing their own land. Includes survey of estates by special magistrates and statistics on estates and lands purchased by laborers. Detailed description given of purchases of plantation "New Orange," Nassau in Demerera. Also contains a report by two African-American visitors from the "Free Coloured People of Baltimore" (January 1840) giving their impressions of British Guiana and Trinidad as possible places to settle and a detailed report by Special Magistrate Wolseley on his visits to plantations in Demerara (July 1841).

173. Great Britain. Parliament. House of Commons. "Letter from the Secretary to the Government of India to the Committee Appointed to Inquire Respecting the Exportation of Hill Coolies. . . . Report Made by that Committee. . . ." *Parliamentary Papers* 1841 (45), vol. 16.

174. Great Britain. Parliament. House of Commons. "Despatch from the Governor of British Guiana to Secretary of State for Colonies.

Transmitting a Report on the State of the Labouring Population of Demerara and Berbice." *Parliamentary Papers* 1841 Sess. II (346), vol. 3. 18 p.

Report written by Mr. Woslely, circuit special magistrate, detailing his visit to the areas where complaints of ill-treatment of Indian laborers first originated. The report gives an account of conditions following the transition to "free labour" and the increase in agricultural production in 1840. Woslely describes new settlements of ex-slaves and relocated Sierra Leone Africans on lands purchased by associations of plantation workers. (Details of purchases provided.) Also describes the process of allocating newly arrived freed Africans from slave ships captured off Brazilian coast. Describes how 145 women, men, and children were divided into groups of fifteen and twenty and sent to plantations in the area. Statistical data provided on crop production and wages (1840) for twenty-nine plantations; census of ninety-one Sierra Leone Africans in Demerara; captured Africans living in Berbice; and total land purchased by former slaves and apprenticed laborers.

175. Great Britain. Parliament. House of Commons. "Papers Relative to the West Indies: Part II Jamaica." *Parliamentary Papers* 1841, sess. II, (344), vol. 3. 401 p.

Significant collection of evidence concerning the transition to "free labour" and the response of the colonial state. Correspondence between Governor Metcalfe and Lord John Russell complaining of the intervention of special magistrates against the interest of landholders. Summary of Jamaican legislation and debates reveals the tensions between property owners and labor. Extensive report on the inadequacies of Jamaican prisons and gaols, with statistics and some prison plans. Contains biannual reports of special magistrates covering labor conditions, landlord-tenant relations, missionary activities, education, wage and labor costs, and production statistics. One report includes a comparison of plantation expenditures under slavery, apprenticeship, and freedom. Also includes statistics on increase in property-owning laborers between 1838 and 1840.

176. Great Britain. Parliament. House of Commons. "Hill Coolies: Letter, Dated 22nd March 1842, from the Court of Directors." *Parliamentary Papers* 1842 (192), vol. 30.

177. Great Britain. Parliament. House of Commons. "Papers Relative to the West Indies; Antigua, Trinidad, St. Lucia, Grenada, 1841–42." *Parliamentary Papers* 1842 (379), vol. 29. 178 p.

Contains special magistrates' reports concerning the performance of free laborers following abolition of apprenticeships. Trinidad material also concerned with immigrant laborers from Sierra Leone and evidence produced by the Agricultural and Immigration Society on the difficulty of finding laborers. Includes population statistics from 1797 to 1838. St. Lucia special magistrates' reports include answers to questionnaire about the general state of the peasantry.

178. Great Britain. Parliament. House of Commons. "Report from the Select Committee on West India Colonies; Together with the Minutes of Evidence, Appendix, and Index." *Parliamentary Papers* 1842 (479), vol. 13. 15, xv, 859 p.

A select committee appointed in March of 1842 "to inquire into the State of the different West India Colonies, in Reference to the existing relations between Employers and Labourers, the Rate of Wages, the Supply of Labour, the System and Expense of Cultivation, and the General State of their Rural and Agricultural Economy." Other related subjects include plantation technology, tenancy, tariffs/taxes, strikes, sugar, internal improvements, rents, religion, rum, police, provision grounds, land purchase by Black-West Indians, family, culture, medical practice/mortality, marriage, the master/servant relationship, magistrates (local administration of the laws), family, immigration, women, women's work, crime, and absenteeism. Documents include the commission's summary report and recommendations, the proceedings of the select committee, and the verbatim testimony of witnesses from St. Vincent, Trinidad, Barbados, British Guiana, Grenada, Antigua, St. Kitts, and Jamaica. Witnesses were mostly proprietors or estate managers, but others came from across the social spectrum. Supporting correspondence and documents (bills, ordinances, orders in council, and material such as reports submitted to the governor by the managers or owners of particular estates) are also appended. A ninety-four-page alphabetical subject index is included.

179. Great Britain. Parliament. House of Commons. "Returns on the Number of Immigrants into the British West India Colonies and British Guiana since 1834, and All Votes of Money for Purposes of Immigration, and Annual Expenditure of the Same for the Like Period." *Parliamentary Papers* 1843 (136), vol. 33.

Statistical returns for all colonies, broken down by colony, year, sex, immigrants (European), and "Captured Africans." Good example of occasional returns which have statistical value as they cover period between 1834 and 1842 (exact years vary by colony).

180. Great Britain. Parliament. House of Commons. "Regulations and Orders for the Protection of Coolies (Labourers), Proceeding to and from Mauritius or Any Other Place." *Parliamentary Papers* 1843 (148), vol. 35.

181. Great Britain. Parliament. House of Commons. "Correspondence Relating to the Return of Coolies from British Guiana to India." *Parliamentary Papers* 1843 (404), vol. 35.

Rich and detailed accounts of the difficult process of repatriating Indian laborers after the lapse of their five-year contracts. Includes accounts of special magistrates' and Governor Light's personal interventions in relations between proprietors and Indian workers as well as his admission of the previous "fatal neglect" of Indian workers on the estates of Demerara's west coast. Offers details on individual workers' savings upon date of departure for Calcutta as well as disputes over final payments and allowances and reports of Indian men remaining behind, buying land, and marrying local women.

182. Great Britain. Parliament. House of Commons. "Papers Relative to Emigration from the West Coast of Africa to the West Indies." *Parliamentary Papers* 1843 (438), vol. 34. 56 p.

Correspondence concerning the possibility of recruiting Africans to come to British Guiana. Includes Lord Stanley's circular dispatch to all West Indies Colonies (February 1843) recommending legislation to promote such emigration. Also contains Governor Light's personal observations of conditions of African immigrants he visited on plantations in Berbice and Demerara and a description of a failed European settlement on the Niger river in west Africa. A letter from Lord Stanley to the Earl of Aberdeen compares the labor situation in Jamaica with that of Barbados, Antigua, St. Christopher, and Trindidad. Stanley counters charges made by the Spanish that the Jamaican colony was forcing Africans from Sierra Leone to become laborers. Also includes instructions for Governor MacDonald of Sierra Leone about future emigration.

183. Great Britain. Parliament. House of Commons. "Correspondence Relative to the Late Disturbances Among the Negroes in the Island of Dominica." *Parliamentary Papers* 1844 (640), vol. 34. 15 p.

Correspondence between Governor FitzRoy and Lord Stanley explaining disturbances as a response to attempts to carry out a census of the rural population. According to Governor FitzRoy, rumors existed among laborers "that the Government intended to reconvert them into slaves." Reportedly many of those involved were refugees from French islands, where they had escaped enslavement. Includes detailed accounts of events by Dominica's President Laidlaw.

184. Great Britain. Parliament. House of Commons. "Extracts of Despatches Relating to the Disturbances in the Island of Dominica." *Parliamentary Papers* 1845 (146), vol. 31. 103 p.

Includes special reports from special magistrates concerning the September 1844 disturbances. President Laidlaw also comments on the political nature of the conflict between "emancipated negroes and coloured people" over political rights and rights to property. Describes causes of the disturbances and of the militia's firing without orders and also gives lists of prisoners and sentences and minutes of trials. Includes a petition from the prisoners to Queen Victoria asking for pardons in which they explain that they thought census was to be used to make them slaves again.

185. Great Britain. Parliament. House of Commons. "Copies of the Last Census of the Population taken in each of the British West Indian Islands and British Guiana. Together with Information Received in the Colonial Department Relative to the Number of Emancipated Negroes Who Have Become Freeholders, the Extent of land Purchased by Them, and the Sums of Money paid for Such Purchase." *Parliamentary Papers* 1845 (426), vol. 31. 43 p.

Gives results of the 1844 census—including the troubled Dominican one—for most of the British West Indies. Figures reported by sex, race, ethnicity, occupation, and number of slaves. Completeness varies by colony. There is also a return listing estates and abandoned estates in British Guiana that were purchased by agricultural laborers.

186. Great Britain. Parliament. House of Commons. "Correspondence relative to the Labouring Population in the West Indies." *Parliamentary Papers* 1845 (642), vol. 31. 200 p.

Contains a collection of various special magistrates' reports for 1844 and 1845 in a number of colonies, with a focus on British Guiana. Includes a report on the "metayer system" (sharecropping) and replies by special magistrates to the British Anti-Slavery Society on "Emancipation in the British Colonies."

187. Great Britain. Parliament. House of Commons. "Despatches and Correspondence between the Colonial Office and the Authorities in Each of the West Indian Colonies, Relative to a Proposed Loan of Money in Aid of the Immigration of Labour into those Colonies. Also Resolutions Passed by the Legislative Assemblies of Each

Colony, in Relation to the Said Proposed Loan." *Parliamentary Papers* 1843 to 1845, 1846 (322), vol. 30. 202 p.

Papers establishing the reintroduction of emigration from India to Jamaica, British Guiana, Trinidad, and St. Lucia. Outlines the number of immigrants for each colony and the amount of British loans for their transport. Includes applications for laborers from various plantations; details of ships carrying immigrants from India to the West Indies; description of reception of Indian workers in Jamaica (1845); and conditions of African workers, including investigations into their efficiency as laborers carried out in Vere and Clarendon Parishes, Jamaica. Trinidad material includes statistics on immigrants for 1844 and 1845 by age, sex, and place of origin. British Guiana correspondence includes initial signs of political crisis in the government over the extension of the Civil List, which occurred at the same time as the immigration loan vote.

188. Great Britain. Parliament. House of Commons. "Rules Issued by the Colonial Land and Emigration Commissioners dated the 27th Day of October 1843, and Sanctioned by the Secretary of State for the Colonies, Relating to the Immigration of Chinese Labourers from the British Settlements in the Straits of Malacca into the Colonies of Guiana, Trinidad, and Jamaica. Despatch Addressed by Lord Stanley to the Governor of Jamaica dated the 26th Day of October 1843, Relating to Contracts with Labourers; Despatch Addressed to the Governor of Trinidad, Relative to the Regulations of the Rights of Masters and Servants." *Parliamentary Papers* 1846 (323), vol. 27. 20 p.

Dispatch from Gladstone to Governors of the British West Indies on measures for promoting immigration of laborers to the West India colonies. Contains Gladstone's correspondence with the West India Committee in London regarding the need to reintroduce emigration from East India. Shows the influence of the West India Committee on colonial policy. At first Gladstone agrees to repeal ban on contracts of service with Africans and others from Europe and North America (see Order in Council in [1846 (168), vol. 27]), but this is later rescinded after criticism from Spain that British were continuing the importation of slaves from areas where they had recently been freed. The decision is then reached to reopen emigration from India and the west coast of Africa.

189. Great Britain. Parliament. House of Commons. "Regulations or Instructions under which the Crown Lands in the West India Colonies and British Guiana Are Permitted to be Put up for Sale." *Parliamentary Papers* 1846 (514), vol. 30. 40 p.

Contains an important statement by Lord Glenelg to the governors of the West Indian colonies (30 January 1836) on the issue of alienation of land to free laborers. Glenelg's argument concerns the dilemma of how to keep laborers working at the "cultivation of exportable produce" while allowing them the "freedom" to purchase their own land, including the suggestion that each colony should set the price of available Crown land "out of reach of persons without capital." Provides minimum price guidelines and government notices from colonies respecting these prices. Followed by debate over how to handle squatters on Crown lands.

190. Great Britain. Parliament. House of Commons. "Order in Council, 1838, for Regulating within the Colonies of British Guiana, &c. the Relative Rights and Duties of Masters and Servants." *Parliamentary Papers* 1846 (in 168), vol. 27.

191. Great Britain. Parliament. House of Commons. "Correspondence Relative to the Supply of Labour to the British Colonies in the West Indies and Mauritius." *Parliamentary Papers* 1847 (in 325), vol. 39.

Contains circulars to governors of the British West Indies from Earl Grey (September 1846–January 1847) outlawing the practice of paying bounty for laborers brought from one colony in the West Indies to work in another. Also discusses "evils experienced from the unsteady habits of certain classes of immigrants," the number of special magistrates, and the education of laboring classes. Jamaican responses include Major General Berkeley's correspondence with Gladstone and Earl Grey. Transmits opinion of Jamaican Assembly that Indian emigration is too costly and that Africans should instead be brought from the "Kroo Coast" by British steamships. Governor Light of British Guiana comments on the "moral effect" on Creole laborers of the introduction of coolies; protests from missionaries against an 1846 Employer and Servant Ordinance; half-yearly special magistrates' reports for 1847; and a report on the workings of the "metayer system" in British Guiana. Trinidad material includes information on immigration of one thousand Indian laborers, Portuguese from Madeira, and Africans from the "Kroo Coast."

192. Great Britain. Parliament. House of Commons. "First Report from the Select Committee on Sugar and Coffee Planting in the East and West Indies and the Mauritius together with the Minutes of Evidence, and Appendix." *Parliamentary Papers* 1847–48 (123), vol. 23, part I.

193. Great Britain. Parliament. House of Commons. "Memorial of the West India Association, on the Present State of the British West India Colonies, Addressed to Lord John Russell, First Lord of Her Majesty's Treasury." *Parliamentary Papers* 1847–48 (17), vol. 45. 5 p.

Pleading imminent financial ruin, this London-based group of planters requested differential duties on slave-grown sugar, labor migration to the West Indies, loan guarantees for agricultural improvements, changes in the regulations and duties on rum and rum production, and permission to market their sugar in any convenient form. Memorial dated 25 October 1837.

194. Great Britain. Parliament. House of Commons. "Despatches from Lord Stanley, Mr. Secretary Gladstone, and Earl Grey, Dated in 1844 and Subsequent Years, to Governor Light, Authorising the Introduction of Coolies into British Guiana." *Parliamentary Papers* 1847–48 (370), vol. 44.

Includes correspondence from Lord Stanley to Governor Light (31 July 1844) authorizing immigration of Indian laborers into British Guiana. Gives authorized number of workers and cost estimate. Other enclosures give higher estimates and numbers to be sent as well as numbers for Jamaica and Trinidad. Information on subsequent dealings with contractors and shippers are included.

195. Great Britain. Parliament. House of Commons. "Despatches relating to the Distress prevailing in the West India Colonies and the Mauritius." Despatches from the Governors of the West India Colonies and Mauritius relative to their General condition, and the Measures in Progress for the Promotion of Immigration; also, of the answers of the Secretary of State to any of the Above Communications." *Parliamentary Papers.* 1847–48 (399), vol. 45.

Collection of dispatches from governors to the Colonial Office requesting immediate relief, such as the possible raising of duties on their competitors' sugar. Earl Grey's response to Governor C. E. Grey of Jamaica is critical of the performance of government and planters since abolition, blaming them for the poor return they receive because production costs and wages remain too high. Remainder of collection contains correspondence on emigration, including Africans from Sierra Leone. Reports on racial tensions between workers, including work stoppages by Creoles in British Guiana. Also includes report on "Coolie" labor in Jamaica containing replies from estates on desertion and vagrancy (1847). Special magistrates' reports from Tobago, St. Lucia and Montserrat, along with governor's reports, portray tense labor relations. The crisis, especially in British Guiana, is attributed to the inability of owners to pay wages due to the collapse of many local and London banks in 1848. The failure of the West India Bank at Nevis is described.

196. Great Britain. Parliament. House of Commons. "Acts for the Suppression of Vagrancy, for the Prevention of Squatting, or for the Encouragement and Enforcement of Labour Contracts, Passed by any of the Colonial Legislatures or Councils since the Year 1834, but Disallowed by the Secretary of State for the Colonies." *Parliamentary Papers* 1847–48 (419), vol. 45.

Includes the text of the acts devised in the colonies to regulate labor and living conditions, but which were deemed too harsh by the Colonial Office. Most fall between the years 1836 to 1838, but some are from the 1840s. Indicates the extent to which colonial legislatures went in their attempts to induce more productivity from ex-slaves and immigrants and how a portion of such legislation offended British sensibilities.

197. Great Britain. Parliament. House of Commons. "Laws, Ordinances, and Rules, not hitherto printed, now in Force in each of the West India Colonies, for the Regulation of Labour between Masters and Labourers and Starting Dates of their being put in Force." *Parliamentary Papers*. [In continuation of 27 March 1846, no. 168; May 1846, no. 323; 26 August 1846, no. 196, part III; and 27 April 1847, no. 325] 1847–48 (63), vol. 45. 62 p.

198. Great Britain. Parliament. House of Commons. "Correspondence between the Secretary of State and the Governors of the Sugar Growing colonies, as to the Distress now Existing in those Colonies." *Parliamentary Papers* 1847–48 (749), vol. 46.

Collection shows widespread breakdown in the immigration system with the decline in sugar revenues. Consists primarily of correspondence—including Blue Books and extracts from immigration and special magistrates' reports—on the inability of colonies to pay for immigrants and requests for emergency loans. Governor Light, of British Guiana, argues in favor of emergency assistance. Governor Light warns that if laborers were to buy up foreclosed farms and plantations, "civilization would not benefit from this change of hands." Includes texts of legislative meetings in various colonies on the issue of "distress."

199. Great Britain. Parliament. House of Commons. "Correspondence with the Governors of Jamaica, Trinidad, and Mauritius, Relating to the General Condition and Government of these Colonies." *Parliamentary Papers* 1849 (280) (280-II), vol. 37.

The Jamaican papers include reports concerning disturbances among the workers in August 1848 caused by rumors of annexation to the United States and the general failure of the sugar economy. Governor Grey requests preferential duty treatment as well as British assistance for new emigration. Governor Grey also accuses Baptist ministers of inciting the Black population with threats of slavery from America and Spain. Includes report of disturbances from a number of parishes. Reports on unrelated attacks on tax collectors and on police in St. Mary and St. Ann parishes are also included. Jamaica reports include: general economic statistics for 1847 and 1848; plans for an Island Bank; and an education report (1848). Part II, covering Trinidad, contains political economy statistics, ordinances against squatters, Governor Harris' reports of opposition from squatters, and information on loans for infrastructure, including a railway.

200. Great Britain. Parliament. House of Commons. "First Report from the Select Committee on Ceylon and British Guiana; together with the Minutes of Evidence, and Appendix." *Parliamentary Papers* 1849 (297), vol. 11. xxxii, 383, vi, 43 p.

These papers were produced by the committee formed to investigate the grievances of colonists in British Guiana and to report how these grievances might best be resolved. The appendices include the petitions from 1847 to 1849 of proprietors, planters, merchants, and others in the colony outlining these grievances, which concerned the "crisis of emancipation, and that of the removal of protection" at a time when other countries were still producing sugar using slaves. Also included here are the report and proceedings of the committee, the minutes of evidence, a list of appendices and the appendices themselves, an index, and a separate list of subject headings used in the index. Materials date from 9 Sept 1840 to 18 May 1849. The witnesses before the Committee were Sir Henry Light (ex-Governor), Charles Cox (of the Colonial Office), William Robertson Sandbach (former member of the Combined Court), Matthew James Higgins (estate owner), and William Henry Holmes (Provost-Marshal). Primary subjects include the civil list, the franchise, political representation, prisons, plantation management, and immigration.

201. Great Britain. Parliament. House of Commons. "Second Report from the Select Committee on Ceylon and British Guiana." *Parliamentary Papers* 1849 (573), vol. 11. 3 p.

A resolution dated 27 July 1849 for a commission to be appointed "to inquire on the spot into the means taken for the repression of the late [1848] Insurrection at Ceylon."

202. Great Britain. Parliament. House of Commons. "Third Report from the Select Committee on Ceylon and British Guiana; together with the Proceedings of the Committee." *Parliamentary Papers* 1849 (591), vol. 11. 7 p.

Consists of the committee's request, dated 31 July 1849, that committee members be reappointed in the following session to continue their investigations into the 1848 Ceylon uprising and its suppression, and that they should have the means to "ensure the attendance" of several key participants.

203. Great Britain. Parliament. House of Commons. "Despatches from the Governor of British Guiana, Showing the State of the Dispute between the Combined Court and the Governor, Respecting the Estimates for the Public Service." *Parliamentary Papers* 1849 (594), vol. 37; 1850 (21), vol. 39; 1851 (154), vol. 36. 200 p., 85 p.

204. Great Britain. Parliament. House of Commons. "Copies of the Correspondence Which Has Taken Place Between the Board of Guardians of St. Pancras and the Poor-Law Board, Relative to the Emigration of Children to the Bermudas: And, of Any Correspondence Which Has Been Transmitted by the Children So Sent Out by the Board of Guardians of St. Pancras, as to Their Condition and Prospects in the Bermudas, and Which Has Been Forwarded by the Aforesaid Board of Guardians to the Poor-Law Board." *Parliamentary Papers* 1851 (243), vol. 40. 20 p.

Correspondence and attachments concerning an inquiry by the Board of Guardians into the transportation of pauper children from the poor house in the parish of St. Pancras, England, to Bermuda, where they were apprenticed as servants until the age of eighteen. The Poor Law Board determined that the emigration of these children was conducted "with a regard for their welfare" but illegal nonetheless. Correspondence dates from 6 March 1850 to 14 February 1851.

205. Great Britain. Parliament. House of Commons. "Papers Relative to Legislative Proceedings in Jamaica." *Parliamentary Papers* 1852–53 (1655), vol. 65; 1854 (1806), vol. 40. 65 p., 144 p.

Concerns the political and economic crises in Jamaica between 1852 and 1853. Governor Grey writes to the Colonial Office explaining the political stalemate over proposed constitutional reforms and changes in property rights. His letter describes social structure of the island's politics, including comments on planters and "Coloureds" and Jews. Includes his speeches to the Council and Assembly. Second volume covers transition from Governor Grey to Governor Barkly, including Grey's instructions to Barkly which sum up the difficulties with the Legislature. Barkly reports on eventual break in the financial stalemate, while the Duke of Newcastle sends a dispatch admonishing Jamaican handling of economy, comparing it with other British West Indian colonies.

206. Great Britain. Parliament. House of Commons. "Correspondence with the Superintendent of British Trade in China, upon the Subject of Emigration from that Country." *Parliamentary Papers* 1852–53 (1686), vol. 68. 102 p.

Correspondence and related documents dated 17 May 1852 to 30 March 1853 focusing on the "abuses" of British shipmasters and others involved in the emigration of Chinese laborers. Most of the material deals with an uprising of Chinese at Amoy (21–24 November 1852) following the attempt of a British merchant to free a "coolie broker" from a local Chinese police station. The British inquiry into the event focused on the question of whether labor migrations were voluntary or coerced. Includes the "Minutes of Evidence" taken at the local Court of Inquiry from British officials, missionaries, ship employees, merchants, "coolie brokers," "coolies," potential Chinese emigrants, and Chinese interpreters. Includes a protest written by local Chinese "Scholars and Merchants" against the entrapment of people by the brokers, as well as a similar proclamation by the local Chinese police promising punishment for such offenders. Though focusing on the China end of the China-West Indies trade, specific shipments of laborers from Amoy to San Francisco (United States), Havana (Cuba), Chincha Island (Peru), and Demerara (British Guiana) are mentioned. Also includes responses of British consuls at various Chinese ports (Shanghai, Ningpo, Canton, and Amoy) regarding the operation of the trade and treatment of the emigrants. Blank labor contracts for Chinese emigrating to Havana and Demerara are included.

207. Great Britain. Parliament. House of Commons. "Returns of the Names of All Persons, of Every Denomination, Who Were in the Service or Pay of Her Majesty's Commissioners for Colonial Land and Emigration on the 1st Day of July 1852, with the Amount of Their Salaries, the Date of Their Appointment, and the Hours of

Attendance Each Day: Of the Name and Tonnage of All Vessels or Ships Chartered by the Commissioners, the Owners' Names, the Price Paid or Agreed To Be Paid for the Conveyance and Victualling Each Statute Adult, and the Number of Statute Adults Taken by Each Ship for the Last Two Years: And, of All Monies Received by the Commissioners under Acts or Votes of Parliament, or from the Sale of Colonial Lands, or from Any Other Source, for the Purpose of Emigration, and How the Same Have from Time to Time Been Disbursed, for the Last Two Years, Being a Continuation of a Return Ordered To Be Printed by the House of Commons, on the 15th Day of August 1850." *Parliamentary Papers* 1852–53 (23), vol. 68. 22 p.

Includes three tables. The second table deals with New South Wales, Victoria, South Australia, Van Diemen's Land, Western Australia, Cape of Good Hope, New Zealand, India to the West Indies, West Indies to India, and Africa and Rio de Janeiro to the West Indies. The third table contains information concerning New South Wales, Victoria, South Australia, Western Australia, Van Diemen's Land, New Zealand, Cape of Good Hope, District of Natal, Falkland Islands, Labuan, Jamaica, British Guiana, and Trinidad, as well as "Colonial Remittances (Australia, &c.)," "Liberated African Services," and "Indian Emigration," among others.

208. Great Britain. Parliament. House of Commons. "Despatches Relative to the Condition of the Sugar-Growing Colonies, Part II, Jamaica." *Parliamentary Papers*. in Continuation of Paper No. 624 of 1851, 1852–53 (76), vol. 67. 361 p.

This collection includes reports on mistreatment of African immigrants in St. Thomas-in-the-East parish, including whipping and refusal to pay wages; cholera outbreak, including medical inspectors report; and disturbances at St. David's parish and Spanish Town over an election in which a colored candidate lost to a white merchant. Governor Grey reports on the cooperation between Blacks and the colored populations in the election disturbances as evidence of their desire for political influence and power. Also contains dispatch from Earl Grey (February 1851) on Jamaican uses of existing labor supply which criticizes the postabolition system of production and wages. Statistics are included showing the shortage of laborers in various parishes.

209. Great Britain. Parliament. House of Commons. "Despatches Relative to the Condition of the Sugar-Growing Colonies, Part III: Trinidad." *Parliamentary Papers* 1852–53 (936), vol. 67. 283 p.

Extensive collection on African immigration, imperial loans, and the desperate financial situation of the colony in 1850. Also contains Governor Harris's account of the riot at Port of Spain (October 1849), which involved the seizure of the government house by the "common people" and then spread to nearby sugar estates. Numerous causes for protest are cited including new prison regulations, cancellation of Sunday markets, rumors of wage reductions, and the removal of squatters. Rumors of new property taxes brought small landowners into the march on Port of Spain. Reports are made of abuses of African immigrants, including accounts by the British Anti-Slavery Society, related to the separation of family members upon arrival in Trinidad. A report on African immigration, including repatriation, is included.

210. Great Britain. Parliament. House of Commons. "Despatches Relating to Chinese Immigrants Recently Introduced into the Colonies of British Guiana and Trinidad." *Parliamentary Papers* 1852–53 (986), vol. 68. viii, 190 p.

Correspondence and attached documents dated 25 August 1851 to 16 August 1853 between governors of British Guiana and Trinidad, the secretary of state's office, the emigration agent in China, and the colonial land and emigration commissioners. Documents focus on the attempts made by planters and officials of British Guiana and Trinidad to introduce Chinese laborers into their colonies. Topics addressed include how workers were secured and transported, legal regulation of the traffic by the various governments involved, discussions of the nature of the contract and its terms, and concerns expressed about various uprisings and strikes, as well as assessments of the value of immigrant labor, the immigration of females, and bounties. Includes reports by special magistrates, immigration agents, health officers, and the "Committee of Immigration Correspondence" (a group of planters in British Guiana interested in immigration). Also includes copies of labor contracts and of ordinances passed between 1851 and 1853 concerning immigration and master/servant relations as well as a detailed chronological subject index.

211. Great Britain. Parliament. House of Commons. "Account of the Declared Value of the various Articles of British Produce and Manufactures Exported to the British West India Colonies, in each of the past Seven Years." *Parliamentary Papers*. Ending the 5th day of January 1853, 1854 (15), vol. 65. 37 p.

212. Great Britain. Parliament. House of Commons. "Correspondence upon the Subject of Emigration from China." *Parliamentary Papers* 1854–55 (0.7), vol. 39. 93 p.

In the wake of the riots in the streets of Amoy in November, 1852 (See 1852–53 [1686], vol. 68), and several other tragedies, these papers document the efforts of the emigration agent in China, the Consul at Canton, the first assistant in the consulate at Amoy, and the governor of British Guiana to figure out whether and under what conditions to continue Chinese emigration. Concerns regarding "the evils resulting from a disparity of the sexes" and the precedent of male communities formed earlier in Australia prompted discussion of the desirability of female emigrants. Marriage and family practices among the Chinese are discussed in detail. Of particular interest is a paper entitled "Marriage, Affinity, and Inheritance in China" and six large charts which map out these relationships. Labor migrations to Chincha Island (Peru) and to Havana are mentioned.

213. Great Britain. Parliament. House of Commons. "Accounts of the Quantities of the Principal Articles Imported into and Exported from the United Kingdom, the British Settlements in Australia, the United States of America, the Canadian Possession, the British West Indies, and Brazil, & c." *Parliamentary Papers* 1856 (351), vol. 55. 34 p.

214. Great Britain. Parliament. House of Commons. "Correspondence between the Governor of British Guiana and the Secretary of State for the Colonies, on the Subject of the Recent Disturbances in that Colony." *Parliamentary Papers* 1856 (432), vol. 44. 89 p.

Contains correspondence mainly from Governor Wodehouse to Secretary of State for Colonies H. Labouchere. Wodehouse identifies the instigator of the disturbances of February 1856 as John S. Orr, an anti-Catholic agitator who allegedly worked "to arouse the passions of the black and coloured populations against the Portuguese immigrants." The looting of Portuguese shops suggests an economic motive for the attack on recently arrived immigrants from Medeira. Includes transcript of John Orr's trial and accounts from rural and town sources about the extent of rioting and speculations on motives. Information on relations between Africans, Creoles, and Portuguese is provided.

215. Great Britain. Parliament. House of Commons. "Recent Communications to or from the Foreign Office, Colonial Office, Board of Trade, and Any Other Department of Her Majesty's Government,

on the Subject of Mortality on Board the 'Duke of Portland,' or Any Other British Ships Carrying Emigrants from China." *Parliamentary Papers* 1857 Sess. 1 (147), vol. 10. 19 p.

Correspondence and attachments dating from 3 October 1856 to 25 February 1857 concerning the 1856 voyages from Hong Kong to Havana of the *Duke of Portland* and the *John Calvin*. Though the figures vary, as many as 305 out of the 627 immigrants on board these ships died on the passage due to "natural death" and suicide. Contains the investigation into these tragedies by the British Foreign Office, including reports of emigration officials, doctors, and ship personnel. Continued by 1857–58 (521), vol. 43.

216. Great Britain. Parliament. House of Commons. "Eighteenth General Report of the Emigration Commissioners, 1858." *Parliamentary Papers* 1857–58 (2395), vol. 24.

217. Great Britain. Parliament. House of Commons. "Correspondence between the Colonial Department and the Governor of Hong Kong, and between the Colonial Department and the Foreign Office, on the Subject of Emigration from Hong Kong, and from the Chinese Empire to the British West Indies, and to Foreign Countries, and Their Possessions, since the 1st Day of January 1853. Part I." *Parliamentary Papers* 1857–58 (481), vol. 43. vii, 84 p.

Correspondence regarding the regulation of emigration from China between the Colonial Department and the governor of Hong Kong and attachments dated 17 May 1853 to 12 April 1858. Includes list of ships bound from Hong Kong between 14 November 1854 and 14 September 1855. Lists numbers of passengers (14,991 total) and their destinations. Abuses on board the *Levant* (a Hawaiian ship), the *Fortuna*, the *Dream* (Macao to Havana), the *Gulnare*, the *Duke of Portland*, and the *John Calvin* are also discussed, with minutes from investigations, letters, depositions, and other supporting documents used in the investigations. Includes a copy of an emigration ordinance. Deals with the British West Indies as well as other destinations for Chinese "coolie" ships, such as Havana.

218. Great Britain. Parliament. House of Commons. "All Letters Addressed by Members of the West India Committee to the Secretary of State for the Colonies, on the Subject of Emigration from China to the Colonies of British Guiana and Trinidad, and of Any Documents Connected Therewith; Also, of Any Replies Either from the Colonial Secretary or the Emigration Commissioners." *Parliamentary Papers* 1857–58 (525), vol. 41. 17 p.

Correspondence and attachments dated 8 March 1858 to 23 June 1858 concerning the introduction of Chinese laborers into the West Indies by private, rather than governmental, means. Includes instructions of the West India Committee to its agent in China regarding a private contract for the shipment of laborers to British Guiana and Trinidad. Names of planters involved in the venture are included.

219. Great Britain. Parliament. House of Commons. "Papers Relating to Immigration to the West Indian Colonies." *Parliamentary Papers* 1859 (2452), vol. 16. xxx, 503 p.

Dispatches from the secretary of state and from the governors and lieutenant governors of British Guiana, Jamaica, Trinidad, Grenada, St. Lucia, and St. Kitts dating from May 1853 to 5 September 1857. Relates to immigration from India, China, Madeira (Portugal), the Cape Verde Islands, and from Panama to the West Indies for the period from 1834 to 1857. Deals with regulating immigration, with the treatment of immigrants, shipboard mortality, the terms of indenture, government and private immigration, the shortage of women, return migration, "coolie children," and questions of immigration funding. An appendix contains copies of acts and ordinances for each of the colonies between 1853 and 1856. A chronological list of documents by colony, gives the subject of each.

220. Great Britain. Parliament. House of Commons. "Correspondence between the Colonial Office and the Governors of the West Indian Colonies and the Mauritius, with Respect to the Condition of the Labouring Population of Such Colonies, both Native and Immigrant, and the Supply of Labour: Part I: British Guiana, Jamaica, Trinidad." And, of the Colonial Acts or Ordinances, regulating the Condition of Imported Labourers, at present in force, and not already laid before Parliament 1859. *Parliamentary Papers* (31 Sess. 2), vol. 20.

221. Great Britain. Parliament. House of Commons. "Correspondence between the Colonial Office and the Governors of the West Indian Colonies and the Mauritius, with Respect to the Condition of the Labouring Population and the Supply of Labours: Part II: St. Lucia, Grenada, Tobago, St. Vincent, St. Kitts, Mauritius." and Colonial Acts, Regulating the Condition of Imported Labourers 1859. *Parliamentary Papers* (31-I, Sess. 2), vol. 21.

222. Great Britain. Parliament. House of Commons. "Immigration Loans: Returns, up to the present date of all Loans made by the British Government, or Guaranteed by it to the Several West Indian

Colonies, British Guiana, and Mauritius for immigration purposes."
Parliamentary Papers 1860 (250), vol. 45.

223. Great Britain. Parliament. House of Commons. "Correspondence between the Secretary of State for the Colonies and the Governor in Chief of the Windward Islands, relating to the Recent Riots at St. Vincent's, and the Proceedings Taken Against the Rioters." *Parliamentary Papers* 1863 (509), vol. 38. 172 p.

Accounts of the September 1862 uprisings of laborers and peasants on the island of St. Vincent. Lieutenant Governor Musgrave's account, along with other reports, provides details of the island-wide uprising. A petition from Barbadian workers involved in the disturbances is included. Charges by the British Anti-Slavery Society of excessive force in putting down the rebellion caused concern in the Colonial Office, prompting the publication of numerous court cases, including witnesses' testimony. Evidence is given by laborers, estate managers, police, and planters. Testimonies reveal the underlying tensions and complaints, particularly toward Portuguese shopkeepers who were also targets of looters. The Colonial Office intervention resulted in charges brought against a white planter who shot one of his workers.

224. Great Britain. Parliament. House of Commons. "Papers Laid before the Royal Commission of Inquiry by Governor Eyre." *Parliamentary Papers* 1866 (3682), vol. 30. 483 p.

On 30 December 1865, Edward Cardwell, secretary of state for the colonies, appointed a Royal Commission headed by Sir Henry Knight Storks to investigate "the origin, nature, and circumstances" of the October 1865 revolt of Jamaican blacks and "the Measures adopted in the course of their Suppression." This compilation of papers consists of documents collected by Governor Eyre to defend his harsh suppression of the rebellion before that committee. The governor rallied support from around the island, asking for, among other things, evidence regarding the scope of the rebellion and of the "disposition" (both political and religious) of the black population before and after the rebellion. The resulting collection of papers includes letters, depositions, and testimony of planters, laborers, Maroons, police officers, local government officials, military officers, and religious leaders. Includes reports (including verbatim testimony) from the trials conducted during the governor's imposition of martial law. Special emphasis is given to the capture, trial, and execution of George William Gordon, an alleged leader of the rebellion. The papers provide information on the organization of plantation labor before and after the revolt; revolt-related organizational activities on the part of the rebels; accounts of the rebellion itself; Afro-Jamaican cultural practices, especially religion; and the political inclinations of planters and laborers. Includes lists of rebels tried and executed, flogged, or imprisoned.

225. Great Britain. Parliament. House of Commons. "Report of the Jamaica Royal Commission, 1866. Part I. Report." *Parliamentary Papers* 1866 (3683), vol. 30. 41 p.

Report of the Royal Commission appointed by Secretary of State for the Colonies Edward Cardwell on the October 1865 rebellion of blacks at St. Thomas-in-the-East, Jamaica, and of its suppression by Governor Eyre. The report, dated 9 April 1866, is a companion piece to part II of the commission's report (see next entry), providing a summary of that evidence and the commission's assessment of the governor's conduct. The report provides a synopsis of events relating to the origin and outbreak of the rebellion itself as well as of its suppression, including the dispatch of troops, the proclamation of martial law, the military occupation of and trials at Morant Bay, Monklands, and Manchioneal, the role of the Maroons in the suppression, and a summary of punishments inflicted. Particular attention is given to the trial of George William Gordon, one of the alleged leaders of the revolt who was executed.

226. Great Britain. Parliament. House of Commons. "Report of the Jamaica Royal Commission, 1866. Part II. Minutes of Evidence and Appendix." *Parliamentary Papers* 1866 (3683), vol. 31. 1162 p.

This compilation of papers consists of verbatim testimony of the witnesses called before the Royal Commission in the course of their investigation into the rebellion of October 1865 and includes documents presented by these witnesses to support their testimony. The witnesses represent a cross section of society, including Afro-Jamaican laborers employed on plantations (both male and female), planters, and government officials, among others. The testimony of the witnesses relates not only to the rebellion itself, but also to political and social relations in Jamaica (especially with regard to the plantations) for the period preceding and following the rebellion. Includes both table of contents and index arranged by the name of the witness, the day of their testimony, and the page number on which that testimony is found. The appendix, for which there is also a table of contents, consists of supplementary documents collected by the commission relating to the rebellion and its suppression. This appendix includes printed copies of correspondence by

Paul Bogle and George William Gordon, the former a principal author of the rebellion and the latter an alleged leader. Also includes copies of military orders and documents created by the military in the course of the suppression, lists of people executed at Morant Bay, Blue Mountain Valley, Port Antonio and Manchioneal, Plantain Garden River District, and Up-Park Camp during the period of martial law, and documents concerning the courts-martial of William Grant, George McIntosh, Samuel Clarke, and the case of George William Gordon. Also contains specific information on the division of labor and payment of wages on the Hordley, Golden Grove, Coley, and St. Jago estates in the Plantain Garden River district, Blue Mountain Valley, and the parish of Clarendon for 1864 and 1865.

227. Great Britain. Parliament. House of Commons. "Letter from Dr. Underhill; Memorial of the Missionaries of the Jamaica Baptist Union; and Correspondence between the Colonial Secretary and the Governor of Jamaica Relative Thereto." *Parliamentary Papers* 1866 (380), vol. 51. 58 p.

Collection concerns allegations made against Baptist ministers about their alleged role in fostering the Morant Bay rebellion. The publication in the local press of a letter by Dr. Underhill, critical of Jamaica's political and social discrimination, was allegedly used by Baptist ministers to help incite the uprising. Allegations and rebuttals concerning Baptists include texts of sermons on such topics as "Suitable Dwellings to the Cultivation of Family Religion" as well as a discussion of the role of African-American Baptist ministers in Jamaica. See also [1866 (3595) vol. 51] which contains Dr. Underhill's letter and more discussion of the "distress of the coloured population" prior to the rebellion.

228. Great Britain. Parliament. House of Commons. "Correspondence in Relation to the Removal of Mr. G. W. Gordon from the Magistracy in Jamaica, and the Circumstances Connected with the Morant Bay Lock-Up Case." *Parliamentary Papers* 1866 (88), vol. 51. 42 p.

Case involves accusations made by George William Gordon, a local magistrate before the Morant Bay Rebellion, about the ill-treatment of prisoners in the "lock-up" at Morant Bay, which was used both for criminals and debtors. Prisoners were forced to clean out a cesspool and to live in unsanitary conditions. On finding the conditions different from those described by Mr. Gordon, a commission of magistrates subsequently found Gordon unfit to continue as a magistrate in St. Thomas-in-the-East. Contains Gordon's letter and his testimony to the commission.

229. Great Britain. Parliament. House of Commons. "Returns of the Mortality among the Coolie Immigrants in Demerara for the Three Years Ending December 1866." *Parliamentary Papers* 1867 (214), vol. 49. 1 p.

230. Great Britain. Parliament. House of Commons. "Correspondence between the Horse Guards and General O'Connor on the Conduct of Military Officers during the Recent Deplorable Occurrences in Jamaica." *Parliamentary Papers* 1867 (33), vol. 42. 28 p.

231. Great Britain. Parliament. House of Commons. "Memorial to the Governor of Hong Kong from the Chief Justice of Hong Kong and the Hon. Mr. Whittal on Coolie Emigration; and, Reply of the Governor Thereto." *Parliamentary Papers* 1867–68 (328), vol. 48. 16 p.

232. Great Britain. Parliament. House of Commons. "Papers on the State of Education in Trinidad." *Parliamentary Papers* 1870 (450), vol. 50. 100 p.

Contains a report (July 1869) written by Patrick Keenan under the orders of the colonial secretary. Report provides historical background on education on the Island, including census data broken down by race and religion from the time of abolition of slavery. Keenan visited over eighty schools and recommended the creation of nondenominational primary and secondary schools run by a state-appointed Board of Education. Includes Keenan's own observations on the lack of morality among the Creole population and the need to incorporate religious education in the curriculum. Report contributed to the Education Ordinance of 1870, which established the state-run Royal College.

233. Great Britain. Parliament. House of Commons. "Correspondence Respecting the Federation of the Leeward Islands." *Parliamentary Papers* 1871 (C. 353), vol. 48. 71 p.

Contains correspondence dated 10 April 1869 to 29 April 1871 between the Colonial Office and island officials of Antigua, St. Kitts, Nevis, Dominica, Virgin Islands, and Montserrat regarding the 1871 Federation of the Leeward Islands. The correspondence relates the political, economic, and social issues relevant to confederation (e.g., education, taxation, commerce, and the penal system), as well as information regarding the political process by which confederation was passed. Includes contents list indicating the dates of each piece of correspondence as well as the names of the authors and recipients. Includes table entitled "Analysis of Votes on Federation," which is organized by island.

234. Great Britain. Parliament. House of Commons. "Report of the Commissioners appointed to Inquire into the Treatment of Immigrant Coolies in British Guiana and Two Appendices." *Parliamentary Papers.* 1871 (C. 393, 393-I, and 393-II), vol. 20. 312 p.

This commission was ordered by Governor Scott in response to allegations made by an ex-special magistrate in Demerara, Mr. Des Voeux, concerning disturbances at sugar plantations involving Chinese, African, and Indian laborers. The subsequent commission's report (23 February 1871) includes testimony taken during visits to estates from forty-six witnesses, including laborers. Appendix II includes details for fifty-five plantations in Demerara, Berbices, and Essequibo. Written evidence includes special magistrates' reports, annual reports of inspectors of estates, and statistical returns on individual estates. Report is excellent source for political economy of sugar estates and descriptions of living and working conditions for Chinese, Indian, and African immigrant laborers. Includes discussion of intermarriage.

235. Great Britain. Parliament. House of Commons. "British Guiana: Correspondence Respecting a Disturbance among the Indian Emigrants Employed on the Devonshire Castle Estate." *Parliamentary Papers* 1873 (C. 879), vol. 49. 21 p.

Letter of Governor Scott of British Guiana to earl of Kimberely (7 October 1872) describes the initial reports of an incident at an estate on the Essequibo coast. The incident allegedly involved two hundred Indian laborers and twenty-four police, with five Indians killed and nine wounded. The disturbance allegedly originated in complaints of low pay and overwork under compulsion. Further investigations include details of similar complaints about working and living conditions on nearby sugar estates. Includes summaries of Indian complaints and testimonies.

236. Great Britain. Parliament. House of Commons. "Returns of the Number and Names of the Ships Employed in Conveying Coolies from India and China to the West Indies since the First Day of January 1872 to the Present Date: and, of the Number of Coolies Taken in These Vessels, the Number of Deaths Which Occurred during the Passage, and the Number of Medical Officers, Qualified and Unqualified, in Whose Medical Charge the Coolies Were Placed on Leaving the Port of Embarkation, and How Many of These Have Been Entered on the Articles of the Ship." *Parliamentary Papers* 1874 (C. 293), vol. 44. 4 p.

Includes information regarding ships involved in the transport of workers from India and China to Jamaica, Trinidad, British Guiana, and Nevis that sailed from January 1872 through mid-December 1873.

237. Great Britain. Parliament. House of Commons. "Coolie Emigration from India: Mr. Geoghegan's Report." *Parliamentary Papers* 1874 (C. 314), vol. 47.

238. Great Britain. Parliament. House of Commons. "Correspondence Respecting the Macao Coolie Trade: 1874–75." *Parliamentary Papers* 1875 (C. 1212), vol. 77. 28 p.

Correspondence and enclosures dated 31 January 1874 to 22 March 1875 between British and Portuguese government officials at Hong Kong, Macao, Canton, and Portugal. Subjects include the passage of an ordinance at Macao to ensure free instead of forced emigration, the skeptical response of the British, and the subsequent closing of the port of Macao to free emigration. Included are a copy of the Macao passenger regulations and a table of "coolie" ships bound out from the ports of Hong Kong, Amoy, Swatow, and Macao and bound to Callao (Peru), Peru, San Francisco (United States), Havana (Cuba), Sydney (Australia), Pondicherry (India), and Demerara (British Guiana) on which mutinies or disasters occurred between 1845 to 1872.

239. Great Britain. Parliament. House of Commons. "Papers Relating to the Late Disturbances in Barbados." *Parliamentary Papers* 1876 (C. 1539), vol. 53. xii, 247 p.

Between 18 and 22 April 1876, laborers throughout the island allegedly plundered as many as eighty-nine estates, reportedly in groups of between 250 and 1,500 persons. The Barbados House of Assembly passed a unanimous resolution to petition for a royal commission of inquiry. The resolution further called for the recall of the governor and certain members of the Executive Council in the event that the inquiry proved that the governor's conduct in promoting a confederation was unconstitutional. Much of the evidence in these documents focuses on the question of whether these were "potato riots" or protests over confederation. Papers reflect the actions and opinions of the colonial officials, the Colonial Office, the West India Committee, the Barbados Defence Association (a group of landed proprietors and small shopkeepers formed to resist confederation), police, and artisans, as well as the colony's laborers. The records relate to the debates in assembly, events surrounding public meetings formed throughout the island in response to the proposed federation (especially those of the Defence Association), the responses of Barbadian laborers, the trial of several supposed "ringleaders," and the investigations themselves. Among the social and political issues discussed are the nature of the existing constitution and treasury, wages and conditions of plantation labor in the sugar industry, emigration and immigration, the military, the penal system, taxation, education, and public works. This volume contains correspondence and papers dated 8 September 1871 to 15 May 1876. Further papers can be found in 1876 [C. 1559], vol. 53; 1877 [C. 1679], vol. 61; 1877 [C. 1687], vol. 61. Each of the four documents includes tables of contents that briefly describe the subjects of the correspondence and papers, their dates, and the names of either the author or recipient.

240. Great Britain. Parliament. House of Commons. "Papers Relating to the Late Disturbances in Barbados." *Parliamentary Papers* 1876 (C. 1539), vol. 53. 247 p.

Correspondence and papers dated 8 September 1871 to 15 May 1876, regarding the attempts of the Colonial Office and the governor of Barbados to federate the Windward Islands and the response of the residents of Barbados to these attempts. Includes information on the actions and opinions of the Earl of Carnarvon, Acting Governor Sanford Freeling, Governor J. Pope Hennessy, the West India Committee, and the Barbados Defence Association. The records relate to the debates in the Assembly, events surrounding public meetings formed throughout the island in response to federation, cane burnings, riots, wages, and conditions of plantation labor in the sugar industry, emigration and immigration, the military, the penal system, taxation, education, and public works. Includes table of contents that briefly describes the subjects of the correspondence and papers, their dates, and the names of either the author or recipient.

241. Great Britain. Parliament. House of Commons. "Further Papers Relating to the Late Disturbances in Barbados (In Continuation of [C. 1539.] of 1876.)." *Parliamentary Papers* 1876 (C. 1559), vol. 53. x, 220 p.

Material dated 11 April 1876 to 5 July 1876. For further papers see 1877 [C. 1679], vol. 61 and 1877 [C. 1687], vol. 61.

242. Great Britain. Parliament. House of Commons. "Return of the Number of Coolies, of the Money Expended on Immigration, together with Particulars as to certain Taxes, for the Islands of St. Vincent, West Indies, during the Fifteen Years since the Origination of the

Immigration Fund in that Island." *Parliamentary Papers* 1876 (C. 249), vol. 53.

243. Great Britain. Parliament. House of Commons. "Further Papers Relating to the Late Disturbances in Barbados. (In Continuation of [C. 1559] of 1876.)." *Parliamentary Papers* 1877 (C. 1679), vol. 61. iv, 66 p.

Material dated 14 January 1876 to 10 August 1876. For previous and subsequent reports see 1876 (C. 1539), vol. 53; 1876 (C. 1559), vol. 53; and 1877 (C. 1687), vol. 61.

244. Great Britain. Parliament. House of Commons. "Further Papers Relating to the Late Disturbances in Barbados (In Continuation of [C. 1679] of 1877.)." *Parliamentary Papers* 1877 (C. 1687), vol. 61. v, 70 p.

Material dated 1 March 1876 to 29 September 1876. For previous and subsequent reports see 1876 (C. 1539), vol. 53; 1876 (C. 1559), vol. 53; and 1877 (C. 1679), vol. 61.

245. Great Britain. Parliament. House of Commons. "Correspondence with the West India Committee Relating to the Sugar Bounty Question." *Parliamentary Papers* 1877 (C. 1838), vol. 84. 10 p.

Correspondence dated 9 March 1876 to 2 February 1877 between the Foreign Office and the West India Committee (a London-based group of planters and others with a financial stake in the West Indies) concerning the Brussels Sugar Convention of 1875 and the continental conference on sugar which met in Paris in 1876. Reflects committee's desire to secure international free trade in sugar.

246. Great Britain. Parliament. House of Commons. "Memorial Signed in the British West Indies on the Sugar Bounty Question, and Presented to the Secretary of State for the Colonies on the 8th Day of May 1878, together with the Copy of Statement Which Was Read to Him on that Occasion on Behalf of the Deputation: and of Any Memorials from the Sugar Trade, Chambers of Commerce, or Any Other Public Body, on the Same Subject, with Any Correspondence Relating Thereto." *Parliamentary Papers* 1878 (C. 395), vol. 68. 6 p.

The petitioners include planters, merchants, clergymen, district medical officers, schoolmasters, tradesmen, and others who desired the elimination of bounties by their foreign competitors (France, Belgium, Holland, Austria, and Russia) in the sugar trade.

247. Great Britain. Parliament. House of Commons. "Papers Relative to the Condition of Indian Immigrants in Grenada." *Parliamentary Papers* 1878–79 (C. 2249), vol. 51. 22 p.

248. Great Britain. Parliament. House of Commons. "Correspondence relative to the Financial Arrangements for Indian Coolie Immigration into Jamaica." *Parliamentary Papers* 1878–79 (C. 2437), vol. 51. 130 p.

249. Great Britain. Parliament. House of Commons. "Report on the Condition of Indian Immigrants and the Working of the New Immigration Law in Grenada," by Mr. O. W. Warner, inspector of immigrants, Trinidad, in continuation of 1879 (C. 2249), *Parliamentary Papers* 1880 (C. 2602), vol. 49. 17 p.

250. Great Britain. Parliament. House of Commons. "Correspondence (1877) Respecting the Constitution and Administration of Barbados." *Parliamentary Papers* 1880 (C. 2645), vol. 49. 9 p.

Correspondence and enclosures dated 16 November 1877 to 25 January 1878 between the Colonial Office, the Barbados Legislative Council, and the House of Assembly. The Colonial Office urged constitutional and administrative reform to extend representation.

251. Great Britain. Parliament. House of Commons. "Correspondence Relating to a Memorial or Memorials Received from Jamaica Setting Forth the Grievances Which Have Arisen under the System of Crown Government in that Island, with the Prayer or Prayers of Such Memorials, and the Number of Signatures Attached Thereto." *Parliamentary Papers* 1881 (C. 425), vol. 65. 16 p.

About twenty-five hundred people signed this memorial, which was put together by the Jamaica Association to protest Crown colony government, including the denial of political representation, which the memorial blamed for financial mismanagement. Includes additional correspondence between the Association, the Colonial Office, and the governor of Jamaica, dated 20 November 1876 to 14 June 1877.

252. Great Britain. Parliament. House of Commons. "Report of the Royal Commission Appointed in December 1882, to Inquire into the Public Revenues, Expenditure, Debts, and Liabilities of the Islands of Jamaica, Grenada, St. Vincent, Tobago, and St. Lucia, and the Leeward Islands; with a Despatch thereon from the Secretary of State to Governor Sir Henry Norman, K.C.B., C.I.E. Part I.—Jamaica. (With Map)." *Parliamentary Papers* 1884 (C. 3840), vol. 46. 246 p., foldout map.

The royal commissioners were Colonel William Crossman and George Smyth Baden-Powell. Each of parts I, II, and III (also see 1884 [C. 3840-I] [C. 3840 II], vol. 46, for parts II and III), consist of the commission's report dealing with "debt and liabilities," "civil establishments and other expenditure," and "revenue and the mode of raising it." The report is followed by a digest of evidence taken formally and informally as well as documents (such as letters and petitions) laid before the commission. Evidence was taken from "all classes," according to the commissioners and touches on aspects of government expense and revenue including elementary schools, poor relief, labor immigration, government employees and their salaries, imports and exports, and agricultural production. Cumulative imports and exports are listed for the previous thirty-year period. Part I has table, "Profits of Provision Grounds, Jamaica." Also see part IV [C. 3840-III], vol. 46, for supplementary remarks.

253. Great Britain. Parliament. House of Commons. "Report of the Royal Commission Appointed in December 1882, to Inquire into the Public Revenues, Expenditure, Debts, and Liabilities of the Islands of Jamaica, Grenada, St. Vincent, Tobago, and St. Lucia, and the Leeward Islands. Part II. Grenada, St. Vincent, Tobago, and St. Lucia." *Parliamentary Papers* 1884 (C. 3840-I), vol. 46. 203 p.

See 1884 (C. 3840), (C. 3840-II), (C. 3840-III), vol. 46, for the remaining regular and supplementary reports and evidence.

254. Great Britain. Parliament. House of Commons. "Report of the Royal Commission Appointed in December 1882, to Inquire into the Public Revenues, Expenditure, Debts, and Liabilities of the Islands of Jamaica, Grenada, St. Vincent, Tobago, and St. Lucia, and the Leeward Islands. Part III. The Leeward Islands." *Parliamentary Papers* 1884 (C. 3840-II), vol. 46. 193 p.

Commissioners visited Tortola, Virgin Gorda, St. Christopher, Nevis, Montserrat, and Dominica. See 1884 (C. 3840), vol. 46.

255. Great Britain. Parliament. House of Commons. "Report of the Royal Commission Appointed in December 1882, to Inquire into the Public Revenues, Expenditure, Debts, and Liabilities of the Islands of Jamaica, Grenada, St. Vincent, Tobago, and St. Lucia, and the Leeward Islands. Part IV.—Supplementary Remarks. (With Maps.)." *Parliamentary Papers* 1884 (C. 3840-III), vol. 46. 24 p., 2 foldout maps.

Continues discussions in parts I–III concerning debt, expenditure, and liability in the colonies. Includes section entitled "Capital and Labor," which includes a discussion of the labor supply in the islands. The appendix includes a chart entitled "Comparative Account of Tropical Colonies.—English and Foreign," which discusses the British West Indian colonies, Bermuda, Ceylon, Fiji, Mauritius, Martinique, Guadeloupe and dependencies, St. Thomas, St. Croix, Puerto Rico, and Cuba. Includes figures on size, population, government expenditure, imports and exports, revenue and import duties. See 1884 [C. 3840], [C. 3840-I], and [C. 3840-II], vol. 46, for the reports and evidence.

256. Great Britain. Parliament. House of Commons. "Petition from the Inhabitants of Jamaica for a Change in the Constitution of that Colony; Together with the Reply of Her Majesty's Government Thereto, and Accompanying Correspondence." *Parliamentary Papers* 1884 (C. 3854), vol. 55. 16 p.

Correspondence and attachments between the governor and the Colonial Office. Attachments include petition signed by 4,677 Jamaicans complaining of their "political disabilities." The forthcoming report of the Royal Commission on the franchise is discussed. Continued by 1884 [C. 4140], vol. 55.

257. Great Britain. Parliament. House of Commons. "Further Correspondence respecting the Constitution of the Legislative Council in Jamaica. (In Continuation of [C. 3854] February 1884.)." *Parliamentary Papers* 1884 (C. 4140), vol. 55. 47 p.

Includes petitions for an expanded electorate and a more representative Legislative Assembly. Also includes recommendations of the Royal Commission established to consider the idea of a new Jamaican Constitution and from George Stieble on education and property requirements for voters. Stieble gives statistics about race, arguing that double requirements would discriminate. The subsequent Order in Council (19 May 1884) on the new Jamaican constitution is included. Statistics on number of voters in each parish added after changes in qualifications are also included. See 1884 [C. 3854], vol. 55 for additional petitions and requests for an expanded Jamaican electorate.

258. Great Britain. Parliament. House of Commons. "Further Correspondence Respecting the Constitution of the Legislative Council in Jamaica (In Continuation of [C. 3854] February 1884.)." *Parliamentary Papers* 1884 (C. 4140), vol. 55. iv, 47 p.

Continues 1884 [C. 3854], vol. 55. Correspondence between colonial officials and attachments dated 11 January 1884 to 30 June 1884. Includes resolutions and protests passed at several public meetings requesting more popular representation on the Legislative Council and the report of the Franchise Commission dated 7 February 1884.

259. Great Britain. Parliament. House of Commons. "Correspondence Respecting the Recent Coolie Disturbance in Trinidad at the Mohurrum Festival with the Report Thereon, by Sir H. W. Norman." *Parliamentary Papers* 1884–85 (C. 4366), vol. 53.

Investigation into shooting of Indian male workers by police during the "Hosein [*sic*] Festival" (30 October 1884) in San Fernando, Naparima District. Details of the 107 wounded and killed, giving names, estates, age, and nature of wounds. Testimony of numerous participants in the religious festival, which had been banned by the colonial government. Evidence reveals aspects of relations between Indians (Hindus and Muslims), Indians and Creoles, free and indentured laborers, as well as between workers and government administration. Detailed descriptions of events by participants and police.

260. Great Britain. Parliament. House of Commons. "Papers Relating to the Proposed Union of the Islands of Grenada, St. Lucia, St. Vincent, and Tobago." *Parliamentary Papers* 1884–85 (C. 4482), vol. 53. v, 46 p.

Correspondence and enclosures dated 6 May 1884 to 4 June 1885 between colonial officials and the Colonial Office concerning the creation of the Federation of the Windward Islands. Includes protests against confederation and discussions of various forms of colonial governance. The Orders in Council and the Letters Patent for the new federation are reprinted. Table of contents.

261. Great Britain. Parliament. House of Commons. "Return of Clauses in Treaties between Great Britain and China Relating to the Treatment of Immigrants." *Parliamentary Papers* 1888 (C. 5374), vol. 98. 5 p.

Texts of treaties and agreements dated 29 August 1842 to 6 May 1886.

262. Great Britain. Parliament. House of Commons. "Annual Report of the Protector of Immigrants of for 1888: Jamaica." *Parliamentary Papers* 1889 (C. 5620–11), vol. 54.

263. Great Britain. Parliament. House of Commons. "Return Showing Particulars Relating to Immigration of Indian and Chinese Coolies into Trinidad since 1871." *Parliamentary Papers* 1892 (C. 26), vol. 56. 2 p.

264. Great Britain. Parliament. House of Commons. "Return Showing Particulars Relating to Immigration of Indian and Chinese Coolies

into British Guiana since the Report of the Commission of Inquiry in 1871." *Parliamentary Papers* 1892 Sess. 1 (C. 25), vol. 56. 5 p.

Letter dated 9 September 1891 from the lieutenant governor of British Guiana to Lord Knutsford, along with returns which provide a demographic breakdown of Indian and Chinese laborers in British Guiana as well as the rate of wages on sugar estates. See also "Returns . . . Trinidad," 1892 Sess. 1 (26), vol. 56.

265. Great Britain. Parliament. House of Commons. "Correspondence Respecting Change in the Constitution of the Legislative Council of Jamaica." *Parliamentary Papers* 1893–94 (C. 6997), vol. 60. 6 p.

Correspondence dated 8 August 1892 to 31 January 1893. Includes the Queen's Order in Council making changes to the Legislative Council, including the substitution of the governor for a president nominated by the Crown.

266. Great Britain. Parliament. House of Commons. "Correspondence respecting Change in the Constitution of the Legislative Council of Jamaica." *Parliamentary Papers* 1893–94 (C. 6997), vol. 60. 6 p.

267. Great Britain. Parliament. House of Commons. "Report of the Royal Commission to Inquire into the Condition and Affairs of the Island of Dominica, and Correspondence Relating Thereto." *Parliamentary Papers* 1894 (C. 7477), vol. 57. 204 p.

Report by Sir Hamilton (10 March 1894), commissioned to investigate the social and political crises on the island. Hamilton gives brief history of the island, including discussion of rebellions, labor, coffee and sugar cultivation, finance, taxation, and politics. Includes summary of oral evidence taken in Roseau and seven rural centers. Written evidence, including that of Dr. H. A. Nicholls, medical officer of public institutions, provides discussion of labor grievances and "racial prejudices."

268. Great Britain. Parliament. House of Commons. "Correspondence Relating to the Sugar Industry in the West Indies." *Parliamentary Papers* 1897 (C. 8359), vol. 61. ix, 111 p.

Correspondence and attachments (including petitions and memorials, ordinances, and financial documents) between the colonial governors, the colonial office, planters, planters' associations, agricultural organizations, and others with a stake in the colonial sugar industry, complaining of their desperate financial condition and discussing methods used and proposed for their improvement. Material is arranged chronologically, including by colony British Guiana, Trinidad, the Leeward Islands

(Antigua and St. Kitts-Nevis), Barbados, the Windward Islands (St. Lucia and St. Vincent), and Jamaica. Final section includes documents ordering the formation of the Norman Commission and outlining its tasks (see below). Includes table of contents and documents dated from 13 September 1894 to 12 January 1897.

269. Great Britain. Parliament. House of Commons. "Report of the West India Royal Commission. Appendix C., Vol. I., Containing Part I., Minutes of Proceedings, Reports of Evidence, and Copies of Certain Documents Received in London." *Parliamentary Papers* 1898 (C. 8656), vol. 50. 213 p.

Contains the verbatim minutes of the proceedings held by the Norman Commission in London prior to its departure for the West Indies. Commissioners interviewed the chairman of the West India Committee, the chairman of the Colonial Bank, merchants, owners, and managers of West Indian estates, officials from the Board of Trade and the Board of Inland Revenue, sugar refiners in England, sugar brokers, government officials from the West Indies, an owner of gold mines in British Guiana, as well as an estate manager and an estate owner from Queensland. Documents prepared for the commission by witnesses are also included. A few provide data on sugar production in places outside the West Indies, including Germany, Egypt, Queensland, Mauritius, and the United States. For the remaining volumes of the report, see below.

270. Great Britain. Parliament. House of Commons. "Report of the West India Royal Commission. Appendix C., Vol. II., Containing Parts II., III., IV., and V., Proceedings, Evidence, and Documents Relating to British Guiana, Barbados, Trinidad, and Tobago." *Parliamentary Papers* 1898 (C. 8657), vol. 50. 365 p.

Contains the minutes of proceedings and evidence collected by the Norman Commission during its investigations in British Guiana, Barbados, Trinidad, and Tobago. Witnesses include planters, plantation managers and overseers, estate attorneys and engineers, agricultural laborers, a small tobacco farmer, agricultural scientists, government officials (including special magistrates), doctors, merchants, newspaper editors, professors, barristers, clergymen, and tradesmen. Societies of agriculturalists and merchants are also represented. Includes a foldout map of British Guiana focused on gold mining and logging. For the remaining volumes of the report see below.

271. Great Britain. Parliament. House of Commons. "Report of the West India Royal Commission. Appendix C., Vol. III., Containing Parts VI.

to XIII. Proceedings, Evidence, and Documents Relating to the Windward Islands, the Leeward Islands, and Jamaica." *Parliamentary Papers* 1898 (C. 8669), vol. 51. 430 p.

Further minutes of proceedings and evidence collected by the Norman Commission during its investigations in the Windward Islands, the Leeward Islands, and Jamaica. Witnesses include planters, plantation managers and overseers, estate attorneys, agricultural laborers, peasant proprietors, agricultural scientists, government officials, merchants, newspaper editors, school officials, a professor, an engineer, a foundry owner, barristers, clergymen, and tradesmen. For partial index to the report, see below.

272. Great Britain. Parliament. House of Commons. "Report of the West India Royal Commission. Appendix C., Vol. IV., Containing Analysis of Verbal Evidence." *Parliamentary Papers* 1898 (C. 8799), vol. 51. 28 p.

Arranged by colony, then by the name of the witness, with a list of the subjects addressed in the testimony of each witness. Can be used as an index to the Norman Commission Report. See 1898 [C. 8655], [C. 8656], [C. 8657], vol. 50, and 1898 [C. 8669], vol. 51.

273. Great Britain. Parliament. House of Commons. "Special Reports on Educational Subjects: Volume 4: Educational Systems of the Chief Colonies of the British Empire." *Parliamentary Papers* 1900 (Cd. 416), vol. 21. 312 p.

274. Great Britain. Parliament. House of Commons. "Papers Relating to the Recent Disturbances at Port of Spain, Trinidad." *Parliamentary Papers* 1903 (Cd. 1661), vol. 44.

Correspondence concerns the burning of the Government House and subsequent killings of unarmed protesters by police on 23 March 1903. The protest was allegedly prompted by an attempt to charge residents for water through a meter system. Members of the Ratepayers Association were apparently joined by members of the colored population of the city in the protest. Governor Moloney contends that the disturbance was caused by agitation for representative government. Lists of killed and wounded include men and women. The commission's findings (1903 [Cd. 1662], vol. 44) give a detailed narrative of events, including the estimates of four to five thousand protestors and the firing of 471 rounds of ammunition by the police. A further investigation (1904 [Cd. 1988], vol. 60) by the chief justice of British Guiana recommended bringing charges against police.

275. Great Britain. Parliament. House of Commons. "Coolie Immigration Ordinances (Trinidad and British Guiana)." *Parliamentary Papers* 1904 (Cd. 1989), vol. 59. 153 p.

276. Great Britain. Parliament. House of Commons. "Educational Systems of the Chief Crown Colonies and Possessions of the British Empire, including Reports of the Training of Native Races. Vol. 12: Part I: West Indies and Central America; St. Helena; Cyprus and Gilbratar." *Parliamentary Papers* 1905 (Cd. 2377), vol. 25. 400 p.

277. Great Britain. Parliament. House of Commons. "Correspondence relating to Disturbances in British Guiana." *Parliamentary Papers* 1906 (Cd. 2822), vol. 77. 63 p.

Correspondence from Governor Sir Hodgson (1905) reporting series of "disturbances" involving "wharf labourers" and shooting of rioters by police. Includes information on a general strike of casual laborers (both black and Creole) on the wharfs and details of casualties. Reports enclosed on effect of strike in Georgetown and on "negro labourers" on the nearby sugar estates. Includes petition signed by 5,750 people protesting economic conditions, treatment by police during riots, the settlement of the strike, court hearings and punishments. Also includes petition against more state-aided immigration of Indian laborers. Statistics compare land held by blacks to land held by Indians. Includes reports from immigration agents on the labor market, wages, and relations between Creole, Indian, and African workers. See also "Further Correspondences relating to Disturbances" (1906 [Cd. 3026], vol. 77) which includes newspaper accounts of growing opposition to immigrant labor and lingering tensions between African and Indian labor.

278. Great Britain. Parliament. House of Commons. "A List of the Laws Dealing with the Emigration of Labourers from the British West Indian Colonies to Foreign Countries." *Parliamentary Papers* 1908 (Cd. 3827), vol. 73. 1 p.

Lists titles and dates of laws, acts, and ordinances by colony from 1864 through 1907.

279. Great Britain. Parliament. House of Commons. "Despatches from his Majesty's Minister at Panama Respecting the Employment of British West Indian Labour in the Panama Canal Zone." *Parliamentary Papers* 1908 (Cd. 3960), vol. 107.

Includes text of the contract from employment of British West Indian workers by the Isthmian Canal Commission of the United States (June 1907). Contract stipulates payment of ten cents U.S. currency per hour plus medical attention and living quarters. Laborers are to provide bedding and food. Also includes dispatches from the British minister in Panama with statistics, including wages, remittances, and "deaths per 1000 of Coloured Employees" from each British West Indian Colony. Majority of British West Indian workers were from Barbados, Trinidad, and Jamaica.

280. Great Britain. Parliament. House of Commons. "Report of the Committee on Emigration from India to the Crown Colonies and Protectorates." *Parliamentary Papers* 1910 (Cd. 5192) (Cd. 5193) (Cd. 5194), vol. 27. 107 p, 446 p, 171 p.

The 107-page report (26 April 1910) examines the future and history of emigration from India to British West Indies. Recommends future emigration to British Guiana and Trinidad and to a lesser extent Jamaica. Combined with 5193, in the same volume, includes over five hundred pages of evidence provided by eighty-three witnesses, including members of the West India Committee in London, academics, church representatives, colonial opponents to further immigration, and one Indian barrister raised in Trinidad. Evidence contains information on savings and remittances of Indians and discussion of conditions of labor for Indian women in British Guiana and Trinidad. Particularly valuable information on state of Indian laborers from 1906 to 1910.

281. Great Britain. Parliament. House of Commons. "The Imperial Department of Agriculture in the West Indies. A Summary by Sir D. Morris, K.C.M.G." *Parliamentary Papers* 1911 (C. 5515), vol. 52. 16 p.

A summary of the activities of the Imperial Department of Agriculture from its creation in 1898 to 1911. This is an update of an 1883 report by Morris entitled "Planting Industries in the West Indies," [C. 3794] focused on the effects of "scientific agriculture" on the region and the department's efforts concerning sugar (including the establishment of central sugar factories), cacao, rice, tobacco, cotton, limes, and rubber. Also outlines the department's efforts to promote the distribution of experimental plants and in agricultural education in primary and secondary schools.

282. Great Britain. Parliament. House of Commons. "Report on the Administration of the Imperial Parliamentary Grant-in-Aid of Roads and Land Settlement in St. Vincent from 1898 to 1910–11." *Parliamentary Papers* 1911 (Cd. 5742), vol. 52. 24 p.

This paper describes the operations and administration of the Roads and Land Settlement Fund in St. Vincent from 1898 to 1911. Administration of the fund involved the purchase of estate land by the colonial government through an imperial grant-in-aid and the resale of that land, in parcels as small as one acre, to peasant proprietors. Proprietors were to manage their land in accordance with government instructions, to live on the land for sixteen years, and to comply with the repayment terms for any government loans they received, or forfeit without appeal the allotment, all crops and all payments made. Town house lots were also made available through this plan. Appendices A and B are statements of revenue and of expenditure, respectively, for the local administration of the plan. Appendix C shows the "Number of Lots disposed of on each Estate, together with the Acreage and Date and Total Cost of Acquisition." Includes map of St. Vincent.

283. Great Britain. Parliament. House of Commons. "Report to the Government of India on the Conditions of Indian Immigrants in Four British Colonies and Surinam, by Messrs. James McNeil and Chinian Lal. Part I. Trinidad and British Guiana." *Parliamentary Papers* 1914–16 (Cd. 7744), vol. 47.

Report commissioned by Indian government to investigate health, housing, working conditions, wages, administration of justice, freedom of movement, relations between employers and laborers, marriage, religious rights, repatriation, and position of free Indians in Trinidad and British Guiana. The investigation was a response to complaints of excessive numbers of prosecutions of Indian laborers. The investigators traveled from India and visited several estates and labor settlements in each colony. Includes account of disturbance in Berbice, British Guiana, in which an Indian laborer was convicted for the killing of a police officer. Valuable source for economic situation of Indians, both indentured and free. Also contains statistics on property owned by Indians over period between 1890 and 1913 in British Guiana, population statistics, savings, and repatriation.

284. Great Britain. Parliament. House of Commons. "Report to the Government of India on the Conditions of Indian Immigrants in Four British Colonies and Surinam, by Messrs. James McNeil and Chinian Lal. Part II. Surinam, Jamaica, Fiji, and General Remarks." *Parliamentary Papers* 1914–16 (Cd. 7745), vol. 47.

Report by James McNeill contains a forty-three-page report on Indian laborers in Jamaica, covering topics including housing, health, working conditions, justice, relations between employers and laborers, repatriation, "Free Indians," and education. Contains a collection of statistics on wages broken down by name of worker, employer, sex, and plantation. Also lists complaints against laborers between 1910 and 1912 and occupations of "free Indians."

285. Great Britain. Parliament. House of Commons. "Report by the Honourable E. F. L. Wood, MP, Parliamentary Under-Secretary of State for the Colonies on His Visit to the West Indies and British Guiana, 1921–22." *Parliamentary Papers* 1922 (Cmd. 1679), vol. 16. 101 p.

286. Great Britain. Parliament. House of Commons. "Correspondence between His Majesty's Government and the Cuban Government Respecting the Ill-treatment of British West Indian Labourers in Cuba." *Parliamentary Papers* 1924 (Cmd. 2158), vol. 26. 21 p.

287. Great Britain. Parliament. House of Commons. "Report of the British Guiana Commission." *Parliamentary Papers* 1927 (Cmd. 2841), vol. 7. 67 p.

Report of a three-member commission that visited British Guiana in November 1927 to investigate economic conditions. Report covers topics including finance, agriculture, interior regions, population, immigration, health, constitution, and education. Gives budget deficits in period between 1921 and 1927 and population statistics from 1911 and 1921 census. Recommendations for development involve exploitation of the interior and use of financial resources to recruit labor from elsewhere in British West Indies rather than India or Africa.

288. Great Britain. Parliament. House of Commons. "Report of the West Indian Sugar Commission." *Parliamentary Papers* 1929–30 [Cmd. 3517], vol. 8, 793. 124 p.

Commission established in 1929 to examine the causes of depression in the sugar industry and possible measures to relieve it including the possibility of moving laborers to new settlements. The interim report recommends rationalization of British buying and selling of sugar, and the final report gives account of the effects of the world depression in the British West Indies. Examines labor conditions, describing poverty and living conditions on sugar estates. Recommends improvements in housing and the establishment of peasant farming to help ensure stability of work force.

289. Great Britain. Parliament. House of Commons. "Correspondence Relating to the Position of the Sugar Industry." *Parliamentary Papers* 1930–31 (Cmd. 3705), vol. 23, 129. 77 items, 79 p.

Covers emergency assistance to the sugar industry in the British West Indian colonies. Provides details of budgets and costs of production and shipping. Also includes budgetary items for improvement of laborers' living conditions on estates, according to recommendations of the Sugar Commission (see 1929–30 [Cmd. 3517], vol. 8). Detailed descriptions are given of unemployment in sugar industry for each colony.

290. Great Britain. Parliament. House of Commons. "Report of the Royal Commission on West India." *Parliamentary Papers* 1944–45 (Cmd. 6607), vol. 6. 483 p.

The report, known properly as the "Moyne Commission Report," was submitted in 1939 but was not issued because of outbreak of World War II. Includes historical data from pre-1930 period. Links current poverty and political crises to the history of slavery and immigration of laborers. Gives population statistics for 1896, 1921, and 1936 as well as information on birth rates and agricultural product values. Also includes sections on colonial administration, the status of women, and East Indians.

SECONDARY SOURCES

---

291. Adamson, Alan. "The Reconstruction of Plantation Labor After Emancipation: the Case of British Guiana." In *Race and Slavery in the Western Hemisphere: Quantitative Studies*, edited by Stanley L. Engerman and Eugene D. Genovese. Princeton: Princeton University Press, 1975.

Describes the transformation in the sources and uses of labor following emancipation in British Guiana. Political control of the state by sugar plantation owners resulted in legislation beneficial to planters in a number of areas including the control and regulation of Creole labor; the control of the former slave peasantry; the immigration of workers from Madras and Calcutta; the development of the indenture contract system; and the control of the state's fiscal policy to assist sugar plantations. Discusses how the sugar industry's monopoly of power permitted profitability in Guiana well into the nineteenth century at high cost to laborers and to the development of other areas of the local economy.

292. Adamson, Alan H. *Sugar Without Slaves: The Political Economy of British Guiana, 1838–1904.* New Haven: Yale University Press, 1972. 315 p.

293. Albert, Bill, and Adrian Graves. *Crisis and Change in the International Sugar Economy, 1860–1914.* Norwich: ISC Press, 1984. 381 p.

A collection of essays, mostly on the period from 1860 to 1914, examining sugar diplomacy, the political economy of sugar, labor relations, and the effects of both slavery and emancipation in places such as Russia, Germany, the Balkans, British West Indies, Brazil, Cuba, Puerto Rico, Trinidad, Argentina, Mexico, Peru, Egypt, the Portuguese Empire, Natal, and Hawaii.

294. Alexander, Jack. "Love, Race, Slavery, and Sexuality in Jamaican Images of the Family." In *Kinship Ideology and Practice in Latin America.* Ed. Raymond T. Smith. Chapel Hill: University of North Carolina Press, 1984.

Investigates attitudes of middle-class Jamaicans during the 1960s towards issues of race, class, and gender identity. Based on a series of lengthy interviews with eleven middle-class Jamaican informants collected between 1967 and 1969. Author explores views on kinship, affinity, illegitimacy, the role of male in the family, race, class, and status. Considers the middle-class "myth of origin" that locates the beginnings of this class in the nonlegal union of white male masters and slave women of African descent.

295. Alonso, Ana Maria. "Men in 'Rags' and the Devil on the Throne: A Study of Protest and Inversion in the Carnival of Post-Emancipation Trinidad." *Plantation Society in the Americas* (1990): 73–120.

296. Ashdown, Peter. "Marcus Garvey, the UNIA and the Black Cause in British Honduras, 1914–1949." *Journal of Caribbean History* 15 (1981): 41–55.

Examines the development of a Universal Negro Improvement Association (UNIA) branch in British Honduras against the backdrop of racial tensions between Blacks, Metizos, Creoles, and whites. Based on Colonial Office records and local newspaper accounts. Discusses the political role of the UNIA including description of a July 1921 visit by Marcus Garvey. Considers how the UNIA functioned as a multiracial political organization in the 1920s but was subsequently eclipsed by new forms of class and race politics during the nationalist period of the 1950s.

297. August, Thomas. "Jewish Assimilation and the Plural Society in Jamaica." *Social and Economic Studies* 36 (June 1987): 109–22.

Describes the history of the Jewish population in Jamaica. Argues that prior to the 1870s Jews were viewed by the white population as a distinct group but that they became increasingly assimilated with the white elite following the 1865 rebellion. By 1914, many Jews had merged with the white elite.

298. Bakan, Abigail B. *Ideology and Class Conflict in Jamaica: the Politics of Rebellion.* Montreal: McGill-Queen's University Press, 1990. 183 p.

Examines continuities in Jamaican workers' protest as exemplified by the 1831 "Baptist War," the 1865 Morant Bay Rebellion, and the labor rebellion of 1938. Examines the social history of Jamaican workers including the expression of workers' demands through a "religious idiom" and their appeals to the British Crown as a potential source of fair treatment and justice. Includes accounts of Alexander Bustamante's ideology and use of religion in his speeches during the events between 1937 and 1938.

299. Barron, T. J. "James Stephen, the 'Black Race' and British Colonial Administration, 1813–47." *Journal of Imperial and Commonwealth History* 5 (January 1977): 131–50.

Investigates the career of James Stephen, an important British Colonial Office official who served as legal counsel, assistant under-secretary, and permanent under-secretary to the Colonial Office. Emphasizes Stephen's ideas about the role of the "Black race" within the British colonial system. Details his family's strong link to missionary work in Sierra Leone and the influence of this link on his attitudes towards the ending of slavery and the apprenticeship system in the British West Indies. Includes quotations from Stephen's writings.

300. Barrow, Christine. "Ownership and Control of Resources in Barbados: 1834 to the Present." *Social and Economic Studies* 32 (September 1983): 83–120.

Discusses the political economy of Barbados from emancipation to the 1980s with special attention to the position of elite property owners' responses to challenges from former slaves, workers, and peasants. Discusses the importance of land shortages and the planters' response to the sugar crisis of the 1880s and early 1900s. Includes a discussion of the 1930 riots and their aftermath.

301. Basdeo, Sahadeo. *Labour Organisation and Labour Reform in Trinidad, 1919–1939.* St. Augustine: Institute of Social and Economic Research, University of the West Indies, 1983. 285 p.

Examines the campaign by organized labor in Trinidad to persuade the Colonial Office, the Trinidad government, and employers to recognize their demands for new labor laws and the negotiations between the Colonial Office and the Trinidad government over labor. Discusses the role of the British Trade Union Congress, the Labour Party's Fabian

Colonial Bureau, and the International Labor Organization as well as the demands, protests, and organization of major Trinidadian labor organizations, including A. A. Cipriani's Trinidad Workingman's association, the East Indian National Association, the Trinidad and Tobago Trades Union Council, and the Trinidad Labour Party. Presents data on sugar estate wages for the 1930s as well as a bibliography of primary and secondary sources.

302. Basdeo, Sahadeo. "The Role of the British Labour Movement in the Development of Labour Organization in Trinidad, 1929–1938." *Social and Economic Studies* 31 (March, 1982): 40–73.

Analyzes the role of the British Labour Party and trade union leaders in trade union activity in Trinidad during the 1930s, including the activities of A. A. Cipriani, W. Arthur Lewis, and Susan Lawrence. Based primarily on Colonial Office records.

303. Beachley, R. W. *The British West Indies Sugar Industry in the Late 19th Century.* 1957. Reprint. Westport, Conn.: Greenwood Press, 1978.

Institutional history of the sugar industry in the British West Indies from 1854 to 1903. Includes discussion of the transfer of estates from bankrupt owners to solvent owners and the role of the Encumbered Estates Court in that process. Discusses production and economic performance of the major sugar producing colonies during and following the U.S. Civil War as well as evidence of increased concentration of property as the U.S. market developed. Also includes sections on sugar cane cultivation and labor and wage issues. Concludes with a discussion of competition between beet sugar and West Indian cane, and the end of prosperity for West Indian cane planters.

304. Beckford, George. "Peasant Movements and Agrarian Problems in the West Indies: Part II—Aspects of the Present Conflict between the Plantation and the Peasantry in the West Indies." *Caribbean Quarterly* 18 (March 1972): 47–58.

305. Beckford, George L. *Persistent Poverty: Underdevelopment in Plantation Economies of the Third World.* New York: Oxford University Press, 1972. 303 p.

A comparative history of plantation societies in Latin America, the Caribbean, Asia and Africa. Examines the role of European capital in the formation of plantation economies in the nineteenth and twentieth centuries. Considers the transformation of plantation labor and society following emancipation and the emergence of distinctions by race, caste, and class in Jamaica and elsewhere in the British West Indies.

306. Beckles, Hillary and Verene Shepard, eds. *Caribbean Freedom: Society and Economy from Emancipation to the Present.* London: Currey, 1993. 581 p.

Essays on emancipatory struggles and movements from the late eighteenth century through the present in the Caribbean including Saint Domingue (and Haiti), Cuba, Jamaica, Martinique, Guadeloupe, the Bahamas, Trinidad, British Guiana, Barbados, Grenada, and Puerto Rico. Themes include planter-peasant relations, indentured labor, popular revolts, women and gender, the labor movement, the sugar industry, and nationalist and socialist movements.

307. Bennett, J. Harry. *Bondsmen and Bishops: Slavery and Apprenticeship on the Codrington Plantations of Barbados, 1710–1838.* Berkeley: University of California Press, 1958.

A microstudy of life on a Barbadian sugar plantation, including the transition from slave to apprenticed labor. The eight-hundred-acre Codrington plantations were bequeathed in 1710 to the Society for Propagation of the Gospel in Foreign Parts. The day-to-day details of the estate were recorded and sent to the Society in London, creating a useful record of plantation life. Major themes discussed include the development of abolitionist thought within the Society and its impact on the running of a slave plantation; the period of "amelioration" (1793–1823), which saw attempts to improve living and working conditions of slaves; and the experiences of former slaves as apprentices in the immediate postemancipation period from 1834 to 1838. During this latter period, the Society experimented with an "allotment system," providing former slaves land in order to entice them to remain working on the estate.

308. Berleant-Schiller, Riva. "The Failure of Agricultural Development in Post-Emancipation Barbuda: A Study of Social and Economic Continuity in a West Indian Community." *Boletin de Estudios Latinoamericanos y del Caribe* 25 (December 1978): 21–36.

309. Bernal, Richard. "The Great Depression, Colonial Policy and Industrialization in Jamaica." *Social and Economic Studies* 37 (1988): 33–64.

Describes the impact of the Great Depression on the Jamaican economy. Compares the Jamaican economy prior to the 1930s with those of Latin American countries and explores the impact of colonialism on industrialization. Includes tables comparing the economic performance of Latin American countries and Jamaica.

310. Besson, Jean. "Family Land and Caribbean Society: Toward an Ethnography of Afro-Caribbean Peasantries." In *Perspectives on Caribbean Regional Identity*. Edited by Elizabeth M. Thomas-Hope. Liverpool: Centre for Latin American Studies, University of Liverpool, 1984.

Ethnography of Martha Brae, a rural Jamaican village in Trelawny Parish. Based on ethnographic fieldwork carried out from 1969 to 1978. Explores indigenous forms of land tenure, particularly the institution of "family land" as practiced among the population of nearly eight hundred in the village. Explores the relationship of "family land" to African and European land tenure traditions and suggests a comparative framework for understanding rural land tenure practices in the Caribbean. Includes a historical study of land practices in Trelawny in the 1830s and 1840s following emancipation. Includes additional references for Caribbean land tenure history.

311. Besson, Jean. "Symbolic Aspects of Land in the Caribbean: The Tenure and Transmission of Land Rights among Caribbean Peasantries." In *Peasants, Plantations and Rural Communities in the Caribbean* edited by Malcolm Cross and Arnaud Marks. Surrey: Department of Sociology, University of Surrey, 1979.

Discusses land tenure, land transfer, and inheritance in the Caribbean. Considers the relationship between land tenure and migration. The author's own work on the concept of "family land" operative in rural Jamaica is used to suggest a more complex typology of land tenure that accounts for the absence of individuals from the rural home as the Jamaican economy has historically created the need for migration to urban areas or overseas for work. Extensive references are included.

312. Besson, Jean. "Land Tenure in the Free Villages of Trelawny, Jamaica: A Case Study in the Caribbean Peasant Response to Emancipation." *Slavery and Abolition* 5 (May 1984): 3–23.

313. Besson, Jean, and Janet Momsen, eds. *Land and Development in the Caribbean*. London: Macmillan Caribbean, 1987. 228 p.

A collection of essays that consider traditional attitudes toward land, the effect of more recent political and economic changes on these attitudes, and conflicts surrounding rural development. Includes essays on Guyana, Barbados, Jamaica, the Bahamas, St. Vincent, Dominica, and Grenada as well as Nevis and Barbuda.

314. Bolland, Nigel and Assad Shoman. *Land in Belize, 1765–1871.* Law and Society in the Caribbean, no. 6. Kingston: Institute of Social and Economic Research, University of the West Indies, 1977. 142 p.

A history of land use, the development of the timber industry, and the creation of a peasantry following emancipation in Belize. Using Colonial Office records the authors trace white settler land use and struggles over labor and land in the postemancipation period from 1831 to 1871. Topics covered for the postemancipation period include the growth of commercial agriculture, the monopolization of freehold land, immigration of former slaves from other areas of the Caribbean, and the dispossession of the Maya, Carib, and African populations. Appendices include timber and sugar export data, distribution of freehold land, and acreage of cane on estates with steam machinery in 1868.

315. Bolland, O. Nigel. "Creolization and Creole Societies: A Cultural Nationalist View of Caribbean Social History." In *Intellectuals in the Twentieth Century Caribbean: Volume I: Spectre of the New Class: The Commonwealth Caribbean,* edited by Alistair Hennessy. London: Macmillan Education, 1992.

Examination of "creole society" theories and their importance in both Caribbean history and Caribbean historiography.

316. Bolland, O. Nigel. "Systems of Domination after Slavery: The Control of Land and Labor in the British West Indies after 1838." *Comparative Studies in Society and History* 23 (October 1981): 591–619.

Consideration of relations between planters and laborers after emancipation with a focus on Belize.

317. Bolland, O. Nigel. "Reply to William A. Green's 'The Perils of Comparative History'" *Comparative Studies in Society and History* 26 (January 1984): 120–25.

318. Bolland, O. Nigel. "Labour Control and Resistance in Belize in the Century After 1838." *Slavery and Abolition* 7 (September 1986): 175–87.

Analysis of strategies used by employers and the state to control laborers in Belize following the end of the apprenticeship system in 1838. Includes discussion of the mahogany trade. Based on records from the British Colonial Office and Belize.

319. Bolland, O. Nigel. *The Formation of A Colonial Society: Belize, from Conquest to Crown Colony.* Baltimore: Johns Hopkins University Press, 1977. 240 p.

History of Belize from conquest and settlement to the establishment of crown colony rule in 1871. Discusses the transition from slavery to free labor and the efforts to limit the growth of a peasantry after emancipation. Considers the roles of Maya, Black 'Caribs,' Creoles, and migrants from China, South Asia, and elsewhere in the Caribbean in plantation labor following the end of slavery.

320. Boomgaard, Peter, and Gert J. Oostindie. "Changing Sugar Technology and the Labour Nexus: the Caribbean, 1750–1900." *Nieuwe West-Indische Gids/New West Indian Guide* 63 (1989): 3–22.

321. Brathwaite, Edward Kamau. "The Slave Rebellion in the Great River Valley of St. James, 1831/32." *Jamaican Historical Review* 13 (1982): 11–30.

322. Brathwaite, Edward Kamau. "Caliban, Ariel, and Unprospero in the Conflict of Creolization: A Study of the Slave Revolt in Jamaica in 1831–32." *Comparative Perspectives on Slavery in New World Plantation Societies*. Annals of the New York Academy of Sciences. Edited by Vera Rubin and Arthur Tuden. New York: New York Academy of Sciences, 1977.

Discusses the Christmas Rebellion in Jamaica (1831–32), creolization, and Creole identity in the postemancipation period.

323. Brereton, Bridget. *Race Relations in Colonial Trinidad, 1870–1900*. Cambridge: Cambridge University Press, 1979. 251 p.

History of the social and economic conditions of Trinidadian society in the last three decades of the nineteenth century including relations between the Creole population, white elite, rural black population, and Indians. Describes class formation, education, and social mobility among the island's Creoles and the development of a racially divided society. Includes discussion of carnival and "drum dances" in the late nineteenth century.

324. Brodber, Erna. "Afro-Jamaican Women at the Turn of the Century." *Social and Economic Studies* 35 (September 1986): 23–50.

Investigates how Afro-Jamaican women born in the immediate postemancipation period (1861–1900) perceived the economic role of men in their lives as independent farmers. Based on the life-histories of four women born in 1861, 1875, 1887, and 1900, respectively.

325. Bryan, Patrick. *The Jamaican People, 1880–1902: Race, Class and Social Control*. London: MacMillan Caribbean, 1991. 300 p.

Considers race and class and distinctions following emancipation in the contexts of law; religion; marriage and family; childhood, youth, and education; health and poor relief; and leisure.

326. Burn, W. L. *Emancipation and Apprenticeship in the British West Indies.* 1937. Reprint. London: Jonathan Cape, 1970. 398 p.

History of the apprenticeship system in the British West Indies. Includes detailed chapters on special magistrates—colonial officials who were given the responsibility for overseeing the smooth running of the apprenticeship system and checking abuses by employers. Discusses careers of the Marquis of Sligo and Lionel Brown as governors of Jamaica during the apprenticeship period.

327. Burt, Arthur E. "The First Installment of Representative Government in Jamaica, 1884." *Social and Economic Studies* 11 (September 1962): 241–59.

Considers the creation of representative government in Jamaica in 1884 including franchise requirements and the role of immigration from India as an election issue.

328. Bush, Barbara. "Towards Emancipation: Slave Women and Resistance to Coercive Labour Regimes in the British West Indian Colonies, 1790–1838." *Slavery and Abolition* 5 (December 1984): 222–43.

Examines the contribution of slave women to labor protest and resistance throughout the British West Indies, including discussion of their roles in both the plantation and informal economies and in family and community life.

329. Butler, Kathleen Mary. *The Economics of Emancipation: Jamaica and Barbados, 1823–1843.* Chapel Hill: University of North Carolina Press, 1995. 198 p.

History of the effects of British payments to former slaveowners in compensation for abolition on the development of Barbados and Jamaica. Focused on the period 1823 to 1843, the book examines planter indebtedness, the availability of credit, and the impact of compensation payments on the value of plantation land, access of former slaves to land, and role of white women as creditors and plantation owners. Based mainly on records from large-scale plantations employing fifty slaves or more, including compensation records, deed of land sales or mortgages, attorney and merchant letter books, and the records of the colonial courts of chancery.

330. Campbell, Carl. "Towards an Imperial Policy for the Education of Negroes in the West Indies after Emancipation." *Jamaican Historical Review* 7 (1967): 68–102.

331. Campbell, Carl. "Social and Economic Obstacles to the Development of Popular Education in Post-Emancipation Jamaica, 1834–1865." *Journal of Caribbean History* 1 (November 1970): 57–88.

332. Campbell, Mavis Christine. *The Dynamics of Change in a Slave Society: A Sociopolitical History of the Free Coloreds of Jamaica, 1800–1865.* Rutherford, N.J.: Fairleigh Dickinson University Press, 1976. 393 p.

History of the Free Coloreds of Jamaica from the early nineteenth century to the Morant Bay rebellion in 1865. Focuses on their role in the Jamaican Legislative Assembly from the time of their enfranchisement in 1830 until their decisive contribution to the defeat of the 1865 Constitution. Considers role of Free Coloreds as mediators between the majority population of ex-slaves and the ruling white elite. Provides a partially annotated bibliography of primary and secondary sources.

333. Caribbean Colloquium. *Peasants, Plantations, and Rural Communities in the Caribbean.* Edited by Malcolm Cross and Arnaud Marks. Department of Sociology, University of Surrey, 1979. 304 p.

Edited collection including case studies of Trinidad, Haiti, Jamaica, Barbuda, Surinam, Barbados, and Martinique.

334. Carnegie, James. *Some Aspects of Jamaica's Politics, 1918–1938.* Cultural Heritage Series, vol. 4. Kingston: Institute of Jamaica, 1973. 194 p.

Examines the political history of Jamaica, including both elite and working-class politics, in the two decades prior to the 1938 labor strikes. Considers organizations such as the National Reform Association, the People's National Party, Garvey's United Negro Improvement Association, and the Bustamante Industrial Trades Union. Also includes a detailed section of the Jamaican press during the period. Includes photos of many national and trade union leaders.

335. Cell, John W. *British Colonial Administration in the Mid-Nineteenth Century: The Policy-Making Process.* New Haven: Yale University Press, 1970. 344 p.

Describes the transfer of specific powers in the 1850s from the Colonial Office in London to the colonies. Includes a discussion of diplomacy between the French and the British over recruitment of South Asian and African laborers after emancipation. Includes appendix with a select list of colonial governors, with brief biographical sketches.

336. Chace, Russel, Jr. "Protest in Post-Emancipation Dominica: the 'Guerre Negre' of 1844." *Journal of Caribbean History* 23 (1989): 118–41.

Examines the "Guerre Negre" of June 1844. The week-long armed protest focused on the taking of a census, which some former slaves perceived as a step towards their re-enslavement. Based primarily on British Colonial Office records and the *British Parliamentary Papers*.

337. Chamberlain, Mary. "Renters and Farmers: The Barbadian Plantation Tenantry System, 1917–1937." *Journal of Caribbean History* 24 (1990): 195–225.

Describes the work and living conditions of tenant contract laborers in Barbados. Considers the Barbados plantation tenantry system, in which contract laborers rented land on an employer's estate and promised to work exclusively for the landowner. Based on interviews with contract workers, most of whom were born in the early twentieth century and grew up in the plantation tenantry system prior to its repeal in 1937.

338. Chan, V. O. "The Riots of 1856 in British Guiana." *Caribbean Quarterly* 16 (March 1970): 39–50.

Describes how protests in Georgetown spread to the nearby sugar estates in Demerara in February of 1856. Discusses role of John Sayers Orr, a Creole born in Georgetown, who allegedly sparked the 1856 disturbances.

339. Chase, Ashton. *A History of Trade Unionism in Guyana 1900 to 1961. With an epilogue to 1964.* Edited by Audrey Chase. Demerara: New Guyana Company, 1966. 327 p.

A detailed history of the trade union movement in Guyana. The author, who served as general secretary of the British Guiana Labour Union and helped found the People's Progressive Party, provides details of the formation of trade unions on the sugar plantations and in urban areas. Describes early attempts at labor organizing and strikes by sugar workers and dockworkers in response to government labor laws. Outlines the growth of trade unions after World War I and the subsequent formation of the People's Progressive Party. Also includes details on Pan-African and Pan-West Indian labor and political organization. An appendix provides names and relevant dates of 120 trade unions formed between 1922 and 1962.

340. Clarke, Colin G. *Kingston, Jamaica: Urban Development and Social Change, 1692–1962.* Berkeley: University of California Press, 1975. 270 p.

Examines the spatial, demographic, and economic growth of Kingston, Jamaica. Divides discussion between the period of slavery (1692–1820), the postemancipation period (1820–1938), post–World War II (1944–60), and postindependence. Explores the physical and social aspects of urban growth, with particular attention to changes in the political economy in the postemancipation period. Includes maps, demographic data, and photographs.

341. Clarke, Colin, ed. *Society and Politics in the Caribbean.* London: St. Martin's Press, 1991. 295 p.

342. Clarke, Edith. *My Mother Who Fathered Me: A Study of the Family in Three Selected Communities in Jamaica.* London: George Allen and Unwin, 1957. 215 p.

An anthropological study of family life in three Jamaican communities during the 1950s. The author spent two years as a "participant observer" in the sugar-worker communities of Sugartown, Orange Grove, and Mocca. Combines household surveys and interviews to explore issues of work, family, marriage, kinship, community, and labor organizations. Appendices provide survey results and a description of the death and burial of local woman.

343. Cole, Joyce. "Official Ideology and the Education of Women in the English-Speaking Caribbean, 1835–1945." *Women in the Caribbean Project.* Cave Hill, Barbados : University of the West Indies, Institute of Social and Economic Research, 1982.

344. Comitas, Lambros. "Occupational Multiplicity in Rural Jamaica." In *Work and Family Life: West Indian Perspectives*, edited by Lambros Comitas and David Lowenthal. Garden City, N.Y.: Anchor Press, 1973. 422 p.

An anthropological discussion of work patterns in five coastal settlements in rural Jamaica. Focuses on the multiple work strategies of men who were viewed officially as fishermen, but who engaged in multiple work strategies.

345. Conniff, Michael L. *Black Labor on a White Canal: Panama, 1904–1981.* Pittsburgh: Pittsburgh University Press, 1985. 221 p.

Examines the role of West Indian laborers in the building of the Panama Canal and Panamanian society. Considers how the United States government sought to maintain a steady supply of labor and separated foreign workers from the local labor force. Includes discussion of labor organization among West Indian workers.

346. Cowley, John. *Carnival, Camboulay, and Calypso: Traditions in the Making*. Cambridge: Cambridge University Press, 1996. 293 p.

Describes the evolution of Carnival and other forms of Black secular music in the Caribbean from 1783 to the first two decades of the twentieth century. Draws on newspaper accounts, colonial documents, oral histories, and folklore.

347. Cox, Edward. "The Free Coloureds and Slave Emancipation on the British West Indies: the Case of St. Kitts and Grenada." *Journal of Caribbean History* 22 (1988): 68–87.

Outlines the responses of the free colored populations on St. Kitts and Grenada to the demands for emancipation and the implementation of the apprenticeship system during the 1820s and 1830s. Provides data showing the demographic importance of the free colored populations on both islands. Provides examples of free colored political appeals and petitions to the British Colonial Office. Outlines the political career of Ralph B. Cleghorn, a free colored political figure active in Britain in the 1830s. References to Colonial Office primary sources are provided.

348. Craton, Michael. *A History of the Bahamas*. London: Collins, 1962. 320 p.

349. Craton, Michael. "Continuity Not Change: The Incidence of Unrest Among Ex-Slaves in the British West Indies, 1838–1876." *Slavery and Abolition* 9 (September 1988): 144–70.

Investigates continuities between postemancipation peasant protests in the West Indies and earlier traditions of slave revolts and protests. Examines the riots of February 1856 in Georgetown, British Guyana, led by John Sayers Orr; the 1865 Morant Bay rebellion in Jamaica, and the rebellion in Barbados of March and April of 1876.

350. Craton, Michael. *Empire, Enslavement and Freedom in the Caribbean*. Oxford: James Currey, 1997. 520 p.

A collection of the author's essays written over roughly a thirty-year period. Organized into three sections, the first of which deals with themes of colonialism and imperialism, addressing topics such as the plantation model, the role of land tenure in creating a British West Indian "plantocracy," and the establishment of the Caribbean vice admiralty courts. Part II focuses on issues of slavery and slave society in the Americas, particularly the British West Indies. Part III discusses emancipation and resistance in the British West Indies and British West Indian slave culture.

351. Craton, Michael. "The Passion to Exist: Slave Rebellions in the British West Indies, 1650–1832." *Journal of Caribbean History* 13 (1980): 1–20.

352. Craton, Michael. *Testing the Chains: Resistance to Slavery in the British West Indies.* Ithaca: Cornell University Press, 1982. 389 p.

History of slave resistance in the Caribbean, including the influence of such resistance on emancipation. Investigates the working of a Jamaican plantation, Worthy Park estate in St. John's Parish, and Maroon activity from 1600 to 1775. Describes the African influence on slave resistance, with examples from the Lesser Antilles, Barbados, Antigua, Dominica, St. Vincent, Tobago, Grenada, and the East Coast of Demerara in British Guiana. Rebellions in the early nineteenth century are described, including Bussa's rebellion in Barbados (1816); the Demerara revolt (1823); and the so-called "Baptist War" (1831–32) in Jamaica.

353. Craton, Michael, and James Walvin. *A Jamaica Plantation: The History of Worthy Park, 1670–1970.* Toronto: University of Toronto Press, 1970. 344 p.

Presents a detailed history of a large sugar estate, Worthy Park, located in St. John's Parish, Jamaica. Based on extensive estate records. Includes discussion of the transition to apprenticeship and free labor in the 1830s and 1840s and the decline of the estate as labor costs increased and sugar prices decreased between 1840 and 1860. Important source for understanding attempts by estate owners to maintain labor supply following emancipation.

354. Craton, Michael, ed. *Roots and Branches: Current Directions in Slave Studies, Historical Reflections.* Toronto: Pergamon Press, 1979. 292 p.

Presents papers and commentaries from a 1979 international conference entitled "Slave Studies: Directions in Current Scholarship" held in Waterloo, Ontario. Includes a paper by Herbert Gutman on the slave family with commentaries by Barry Higman and Stanley Engerman; a paper by Sidney Mintz on slavery and the rise of peasantries with commentaries by Woodville Marshall, Mary Karasch, and Richard Frucht; and a paper by Walter Rodney on slavery and underdevelopment with commentary by Orlando Patterson.

355. Craton, Michael, James Walvin and David Wright. *Slavery, Abolition and Emancipation: Black Slaves and the British Empire. A Thematic Documentary.* London: Longman, 1976. 347 p.

356. Craton, Michael, with the assistance of Garry Greenland. *Searching for the Invisible Man: Slaves and Plantation Life in Jamaica.* Cambridge, Mass.: Harvard University Press, 1978. 439 p.

Examines the lives of slaves and ex-slaves working on the large sugar estate of Worthy Park in St. John's Parish Jamaica. Includes a section on the transition to free-wage labor (1838–46) that provides comparable wage rates and work requirements for the period. Discusses how increased labor cost coupled with declining world sugar prices led to a restructuring of production in the 1850s. Other sections explore the genealogies of families as they moved from slavery to status as peasant workers. Also contains a selection of photos and illustrations of plantation life and postemancipation rural life.

357. Craton, Michael. "Emancipation from Below? The Role of the British West Indian Slaves in the Emancipation Movement, 1816–34." In *Out of Slavery: Abolition and After*, edited by Jack Hayward. London: Frank Cass, 1985.

Discusses contributions by slaves and slave protests to emancipation. Presents brief summaries of slave rebellions and strikes, including Bussa's rebellion of April 1816 in Barbados, and the larger rebellions in Demerara, British Guiana, in August and September 1823 and the Baptist Wars of December 1831 and February 1832. Considers the so-called interaction between slave politics in the Caribbean and abolitionist politics in London.

358. Cronon, E. David. *Black Moses: the Story of Marcus Garvey and the Universal Negro Improvement Association.* Madison: University of Wisconsin Press, 1968. 278 p.

359. Cross, Malcolm and Arnaud Marks, eds. *Peasants, Plantations and Rural Communities in the Caribbean.* Surrey: Department of Sociology, University of Surrey, 1979. 304 p.

Collection of papers originally presented at the Third Caribbean Colloquium held in December, 1977. Relevant papers include the following: Gad Heuman on the franchise in postemancipation Jamaica; David Harrison on the Trinidad peasantry following emancipation; Jean Besson on land tenure and land inheritance in the Caribbean; Wout van der Bor on peasants and emancipation on St. Eustatius and Saba; David Lowenthal and Colin Clark on common lands on Barbuda; Eric Hanley on rice cultivation by East Indians in Guyana; and Michael Allen comparing the white elites in Barbados and Martinique following emancipation.

360. Cross, Malcolm, and Gad Heuman, eds. *Labour in the Caribbean: From Emancipation to Independence.* London: Macmillan Publishers, 1988. 352 p.

361. Cumper, G. E. "A Modern Jamaican Sugar Estate." *Social and Economic Studies* 3 (September 1954): 119–60.

362. Cumper, G. E. "Labour Demand and Supply in the Jamaican Sugar Industry, 1830–1950." *Social and Economic Studies* 2 (March 1954): 37–86.

363. Curtin, Philip D. "The British Sugar Duties and West Indian Prosperity." *Journal of Economic History* 14 (Spring 1954): 157–64.

   Examines the effects of the British Government's Sugar Act of 1846 on the economy of the British West Indies. A victory for proponents of free trade in Britain, the Sugar Act removed protection of West Indian sugar prices and left planters to face world sugar prices and competition from those areas still using slave labor, notably Brazil and Cuba. Based primarily on the *British Parliamentary Papers.*

364. Curtin, Philip D. *Two Jamaicas: The Role of Ideas in a Tropical Colony, 1830–1865.* Cambridge, Mass.: Harvard University, 1955. 270 p.

   Examines Jamaican politics and the transformation of labor and race relations in the immediate postemancipation period.

365. Dabydeen, David and Brinsley Samaroo, eds. *Across the Dark Waters: Ethnicity and Indian Identity in the Caribbean.* London: Macmillan, 1996. 222 p.

   Papers from a May 1988 conference at the University of Warwick on the theme of East Indians in the Caribbean, grouped under four themes: "Race Relations," "Religious and Cultural Practices," "Bibliography," and "Early History."

366. Davenport, William. "The Family System of Jamaica." *Social and Economic Studies* 10 (December 1961): 420–54.

   Discusses contemporary family structure, marriage, kinship, and land tenure in Jamaica.

367. Davis, David Brion. "Capitalism, Abolitionism, and Hegemony." In *British Capitalism and Caribbean Slavery,* edited by Barbara Solow and Stanley Engerman. Cambridge: Cambridge University Press, 1987.

   Discusses ideologies of abolition and free labor among British and American abolitionists.

368. Davis, David Brion. "British Emancipation as a New Moral Dispensation." *Rice University Studies* 67 (Winter 1981): 43–56.

Discusses British abolitionists' perceptions of the West Indies and Americas during the 1830s. Considers the works of major abolitionist writers such as Ralph Wardlaw and Thomas Clarkson.

369. Davis, David Brion. *Slavery and Human Progress.* New York: Oxford University Press, 1984. 374 p.

370. Deerr, Noel. *The History of Sugar.* 2 vols. London: Chapman and Hall, 1949–50.

Examines the role of sugar throughout world history, including a comparative discussion of sugar workers during the transition from slave to free labor. Volume I includes extensive quantitative data on sugar production for British colonies from the late seventeenth to the mid-twentieth centuries as well as plate illustrations of estate life and detailed plans of a Barbados sugar mill. Volume II explores the history of sugar workers, covering the following areas: slavery; the plantation and planters; the British colonies after emancipation; free immigrant labor; indentured Asian workers; and the Chinese "Coolie" trade. Also includes comparative material on sugar production in each West Indian colony following emancipation and extensive quotations from primary sources.

371. Delle, James A. *An Archaeology of Social Space: Analyzing Coffee Plantations in Jamaica's Blue Mountains.* New York: Plenum Press, 1998. 243 p.

History of coffee plantations in Jamaica from 1790 to 1865.

372. De Verteuil, Anthony. *The Years of Revolt: Trinidad, 1881–1888.* New Town, Port-of-Spain, Trinidad: Paris Publishing, 1984. 294 p.

A study of the social and political history of the Carnival riots by Blacks in 1881 and the Hosay riots by East Indians in 1884, together with the 1887 political reform movement that developed in the aftermath.

373. Domar, Evsey D. "The Causes of Slavery or Serfdom: A Hypothesis." *Journal of Economic History* 30 (1970): 18–32.

Seminal article offering a theory to explain the origins of unfree labor and why it takes the form of serfdom or slavery. Argues that the crucial variable is the land-labor ratio of a given society as mediated by political power relations.

374. Dookhan, Isaac. "The Elusive Nirvana: Indian Immigrants in Guyana and the Des Voeux Commission, 1870–71." *Revista/Review Interamericana* 17 (Fall/Winter 1987): 54–89.

Describes the conditions of South Asian sugar estate workers in British Guyana during the 1870s. Based on the papers of the Des Voeux Commission.

375. Drescher, Seymour. *Capitalism and Antislavery: British Mobilization in Comparative Perspective.* New York: Oxford University Press, 1987. 300 p.

Like the work of David Brion Davis, that of Seymour Drescher is focused primarily on antislavery organization prior to final abolition but is crucial for understanding postemancipation colonial ideology.

376. Eisner, Gisela. *Jamaica, 1830–1930: A Study in Economic Growth.* Manchester: Manchester University Press, 1961. 399 p.

Economic history of Jamaica based on colonial statistical data. Provides extensive information related to national income, population growth, production, public finance, and trade. Includes chapters on the transformation of the plantation economy in the postemancipation period and the growth of a peasantry. Also examines major social issues in the period as they relate to changes in productivity and labor supply. An appendix presents comparative wage rates from 1832 to 1932 for day workers, tradesmen, domestic workers, and professionals (lawyers and doctors).

377. Elkins, W. F. "Black Power in the British West Indies: the Trinidad Longshoremen's Strike of 1919." *Science and Society* 33 (Winter 1969): 71–75.

Analysis of the December 1919 dockworker's strike in Port-of-Spain, Trinidad. Discusses role of Afro-Caribbean soldiers just returned from the European front, the Trinidad Workingmen's Association, and the Universal Negro Improvement Association. Provides quotations and citations from British colonial records concerning the strike.

378. Elkins, W. F. "Marcus Garvey: 'The Negro World' and the British West Indies, 1919–1920." *Science and Society* 36 (Spring 1972): 63–77.

Outlines the reception, and often official censorship, of Marcus Garvey's Universal Negro Improvement Association and its paper *The Negro World* in British Honduras, British Guiana; the Windward Islands of St. Vincent, St. Lucia and Grenada; Trinidad, Jamaica, Barbados, and Bermuda; and the Panama Canal Zone. Based on British colonial records.

379. Eltis, David. "Abolitionist Perceptions of Society after Slavery." In *Slavery and British Society, 1776–1846,* edited by James Walvin. Baton Rouge: Louisiana State University Press, 1982.

Examines British abolitionists' views on economic and social conditions in postemancipation British West Indies.

380. Eltis, David. "Labour and Coercion in the English Atlantic World from the Seventeenth to the Early Twentieth Century." *Slavery and Abolition* 14 (April 1993): 207–26.

Discusses the similarities and differences in unfree labor systems in Britain and the British American colonies. Examines the circumstances that prompted the importation of African slaves.

381. Engerman, Stanley L. "Economic Change and Contract Labor in the British Caribbean: The End of Slavery and the Adjustment to Emancipation." *Explorations in Economic History* 21 (1984): 133–50.

Analyzes land-to-labor ratios in the British West Indies immediately following emancipation as well as other data related to annual sugar production.

382. Engerman, Stanley L. "Contract Labor, Sugar, and Technology in the Nineteenth Century." *Journal of Economic History* 43 (1983): 635–59.

Examines macrolevel trends in sugar production, technology, and the movement of contract laborers from India, China, and Africa to areas of large-scale sugar plantations, such as the British West Indies. Includes statistical data on the following: estimates of intercontinental flows of contract labor for the period from 1838 to 1915; outflows of labor from India including where Indian workers were received for the period from 1842 to 1920; and world output of cane sugar by type of labor for 1871/72 and 1880/81–1884/5. Explores attempts in the British West Indies by planters to gain access to the labor of former slaves and the turn to contract labor from overseas.

383. Engerman, Stanley R. "Economic Adjustments to Emancipation in the United States and British West Indies." *Journal of Interdisciplinary History* 13 (Autumn 1982): 191–20.

Compares data on labor production and income for ex-slaves in the British West Indies and the United States following emancipation. Includes statistical data for various British West Indian colonies on slave price (1822–30); land to labor ratios; and percentage change in annual sugar production between 1824 and 1833 and from 1839 to 1846. Compares capita income of former slaves in the British West Indies to that of former slaves in the U.S. South during 1860 and 1900.

384. Farley, Rawle. "The Rise of the Village Settlements of British Guiana." *Caribbean Quarterly* 3 (1953): 101–109.

Discusses the development of village settlements by slaves and ex-slaves during and immediately following emancipation in British Guiana. Statistics on the population of freeholders and examples of the amounts paid for specific village settlements are provided.

385. Farley, Rawle. "The Rise of the Peasantry in British Guiana." *Social and Economic Studies* 2 (1954): 87–103.

386. Feuer, Carl Henry. "Better Must Come: Sugar and Jamaica in the 20th Century." *Social and Economic Studies* 33 (December 1984): 1–49.

Discusses the development of the Jamaican sugar industry from the late nineteenth century to the reformist policy initiatives of the Jamaican state from 1972 to 1980, based primarily on secondary sources.

387. Foner, Eric. *Nothing but Freedom: Emancipation and Its Legacy.* Baton Rouge: Louisiana State University Press, 1983. 142 p.

Three essays on postemancipation labor systems in the Caribbean, Africa, and the United States. First essay discusses postemancipation labor in the British West Indies and Haiti. Second essay considers impact of the Caribbean experience on North American slavery and compares postemancipation society in the Caribbean and United States. Final essay is a comparative analysis of a strike by South Carolina sugar workers during the Reconstruction period.

388. Frucht, Richard. "Emancipation and Revolt in the West Indies: St. Kitts, 1834." *Science and Society* 39 (Summer 1975): 199–214.

Discusses resistance to the implementation of the apprenticeship system on St. Kitts.

389. Gocking, C. V. "Early Constitutional History of Jamaica (With Special Reference to the Period 1836–1866)." *Caribbean Quarterly* 6 (May 1960): 114–33.

Examines the creation of representative government in Jamaica following emancipation. Focuses on the British Cabinet Memorandum of 19 January 1839 on the "Course to be followed with West Indian Assemblies," including the memorandum's consideration of the role of the "coloured population." Also considers the Jamaican Constitution Act of 1854 and Jamaican opposition to "responsible government."

390. Gomes, P. I., ed. *Rural Development in the Caribbean.* London: C. Hurst, 1985. 246 p.

Collection of essays on the history of peasants in the Caribbean. Geographical areas covered include Barbados, Martinique, St. Lucia, Dominica, Tobago, Jamaica, Grenada, Cuba, and Trinidad.

391. Green, Pat. "'Small Settler' Houses in Chapelton: Microcosm of the Jamaican Vernacular." *Jamaica Journal* 17: 39–45.

Examines the architectural legacy of houses built by ex-slaves who chose to live on their own land rather than remain on the estates. The houses, defined as "small settler," represent an eclectic blend of Georgian proportions and scale and African technology and decorations. Includes photographs of houses from the area near Chapelton in the upper Clarendon region.

392. Green, William. "Parliament and the Abolition of Negro Apprenticeship, 1835–1838." *English Historical Review* 96 (1981): 560–76.

393. Green, William A. *British Slave Emancipation: The Sugar Colonies and the Great Experiment, 1830–1865.* Oxford: Clarendon, 1976. 449 p.

History of emancipation based mainly on Colonial Office records. Discusses apprenticeship, free trade, immigrant labor, and changes in the plantation economy, race relations, politics, and religion. Concludes with a discussion of Morant Bay rebellion.

394. Green, William A. "The Perils of Comparative History: Belize and the British Sugar Colonies after Slavery." *Comparative Studies in Society and History* 26 (1984): 112–19.

Green's response to a 1981 article by Nigel Bolland on postemancipation Belize.

395. Green, William A. "The Planter Class and British West Indian Sugar Production, before and after Emancipation." *Economic History Review* 26 (August 1973): 448–63.

396. Green, William A. "The Creolization of Caribbean History: The Emancipation Era and a Critique of Dialectical Analysis." *The Journal of Imperial and Commonwealth History* 14 (May 1986): 149–69.

Discussion of different scholarly approaches to relations between planters, former slaves, and other groups in the British West Indies during emancipation.

397. Gross, Izhak. "Parliament and the Abolition of Negro Apprenticeship, 1835–1838." *English Historical Review* 96 (1981): 560–76.

Discusses the debate in the British Parliament and the Colonial Office over the abolition of the apprenticeship system. Investigates the role of the London Anti-Slavery Society and public opinion. Based on personal papers, newspapers, and Colonial Office records.

398. Hall, Douglas. *Five of the Leewards 1834–1870: The Major Problems of the Post-Emancipation Period in Antiqua, Barbuda, Montserrat, Nevis and St. Kitts*. St. Laurence, Barbados: Carib University Press, 1971. 210 p.

Discusses the postemancipation labor question in the Leeward Islands, emphasizing the debates over apprenticeship following abolition. Considers the transition from slave to free labor and the increasing importance of wage labor on plantations for former slaves after 1846. Appendices include lists of Antigua estates by proprietor and size for the period between 1829 and 1921 and import duties on selected items in 1848 and 1855 for the five islands.

399. Hall, Douglas. *Free Jamaica, 1838–65: An Economic History*. New Haven: Yale University Press, 1959. 290 p.

Economic and political history of Jamaica focused on the abolition of apprenticeship in 1838, the 1846 British Sugar Duties Act, and the 1865 Morant Bay rebellion. Details economic factors motivating ex-slaves "flight" from the sugar estates and the "rise of the peasantry." Appendices include population and occupation statistics by race, age, and place of birth from the 1844 and 1861 censuses; sugar exports and prices from 1831 to 1865; immigration statistics from 1834 to 1865; revenues, expenditures, and revenue sources from 1840 to 1865; and import data from 1841 to 1865.

400. Hall, Douglas. "Absentee-Proprietorship in the British West Indies to About 1850." *Jamaican Historical Review* 4 (October 1964): 15–35.

Investigates contemporary perceptions of the West Indian absentee property owner in the eighteenth and nineteenth centuries. European observations on the perceived negative aspects of absenteeism are presented, particularly the argument that it reduced the white elite population in the colonies.

401. Hall, Douglas. "The Flight from the Estates Reconsidered: The British West Indies, 1838–42." *Journal of Caribbean History* 10–11 (1978): 7–24.

Considers different explanations for the massive movement of former slaves from estates in the British West Indies following the end of apprenticeships in 1838. Based on evidence presented to the Select Committee of the House of Commons on the West India Colonies of 1842. Includes materials on Jamaica, Barbados, Trinidad, and British Guiana.

402. Hall, Douglas G. *Ideas and Illustrations in Economic History*. New York: Holt, Rinehart and Winston, 1964.

Includes an account of the early banana trade in Jamaica during the period between 1868 and 1905.

403. Hamilton, Jill. *Women of Barbados: Amerindian Era to the mid 20th Century*. Bridgetown, Barbados: Letchworth Press, 1981. 91 p.

Overview of the living and social conditions of women in Barbados, emphasizing the individual achievements and community service of prominent women. Discusses changes in marriage and property laws in the nineteenth century, as well as developments in girls' education.

404. Handler, J. S. "The History of Arrowroot and the Origin of Peasantries in the British West Indies." *Journal of Caribbean History* 2 (May 1971): 46–93.

405. Haraksingh, Kusha. "Control and Resistance among Overseas Indian Workers: a Study of Labour on the Sugar Plantations of Trinidad." *Journal of Caribbean History* 14 (1981): 1–17.

Describes the working and living conditions of Indian workers in Trinidad during the period of indentured service from the 1840s to 1917. Outlines the experiences of Indian workers, of whom 143,000 ventured to Trinidad before 1917 and of whom fewer than 25 percent returned to India. Describes forms of control used in the labor process and in plantation life on the sugar estates, as well as specific forms of worker resistance. Such resistance is described in relation to older forms of association and cooperative assistance found in different regions of India.

406. Hart, Ansell. "The Banana in Jamaica: Export Trade." *Social and Economic Studies* 3 (September 1954): 212–29.

Considers the origins and growth of the banana export trade in Jamaica from the 1870s through 1953. Includes information on prices and number of acres cultivated as well as on exports from 1910 to 27, banana prices per count bunch from 1918 to 1927, comparisons between prices of the United Fruit Company and of the Jamaica Banana Producers' Association, and the values of exported products for various periods between 1700 and 1953.

407. Hart, Richard. "The Formation of a Caribbean Working Class." *The Black Liberator* 2 (1973/4): 131–48.

408. Hayward, Jack, ed. *Out of Slavery: Abolition and After*. London: Frank Cass, 1985. 200 p.

Collection of lectures given in 1983 in commemoration of the 150th anniversary of William Wilberforce's death and the abolition of slavery in the British West Indies. Lectures discuss the legacy of Wilberforce and different aspects of slavery and abolition in the British West Indies. Lecturers include Jack Hayward, Orlando Patterson, James Walvin, Fiona Spiers, Ian Bradley, Howard Temperley, Michael Craton, Lloyd Best, Shridath S. Ranphal, and Lord Scarman.

409. Henriques, Fernando. "Kinship and Death in Jamaica." *Phylon* 12 (1951): 272–78.

Discusses family structure and funeral rituals.

410. Heuman, Gad J. *Between Black and White: Race, Politics, and the Free Colureds in Jamaica, 1792–1865.* Westport, Conn.: Greenwood Press, 1981. 231 p.

Investigates the social and political roles of free people of color in Jamaica prior to and following emancipation. Describes the free coloreds' campaigns for civil rights prior to 1830, the role of coloreds and Blacks in the Legislative Assembly from 1830 to 1865, and the politics of colored opposition in the period leading up to the Morant Bay rebellion. Includes a bibliographical essay on primary source materials including private papers.

411. Heuman, Gad J. "White over Brown over Black: The Free Coloureds in Jamaican Society during Slavery and after Emancipation." *Journal of Caribbean History* 14 (1981): 46–69.

Examines the status of free people of color in Jamaica from the eighteenth century through the period following emancipation. Includes material on social and religious life, education, employment, and biographies of free people of color.

412. Heuman, Gad J. *The Killing Time: The Morant Bay Rebellion in Jamaica.* Knoxville: University of Tennessee Press, 1994. 199 p.

History of the Morant Bay rebellion from its origins to the immediate aftermath.

413. Higman, B. W. "The West India 'Interest' in Parliament, 1807–1833." *Historical Studies* 13 (October 1967): 1–19.

414. Higman, B. W. "Theory, Method and Technique in Caribbean Social History." *Journal of Caribbean History* 20 (1985–86): 1–29.

Review of different approaches to aspects of Caribbean history including kinship and family, social movements, material culture, and oral history.

415. Higman, B. W. *Slave Population and Economy in Jamaica, 1807–1834.* Cambridge: Cambridge University Press, 1976. 327 p.

History of Jamaican slave populations based on Jamaican primary sources as well as the British Colonial Office's "Slave Registration and Compensation Records." Includes extensive parish-level data related to topics such as population distribution, productivity, death and birth rates, marriages, manumissions, and runaways. Transformations in labor productivity during the period are discussed in the context of Jamaica's position in the world economy and the movement toward free labor.

416. Higman, B. W. *Slave Populations of the British Caribbean: 1807–1834.* Baltimore: Johns Hopkins University Press, 1984. 781 p.

Presents extensive demographic evidence related to slave populations of the British West Indies based primarily on colonial slave registrations from 1807 to 1834. A complement to author's earlier work on Jamaica, this compendium provides evidence for other colonies related to the physical and economic environments; growth and distribution of the slave population; structure of the slave populations, including gender, race, and age difference; differences between rural and urban areas in work, occupation, housing, and incentives to labor; health, fertility, mortality; and data on manumission, marronage, and rebellions. Includes a three hundred-page statistical supplement with demographic data derived from colonial sources.

417. Higman, B. W., ed. *Trade, Government and Society in Caribbean History, 1700–1920: Essays Presented to Douglas Hall.* Kingston, Jamaica: Heinemann Education Books Caribbean, 1983. 172 p.

Essays include Richard B. Sheridan's discussion of the slave trade to Jamaica from 1702 to 1808; Woodville K. Marshall's analysis of the St. Vincent riots of 1862, and Barry Higman's examination of domestic service in Jamaica since 1750. Other relevant essays discuss the role of slavery in three West Indian towns and the crown colony government in Trinidad before and after emancipation.

418. Higman, B. W. *Montpelier, Jamaica: A Plantation Community in Slavery and Freedom, 1739–1912.* Barbados: University of the West Indies Press, 1998. 384 p.

Reconstruction of daily life in a plantation village using archeological as well as documentary evidence. Examines the property ownership, labor, settlement patterns, organization of workers' villages, village architecture, and the material contents of individual houses. Discusses role of Montpelier in the slave rebellion between 1831 and 1832.

419. Higman, B. W. "Remembering Slavery: The Rise, Decline and Revival of Emancipation Day in the English-speaking Caribbean." *Slavery and Abolition* 19 (April 1998): 90–105.

420. Higman, Barry W. "Jamaican Coffee Plantations, 1780–1860: A Cartographic Analysis." *Caribbean Geography* 2 (October 1986): 73–91.

421. Higman, Barry W. "Slavery Remembered: The Celebration of Emancipation in Jamaica." *Journal of Caribbean Geography* 12 (1979): 55–74.

422. Higman, Barry W. "The Spatial Economy of Jamaican Sugar Plantations: Cartographic Evidence from the Eighteenth and Nineteenth Centuries." *Journal of Historical Geography* 13 (January 1987): 17–39.

    Presents a cartometrical analysis of 156 plans of sugar plantations over the period 1750 and 1880. Analyzes land-use patterns, including the distance between residential and workplace based on the location of sugar fields, laborers' villages, and the great house.

423. Higman, Barry W. "The Internal Economy of Jamaican Pens, 1760–1890." *Social and Economic Studies* 38 (1989): 61–86.

    Outlines the economic history of livestock pens during the eighteenth and nineteenth centuries in Jamaica.

424. Holt, Thomas C. "'An Empire over the Mind': Emancipation, Race, and Ideology in the British West Indies and the American South." In *Region, Race, and Reconstruction: Essays in Honor of C. Vann Woodward*, edited by J. Morgan Kousser and James M. McPherson. New York: Oxford University Press, 1982.

    Compares the ideologies of British and American officials toward emancipated laborers in the British West Indies and U.S. South. Focuses on the writings of Henry Taylor, a middle-level bureaucrat in the British colonial office.

425. Holt, Thomas C. *The Problem of Freedom: Race, Labor, and Politics in Jamaica and Britain, 1832–1938.* Baltimore: Johns Hopkins University Press, 1992. 517 p.

    A political, social, and economic history of the transformations in Jamaica from emancipation to the 1938 labor rebellion. Explores colonial and Jamaican political debates over the meaning of free labor and the realities of ex-slave peasant life. Examines contradictions within liberal democracy and free market ideologies. Presents extensive data on land and labor, and analyzes the 1865 Morant Bay Rebellion. Concludes with a discussion of twentieth-century working-class history and the 1938 labor unrest. Appendices provide sources for the analysis of data on land-holdings and migration, as well as sources for and analysis of data on the Jamaican Assembly.

426. Holt, Thomas C. "The Essence of the Contract: The Articulation of Race, Gender, and Political Economy in British Emancipation Policy, 1838–1866." In Frederick Cooper, Thomas C. Holt, and Rebecca J. Scott, *Beyond Slavery: Explorations of Race, Labor, and Citizenship in Postemancipation Societies*. Chapel Hill: University of North Carolina Press, 2000.

Expands on author's monograph (above), with a focus on Jamaica. Explores the dimension of gender in free labor ideology.

427. Horowitz, Michael. *Peoples and Cultures of the Caribbean: An Anthropological Reader*. Garden City, N.Y.: Natural History Press (1971). 606 p.

Wide-ranging collection of anthropological essays on the Caribbean. Themes include culture and history, language, race, ethnicity and class, plantations, peasants and communities, land tenure, labor, economics and internal markets, domestic organization, and the place of religion and folklore.

428. Hum, Derek and Alexander Basilevsky. "Economic Activity and Cyclical Variation in Birthrates: Some New Evidence for Jamaica." *Social and Economic Studies* 27 (June 1978): 197–203.

Statistical analysis of birth rate cycles and production cycles in major agricultural export crops in Jamaica between 1880 and 1938.

429. *Jamaican Historical Review* 14 (1984). Special issue commemorating the 150th anniversary of slave emancipation in Jamaica.

430. Johnson, Howard. "The Anti-Chinese Riots of 1918 in Jamaica." *Caribbean Quarterly* 28 (September 1982): 19–32.

Examines anti-Chinese violence in St. Catherine, St. Mary, St. Ann, and Clarendon parishes. Considers position of the Chinese in Jamaican society as well as tensions between working-class Creoles and Chinese traders.

431. Johnson, Howard. "Barbadian Immigrants in Trinidad, 1870–1897." *Caribbean Studies* 13 (October 1973): 5–30.

Examines the migration of ex–slaves from Barbados to work on the sugar plantations of Trinidad. Explores the motives for migration to Trinidad and the use of labor recruiters in Barbados after 1870.

432. Johnson, Howard. "The Origins and Early Development of Cane Farming in Trinidad, 1882–1906." *Journal of Caribbean History* 5 (November 1972): 46–74.

Examines the evolution of cane farming from 1882 to early twentieth century, including motivations and organization of the system and conflicts between planters and cane farmers.

433. Johnson, Howard. "Labour Systems in Postemancipation Bahamas." *Social and Economic Studies* 37 (1988): 181–201.

434. Johnson, Howard. *The Bahamas from Slavery to Servitude, 1783–1933.* Gainesville: University Press of Florida, 1996. 218 p.

435. Johnson, Howard. *The Bahamas in Slavery and Freedom.* London: James Currey, 1991. 184 p.

A series of essays on labor in the Bahamas including the self-hire system during slavery, the development of sharecropping and tenancy during the immediate postemancipation period, and the increased exploitation of peasants at the end of the nineteenth century. Concludes with chapters on West Indian migration in the 1920s as well as labor migration to Florida in the nineteenth and twentieth centuries.

436. Joseph, Cedric L. "The Strategic Importance of the British West Indies, 1882–1932." *Journal of Caribbean History* 7 (November 1973): 23–67.

History of the decline of British military presence in the West Indies.

437. *Journal of Caribbean History* 22 (1988). Special issue "to commemorate the 150th anniversary of slave emancipation in the British Caribbean."

438. Karch, Cecilia. "The Growth of the Corporate Economy in Barbados: Class/Race Factors, 1890–1977." In *Contemporary Caribbean: A Sociological Reader*, vol. 1, edited by Susan Craig. Maracas: Susan Craig/College Press, 1981.

Overview of key changes in economy of Barbados.

439. Kilkenny, Roberta. "Sugar and Socioeconomic Transformation in Post-Indenture British Guiana, 1880–1948." *Historia y Sociedad* 3 (1990): 78–95.

440. Klein, Herbert S., and Stanley L. Engerman. "The Transition from Slave to Free Labor: Notes on a Comparative Economic Model." In *Between Slavery and Free Labor: The Spanish-Speaking Caribbean in the Nineteenth Century*, edited by Manuel Moreno Fraginals, Frank Moya Pons, and Stanley L. Engerman. Baltimore: Johns Hopkins University Press, 1985.

Discusses possible points of comparison for the study of the transition from slave to free labor in the Caribbean, including "Postemancipation Conflicts," "Land and Natural Resources," "Demographic Characteristics and the Land-Labor Ratio," "Government Policies and Their Determinants," "World Market Conditions," "Technologies of Crop Production," and "Patterns in Transition."

441. Klingberg, Frank J. "The Lady Mico Charity Schools in the British West Indies, 1835–1842." *Journal of Negro History* 24 (July 1939): 291–344.

A history of the Lady Mico Charity Schools, which were developed and funded by British abolitionists with the goal of educating former slaves in the British West Indies. Based on the reports and letters written by Mico teachers in the West Indies to the Charity's trustees in London. Includes quotations from instructors and administrators on the workings of the Mico schools.

442. Knaplund, Paul. *James Stephen and the British Colonial System, 1813–1847*. Madison: University of Wisconsin Press, 1953. 315 p.

A biography of the Colonial administrator James Stephen who worked as a legal advisor in the suppression of the slave trade, abolition, and the protection of former slaves' rights in the British West Indies. Includes a speech made by Stephen in 1858 entitled "Colonization as a Branch of Social Economy." Based on Colonial Office Record Group 323, which concerns legal counsel to the Colonial Office during the period of emancipation.

443. Knight, Franklin. "Jamaican Migrants and the Cuban Sugar Industry, 1900–1934." In *Between Slavery and Free Labor: the Spanish-Speaking Caribbean in the Nineteenth Century*, edited by Manuel Moreno Franginals, Frank Moya Pons, and Stanley Engerman. Baltimore: Johns Hopkins University Press, 1985.

Investigates the migration of Jamaican workers to Cuba during the early decades of the twentieth century. Provides data on number of migrants and occupational status in Cuba and discusses official views in Cuba toward Jamaican workers. Includes three life histories of former migrants to Cuba, which are based on the author's fieldwork.

444. Knight, Franklin and Colin A. Palmer, eds. *The Modern Caribbean.* Chapel Hill: University of North Carolina Press, 1989. 382 p.

A reader consisting of individually authored essays on the history, economics, politics, and culture of the Caribbean region from the Haitian Revolution through the twentieth century. Includes discussion of Haiti, Jamaica, Trinidad, Puerto Rico, and Cuba. Essay by Francisco Scarano on land and labor in the Spanish-speaking Caribbean is of particular relevance for comparative purposes.

445. Knox, A. J. G. "Opportunities and Opposition: the Rise of Jamaica's Black Peasantry and the Nature of the Planter Resistance." *The Canadian Review of Sociology and Anthropology* 14 (November 1977): 381–95.

Outlines the history of peasant resistance in Jamaica from the end of apprenticeship in 1838 to the Morant Bay rebellion of 1865. Discusses primary sources and secondary literature related to Jamaican peasant life and resistance with an emphasis on the interaction between planters, the state, the British government, and rural populations. Also reviews the role of Baptist missionaries who supported the demands of rural people after emancipation.

446. Knox, B. A. "British Government and the Governor Eyre Controversy, 1865–1875." *Historical Journal* 19 (December 1976): 877–900.

Examines how successive British Governments responded to Governor Eyre's handling of the Morant Bay rebellion of 1865. Based on the private papers of British political leaders.

447. Knox, Bruce. "The Queen's Letter of 1865 and British Policy towards Emancipation and Indentured Labour in the West Indies, 1830–1865." *Historical Journal* 29 (June 1986): 345–67.

Discusses ideological background to Henry Taylor's 1865 response to a petition for land and aid from "certain poor people" of St. Ann's parish in Jamaica. Also considers the Colonial Land and Immigration Commission's report of 1858, which sanctioned immigration of Chinese workers to the West Indies.

448. Knox, Graham. "Political Change in Jamaica (1866–1906) and the Local Reaction to the Policies of the Crown Colony Government." In *The Caribbean in Transition*, edited by F. Andic and T. Mathews. Puerto Rico: University of Puerto Rico Press, 1965.

449. Knox, Graham. "British Colonial Policy and the Problems of Establishing a Free Society in Jamaica, 1838–1865." *Caribbean Studies* 2 (January 1963): 3–13.

Overview of the major problems facing colonial government in Jamaica from the end of apprenticeship to the Morant Bay rebellion including political representation; free trade and the loss of sugar protection; elimination of foreign slavery; completion of emancipation; labor shortages and indentured labor; needs of the newly independent peasantry; and the increasingly wide gap between rich and poor.

450. Kopytoff, Barbara Klamon. "Jamaican Maroon Political Organization: The Effects of the Treaties." *Social and Economic Studies* 25 (June 1976): 87–105.

Discusses 1739 treaties between the government of Jamaica and two separate groups of Maroons and the treaties' effects on Maroon political stability. Describes the pretreaty political organization of Maroons; political disturbances in the posttreaty period; and efforts by the colonial state to destabilize Maroon society.

451. Laurence, K. O. *A Question of Labour: Indentured Immigration into Trinidad and British Guiana, 1875–1917.* New York: St. Martin's Press, 1994. 648 p.

An examination of the recruitment and structure of Indian indentured labor. Discusses enforcement of indentures, the health and social conditions of the immigrants, and the financing of the system and its eventual abolition.

452. Laurence, K. O. "The Development of Medical Services in British Guiana and Trinidad, 1841–1873." *Jamaican Historical Review* 4 (October 1964): 59–67.

Details the development of medical services in rural areas and the enforcement of colonial indentured service laws in Trinidad and British Guiana. Based on Colonial Office records and the *British Parliamentary Papers*.

453. Laurence, K. O. "The Establishment of the Portuguese Community in British Guiana." *Jamaican Historical Review* 5 (November 1965): 50–74.

A history of Portuguese immigration to British Guiana in the nineteenth century. Discusses role of Portuguese in sugar industry and retail trade as well as relations between Portuguese, East Indians, and former slaves. Based on the *British Parliamentary Papers* and records of the Colonial Office.

454. Laurence, K. O. "The Evolution of Long-term Labour Contracts in Trinidad and British Guiana, 1834–1863." *Jamaican Historical Review* 5 (May 1965): 9-27.

Examines regulations and ordinances concerning long-term labor contracts following emancipation. Discusses Colonial Office's regulation of contracts for different groups of workers including former slaves, African-American immigrants from the United States, and immigrants from India and China. Based on the *British Parliamentary Papers* and records of the Colonial Office.

455. Levy, Claude. *Emancipation, Sugar, and Federalism: Barbados and the West Indies, 1833–1876.* Gainesville: University Press of Florida, 1980. 206 p.

Examines the transition from slavery to free labor in Barbados. Includes discussion of abolition of slavery apprenticeship and the advent of free labor. Based on archival records from Barbados and the Colonial Office.

456. Lewis, Lancelot S. *The West Indian in Panama: Black Labor In Panama, 1850–1914.* Washington, D.C.: University Press of America, 1980. 271 p.

History of West Indian migrant workers in Panama from the building of the Panama Railroad in the 1850s through the completion of the Panama Canal. Discusses working and housing conditions, education, and racism in Panama. Appendices include copies of signed statements by migrants detailing their experiences in Panama and service contracts as well as statistical data on migrants.

457. Lewis, Rupert. *Marcus Garvey: Anti-Colonial Champion.* Trenton, N.J.: Africa World Press, 1988. 301 p.

Biography of Marcus Garvey with special emphasis on the role of Garvey's Universal Negro Improvement Association (UNIA) in Jamaican politics and social protests. Includes discussion of Garvey's family and early influences, including Robert Love and Alexander Bedward. Charts the development of the UNIA and its impact in Cuba, Panama, and Costa Rica as well as Garvey's influence in the United States and Africa. Covers the UNIA's role in municipal and national politics in Jamaica and Garvey's influences on the labor protests between 1937 and 1938.

458. Lewis, Rupert and Patrick Bryan, eds. *Garvey: His Work and Impact.* Mona, Jamaica: Institute of Social and Economic Research and Department of Extramural Studies, University of the West Indies, 1988. 334 p.

A collection of individually-authored papers originally presented at a conference held at the University of the West Indies in November 1987.

459. Liverpool, Hollis "Chalkdust." *Rituals of Power and Rebellion: The Carnival Tradition in Trinidad and Tobago, 1763–1962.* Chicago: Research Associates School Times Publications/Frontline Distribution, 2001. 518 p.

Study drawing on extensive primary printed sources, recordings, oral interviews with calypsonians, and author's experiences as composer and performer. Parts II and III deal with postemancipation period. Based on author's doctoral dissertation.

460. Lobdell, Richard. *Economic Structure and Demographic Performance in Jamaica, 1891–1935.* New York: Garland Publishing, 1987. 259 p.

An economic and demographic history of Jamaica based on parish-level data from 1891 to 1935. Investigates the relationship between economic activity and demographic patterns following the demise of the sugar plantation economy and the rise of banana and other staple crop production by small holders. Provides statistical data on parishes between 1871 and 1943.

461. Lobdell, Richard. "Women in the Jamaican Labour Force, 1881–1921." *Social and Economic Studies* (37): 1988. 203–40.

Considers women's participation in the Jamaican labor force from 1881 to 1921. Draws on the decennial censuses. Notes a significant rise in the number of women categorized as agricultural workers and planters between 1881 and 1921.

462. Lobdell, Richard A. "Patterns of Investment and Sources of Credit in the British West Indian Sugar Industry, 1838–97." *Journal of Caribbean History* 4 (May 1972): 31–53.

463. Look Lai, Walton. *Indentured Labor, Caribbean Sugar: Chinese and Indian Migrants to the British West Indies, 1838–1918.* Baltimore: Johns Hopkins University Press, 1993. 370 p.

History of contract and indentured labor systems in the British West Indies. Examines the experience of Chinese and Indian immigrants and migrants in the Caribbean, detailing life and labor on the plantations for each group as well as relations with Creole and ex-slave populations. Investigates the social mobility of Chinese and Indian immigrants, assimilation, and contributions of each group to West Indian economy and culture. Appendices include statistical data on Asian migration and immigration; laws on immigration in Trinidad, British Guiana, and Jamaica; and examples of indenture contracts.

464. Lowenthal, David. "Post-Emancipation Race Relations: Some Caribbean and American Perspectives." *Journal of Inter-American Studies and World Affairs* 13 (July–October 1971): 367–77.

Comparison of race relations following emancipation in the West Indies and United States.

465. Lowenthal, David and Lambros Comitas. *The Aftermath of Sovereignty: West Indian Perspectives.* Garden City: Anchor Books, 1973. 422 p.

Collection of essays on politics and identity in the West Indies after decolonization.

466. Malmsten, Neal R. "The British Labour Party and the West Indies, 1918–39." *Journal of Imperial and Commonwealth History* 5 (January 1977): 172–205.

Investigates the British Labour Party's influence on colonial policy and trade union organizations in the West Indies. Discusses the West Indian Labour Conference, the Trinidad Workers' Association, and the British Guiana Labour Union. Addresses development assistance, development ideology, and labor unrest in the late 1930s as well as the role of Labour MP Arthur Creech Jones, who served as colonial secretary after World War II.

467. Mangru, Basdeo. *Indenture and Abolition: Sacrifice and Survival on the Guyanese Sugar Plantations.* Toronto: TSAR, 1993. 146 p.

Essays on the contribution of East Indians to Guyanese sugar plantations. Author examines the initial "seasoning" of the immigrants at Calcutta for the impending voyage, the role of James Crosby as the protector of the Indians, "Tadjah" festivals, the establishment of East Indian villages, the Rose Hall riots of 1913, the campaign against indenture from 1908 to 1918, and postabolition labor schemes of Guyanese planters and resistance to those schemes by Indian nationalists and the Government of India.

468. Marks, Shula and Peter Richardson, eds. *International Labour Migration: Historical Perspectives.* Hounslow, Middlesex: Institute of Commonwealth Studies/M. Temple Smith, 1984. 280 p.

A collection of essays on labor migration in the British Empire and Commonwealth from 1780 to the twentieth century. Includes studies of English indentured servants, the failure of contract labor in the nineteenth-century United States, the importation of British Indians into Surinam, migrant labor in South Africa, and coerced labor in New Zealand, Northern Nigeria, and Australian New Guinea.

469. Marsala, Vincent John. *Sir John Peter Grant, Governor of Jamaica, 1866–1874*. Cultural Heritage Series, vol. 3. Kingston: Institute of Jamaica, 1972. 125 p.

A biography of Governor Grant, who took over as governor of Jamaica following the Morant Bay rebellion. Provides a brief account of the Morant Bay rebellion of 1865, noting the implications of the rebellion for debates over crown colony status and bureaucratic reforms. Documents the activities of Governor Grant and his administration from 1866 to 1873, particularly in terms of education, financial reform, assistance to sugar planters, and public works projects. Includes a bibliography of relevant Jamaican primary sources.

470. Marshall, Dawn I. "Vincentian Contract Labor Migration to Barbados: The Satisfaction of Mutual Needs?" *Social and Economic Studies* 33 (1984): 63–92.

Examines relative economic differentials in St. Vincent and Barbados that prompted labor migrations and changes over time.

471. Marshall, K. "Notes on Peasant Development in the West Indies since 1838." *Social and Economic Studies* 17 (September 1968): 252–63.

Offers a typology and periodization for understanding the history of West Indian peasantries since emancipation. Includes statistical tables showing the distribution of land holdings.

472. Marshall, W. K., ed. *Emancipation II: Aspects of the Post-slavery Experience in Barbados*. Bridgetown, Barbados: Department of History, University of the West Indies, 1987. 143 p.

473. Marshall, W. K. "Metayage in the Sugar Industry of the British Windward Islands, 1838–1865." *Jamaican Historical Review* 5 (May 1965): 28–55.

Considers the emergence and decline in the British Windward Islands of the metayage system of sugar production, a form of labor in which wages were paid in kind rather than in cash. Discusses contracts, grievances of the "metayers" (laborers), role of courts, and the levels of sugar production. Describes planters' growing opposition to the system.

474. Marshall, Woodville. "The Establishment of a Peasantry in Barbados, 1840–1920." In *Social Groups and Institutions in the History of the Caribbean*. Association of Caribbean Historians, 1975: 84–105.

475. Marshall, Woodville K. "Social and Economic Problems in the Windward Islands, 1838–1865." In *The Caribbean in Transition*,

edited by F. Andic and T. Mathews. Puerto Rico: University of
Puerto Rico Press, 1965.

476. Marshall, Woodville K. "The Termination of Apprenticeship in
Barbados and the Windward Islands: An Essay in Colonial
Administration and Politics." *Journal of Caribbean History* 2 (May
1971): 1–45.

Detailed examination of efforts by the governor-in-chief of the Windward Islands to abolish the apprenticeship system.

477. Marshall, Woodville, ed. *Emancipation III.* Cave Hill, Barbados:
Department of History, University of the West Indies, 1988. 122 p.

Lectures by different authors delivered in 1987 to commemorate the
150th anniversary of emancipation in Barbados. Emphasis is on the first
four decades of the twentieth century. Themes include village formation,
political and trade union organization, the 1937 riots and the relationship of Barbados to the Confederation of the West Indies in the 1950s
and 1960s.

478. Martin, Tony. *Race First: The Ideological and Organizational
Struggles of Marcus Garvey and the Universal Negro Improvement
Association.* Westport, Conn.: Greenwood Press, 1976. 421 p.

History of Marcus Garvey (1884–1940) and the United Negro Improvement Association (UNIA). Describes Garvey's formative years in Jamaica
and aspects of his philosophy and political agenda including the concepts
of "race first" and self-reliance, and his writings concerning nationhood,
religion, history, Africa, and the Black Star Line. Also considers topics
such as Garvey's relations with the FBI and the NAACP as well as his court
battles, imprisonment and exile. Includes a table showing the distribution of UNIA branches in the United States, the West Indies, Central, and
South America in 1926.

479. Mason, Peter. *Bacchanal! The Carnival Culture of Trinidad.*
Philadelphia: Temple University Press, 1998. 191 p.

480. Mathieson, William Law. *British Slave Emancipation, 1838–1849.*
London: Longmans, 1932. 243 p.

A history of the political and economic crises confronting the British
colonies during the period immediately following emancipation. Discusses tensions over sugar price subsidies for Antigua, Barbados, Jamaica, Trinidad, and British Guiana and the impact of emancipation on
the supply of labor to sugar estates in these colonies. Based on the *British Parliamentary Papers* and contemporary accounts. Considers land

ownership by former slaves; attempts to supply labor through immigration from China, Africa, and India; social conditions following emancipation; the 1846 Sugar Price Act; and free trade.

481. Mathieson, William Law. *British Slavery and Its Abolition, 1823–1838.* London: Longmans, 1926. 318 p.

History of the abolition of slavery in the British colonies. Based primarily on the *British Parliamentary Papers* and published accounts by European observers.

482. McGlynn, Frank and Seymour Drescher, eds. *The Meaning of Freedom: Economics, Politics, and Culture after Slavery.* Pittsburgh: Pittsburgh University Press, 1992. 333 p.

Collection of individually-authored chapters originally presented at a conference on postemancipation societies held at the University of Pittsburgh in August 1988. Authors include Stanley Engerman on economic responses to emancipation; O. Nigel Bolland on the politics of freedom in the British Caribbean; Michel-Rolph Trouillot on free people of color and politics in postemancipation Dominica and Saint-Domingue/Haiti; Jean Besson on community and family life in the British West Indies; Diana Austin-Broos on Christianity in postemancipation Jamaica; Sidney Mintz on the historiographical meaning of freedom; and Raymond T. Smith on race, class, and gender during the transition to freedom.

483. McLewin, Philip J. *Power and Economic Change: the Response to Emancipation in Jamaica and British Guiana, 1840–1865.* New York: Garland Publishing, 1987. 271 p.

Comparative history of Jamaica and British Guiana after emancipation. Discusses problems of land, plantation technology, capital, and labor supply in each colony. Considers the politics of planters in each colony and different approaches to finding labor for sugar estates. Considers the proprietary village, the metayer system, immigrant labor and communal villages in British Guiana. In the case of Jamaica, addresses efforts by planters to shape the working class and rent policies for landless peasants. Appendices include information on a Guiana estate; the constraints of English immigration policy; production techniques for Jamaican sugar; Jamaican agricultural and criminal laws; and the Jamaica Baptist Mission.

484. Mills, Charles W. "Race and Class: Conflicting or Reconcilable Paradigms?" *Social and Economic Studies* 36 (June 1987): 69–108.

Discussion of theoretical approaches to race and class in Caribbean society.

485. Mintz, Sidney W. *Caribbean Transformations*. Chicago: Aldine, 1974. 355 p.

A collection of the author's essays on slavery, forced labor, and the plantation system in Puerto Rico and peasantries in the Caribbean more generally. Discusses the historical sociology of Jamaican villages, including the origins of free villages following emancipation and the origins of the Jamaican market system. Explores the uses and symbolic meaning of houses and yards among Caribbean peasantries.

486. Mintz, Sidney W. "Labor and Sugar in Puerto Rico and in Jamaica, 1800–1850." *Comparative Studies in Society and History* 1 (March 1959): 273–80.

A comparative analysis of the growth of sugar plantation agriculture in Puerto Rico and Jamaica. Compares the land tenure and land use patterns of peasantries in both colonies and discusses the relationship between the decline of the sugar economy in Jamaica and the rise of sugar in Puerto Rico in the second half of the nineteenth century. Followed by a brief commentary by Elsa V. Goveia.

487. Mintz, Sidney W. "The Rural Proletariat and the Problem of Rural Proletarian Consciousness." *Journal of Peasant Studies* 1 (April 1974): 291–325.

Examination of conceptual issues in defining the class status of rural labor. Discusses the analytical and terminological difficulties in extant literature, the character of rural proletariat and peasant communities, and the process of rural proletarianization.

488. Mintz, Sidney W. *Sweetness and Power: The Place of Sugar in Modern History*. New York: Viking Books, 1985. 274 p.

Traces the relationship between Europeans' increasing consumption of sugar and the development of Caribbean sugar production based on slavery. Discusses the ways in which the increased importance of sugar consumption in Europe contributed to the development of European capitalism in the eighteenth and nineteenth century and European reliance on colonies and slave plantation economies in the Caribbean. Considers production of sugar and the international sugar trade. Includes images of sugar production in the West Indies.

489. Mintz, Sidney W. "A Note on the Definition of Peasantries." *The Journal of Peasant Studies* 1 (October 1973): 91–106.

490. Mintz, Sidney W. and Richard Price. *The Birth of African-American Culture: An Anthropological Perspective*. Boston: Beacon Press, 1992. 121 p.

A series of essays originally written in 1972 and 1973 on African-American history. Engages Melville Herskovits's works concerning African cultural survivals in the New World. Authors consider topics including the encounter model, sociocultural contact and flow in slave societies; slavery as a social system; the beginnings of African-American societies and cultures; retentions and survivals; and kinship and sex roles.

491. Moberg, Mark. *Myths of Ethnicity and Nation: Immigration, Work and Identity in the Belize Banana Industry.* Knoxville: University of Tennessee Press, 1997. 218 p.

Describes the racial and ethnic segmentation of the labor force in the Belizian banana industry since the early 1980s, its relation to local and political constraints affecting banana production, and the various forms by which immigrant labor is recruited and deployed. Includes a detailed discussion of relations between labor processes, ethnic tensions, and efforts at unionization.

492. Moohr, Michael. "Economic Impact of Slave Emancipation in British Guiana, 1832–1852." *Economic History Review* 25 (November 1972): 588–607.

493. Moore, Brian L. *Cultural Power, Resistance and Pluralism: Colonial Guyana, 1839–1900.* Montreal: McGill-Queen's University Press, 1995. 376 p.

A cultural history of British Guiana in the nineteenth century following emancipation. Discusses elite Victorian, Afro-Creole Folk, Indian Bhojpuri, Portuguese Latin, and Chinese Hua-Qiao cultures. Discusses value-systems, naming, food, language, dress, and rites of passage. Contains numerous historical photographs.

494. Moore, Brian L. *Race, Power and Social Segmentation in Colonial Society: Guyana After Slavery, 1838–1891.* New York: Gordon and Breach Science Publishers, 1987. 310 p.

A history of class, race, and ethnicity in British Guiana. Investigates how the white elite used state power to coerce former slave, indentured Indian, and Chinese populations. Examines plantation life and labor routines, attempts by former slaves to engage in peasant production, and planters' attempts to influence postemancipation politics. Compares experience of Portuguese immigrants with those of Chinese and Indian immigrants to the colony. Based on records from the British Colonial Office and Guyana.

495. Morison, J. L. *The Eighth Earl of Elgin: A Chapter in Nineteenth-Century Imperial History*. London: Hodder and Stoughton, 1928. 317 p.

Biography of one of the most influential governors of Jamaica during its transition to a free wage labor system in the 1840s.

496. Murray, D. J. *The West Indies and the Development of Colonial Government, 1801–1834*. Oxford: Clarendon Press, 1965. 264 p.

A narrative history of British colonial governments in the West Indies from the beginning of the Colonial Office to the beginning of apprenticeship. Analyzes the role of colonial governments in the abolition of the slave trade and increasing pressures in Britain for the abolition of slavery. Also discusses the growth of the Colonial Office during the first quarter of the nineteenth century. Details the British occupations of Martinique, Guadaloupe, and St. Lucia following France's defeat in 1794. Also discusses the British acquisition of Trinidad from Spain in 1802.

497. Myers, Robert. "Post-Emancipation Migrations and Population Change in Dominica, 1834–1950." *Revista/Review Interamericana* 11 (1981): 87–109.

498. Naylor, Robert. "The Mahogany Trade as a Factor in the British Return to the Mosquito Shore in the Second Quarter of the 19th Century." *Jamaican Historical Review* 7 (1967): 40–67.

499. Nevadomsky, Joseph. "Social Change and the East Indians in Rural Trinidad: A Critique of Methodologies." *Social and Economic Studies* 31 (1982): 90–126.

Discusses different approaches to the study of the history of East Indians in Trinidad from 1834 onward.

500. Newton, Velma. *The Silver Men: West Indian Labour Migration to Panama, 1850–1914*. Kingston: Institute of Social and Economic Research, University of the West Indies, 1984. 218 p.

A history of British West Indian emigration to Panama. Highlights the role of West Indians in the building of the Panama railroad in the 1850s and efforts to construct a canal across Panama during the period from 1881 to 1914. Investigates push and pull factors leading to migration, including the depressed sugar economy in most of the West Indies, increased population pressures on small peasant landholdings, and the recruitment of workers by agents of canal-related companies. Details the demographic, economic and social effects of emigration, with a focus on Jamaica and Barbados.

501. Nurse, Lawrence. *Trade Unionism and Industrial Relations in the Commonwealth Caribbean: History, Contemporary Practice, and Prospect.* Westport, Conn.: Greenwood Press, 1992. 157 p.

History of industrial relations and trade union practices in the Caribbean. Examines values in the workplace; the historical origins and character of trade unions; the practice of collective bargaining; state attempts to redefine labor-employer relations after the 1960s; and prospects for the future of trade unions in the Caribbean. Focuses mainly on the period after 1960, but includes discussion of trade union origins.

502. Nwulia, Moses D. E. "The 'Apprenticeship' System in Mauritius: Its Character and its Impact on Race Relations in the Post-Emancipation Period, 1839-1879." *African Studies Review* 21 (April 1978): 89–101.

Examines the apprenticeship system in Mauritius from 1835 to 1839. The apprenticeship system is described both in legal and practical terms using Colonial Office correspondence and investigations. Makes comparisons with apprenticeship in the British West Indies including a discussion of how East Indian labor was used to compensate for the loss of African ex-slaves who retreated from the sugar-plantation labor market during the apprenticeship period.

503. Olivier, Lord [Sydney Haldane]. *The Myth of Governor Eyre.* London: Hogarth Press, 1933. 348 p.

A dissection of the administration of Governor Eyre and the causes of the Morant Bay Rebellion by a twentieth-century governor of Jamaica.

504. Paget, Hugh. "The Free Village System in Jamaica." *Jamaican Historical Review* 1 (June 1945): 31–48.

505. Patterson, Orlando. "Persistence, Continuity, and Change in the Jamaican Working-Class Family." *Journal of Family History* 7 (Summer 1982): 135–61.

Investigates continuities in family organization from slavery to modern-day urban poverty. Based on secondary literature on the West Indian family during slavery and in the postemancipation period. Includes demographic data on household composition under slavery and data on sugar plantation employment between 1834 and 1973.

506. Patterson, Orlando. "Slavery: The Underside of Freedom." *Slavery & Abolition* 5 (September 1984): 87–104.

507. Petras, Elizabeth McLean. *Jamaican Labor Migration: White Capital and Black Labor, 1850–1930.* Boulder: Westview, 1988. 297 p.

Investigates the creation of a labor reserve in Jamaica during the nine-teenth century and the history of labor out-migration, particularly to Panama and Cuba. Discusses the political economy of Jamaica at the time of emancipation, the free labor debate, and the creation of a rural population dependent on wage labor for family survival. Examines Jamaican laborers' role in building the Panama Canal and the sugar estates and as domestic workers in Cuba. Concludes with a discussion of Jamaican workers as international workers and the impact of migration on family and household structure.

508. Phelps, O. W. "Rise of the Labour Movement in Jamaica." *Social and Economic Studies* 9 (December 1960): 417–68.

A history of the Jamaican trade union movement from 1919 to 1955. Discusses the beginnings of legal trade unionism (1919–34); the labor revolt in Jamaica of 1938; and the struggle between Alexander C. Bustamante's Industrial Trade Union (BITU) and Norman Manley's Trade Union Council (TUC) for control of the labor movement in the 1930s and 1940s. Provides a detailed account of the 1938 disturbances and the biographies of Manley and Bustamante. Includes statistics on labor participation, wages, and descriptions of government labor legislation.

509. Post, Ken. *'Arise Ye Starvelings': The Jamaican Labour Rebellion of 1938 and Its Aftermath.* The Hague: Martinus Nijhoff, 1978. 502 p.

A history of the 1938 labor rebellion in Jamaica. Analyzes modes of production in Jamaica after emancipation and the impact of peasant-worker social relations on political and labor organization. Discusses the roles of Jamaican Ethiopianism, Garveyism, and Bedwardism in the politics of rural and urban working populations in the early twentieth century.

510. Ramdin, Ron. *From Chattel Slave to Wage Earner: A History of Trade Unionism in Trinidad and Tobago.* London: Martin Brian & O'Keeffe, 1982. 314 p.

Focuses on the 1937 labor actions in Trinidad. Briefly discusses slave labor and early indentured labor from India. Includes a history of early attempts at trade union recognition, the Trinidad Working Men's Association, and the strike of 1919. Includes biographical material on many trade union leaders, including Arthur Cipriani, Adrian Rienzi, and Uriah Butler. Bibliography contains a list of relevant British Colonial Office files and other primary source materials.

511. Ramesar, Marianne. "Patterns of Regional Settlement and Economic Activity by Immigrant Groups in Trinidad: 1851–1900." *Social and Economic Studies* 25 (September 1976): 187–215.

A demographic history of Trinidad's four main population groups: Creoles, British West Indians, natives of India and their descendants, and natives of Africa and their descendants. Based primarily on decennial censuses between 1851 and 1901. Discusses population trends in the period including the involvement of Asian laborers in the sugar and cocoa industries. Provides data from annual reports and censuses in tabular form including information on Ward Unions, occupations, and sales of crown land.

512. Ramesar, Marianne. *Survivors of Another Crossing: A History of East Indians in Trinidad, 1880–1946.* St. Augustine, Trinidad and Tobago: University of the West Indies, School of Continuing Studies, 1994. 190 p.

513. Reckord, Mary. "The Colonial Office and the Abolition of Slavery." *Historical Journal* 14 (December 1971): 723–34.

Examines the political negotiations between the British Colonial Office and its representatives in the British West Indies, particularly Jamaica, over the amelioration and abolition of slavery between 1823 and 1831. Based primarily on Colonial Office correspondence. Discusses the relationship between the Colonial Office and abolitionists in Britain and Jamaica and the large body of evidence collected through various official investigations of slavery. Includes references to the *British Parliamentary Papers*.

514. Reddock, Rhoda. "Indian Women and Indentureship in Trinidad and Tobago, 1845–1917." *Economic and Political Weekly* 20 (October 26, 1985): 79–88.

515. Reddock, Rhoda E. *Women, Labour and Politics in Trinidad and Tobago: A History.* London: ZED Books, 1994. 346 p.

A history of women in Trinidad and Tobago with special emphasis on the growth of trade unions and women's political organizations in the period between 1898 and 1960. Includes a discussion of the gender division of labor during slavery and indentureship, including African and Indian women's work. Explores the rise of trade unions and other political organizations as well as relations between middle-class and working-class women. Details the political career of Elma Francois and others involved in the creation of a women's movement in Trinidad and Tobago.

Includes data on women's work and wages and chronology of trade union history from 1919 to 1960.

516. Rich, Paul B. *Race and Empire in British Politics.* 2d ed. Cambridge: Cambridge University Press, 1986. 272 p.

Explores British racial thought from the 1890s to the early 1960s. Investigates the influence of Mary Kingsley and ideas of cultural relativism; racial segregation and the Commonwealth; the roles of sociology, anthropology; and race riots in London, Liverpool, and other areas.

517. Richardson, Bonham. "Slavery to Freedom in the British Caribbean: Ecological Considerations." *Caribbean Geography* 1 (1984): 164–75.

518. Richardson, Bonham C. "Depression Riots and the Calling of the 1897 West India Royal Commission." *New West Indian Guide/ Nieuwe West-Indische Gids* 66 (1992): 169–92.

519. Richardson, Bonham C. "Human Mobility in the Windward Caribbean, 1884–1902." *Plantation Society in the Americas* 2 (May 1989): 301–19.

520. Richardson, Bonham C. *Caribbean Migrants: Environment and Human Survival on St. Kitts and Nevis.* Knoxville: University of Tennessee Press, 1983. 207 p.

A history of human migration on the islands of St. Kitts and Nevis. Provides demographic and historical evidence related to slave society; patterns of migration in the postemancipation period, particularly to Trinidad and British Guiana; and subsequent labor migration patterns to Bermuda and Santa Domingo in the twentieth century.

521. Richardson, David, ed. *Abolition and its Aftermath: the Historical Context, 1790–1916.* London: Frank Cass, 1985. 279 p.

Collection of individually-authored chapters presented at a conference commemorating the 150th anniversary of the abolition of slavery. Divided into four sections, the papers cover the following themes: the historical context of British abolition; slaves and the emancipation process; connections between British and Continental European abolitionist movements; postemancipation society. Includes Barbara Bush, "Towards Emancipation: Slave Women and Resistance to Coercive Labour Regimes in the British West Indian Colonies, 1790–1838"; W. K. Marshall, "Apprenticeship and Labour Relations in Four Windward Islands"; and Stanley L. Engerman, "Economic Change and Contract Labour in the British Caribbean: The End of Slavery and the Adjustment to Emancipation."

522. Riviere, W. Emanuel. "Labour Shortage in the British West Indies after Emancipation." *Journal of Caribbean History* 4 (May 1972): 1–30.

523. Roberts, George W. *The Population of Jamaica.* Cambridge: Cambridge University Press, 1957. 356 p.

A historical demography of Jamaica from 1658 to the 1950s. Material is organized into four main historical periods as the early slave period; the period covering the last years of slavery and apprenticeship; the period of census records and indenture migration (beginning in the 1840s); and the period of civil registration (after 1878). Discusses population growth in each period by parish with data on age, race, sex, education, and occupational status. Also includes data on indenture and immigration and trends in outmigration, internal migration, mortality, birthrates, fertility, and illegitimacy, as well as population growth forecasts.

524. Roberts, W. Adolphe. *Six Great Jamaicans: Biographical Sketches.* Kingston: Pioneer Press, 1951. 122 p.

Includes biographical information on six prominent historical figures in Jamaican history including Edward Jordon, a prominent colored freeman who fought during the 1830s for abolition and emancipation in the Jamaican Assembly; George William Gordon, a colored politician assassinated during the Morant Bay rebellion; Thomas Henry MacDermot, a prominent journalist and literary figure at the turn of the century; Herbert George de Lisser, prominent conservative politician and author in the 1930s; Archbishop Enos Nuttall, the Anglican Archbishop from 1893 to 1916; and Dr. Robert Love, a Black newspaper editor who founded the "Jamaica Advocate" in 1894 and was elected to the Jamaican Assembly for St. Andrew in 1916. Includes photographs.

525. Robotham, Don. *"The Notorious Riot": The Socio-Economic and Political Base of Paul Bogle's Revolt.* Working Paper Number 28. Jamaica: Institute of Social and Economic Research, University of the West Indies, 1981. 95 p.

Discusses the Morant Bay rebellion and the role of Paul Bogle in the revolt. Contains quotations from Bogle's testimony to the Jamaican Royal Commission following the Morant Bay rebellion and other data produced by the Commission and published in the *British Parliamentary Papers.*

526. Robotham, Don. "Pluralism as an Ideology." *Social and Economic Studies* 29 (March 1980): 69–89.

Discussion of Jamaican anthropologist M. G. Smith's, *The Plural Society in the British West Indies* (1965).

527. Robotham, Don. "The Why of the Cockatoo." *Social and Economic Studies* 34 (June 1985): 111–51.

Continues a debate between the author and M. G. Smith over the latter's "plural society" theory. See item 559.

528. Rodney, Walter. *A History of the Guyanese Working People, 1881–1905*. Baltimore: Johns Hopkins University Press, 1981. 282 p.

A social, political, and economic history of British Guiana. Considers the class struggle between the sugar planter elite and the African and Indian working classes. Addresses the political economy of the sugar estates and peasant production outside of the sugar economy. Discusses the role of race as an impediment to worker solidarity and details the difficulties of multiracial alliances prior and during the 1905 riots in Georgetown and on the sugar estates. Appendices include statistics on production, land distribution, wages, immigration, and racial and ethnic composition of the Guyanese population at the turn of the twentieth century.

529. Rooke, Patricia. "Slavery, Social Death, and Imperialism: The Formation of a Christian Black Elite in the West Indies, 1800–1845." In *Making Imperial Mentalities: Socialisation and British Imperialism*, edited by J. A. Mangan. Manchester: Manchester University Press, 1990.

Examines Protestant evangelization and missionary education in the immediate postemancipation period. Details evangelical work among slave communities during the period from 1800 to 1834 by the Christian Missionary Society (cms) missions in Demerara, British Guiana and the role of Creole missionaries in evangelical work following emancipation.

530. Rooke, Patricia T. "Evangelical Missionaries, Apprentices, and Freedmen: The Psychosociological Shifts of Racial Attitudes in the British West Indies." *Caribbean Quarterly* 25 (March–June 1979): 1–14.

Investigates relations between ex-slaves and European Missionaries in the immediate postemancipation period. Examines the views of leading missionaries during the apprenticeship period (1834–38) among the four major Protestant missions: the Church Missionary Society (cms), the London Missionary Society (lms), the Baptist Missionary Society (bms), and the Wesleyan Methodist Missionary Society (WMMS). Provides references to missionary papers as well as British Parliamentary debates and reports concerning education policies following emancipation.

531. Rubin, Vera, ed. *Caribbean Studies: A Symposium.* Seattle: University of Washington Press, 1971. 124 p.

Collection of essays delivered at 1956 conference. Includes influential essays by Charles Wagley, Eric Williams, M. G. Smith, Raymond T. Smith, and others, many of which address interpretive issues related to postemancipation societies.

532. Rubin, Vera and Arthur Tuden, eds. *Comparative Perspectives on Slavery in New World Plantation Societies.* Annals of the New York Academy of Sciences, vol. 292. New York: New York Academy of Sciences, 1977. 618 p.

Collection of papers originally presented at a 1977 conference of the same title. Discusses development of plantation systems and slave societies; metropolitan slave codes and slave demography; social institutions and slave societies; slave images and identities; slave revolts, resistances, marronage, and implications for postemancipation society; research tools and resources; and research problems and implications for contemporary society. Postemancipation studies cover the British West Indies (including St. Kitts and Jamaica) and Puerto Rico.

533. Safa, Helen I. "Economic Autonomy and Sexual Equality in Caribbean Society." *Social and Economic Studies* 35 (September 1986): 1–21.

Explores traditions of female autonomy in Caribbean history.

534. Satchell, Veront. "Squatters or Freeholders? The Case of the Jamaican Peasants during the Mid-Nineteenth Century." *Journal of Caribbean History* 23 (1989): 164–77.

535. Satchell, Veront M. *From Plots to Plantations: Land Transactions in Jamaica, 1866–1900.* Mona, Jamaica: Institute of Social and Economic Research, University of the West Indies, 1990. 197 p.

A statistical analysis of land conveyance deeds in rural Jamaica during the period from 1866 to 1900. The analysis is divided into four periods: 1867 to 1869, when there was little interest in land acquisition by the wealthier landowners; 1870 to 1879, when government land policies forced squatters off lands, and unclaimed lands were sold off, with a noticeable increase in banana cultivation by small settler planters; 1880 to 1889, witnessing the rapid growth of the banana industry in northeastern and southern parishes and the further decline of the sugar industry; and the period from 1890 to 1900, with consolidation of the banana industry. Includes tables showing parish-level land transactions with price and acreage information.

536. Saunders, D. Gail. *Slavery in The Bahamas, 1648–1838*. Nassau: D. G. Saunders, 1985. 249 p.

A history of slavery in the Bahamas, with particular emphasis on the period between 1807 and 1834. Provides demographic information including data on births and deaths, manumission and runaways, discipline and punishment, occupations, and health. Other topics include entertainment and customs, secular music and dance, Junkanoo, story telling, African cooking, and Obeah. Includes sections on settlements of ex-slaves and the apprenticeship system.

537. Saunders, Gail. *Bahamian Society After Emancipation: Essays in Nineteenth and Early Twentieth Century Bahamian History*. Nassau: D. Gail Saunders, 1990. 209 p.

A group of essays by the director of archives for the Bahamas. Coverage includes the 1942 riot in Nassau and the 1937 riot on Inagua, the role of the colored middle class in Nassau from 1890 to 1942, family life, and a description of "Over-the-Hill," a group of towns established by emancipated slaves that become a neighborhood associated with the Black population of Nassau as white elites attempted to segregate the city.

538. Saunders, Kay, ed. *Indentured Labour in the British Empire, 1834–1920*. London: Croom Helm, 1984. 327 p.

A collection of individually-authored essays on indentured labor in the British colonial world in the nineteenth and twentieth centuries. An introductory comparative literature review by the editor is followed by selections on Jamaica, British Guiana, Trinidad, Mauritius, Fiji, Malaya, Queensland (Australia), and the Transvaal. Chapters covering the British West Indies include an essay on Jamaica by William Green, an essay on British Guiana by Alan Adamson, and an essay on Trinidad by Marianne Ramesar.

539. Scarano, Francisco A. "Labor and Society in the Nineteenth Century." In *The Modern Caribbean*, edited by Franklin W. Knight and Colin A. Palmer. Chapel Hill: University of North Carolina Press, 1989.

Discusses major themes in the transformation of Caribbean labor systems in the nineteenth century. Compares the strategies used by planters and the colonial state to maintain a viable and inexpensive labor force in the postemancipation period. Includes discussion of Jamaica, British Guiana, Trinidad, Cuba, and Puerto Rico.

540. Schuler, Monica. *'Alas, Alas, Kongo': A Social History of Indentured African Immigration into Jamaica, 1841–1865.* Baltimore: Johns Hopkins University Press, 1980. 186 p.

Examines the experiences of African indentured workers who were enlisted in Sierra Leone to work on Jamaican sugar estates between 1843 and 1865. Based on the author's 1971 fieldwork with descendants living in Westmoreland and St. Thomas parishes as well as archival and newspaper records. Investigates work routines on the sugar estates, African economic and cultural institutions, and the importance of African religious communities. Includes a discussion of Mayalism, an eighteenth-century religion that combined African and Jamaican traditions. An appendix provides data on immigration, including ship dates, number of passengers, and mortality rates on immigrant ships from St. Helena to Jamaica.

541. Schuler, Monica. "Coloured Civil Servants in Post-Emancipation Jamaica: Two Case Studies." *Caribbean Quarterly* 30 (September–December 1984): 85–98.

Investigates the careers of two colored civil servants working in the colonial administration after emancipation. Discusses Thomas Witter Jackson, who served as a stipendiary magistrate, and David Ewart, who became agent general of immigration in 1848.

542. Sebastien, Raphael. "A Typology of the Caribbean Peasantry—the Development of the Peasantry in Trinidad, 1845–1917." *Social and Economic Studies* 29 (June/September 1980): 107–33.

Presents a typology of peasants in Trinidad and the Caribbean more generally. Discusses squatting, freeholders, small cocoa cultivators, and sugar cane farmers and provides statistical data on cultivated acreage of different crops for the period from 1834 to 1921. Includes references to primary sources on early-nineteenth-century forms of peasant cultivation.

543. Semmel, Bernard. *Jamaican Blood and Victorian Conscience: The Governor Eyre Controversy.* 1963. Reprint. Boston: Westport, Conn.: Greenwood Press, 1976. 188 p.

History of the controversy surrounding Governor Eyre's suppression of the Morant Bay rebellion of 1865 including the roles of John Stuart Mill, Thomas Carlyle, Charles Darwin, John Ruskin, and Thomas Henry Huxley.

544. Senior, Carl. "The Robert Kerr Emigrants of 1840: Irish 'Slaves' for Jamaica." *Jamaica Journal* 42 (1978): 104–16.

545. Senior, Carl. "German Immigrants in Jamaica, 1834–8." *Journal of Caribbean History* 10–11 (1978): 25–53.

546. Sheller, Mimi. "Quasheba, Mother, Queen: Black Women's Public Leadership and Political Protest in Post-Emancipation Jamaica, 1834–1865." *Slavery and Abolition* 19 (December 1998): 90–117.

Discusses Jamaican women's roles in collective labor protests, petitions, demonstrations and riots between 1834 and 1865. Examines agricultural workers' collective protests against plantation policies, particularly during the apprenticeship period, challenges to male control of religion, and uses of urban culture and outdoor public space to demonstrate, riot, and rebel.

547. Shepherd, Verene A. "The Effects of the Abolition of Slavery on Jamaican Livestock Farms (Pens), 1834–1845." *Slavery and Abolition* 10 (September 1989): 187–211.

Examines transformations in production and labor relations on Jamaican livestock farms during the apprenticeship and immediate post-emancipation period. Discusses the exodus of pen workers after 1836, with examples of workers' complaints as presented in special magistrate records and data on the economic decline of livestock farming after emancipation.

548. Shepherd, Verene A. "Alternative Husbandry: Slaves and Free Labourers on Livestock Farms in Jamaica in the Eighteenth and Nineteenth Centuries." *Slavery and Abolition* 14 (April 1993): 41–66.

Detailed history of the evolution, growth, and decline of livestock farms or "pens" from slavery through emancipation, including discussion of character of work regime, gender relations and fertility, and relations with sugar plantations.

549. Shepherd, Verene A. *Transients to Settlers: The Experience of Indians in Jamaica, 1845–1950.* Leeds, England: Peepal Tree, University of Warwick, 1994. 281 p.

Discusses the initial immigration of Indians to Jamaica and their eventual settlement, economic activities, the effects of Christian missionaries, interactions with the education system, attempts to retain distinct social traditions and customs, and attitudes toward political participation.

550. Shepherd, Verene A. "The Apprenticeship Experience on Jamaican Livestock Pens, 1824–38." *Jamaica Journal* 22 (February–April 1989): 48–55.

Examines the relations between employers and workers on Jamaican livestock farms during the apprenticeship period. Includes discussion of "valuation," the process by which plantation and pen owners negotiated the value of their slaves in order to be compensated by the colonial government as well as conflicts over classifications of apprentices under a 1837 act. Based on Colonial Office records.

551. Sheridan, Richard B. "Changing Sugar Technology and the Labour Nexus in the British Caribbean, 1750–1900, with Special Reference to Barbados and Jamaica." *Nieuwe West-Indische Gids/New West Indian Guide* 63 (1989): 59–93.

552. Sheridan, Richard B. "From Chattel to Wage Slavery in Jamaica, 1740–1860." *Slavery and Abolition* 14 (April 1993): 13–40.

553. Sires, Ronald V. "The Experience of Jamaica with Modified Crown Colony Government." *Social and Economic Studies* 4 (June 1955): 150–67.

554. Sires, Ronald V. "The Jamaica Constitution of 1884." *Social and Economic Studies* 3 (June 1954): 64–81.

555. Sires, Ronald Vernon. "Negro Labor in Jamaica in the Years Following Emancipation." *Journal of Negro History* 25 (October 1940): 484–97.

Investigates the conditions of Jamaican workers between 1838 and 1846. Examines the views of planters, Jamaican political leaders, and colonial officials on the postemancipation labor question. Also details the Jamaican Assembly's attempted use of law and punishment to retain labor of former slaves for plantations.

556. Smith, Kevin D. "A Fragmented Freedom: The Historiography of Emancipation and its Aftermath in the British West Indies." *Slavery and Abolition* 16 (April 1995): 101–30.

557. Smith, M. G. "Some Aspects of Social Structure in the British Caribbean about 1820." *Social and Economic Studies* 1 (August 1953): 55–79.

558. Smith, M. G. "Pluralism: Comments on an Ideological Analysis." *Social and Economic Studies* 36 (December 1987): 157–91.

Discusses acculturation and differentiation among Jamaican Africans, Creoles, and whites during the nineteenth century.

559. Smith, M. G. "Robotham's Ideology and Pluralism: A Reply." *Social and Economic Studies* 32 (June 1983): 103–39.

See items 526 and 527.

560. Smith, M. G. *The Plural Society in the British West Indies.* Berkeley: University of California Press, 1965. 359 p.

A collection of essays on Caribbean social structure, race, class, education, land rights, and author's theory of "ethnic and cultural pluralism." Sections most relevant to postemancipation studies include a historical examination of Caribbean social structure in the 1820s; a comparative discussion of slavery and emancipation in Jamaica and Zaria, Northern Nigeria; and a study of land rights and land transfers on the Island of Carriacou (in the Grenadines) for the period from 1904 to 1954.

561. Smith, Raymond T. "Hierarchy and the Dual Marriage System in West Indian Society." In *Gender and Kinship: Essays toward a Unified Analysis*, edited by Jane Fishbourne Collier and Sylvia Junko Yanagisaka. Stanford: Stanford University Press, 1987.

562. Smith, Raymond T. "Race and Class in the Post-Emancipation Caribbean." In *Racism and Colonialism*, edited by Robert Ross. Leiden: Martinus Nijhoff, 1982.

Addresses race and class in the Caribbean, including the importance of British liberalism

563. Smith, Raymond T. "Culture and Social Structure in the Caribbean: Some Recent Work on Family and Kinship Studies." *Comparative Studies in Society and History* 6 (October 1963): 24–46.

Review of sociological and anthropological literature concerning family and social structure in the Caribbean, including works on land tenure, inheritance, marriage, kinship, and status.

564. Spackman, Ann. "Official Attitudes and Official Violence: The Ruimveldt Massacre, Guyana, 1924." *Social and Economic Studies* 22 (September 1973): 315–34.

Discussion of labor protests in British Guiana in 1924, which resulted in the deaths of sugar workers in East Demerara. Discusses the events leading up to the protests of sugar estate workers, including strikes by dockworkers in Georgetown under the leadership of the British Guiana Labour Union (BGLU).

565. Standing, Guy. *Labour Force Participation in Historical Perspective: Proletarianisation in Jamaica.* Geneva: ILO, 1977. 50 p.

566. Stinchcombe, Arthur L. *Sugar Island Slavery in the Age of Enlightenment: The Political Economy of the Caribbean World.* Princeton: Princeton University Press, 1995. 361 p.

Examines the political economy of the Caribbean from the late eighteenth through the late nineteenth centuries. Part I discusses slave societies in the late eighteenth century, including the roles of free labor, finance capital, planters, and race. Part II discusses emancipation, including the impact of the French and Haitian Revolutions, the rise of new labor systems, and politics in Cuba, Puerto Rico, and the Dominican Republic.

567. Sutherland, Anne. *The Making of Belize: Globalization in the Margins.* Westport, Conn.: Bergin and Garvey, 1998. 202 p.

568. Tanna, Laura. *Jamaican Folk-Tales and Oral Histories.* Kingston: Institute of Jamaica Publications, 1984. 143 p.

An anthology of folk tales and oral histories collected by the author in 1973 and 1974 including stories, rhymes, songs, riddles, trickster narratives, and other manifestations of oral tradition collected in rural and urban areas of Westmoreland, St. Elizabeth, Manchester, St. Catherine, St. Mary, Portland, and St. Andrew parishes. Discusses the cultural legacy of West African and Afro-Jamaican storytelling from the period of slavery and postemancipation labor migration. Includes photographs, musical scores, and complete text of many stories.

569. Temperley, Howard. *British Antislavery, 1833–1870.* Columbia, S.C.: University of South Carolina Press, 1972. 298 p.

570. Temperley, Howard. "Capitalism, Slavery and Ideology." *Past and Present* 75 (May 1977): 94–118.

Discussion of abolitionist ideas about slavery and capitalism and their influence on later historians.

571. Thomas, Mary Elizabeth. *Jamaica and Voluntary Laborers from Africa, 1840–1865.* Gainesville: University Presses of Florida, 1974. 211 p.

Examines the efforts of Jamaican sugar planters and the colonial state to obtain laborers from the West Coast of Africa following emancipation. Explores the difficulties experienced by planters immediately after abolition in obtaining sufficient labor at low wages and negotiations between planters and politicians with the Colonial Office on possible strategies for recruiting laborers from outside Jamaica. Includes data on numbers of African immigrants and their wages and occupations in Jamaica.

572. Thomas-Hope, Elizabeth. *Explanation in Caribbean Migration: Perception and the Image—Jamaica, Barbados, St. Vincent.* London: Macmillan Caribbean, 1992. 184 p.

573. Thomas-Hope, Elizabeth M. "The Establishment of a Migration Tradition: British West Indian Movements to the Hispanic Caribbean in the Century after Emancipation." In *Caribbean Social Relations,* edited by Colin G. Clarke. Monograph Series No. 8. Liverpool: Centre for Latin American Studies, University of Liverpool, 1978.

Discusses labor migration from the British West Indies to Panama, Cuba, Costa Rica, and Venezuela. Discusses how the "free wage market" after emancipation created a pull factor as U.S. companies operating in the Spanish-speaking Caribbean paid higher wages than those in the British West Indies. Includes a map showing the net outflow of Jamaican and Barbadian migrants to Panama, Cuba, and Costa Rica and of Trinidadians to Venezuela.

574. Thompson, Alvin O., ed. *Emancipation I.* Cave Hill, Barbados: Department of History, University of the West Indies, 1986. 108 p.

Essays discuss topics including West African societies on the eve of the Atlantic slave trade, the effect of the slave trade on Barbados, the origins of sugar plantations and slave society on Barbados, legal measures leading up to emancipation, and the period from 1838 to 1876.

575. Tinker, Hugh. "Into Servitude: Indian Labour in the Sugar Industry, 1833–1970." In *International Labour Migration: Historical Perspectives,* edited by Shula Marks and Peter Richardson. London: Maurice Temple Smith, 1984. 432 p.

Investigates the political and economic history of Indian indentured labor migration to British Guiana, Trinidad, Mauritius, and Fiji.

576. Tinker, Hugh. *A New System of Slavery: The Export of Indian Labour Overseas, 1830–1920.* Oxford: Oxford University Press, 1974.

A history of Indian indentured and forced emigration in the British Empire. Explores the places of origin of Indian migrants, including methods of recruitment and the passage by ship to numerous destinations. Compares plantation society in different places including British Guiana, Trinidad, Jamaica, and Mauritius. Based on the *British Parliamentary Papers* and Colonial Office records.

577. Trotman, David Vincent. *Crime in Trinidad: Conflict and Control in a Plantation Society, 1838–1900.* Knoxville: University of Tennessee Press, 1986. 345 p.

Examines how crime reflected conflicts and tensions in the plantation system in Trinidad. Discusses new criminal codes created after emancipation in context of the desire of planters to obtain more wage labor. Considers law enforcement agencies, rates and patterns of crime, violence and social disorder, and mechanisms of labor control, as well as topics such as carnival and Obeah. Appendices include data on crime and punishment during the period. Based primarily on British Colonial Office records, the Trinidad Council Papers, and Trinidad newspapers.

578. Trouillot, Michel-Rolph. *Peasants and Capital: Dominica in the World Economy.* Baltimore: Johns Hopkins University Press, 1988. 344 p.

A history of Dominica with a focus on the development of a peasant-worker class following emancipation. Discusses emancipation, land acquisition, indebtedness, and land alienation by the former slaves during apprenticeship and the immediate postemancipation period. Considers peasant-worker communities and gives an ethnographic description of life in the village of Wesley based on the author's fieldwork in the early 1980s.

579. Trouillot, Michel-Rolph. "Discourses of Rule and the Acknowledgment of the Peasantry in Dominica, West Indies, 1838-1928." *American Ethnologist* 16 (1989): 704–18.

580. Turner, Mary. *Slaves and Missionaries: The Disintegration of Jamaican Slave Society, 1787–1834.* Urbana: University of Illinois Press, 1982. 223 p.

Investigates the role of European missionaries in the lives of the slave populations of western Jamaica, with a focus on the "Baptist War" of 1831. Based on records from the British Colonial Office, the Baptist Missionary Society, and the Wesleyan Methodist Missionary Society. Describes relations between missionaries, planters, and slaves in Hanover, St. James, and Westmoreland parishes. Describes internal struggles within the European missions concerning abolition, emancipation, and the apprenticeship system. Details the role of the Native Baptist missions in St. James parish during the Baptist War and retaliation by whites who burned numerous mission chapels in February, 1832.

581. Tyrell, Alex. "The 'Moral Radical Party' and the Anglo-Jamaican Campaign for the Abolition of the Negro-Apprenticeship System." *English Historical Review* 99 (1984): 481–502.

582. Walvin, James, ed. *Slavery and British Society, 1776–1846.* Baton Rouge: Louisiana State University Press, 1982. 272 p.

Collection of essays on British abolitionists and aspects of West Indian emancipation. Includes work by Michael Craton on slave culture, resistance, and emancipation in the British West Indies; Barry Higman on slavery and the industrial revolution; and David Eltis on British abolitionists' perceptions of postemancipation society.

583. Wesley, Charles H. "The Emancipation of the Free Coloured Population in the British Empire." *Journal of Negro History* 19 (1934): 137–70.

Discusses legal rights of free persons of color in the West Indies. Considers the "free coloured"—persons of mixed race—and "free blacks." Includes demographic data on populations of free people of color in the early 1800s in Antigua, Jamaica, Trinidad, Grenada, Barbados, Dominica, Mauritius, St. Lucia, and Montserrat. Describes the struggles of free persons for rights, including the case of Louis Celeste Lecesne and John EscoVery in Jamaica.

584. Will, H. A. *Constitutional Change in the British West Indies, 1880–1903: with Special Reference to Jamaica, British Guiana, and Trinidad.* Oxford: Clarendon Press, 1970. 331 p.

Considers constitutional reforms in Jamaica (1880–95), British Guiana (1880–95), Trinidad (1880–95), and the British West Indies generally (1895–1903). Discusses the role of the Executive Councils of each colony in advising colonial governors and debates over representation. Includes an extensive bibliography of relevant primary and secondary sources.

585. Will, H. A. "Colonial Policy and Economic Development in the British West Indies, 1895–1903." *The Economic History Review.* 2d Series. 23 (April 1970): 129–47.

586. Williams, Eric. *Capitalism and Slavery.* Chapel Hill: University of North Carolina Press, 1944. 285 p.

Foundational study of abolition, much debated in the subsequent scholarship.

587. Williams, Eric. *From Columbus to Castro: The History of the Caribbean, 1492–1969.* New York: Harper and Row, 1971. 576 p.

A general history of the West Indies including areas formerly and currently colonized by the British, French, Spanish, American, Dutch, and Danish. Discusses topics such as the abolition of the Caribbean slave system, the rise of free labor, Asian immigration, and the sugar economy.

588. Wilmot, Swithin. "The Politics of Protest in Free Jamaica—The Kingston John Canoe Christmas Riots, 1840 and 1841." *Caribbean Quarterly* 36 (December 1990): 65–75.

Examines popular protest and local politics in Kingston in the postemancipation period. Discusses how the enfranchisement of Jewish, free Black, and colored men in 1831 changed the composition and nature of the Kingston Common Council.

589. Wilmot, Swithin. "Emancipation in Action: Workers and Wage Conflict in Jamaica, 1838–1840." *Jamaica Journal* 19 (August–October 1986): 55–62.

Examines labor relations in the first years following emancipation and the end of the apprenticeship system. Discusses parish-level protests immediately following emancipation including opposition to East Indian immigration by former slaves. Based on sources from the Colonial Office and Jamaican newspapers.

590. Wilmot, Swithin. "Not 'Full Free': The Ex-Slaves and the Apprenticeship System in Jamaica, 1834–38." *Jamaica Journal* 17 (1984): 2–10.

Describes ex-slaves' resistance to the apprenticeship system after 1834. Also describes elaborate festivities and celebrations marking the first emancipation and the end of apprenticeship. Includes images of cane workers and emancipation celebrations.

591. Wilmot, Swithin. "Race, Electoral Violence and Constitutional Reform in Jamaica, 1830–54." *Journal of Caribbean History* 17 (1982): 1–13.

592. Wilson, Peter J. *Crab Antics: the Social Anthropology of English Speaking Negro Societies of the Caribbean.* New Haven: Yale University Press, 1973. 258 p.

An ethnography of people of African descent on the island of Providencia. Discusses work, family, marriage, kinship, and social structure. Also includes comparative sections that discuss other Caribbean populations of African descent.

593. Wood, Donald. *Trinidad in Transition: The Years after Slavery.* London: Oxford University Press, 1968. 318 p.

Discusses the influx and incorporation of new immigrant groups after the end of the apprenticeship period in 1838. Considers the arrival and treatment of immigrants including liberated Africans from Sierra Leone, African-American freepersons recruited from the southern United

States, and immigrants from Madeira, India, and China. Discusses racial and class tensions in the postemancipation society. Also considers competing religious organizations, problems in education, and the cultural and social difficulties confronting the Creole population.

II British Colonial Africa

EDITOR

Frederick Cooper
New York University

COMPILED BY

Frederick Cooper

Lisa Lindsay
University of North Carolina-Chapel Hill

Timothy Scarnecchia
Washington, D.C.

Kerry Ward
Rice University

INTRODUCTION

The problem of slavery was crucial to the way British officials, missionaries, merchants, and explorers thought about Africa in the nineteenth and early twentieth centuries. Such people often conceived of their own role in history in terms of their contribution to eradicating slavery. The result has been a large body of documentation and considerable difficulties in interpreting it. Through careful analysis, one can learn something about social practices within African societies on the eve of conquest, about the effects of shifting colonial policies on social and economic relationships in them, and on the consequences of a variety of changes of the early colonial era for rich and poor Africans, on the exploited and the exploiting, on powerful kings or lineage heads and their subordinates, on men and women, and on old and young. But one learns at least as much, indeed more, about the colonizing regimes themselves—about their social categories, about their mixed motives, about differences among colonizers, about the way they became caught up in the unintended consequences of their own actions, and about their coming to face the limits of their own power to effect change.

This bibliography is intended to shed some light on this range of questions. It cannot do so in a comprehensive or complete fashion, not only because the slavery question itself was debated so extensively but also because the boundaries of that question are necessarily unclear. The boundary question is in fact one of the most interesting. By the 1860s, after the famous voyages of David Livingstone and the tales of the horrors of slave raids which he brought back from Central Africa, the image of Africa as slave-ridden became an important element of British thinking about the continent. Slave trading and slavery provided a vivid counterpoint to the benign images of Christianity, commerce, and civilization that Livingstone associated with the role of missionaries. Just how important this imagery was to the course of British imperialism is open to debate.[1] The documents below will reveal some of the language in which these issues were discussed at the time. But the difficult task of actually establishing a structure of rule—of collecting revenue and containing conflict—inevitably changed the terms of discussion. The very

---

1. The relationship between the slave emancipation of the British West Indies in the 1830s and the new conquered colonies of British Africa at the end of the nineteenth century is discussed in Frederick Cooper, Thomas C. Holt, and Rebecca J. Scott, *Beyond Slavery: Explorations of Race, Labor, and Citizenship* (Chapel Hill: University of North Carolina Press, 2000).

portrayal of Africa that made European intervention seem progressive seemingly obliged officials to do something about it, and missionaries and the antislavery lobbies kept up considerable pressure. What to do quickly became a thorny question. In some instances, antislavery ideology rationalized the destruction of African regimes, but in others the imperial takeover entailed alliances with rulers or lineage heads who were also involved in the forced recruitment and subordination of women, children, and men. Just as slavery tended to expand into a symbol for many of Africa's alleged failings, after conquest it tended to shrink into a legalistically defined category.[2] Officials not only depended in a number of colonies on the revenue generated by slave labor in agriculture, but their fragile control over diverse populations also depended on understandings with local elites whose nefarious involvement in slavery they had previously emphasized.

The fact of conquest was itself a blow to slave-raiding armies and to established slave trading routes, and rather quickly colonial governments took action to stop the remaining long-distance slave trading activities. Over time, the curtailing of new enslavement would affect the lives of those who were already enslaved in many ways. But the use of slaves within a given social unit, the exchange of slaves within tightly woven local networks, and the biological reproduction of slave populations were problems that proved more difficult for colonial governments to tackle than the phenomenon of the slave trade itself.

Most British colonial governments had to do something, but they often tried to define slavery in narrow terms so that they could more easily declare it abolished. In some instances they were eager to see other forms of elite power and enforced dependence exercised over former slaves. If before conquest, propagandists who professed concern with the situation of African women tried to assimilate marriage into slavery, afterwards officials often tried to assimilate slavery into marriage—so that they would not feel obliged to do something about the coerced basis on which certain women were incorporated into households.

Slaves, however, did not necessarily accept being pawns in a multidecade exercise in hypocrisy. Many seized whatever opportunities conquest offered—from the formalistic structures of laws and courts to opportunities to exit from oppressive relationships. In turn, even those who stayed within their villages or within their status designations faced changed circumstances in which they could reshape their relationship

2. For an excellent study of the history of such a category in another British colony, see Gyan Prakash, *Bonded Histories: Genealogies of Labor Servitude in Colonial India* (Cambridge: Cambridge University Press, 1990).

with their former owners. In many places, the formal abolition of slavery—as part of a wider process of colonial intervention—proved to have more radical effects than the officials who implemented it desired.

Slavery is a problem for modern-day scholars of Africa as well. Much of the problem stems from a set of images centered on the Southern United States and the West Indies, as if those defined what "real" slavery is all about. That such images poorly fit most of Africa is obvious. But it is not clear why one pattern of enslavement and institutionalization of slavery should be the reference point for all others. In principle, the problem of definition is resolvable. Slavery, as Moses Finley and Orlando Patterson have most clearly argued, can be defined as a form of uprooting or natal alienation—the removal of people against their will from the social relationships into which they were born and their reinsertion under terms they could not control into another social milieu.[3] In such a construct, the idea of slaves as property is derivative rather than defining, so that in a society with strong notions of private property, the kinlessness and rootlessness of slaves made them vulnerable to be reduced into the analogue of things. But people could also be reduced to marginal status within a system of social relationships, and they could remain for long periods of time in a liminal position, between their old and new societies, in a prolonged "junior" status that might even last several generations. A village in East Africa, in which an enslaved girl entered relationships not sharply distinguished from marriage, and a sugar plantation in Jamaica, defined very different sorts of existences. Nonetheless, either one retained the possibility of the other, precisely because the process of social and physical displacement so weakened the social resources available to the enslaved person that she was vulnerable to whatever sort of arrangement that luck and her owner provided her.[4] Both formal emancipation—the declaration by a colonizing government that the legal status of slavery would not be recognized or that slaves would be given papers attesting to their "freedom"—and the wider impact of colonization on the power of slave-owning elites to discipline

3. M. I. Finley, "Slavery," *International Encyclopedia of Social Sciences* (New York: Macmillan, 1968) 14: 307–13; Orlando Patterson, *Slavery and Social Death: A Comparative Study* (Cambridge, Mass.: Harvard University Press, 1982).

4. For two quite different approaches to these sorts of issues, see Miers and Kopytoff (in the bibliography which follows) and Frederick Cooper, "The Problem of Slavery in African Studies," *Journal of African History* (1979). For all the reluctance of some Africa specialists to acknowledge that the concept of "slavery" fits Africa, the literature on this subject since the mid-1970s has burgeoned. See the volumes of Joseph Miller, *Slavery: A Worldwide Bibliography* (annotated below), for references.

their slaves had strong effects, in part because such measures gave former slaves new bases on which to challenge the authority of owners.

The documents that follow will allow readers to see colonial administrations, missionaries, and other Europeans trying to talk about slavery in specific ways: attempting to try to define an essential Africa in which the evil of slavery stood out or was effaced and attempting to define colonial roles expansively or minimally. They will allow readers to begin the task of seeing the intended and unintended effects of such interventions. They reveal a problem that would not stay within bounds: slaves often forced governments to take the issue more seriously than they wanted to, while governments themselves tried to conceal their own forms of coercive labor mobilization under a purported civilizing mission, claiming that they were teaching backward Africans the virtues of work. Agricultural innovation—such as the development of cocoa cultivation in the Gold Coast—both drew upon labor resources with strong elements of coercion and over time changed the social relations upon which such coercion had been based.

That Africa, including the parts colonized by Great Britain, is a vast and varied space and that interventions occurred over a long span of time complicates the picture. The foci of humanitarian and official interest varied: from the 1820s, a British presence on the Gold Coast brought to the fore issues about the slave trade, and the increased intrusion from isolated coastal zones in the 1870s made domestic slavery in a wider region a question for colonial administrations. There was a burst of interest in the region near what is now Lake Malawi beginning in the 1860s and becoming critical in the 1880s and 1890s, when the East African slave trade received attention. Zanzibar became the focus of great concern in antislavery circles, in the 1870s because of its role in the slave trade and in the 1890s because of its especially intense form of plantation slavery. On the Kenyan coast, the fact that a considerable number of slaves took refuge in mission stations from the 1870s onward made this region a striking instance of the way in which the actions of slaves forced the issue of slavery onto a reluctant administration. In the Sudan by the 1880s, slavery became a regional, not a local issue, for it was caught up in the uncertain relations of the Sudan with the Ottoman Empire and with Egypt, with the tensions of the Muslim North and the non-Muslim South (and with the racial significance of slave trading) and then with the emergence of militant Islam. By 1900, the role of slaves in the powerful Islamic state structure of northern Nigeria was being much talked about, and the general agreement that the "legal" status of slavery was unacceptable hardly concealed a long, shifting argument among officials and humanitarians over how oppressive this system was and the relative importance of maintaining order and productivity by ensuring the continued strength of its upper class versus the necessity of transforming social relations in a more fundamental way. Finally, Sierra Leone was from the eighteenth century a symbol of British commitment to "freedom," for it was there that slaves liberated by the antislave trade patrols were often sent and from there that some of their descendants, converted to Christianity, fanned out to bring their own interpretation of freedom, progress, and religion to other parts of West Africa. But just inland from the port of Freetown, British officials looked the other way as forms of servitude persisted, until a rather embarrassed administration officially abolished slavery in 1927.

If colonizers, for a time, tried to present themselves as emancipators, they soon found the vocabulary of antislavery turned against some of their own practices, and the ambiguity of what was slavery, what was forced labor, what was traditional service, and what was labor legitimately demanded by a state in the interest of its people emerged in numerous debates. The language which contrasted slavery with freedom did not reveal the subtleties of colonial power any more than it did the particularities of authority relations within African societies, but the history of emancipation in the British empire necessarily framed issues in specific ways. British humanitarian lobbyists raised scandals about "slavery under the British flag" and they were instrumental in focusing attention on the practices of Portuguese colonial regimes and of the formally independent government of Liberia, among others. This language both illuminated and limited debates over the morality of colonial policy in the years up to World War II, when wider mobilizations among Africans made it no longer possible to contain politics within such an ideological framework.[5]

What sort of documents can we point to? Not necessarily the ones we would like. As is so often the case, available documentation comes predominantly from administrators and missionaries. There are a few compilations of slave testimonies, such as those by Mbotela and Wright noted in the following, that have been recorded and which shed light on the uncertain terrain between being "slave" and being "free" in the early stages of colonization, but it remains difficult to get an ex-slave's view of what happened. Scholars have relied on oral sources to do this, and in some instances these have proved surprisingly rich. When I began my own research on the Kenya coast in 1972, more experienced research-

5. This process is discussed at length in Cooper, Holt, and Scott, *Beyond Slavery*.

ers told me the subject was too delicate for people to talk about or to admit what their status had been. To the contrary, I found a significant number of informants quite eager to give me their side of the story—this history was clearly still alive for them—and I was able to get at opposed versions of what had happened in the years before and after formal abolition in 1907. Other secondary works cited in this bibliography also make use of oral sources.

There are two interrelated and available sources that cover a good deal of territory and long periods of time and that offer sufficiently rich material to make the entire enterprise worthwhile. These are the *British Parliamentary Papers*, which are documents originating in a part of the British bureaucracy and collected and printed for the benefit of Parliament. They are available in good research libraries, either in the form of the annual compilations—bound volumes of papers loosely grouped by theme—or (more selectively) in the form of series covering many years around a single theme, notably the Irish University Press multivolume series on the slave trade. There are annual indexes as well as a nineteenth-century cumulative index and another one for the first half of the twentieth century. Our bibliography points to a considerable range of material in the *British Parliamentary Papers*, from correspondence between the Foreign or Colonial Office and representatives in different parts of Africa, to reports on specific topics to published versions of important laws or decrees. The other major source, the *Antislavery Reporter*, can in many ways be seen in dialogue with Parliament because the Foreign and Colonial Offices were in such intensive interaction with the antislavery lobby in Great Britain—sometimes working together, sometimes in opposition. The *Reporter* tried to redefine issues as well as to articulate programs and was very much involved in the creation of images of Africa before the public.

Sources such as these allow the scholar to chart the public discourse about slavery across time and space. With all the limitations of the biases and selectivity involved in making these documents public, they point to the complexity of what was happening on the ground. They can be read against individual travel accounts of different areas and against a number of other sources which are close enough to the front lines of struggles over slavery to provide information and insight.

The most difficult task for the historian is to analyze the production of categories within the documents from the period in question—to see the documents themselves as shaping as well as describing what is happening—and still use the documents as sources. Each of them needs to be read in a nuanced way and in conjunction with other source material, if one is to get at the ways in which the lives of slaves, slaveowners, and others were being reshaped.

Our documents can do no more than open up the complex issues, which need to be studied in particular parts of Africa, and any in-depth study will move beyond the boundaries of the slavery "question" to look at the other dynamics of African societies. The variety of meanings that slavery had in Africa and the different ways in which the colonial intrusion affected social processes on the ground should emerge even from the selected documents included here. Read across regions, the documents can also be used to track the shifting debates over slavery among differing sectors of the British establishment in the course of nineteenth and early twentieth century, and from there one can examine not only how particular parts of Africa were discussed over time but how "Africa" itself emerged as a category of analysis.

FREDERICK COOPER

BIBLIOGRAPHIES, HISTORIOGRAPHICAL ESSAYS, AND INDEXES

1. Cockton, Peter, comp. *Subject Catalogue of the House of Commons Parliamentary Papers, 1801–1900.* 5 vols. Cambridge.: Chadwyck-Healey, 1988.

   This guide is the first complete subject arrangement of the nineteenth-century *British Parliamentary Papers* and is therefore the easiest to use for researching slavery and postemancipation in British Africa. Includes references to the Chadwyck-Healey microform edition of the nineteenth-century *British Parliamentary Papers.* Volume 5 contains the subject index for "The African Colonies" and "Slavery and The Slave Trade."

2. Irish University Press. *The Irish University Press Series of the British Parliamentary Papers Subject Set on Slave Trade (94 Volumes).* Shannon, Ireland: Irish University Press, 1969.

   Describes and indexes, chronologically and by subject, the contents of the ninety-four-volume set of sessional papers the Irish University Press compiled dealing specifically with the slave trade.

3. Miller, Joseph C. *Slavery and Slaving in World History: A Bibliography.* Armonk, N.Y.: M. E. Sharpe, 1999.

Continues the bibliography cited below; includes sections on Africa and on Muslim societies. Many entries treat postemancipation developments although they are not the focus. Not annotated.

4. Miller, Joseph C. *Slavery and Slaving in World History: A Bibliography, 1900–1991*. Millwood, N.Y.: Kraus International, 1993. 556 p.

Continues Miller's bibliographies through 1991. Contains 10,351 entries, organized regionally or by time frame (e.g., "Ancient"). Relevant sections include those on Africa, Muslim societies (including North, West, and East Africa), and the slave trade. Many entries treat postemancipation developments, although they are not the editor's focus. Entries are not annotated. Series of yearly updates, entitled "Slavery: Annual Bibliographical Supplement," resumed in *Slavery and Abolition* with 14,3 (1993); 15,3 (1994); 16,3 (1995); 17,3 (1996); 18,3 (1997); and 19,3 (1998).

5. Miller, Joseph C. *Slavery: A Worldwide Bibliography, 1900–1982*. White Plains, N.Y.: Kraus International, 1985. 451 p.

A comprehensive list of works on slavery and the slave trade, many with relevance to emancipation although that is not Miller's focus. The section on Africa has 328 entries, with others listed in the section on Muslim slavery. All materials compiled between 1983 and 1992 were consolidated into a new bibliography, published as *Slavery and Slaving in World History*, which was followed by another under the same name. See separate entries for those volumes.

PRIMARY SOURCES

6. Anderson-Morshead, A. E. M. *The History of the Universities' Mission to Central Africa, 1859–1898*. 3rd ed. London: Office of the Universities' Mission to Central Africa, 1902. 494 p.

History of mission activities in Central and East Africa describes the links between missionary work and antislavery. See chapter 2, which discusses mission involvement with slavery at Magomero, early 1860s; chapter 4, which treats slavery in Zanzibar, late 1860s; chapter 6, on the antislavery views and actions of the UMCA in the 1870s; and chapters 15 and 18, which describe slavery and antislavery in Zanzibar in the 1890s. Chapter 19, written by C. S. Smith, former British Consul at Zanzibar, focuses on slavery and antislavery efforts both generally and in Zanzibar. Includes an index.

7. Anti-Slavery Society. *The Anti-Slavery Reporter*. London: The Anti-Slavery Society, 1840.

This long-running journal is a valuable research source for British Africa. It is a clearing-house of articles collected from colonial administrators, travelers, "experts," and government documents, concerning the slave trade and domestic slavery. Published by the British and Foreign Anti-Slavery Society, the journal served to pressure the British government towards abolition in the British African territories and colonies. For example, throughout the 1870s there are articles on domestic slavery in the Gold Coast; in the 1890s there is continuous commentary and reporting on slavery in Zanzibar and Pemba. The Anti-Slavery Society and the Aborigines' Protection Society joined forces in 1906 and the journal continued to campaign for emancipation. The Society also began to extend antislavery vocabulary to issues of forced labor in colonial Africa.

8. Baker, Samuel W. *Ismailia: A Narrative of the Expedition to Central Africa for the Suppression of the Slave Trade Organized by Ismail, Khedive of Egypt*. 1874. Reprint. 2 vols. New York: Negro Universities Press, 1969.

Account of expedition into southern Sudan and Uganda (1869–73) to suppress the slave trade and annex territory for Egypt, written by the Khedive's governor-general of Central Africa. Contains descriptions of the violence and degradation associated with the slave trade. Describes Baker's antislavery efforts, battles against slave traders, and treatment of freed slaves. Baker complains about Egyptian officials' involvement with the slave trade and their attempts to thwart his activities. Points out the contradiction between slave trade suppression and extending Egyptian political control, since significant numbers of officials in the southern territories were Egyptian slave dealers (e.g. vol. 1, chapter 5). Indexed.

9. Baker, Samuel White. *The Albert N'yanza: Great Basin of the Nile and Explorations of the Nile Sources*. 2 vols. New York: Horizon Press, 1962.

Narrative covers travels from Khartoum to the source of the Nile in Uganda (1862–65) and contains numerous observations on the slave trade. In chapter 18, Baker refers to the slave trade as a "curse on Africa" and urges European powers to force Egypt to suppress it. Discusses the eradication of the trade in relation to the extension of Christianity and legitimate commerce. Includes an index.

10. Basden, G. T. *Niger Ibos: A Description of the Primitive Life, Customs and Animistic Beliefs, & c., of the Ibo People of Nigeria by One Who, for Thirty-Five Years, Enjoyed the Privilege of their Intimate Confidence and Friendship.* 1938. Reprint. London: Cass, 1966. 456 p.

Ethnology based on observations from around 1900 to 1930. Relevant sections are chapter 17, "Oru and Osu—Slaves of Men and Gods," which describes the slave system and the negligible effects of British emancipation; and chapter 19, "Land Tenure and Inheritance." The 1966 edition contains a bibliographical note by John Ralph Willis and an index.

11. Buchanan, John. *The Shiré Highlands (East Central Africa) as Colony and Mission.* 1885. Reprint. Blantyre: Blantyre Printing and Publishing, 1982. 260 p.

Written by a prosperous planter and former member of the Blantyre mission who later became British vice-consul and a founder of the African Lakes Company. Book attempts to encourage further British agricultural enterprise in Nyasaland and stresses the virtues of free African labor (chapters 4 and 5). Describes daily activities and antislavery work of Blantyre mission (chapter 7), Livinstonia mission (chapter 8), and the UMCA station (chapter 9).

12. Buell, Raymond Leslie. *The Native Problem in Africa.* 1928. Reprint. 2 vols. London: Frank Cass, 1965.

Massive compilation containing sections on the southern African colonies, the Rhodesias and Nyasaland, Kenya, Tanganyika, Uganda, Nigeria, the Gold Coast, Sierra Leone, French and Belgian colonies in Africa, and Liberia. Primarily focuses on land, labor, and administrative policies; some sections discuss education, religion, health, population, and history of the region. Includes discussion of forced labor issues and the League of Nations interventions. Includes an extensive bibliography.

13. Burton, Richard F. and Verney Lovett Cameron. *To the Gold Coast for Gold: A Personal Narrative.* 2 vols. London: Chatto and Windus, 1883.

Account of 1882 expedition to explore the Gold Coast's Kong Mountains and assess prospects for gold mining. Chapters 11 and 12 describe the history, economy, and inhabitants of Sierra Leone and provide a wealth of stereotypes of ex-slaves. Comparing this voyage with a similar one in 1861, Burton asserts that the government of the colony has improved in that it no longer treats inhabitants so "leniently." He complains in particular that the economy suffers because Africans "cannot legally be compelled to work" (vol. 1, p. 342). Appendix I consists of sections on the "Ashanti Scare" of 1881; "The Labour-Question in Western Africa," which calls for the importation of Chinese laborers; and "Gold-digging in North-Western Africa."

14. Buxton, Travers. "Is Slavery Dead in Africa?" *Missionary Review of the World* 44, 11 (1921): 853–55.

Examines the effect of the League of Nations' mandates on continued slavery, particularly in the Portuguese African colonies, German East Africa, Kenya, and Zanzibar. Surveys continued slavery and attempts to impose wage labor with limited time contracts as an alternative.

15. Cave, Basil S. "The End of Slavery in Zanzibar and British East Africa." *Journal of the African Society* 9 (1909): 20–33.

British Consul-General for German East Africa and Zanzibar relates the history of antislavery measures since 1868, emphasizing the importance of British actions in ending the slave trade and the undramatic effects of legal status abolition. Describes the final abolition of slavery in 1908 and its effects on concubines. Cave concludes that emancipation was peaceful and nondisruptive because of its gradual implementation and because of administrators' recognition that slavery was "one of the most elemental factors of Mohammedan social life."

16. Cecil, Robert. *A Great Experiment: An Autobiography.* New York: Oxford University Press, 1941. 390 p.

Account of the origin and work of the League of Nations by a British diplomat and League founder. A useful complement to the *Slavery Convention,* it describes the League's treatment of slavery and matters related to it.

17. Chirnside, Andrew. *The Blantyre Missionaries: Discreditable Disclosures.* London: William Ridgway, 1880. 24 p.

Describes recent abuses by Blantyre missionaries in Nyasaland, including the execution of a mission employee for allegedly murdering his former slave. Introductory section recounts the history of mission activity in Nyasaland.

18. Church Missionary Society. *Church Missionary Society Archives Relating to Africa and Palestine, 1799–1914.* London: Church Missionary Society, n.d.

Microfilms of archival materials from one of the most important mission societies involved in antislavery debates in Great Britain, with encounters with slavery and the emancipation process in several areas of Africa. Available at Northwestern University Library (188 reels) and University of Wisconsin Library (257 reels). Materials are divided into three chronological groups, 1803–20 (1799–1803 are only in committee minutes), 1820–80, and 1880–1914. The first set is arranged chronologically and includes incoming and outgoing letters, journals, and reports. The second set is divided into three sections, containing letter books, which are copies of outgoing material from the CMS office in London; mission books, which are excerpts from letters and reports received at the office in London; and original letters, journals, and papers. The final section is structured like the second, except that mission books are replaced by précis books in which all incoming materials are listed. Records of the CMS's involvement in antislavery debates and policies may be found in sections for the west Africa, Sierra Leone, Yoruba, Niger, South Africa, East Africa, Kenya, Nyanza, Uganda, Tanganyika, and northern Nigeria missions. Helpful references for using this material are the catalogue index in reel 1, Northwestern University's *Guide to Records on Microfilm at the Center for Research Libraries and Northwestern University* (available through interlibrary loan), and Eugene Stock's four-volume *The History of the CMS* (London: CMS, 1899–1914), which is based on the archive.

19. Dougherty, John Anderson. *The East Indies Station; or the Cruise of H.M.S. "Garnet," 1887–90: An Epitome of the Life, Manners, and Customs of the Races Met with in Indian Waters; Also Their Legendary and Historical Records.* Malta: Muscat Printing Office, 1892.

   Ship captain's record of voyage to East Africa and India. Sections on Africa contain substantial information on the interception of slave dhows (chapters 3–5, 17), plus general remarks about slavery and slave trading (pp. 20, 187–8, 215) and references to communities of freed slaves at Rabai and Frere Town (chapter 5). Chapter 17 discusses the abolition of the Zanzibar slave trade, its anticipated effects, and the reaction of the island's Arab inhabitants. Includes an index.

20. Elton, J. Frederic. *Travels and Researches among the Lakes and Mountains of Eastern and Central Africa.* 1879. Reprint. Cass Library of African Studies, Travels and Narratives, no. 31. Edited and completed by H. B. Cotterill. London: Frank Cass, 1968. 417 p.

   Journal written during author's tenure as vice-consul to Zanzibar (1873–75) and Consul to Mozambique (1875–77). Introductory chapter traces Britain's involvement with East and Central Africa and antislavery activities of missionaries and officials. Part I contains information on the slave trade and British attempts to suppress it in Zanzibar and Coastal Kenya; part II describes the author's expedition on and around Lake Nyasa in 1877. Both sections point to the violence and disorder associated with the slave trade and advocate an increased British presence in the region.

21. Fotheringham, L. Monteith. *Adventures in Nyassaland: A Two Years' Struggle with Arab Slave-Dealers in Central Africa.* 1891. Reprint. Blantyre: Malawi Against Polio, 1987. 304 p.

    Head of the African Lakes Company trading station at Karonga describes battles with the armies of Swahili slave dealers between 1887 and 1889. Portrays Company efforts to protect its Wankoude allies, secure its road to Lake Tanganyika, and suppress slaving. Concluding chapter suggests that trading companies should work actively to eradicate slavery in their spheres of operations and to help suppress the slave trade.

22. Fraser, Donald. *The Autobiography of an African: Retold in Biographical Form and in the Wild African Setting of the Life of Daniel Mtusu.* 1925. Reprint. Westport, Conn.: Negro Universities Press, 1970. 210 p.

    Account of the life of Daniel Mtusu (c. 1870–1917), who worked for the Livingstonia mission in Nyasaland first as a houseboy, then as a teacher, and finally as an evangelist. Depicts violence and slave raiding before the European presence. Description of life on the mission station shows missionary efforts to shape a society based on Christianity, trade, and wage labor. Narrative was begun by Mtusu and completed after his death by Fraser, a missionary who moved to Nyasaland in 1897.

23. Furahani, Martin. *The Autobiography of an African Slave-Boy.* Edited and translated by P. L. Jones-Bateman. 3rd ed. London: Universities' Mission to Central Africa, 1894. 27 p.

    Narrative of Martin Furahani, who was born near Uganda and captured during warfare. Chronicles his treatment under various masters and his liberation in 1880, when the dhow in which he was being transported was intercepted by British officials off the coast of Zanzibar. Useful for understanding British notions of African slavery in the era of the crusade against slavery and the slave trade in East and Central Africa.

24. Gessi, Romolo. *Seven Years in the Soudan: Being a Record of Explorations, Adventures, and Campaigns against the Arab Slave Hunters.* Collected and edited by Felix Gessi. 1892. Reprint. Hants, Eng.: Gregg International, 1968. 467 p.

    Collection of diary entries, letters, and journalistic dispatches by an Italian officer of the Egyptian army between 1873 and 1881. Initially Gessi was employed by Charles Gordon to explore the southern Sudan; in

1878 he was charged with suppressing a rebellion in Bahr-el-Ghazal led by Suleiman Bey, the son of the most important slave trader in the Sudan, Zubeir Bey. Describes the Sudanese slave trade, Gordon's suppression efforts, and the campaign against Suleiman. In chapter 27, notes the importance of slavery for Egyptian society and the obstacles to abolishing it. Chapters 29 and 41 include information on the postslave trade society Gessi attempted to establish after defeating Suleiman. Indexed.

25. Glave, E. J. "Glave in Nyassaland. British Raids on the Slave-Traders: Glimpses of Life in Africa, from the Journals of the Late E. J. Glave." *The Century Magazine* 52 (1896): 589–606.

Narrative by journalist who traveled to Nyasaland in 1895. Describes Harry Johnston's military campaigns against slavetraders, ex-slaves in mission stations, and conditions under British administration. Contrasts communities subject to slave raids with the "security to life and property" found in British-controlled areas.

26. Gleichen, Lieut.-Col., ed. *The Anglo-Egyptian Sudan: A Compendium Prepared by Officers of the Sudan Government.* 2 vols. London: Harrison and Sons, 1905.

Contains an extensive description of the slave trade and efforts to suppress it (1860s–1881) in volume 1, part 2 ("History"), chapter 3. Recounts the antislave trade activities of the Egyptian Khedive Ismail, Samuel Baker, and Charles Gordon, highlighting the connections between antislavery and the extension of Egyptian sovereignty into the Sudan, Abyssinia, and Uganda. Points to the continuing power of slave merchants and their connections to the Egyptian government. Attributes the Mahdist uprising in large measure to slave trade suppression. Indexed.

27. Gordon, C. G. *Equatoria under Egyptian Rule: The Unpublished Correspondence of Col. (Afterwards Major-Gen.) C. G. Gordon with Ismail Khedive of Egypt and the Sudan During the Years 1874–1876.* With Introduction and Notes by M. F. Shukry. Cairo: Cairo University Press, 1953. 478 p.

Extensive (118 p.) introduction places in historical context the primary documents that follow, which include letters, dispatches, and telegrams. Both introduction and correspondence link Egypt's antislavery efforts to attempts to extend its power into Sudan and Uganda and to secure support from Great Britain. Introduction also describes slave trade suppression under the administration of Charles Gordon, governor of

Equatoria Province (Egyptian Sudan), and provides background on Gordon's life and efforts to suppress the slave trade (1830s–60s). Some documents were translated from Arabic to English; most are in French. Contains an index of proper nouns.

28. Great Britain. Colonial Office. *Confidential Prints to 1916: C. O. 879/ 1–116, Africa, 1642–1916.* London: Colonial Office.

A collection of papers on various subjects printed for use of Colonial Office officials. Similar to some of the *British Parliamentary Papers*, these papers might contain letters and reports on a topic such as slavery. Although the title claims the collection begins in 1642, the first entry is dated 1848. There is a *List of Colonial Office Confidential Prints to 1916* (London, 1965) that lists the entries by volume. This does not include an index; therefore it may be useful to refer to Ann Vandenburgh's, "A Keyword Index to British Colonial Office Confidential Prints on Africa, 1642–1922," in *Africana Journal*, 11, 3 (1980): 197–231. However Vandenburgh only indexes titles, and came up with only one direct entry on slavery. Available on 101 reels of microfilm at several libraries in the United States.

29. Great Britain. Foreign Office. *Slave Trade: Confidential Prints, 1858– 1892.* [F.O. 541]. London : Foreign Office.

Consists of ten reels of microfilm pertaining specifically to the slave trade.

30. Great Britain. Foreign Office. *Africa: Confidential Prints, 1837–1957.* London: Foreign Office.

A collection of Foreign Office documents and correspondences similar to, but not inclusive of, the *British Parliamentary Papers*. Covers mainly British West Africa, Uganda, and Central and East Africa. The largest library microfilm collection in the United States is eighty-four reels. An index is available for the period between 1891 and 1905 (C.O. 804). Various sections of the entire series are also available.

31. Griffith, W. Brandford. *Ordinances of the Settlements on the Gold Coast and of the Gold Coast Colony, in Force April 7th, 1887.* London: Stevens and Sons, 1887. 777 p.

Laws are listed chronologically and then printed in full. Relevant topics include native celebrations, the abolition of slavery, public lands, master-servant contracts, public health, education, forced labor on public works, and marriage. Particularly useful for indications of increasing colonial control over African living and working conditions.

32. Harris, John H. *A Century of Emancipation.* 1933. Reprint. Port Washington, N.Y.: Kennikat Press, 1971. 287 p.

General description of the work of abolitionists in Britain and elsewhere. Covers postemancipation land and labor systems in Africa and the West Indies. Relatively little detail on British Africa, although there is a description and comparison of colonial land policy in British West and East Africa. Discusses the League of Nations' efforts to combat slavery as well as the Liberian slavery scandal. An extensive index follows.

33. Harris, John H. *Africa: Slave or Free?* New York: E. P. Dutton, 1920. 261 p.

Written in an attempt to direct missionary attention to conditions in Africa, this volume contains general demographic and economic observations as well as criticisms of colonial land and labor policies. Objects to colonial governments' toleration of domestic slavery and use of forced labor for government projects (part 1, chapter 1). Extremely critical chapters on forced labor in the Belgian Congo (part 1, chapter 2) and in Portuguese Africa (part 1, chapter 3). Includes an index.

34. Harris, John H. "Back to Slavery?" *The Contemporary Review* 668 (1921): 190–97.

Responding to the scandal over forced labor in Kenya, Harris compares it to slavery. Asserts that Africans will work if they are given incentives to do so and seems to advocate a system of peasant production similar to that in West Africa. Suggests that this type of free labor will raise productivity and bring colonial prosperity.

35. Harris, John H. *Dawn in Darkest Africa.* 1912. Reprint. London: Frank Cass, 1968. 308 p.

Observations based on author's travels in West Africa and the Congo in 1898. Part 3, chapter 1, links contract labor, forced labor, and domestic slavery and criticizes their persistence in British, French, Portuguese, and Belgian Africa. Chapter 2 discusses how unacceptable labor practices were related to Africans' lack of access to land. Criticizes slavery in Portuguese colonies (chapter 3) and abuses in the Belgian Congo (chapter 4) as violations of international norms governing imperial behavior.

36. Harris, John H. "Liberian Slavery: The Essentials." *The Contemporary Review* 783 (1931): 303–309.

Leading British antislavery leader comments on League of Nations report of 1930 on Liberian forced labor, which details conditions of coerced labor, kidnapping for labor, overseas traffic in workers, and an extensive pawning system, all with government complicity. Urges reorganization of Liberian finances and judicial system, among other reforms, to "save" Liberia.

37. Harris, John H. *Slavery or "Sacred Trust"?* 1926. Reprint. New York: Negro Universities Press, 1969. 195 p.

Primarily focuses on League of Nations efforts' to abolish slavery and conditions alleged to be similar to slavery. Chapters relevant to postemancipation Africa include "Forced Labor," on Kenya; "The Land and Raw Material," on systems of land tenure in Nigeria, Rhodesia, Nyasaland, and Kenya; and "The Coloured Producer," on cocoa production in the Gold Coast colony. Extracts from newspaper articles, official correspondence, and government documents are included in the text, and an index follows.

38. Harris, Joseph B. *Recollections of James Juma Mbotela.* Nairobi: East African Publishing House, 1977. 101 p.

Narrative based on interviews and reminiscences of the son of an ex-slave, who was taken from a captured slave vessel by the British and settled in the mission station at Freretown, now in Kenya. The son describes life in the village of freed slaves and the experience of a literate, Christian, ex-slave in colonial Kenya. (See James Juma Mbotela, *The Freeing of the Slaves in East Africa,* also listed in this bibliography.)

39. Hayford, J. E. Casely. *Gold Coast Native Institutions with Thoughts upon a Healthy Imperial Policy for the Gold Coast and Ashanti.* 1903. Reprint. London: Frank Cass, 1970. 418 p.

Written in an attempt to influence British colonial policy, this is based on information gathered by the author in preparation for a brief for the Executive Committee of the Gold Coast Aborigines' Rights Protection Society dealing with the 1897 Lands Bill, as well as material gathered in his Gold Coast legal practice. Advocates indigenous local government through "native institutions" and stresses the crucial nature of land rights for the colony's inhabitants. Includes a description of the slave system before legal abolition in 1874 (pp. 81–84) and reference to the effects of emancipation on trade and on relations between the colony and Great Britain (pp. 97–98, 143–45). Includes index.

40. Jackson, Frederick. *Early Days in East Africa.* 1930. Reprint. London: Dawsons of Pall Mall, 1969. 399 p.

Account of travel in East Africa between 1884 and 1900. Author later became lieutenant-governor for the East Africa Protectorate (1907) and governor and commander in chief of Uganda (1911–17). Includes some discussion of labor systems, a description of communities of ex-slaves, and a discussion of the role of the railroad in abolition (chapter 24).

41. Jackson, H. C., trans. and ed. *Black Ivory, or the Story of El Zubeir Pasha, Slaver and Sultan, as Told by Himself.* 1913. Reprint. New York: Negro Universities Press, 1970. 118 p.

Autobiography of the most prominent slave trader in the Sudan, who became governor of Shakka and the Bahr el Ghazal in 1873. Recounts military exploits, government administration, and captivity under the Mahdists in the 1880s. Mentions slave trading but plays down Zubeir's involvement in favor of highlighting abilities. Zubeir's ties to Charles Gordon illustrate the governor-general's willingness to overlook slave trading when politically expedient.

42. Johnson, M. *Salaga Papers.* 2 vols. Legon, Ghana: Institute of African Studies, 1965.

Collection of official correspondence relating to Salaga trading station between 1875 and 1897. Many entries relating to the slave trade; less on postemancipation. Of particular interest are acc. no. SAL/5, account of David Asante's visit to Salaga, 1884, in which he describes the effects of a decline in slaving; and acc. no. SAL/112, 1897 Dispatch from the West African Colonial Office which includes a treaty with the King of Salaga establishing British authority over the area and abolishing slavery.

43. Johnson, William Percival. *My African Reminiscences, 1875–1895.* 1924. Reprint. Westport, Conn.: Negro Universities Press, 1970. 236 p.

Autobiography of UMCA Archdeacon, recounting experiences in Zanzibar and Nyasaland, including mission involvement in slave redemptions and the violence and warfare associated with the slave trade. Discusses ex-slave conceptions of freedom, stressing the importance of family and community ties (chapters 3 and 5). In chapter 3, describes mission shelters for ex-slaves in Zanzibar in the late 1870s and complains of the legal constraints on protecting escaped slaves. Chapter 16 contains accounts of fighting slave dealers and the antislavery activities of Commissioner Harry Johnston.

44. Johnston, Harry H. *British Central Africa: An Attempt to Give Some Account of a Portion of the Territories under British Influence North of the Zambezi.* London: Methuen, 1897. 544 p.

An account of the Nyasaland region that traces the establishment of the protectorate and Johnston's military activities but suggests that the establishment of British political and economic security were his primary objectives. A short chapter on the slave trade outlines Johnston's policies: opposition to the slave trade but noninterference with slavery except in cases of cruelty. In a chapter encouraging European settlement (chapter 6), Johnston provides "imaginary letters from a typical planter," one of which reveals his conception of postemancipation labor relations.

45. Johnston, Harry H. *The Story of My Life*. London: Chatto and Windus, 1923. 536 p.

Author was appointed commissioner and consul general of Nyasaland in 1891 with instructions to suppress the slave trade. His autobiography includes accounts of military expeditions against slave traders and early organization of the protectorate. Lacks table of contents and chapter titles, but includes an index.

46. Junker, Wilhelm. *Travels in Africa during the Years 1875–1886*. 3 vols. Trans. by A. H. Keane. London: Chapman and Hall, 1890–92.

Account by German explorer in Egypt, the Sudan, and Uganda, divided into volumes covering 1875–78, 1879–83, and 1882–86. Contains several discussions of Charles Gordon's efforts to suppress the slave trade, its persistence among Egyptian officials and Sudanese traders, and attempts to hide it from European observers. References to the slave trade can be located through the indexes that are included in each volume.

47. Labouret, Henri. "A propos de l'esclavage: l'affaire de Sierra-Leone." *L'Afrique française: renseignements coloniaux* 11 (1927): 405–408.

Discusses the recent Supreme Court decision in Sierra Leone, which allowed an ex-master to use force to retrieve his former slave. Asserts that the sudden abolition of slavery would cause social disorder and that gradually undermining its social and economic basis is the best way of combating slavery. Compares emancipation in Sierra Leone to that in French West Africa, emphasizing the nondisruptive nature of French abolition.

48. League of Nations. Advisory Committee of Experts on Slavery. *Report, 1st–5th Sessions*. C.618.1932.VI; C.159.M.113.1935.VI; C.189(1).M.145.1936.VI; C.188.M.173.1937.VI; C.112.M.98.1938.VI. Geneva, 1932–1938. Report of 1st session issued as "Report of the Committee of Experts on Slavery Provided for by the Assembly Resolution of September 25th, 1931." 27 p., 112 p., 99 p., 83 p., 131 p.

The advisory committee took up the work of the League's Temporary Commission on Slavery. The first two of its reports follow the structure of the Temporary Commission's report, with headings on the status of slavery, slave trading, and so on. This similarity facilitates comparison with the 1925 report. The following three reports contain sections on slave raids and trade, "born slaves," and "other institutions," with subdivisions within each for various geographical regions. All five reports include extensive annexes containing communications to the League from member governments. The dispatches from the British government treat its African possessions, especially, in the fifth session report, Nigeria.

49. League of Nations. Question of Slavery. *Letters from the British Government Transmitting Despatches Showing the Situation with Respect to Slavery in the British Colonies and Protectorates and Territories under British Mandate.* A.25(a).1924.VI. Geneva: Imp. Kundig, 1924. 12 p.

Contains sections describing slavery and emancipation in the following British African possessions: Kenya, Uganda, Zanzibar, Nyasaland, Tanganyika, Gambia, Sierra Leone, Gold Coast, and Nigeria.

50. League of Nations. Question of Slavery. *Memorandum by the Secretary-General.* A.25.1924.VI. Geneva: Imp. J. de G., 1924. 25 p.

Outlines the council's progress in gathering information on slavery and emancipation. Contains the texts of communications from fourteen countries, including France, Belguim, and Liberia. Useful for comparing conditions in non-British Africa.

51. League of Nations. Slavery Convention. "Report Presented to the Assembly by the Sixth Committee." A.104.1926.VI; C.586.M.223.1926.VI. Geneva: Imp. Kundig, 1926. 6 p.

Contains the Sixth Committee's comments on each article of the 1926 *Slavery Convention*, giving background and explanations. Full text of the *Slavery Convention*, which prohibits slavery and conditions analogous to it, follows as an annex.

52. League of Nations. Seventh Assembly. Slavery Convention. *Resolutions Adopted by the Assembly at its Meeting Held on September 25th, 1926, (afternoon).* A.123.1926.VI. Geneva, 1926. 1 p.

Text of four resolutions: 1) approving the *Slavery Convention*; 2) requesting the Council to prepare a yearly report on new slavery laws and regulations passed by member countries; 3) reluctantly permitting forced labor for public works; and 4) requesting the Governing Body of the International Labor Office to study ways of preventing situations "analogous to slavery."

53. League of Nations. Slavery Convention. *Annual Report by the Council.*
A.37.1927.VI; A.37(a).1927.VI; A.37(b).1927.VI; A.24.1928.VI;
A.24(a).1928.VI; A.17.1929.VI; A.17(a).1929.VI; A.71.1929.VI;
A.13.1930.VI; A.13(a).1930.VI; A.13(c).1930.VI; A.13.1931.VI.
Geneva: Imp. Kundig, 1927–1931. 12 p., 1 p., 17 p., 4 p., 3 p., 10 p.,
2 p., 2 p., 2 p., 3 p., 9 p., 6 p.

Yearly reports by the council required by 1926 League resolution. Describes new laws relating to slavery or abolition, working conditions, process of emancipation, and results of emancipation in various colonies. Great Britain submitted information every year on its African colonies, with special emphasis on Sierra Leone and the Gold Coast.

54. League of Nations. Temporary Slavery Commission. *Report to the Council.* A.17.1924.VI. Geneva: Imp. Tribune, 1924. 3 p.

Outlines the proposed tasks of the commission and its methods for achieving them.

55. League of Nations. Temporary Slavery Commission. *Letter from the Chairman of the Commission to the President of the Council and Report of the Commission.* A.19.1925.VI. Geneva: Imp. Kundig, 1925. 15 p.

The Chairman's letter outlines the recommendations of the more lengthy report, which follows. The report describes the existing situation and the committee's suggestions regarding the legal status of slavery, slave-raiding, slave trade, practices restrictive of the liberty of the person, domestic or predial slavery, compulsory labor, and transition to free-wage labor or independent production. Although the geographic focus is general, references to specific locations, for example Liberia, do appear.

56. Livingstone, David. *The Last Journals of David Livingstone, in Central Africa From Eighteen Hundred and Sixty-Five to His Death. Continued by a Narrative of His Last Moments and Sufferings, Obtained from His Faithful Servants Chuma and Susi, by Horace Waller, F.R.G.S.* New York: Harper and Brothers, 1875. 541 p.

Description of Livingstone's travels around Lake Nyasa and through Tanganyika and coastal Kenya between 1866 and 1873. Discusses the warfare and degradation associated with the slave trade, particularly emphasizing the role played by Swahili "Arabs." Also treats his antislavery efforts (chapters 3, 9, and 18), accusations that missionaries are taking slaves for their own gain (chapter 4), and slave escapes (chapters 13 and 19). The publication of these journals fueled British interest in slavery suppression and the possibilities of British administration in Central Africa.

57. Livingstone, David, and Charles Livingstone. *Narrative of an Expedition to the Zambezi and its Tributaries; and of the Discovery of the Lakes Shirwa and Nyassa, 1858–1864.* 1865. Reprint. New York: Johnson Reprint, 1971. 608 p.

Emphasizes the social disruption and warfare caused by Swahili and Luso-African slave-raiding. Contains numerous descriptions of the slave trade and its effects; criticisms of Portuguese involvement in slaving; and accounts of the Universities' Mission to Central Africa station at Magomero, whose members consisted of freed slaves. Influential in focusing British interest on Central African slavery, later resulting in the extension of British control over the area.

58. Lugard, F. D. *The Diaries of Lord Lugard.* Edited by Margery Perham, assistant editor Mary Bull. Northwestern University African Studies Number 3. 4 vols. Evanston: Northwestern University Press, 1959.

Vols. 1–3 cover author's tenure in East Africa from 1889 to 1892; Lugard's period in Nigeria from 1894 to 1895, comprises vol. 4. Vols. 1 and 4 contain a general introduction, and vols. 3 and 4 contain biographical notes, an index of people, and an index of places. Chapters include introductory notes and a summary of contents. Reprints of treaties and correspondence are inserted into the text where relevant. While discussions of slavery, slave trading, and activities of former slaves appear in each volume, vol. 1 is most useful for its extensive treatment of Lugard's plan for slave self-redemption through employment with the British Imperial East Africa Company.

59. Lugard, F. D. *The Dual Mandate in British Tropical Africa.* Edinburgh: William Blackwood and Sons, 1922. 643 p.

Detailed examination of British indirect rule, the problems confronting the colonial administrator, and suggestions for solving them. Part I gives the history of Europe's involvement with tropical Africa and the general principals of British administration. Part II is based on Lugard's 1906 "Instructions" and 1919 "Political Memoranda." Useful sections are "Taxation," "Land Tenure and Transfer," "Slavery in British Africa," "Labour in Tropical Africa," "Education," "Economic Development," and "the Law and Courts of Justice."

60. Lugard, F. D. *Instructions to Political and Other Officers, on Subjects Chiefly Political and Administrative.* London: Waterlow and Sons, 1906. 319 p.

Written when Lugard was British high commissioner for northern Nigeria as a policy guide for district officers. Memo no. 5, "The System of Tribute and Taxes," describes tax policies as a means of promoting free labor. Memo no. 6, "Slavery," gives arguments against both slavery and complete emancipation and discusses methods of turning freed slaves into a landless free labor force. It also addresses methods of "dealing with cases of assertion of freedom," self-redemption schemes, slave trading, pawning, "disposal of freed slaves," and enlistment of former slaves as soldiers and police. Other useful memos are no. 16, "Titles to Lands," and no. 22, "Native Law and Custom re Slaves," which describes types of slaves, working conditions and privileges, marriage, and manumission under Islamic systems.

61. Lugard, F. D. *Political Memoranda: Revision of Instructions to Political Officers on Subjects Chiefly Political and Administrative 1913–1918.* 3rd ed. Cass Library of African Studies, General Studies No. 93. London: Frank Cass, 1970. 479 p.

Update of "Instructions," written in 1919 after the amalgamation of Northern and Southern Nigeria under Lugard's administration. Memo no. 5, "Taxation," describes the tax system as a stimulant to commerce and free labor as well as a corollary of abolition, in that it provides chiefs with income to replace profits from slaving. Memo no. 6, "Slavery— forced labour, etc.," contains similar information to this section in "Instructions," in addition to discussions of the status of slavery laws and the effects they have had, the position of women slaves, and paid and unpaid forced labor. Contains an index and a summary of the contents of each memo.

62. Lugard, F. D. *The Rise of Our East African Empire: Early Efforts in Nyasaland and Uganda.* 1893. Reprint. Cass Library of African Studies General Studies No. 71. 2 vols. London : Frank Cass, 1968.

Attempt by colonial military leader to provide background information to guide future British policy and settlement. Volume 1 includes an extensive discussion of the slave trade and slavery, as well as the options for abolition from which the British government could have chosen. The position of ex-slaves and fugitive slaves is addressed in the context of a discussion of colonies, industrial missions, and self-redemption schemes. Chapter 13 focuses on the labor supply in East Africa and covers slaves, free laborers, wage laborers, and Persian and Indian immigrants. Appendices to this volume include texts of the Indian Act abolishing the legal status of slavery (1843) and the Sultan of Zanzibar's 1890 Anti-Slavery

Edict. Chapter 43 in volume 2 contains information on taxation and land tenure, and an appendix to this volume reprints the Orders for Administration of Witu (British protectorate) regarding land use, slavery, and administration. An index follows.

63. Lugard, F. D. "Slavery in All Its Forms." *Africa: Journal of the International Institute of African Languages and Cultures* 6 (1933): 1–14.

General history of British and League of Nations abolition efforts, followed by an examination of present conditions throughout the world. Contains a brief discussion of the British rationale for abolishing the "legal status of slavery" in British Africa.

64. Lugard, F. D. "Slavery under the British Flag." *The Nineteenth Century* 228 (February 1896): 335–55.

After summarizing the history of British efforts to suppress slavery and the slave trade in East Africa, Lugard describes the status of slavery in Zanzibar as of 1896. Refutes arguments against abolition and describes the potential benefits of a complete transition to free labor.

65. Luke, Harry. *Cities and Men: An Autobiography*. Vol. 3, *Work and Travel in All Continents (1924–1954)*. London: Geoffrey Bles, 1956. 254 p.

Author was acting governor of Sierra Leone when the legal status of slavery was abolished. Describes antislavery legislation and local reaction to the 1927 ordinance (pp. 9–12). Depicts domestic slavery as benign and hints that abolition was more the result of political necessities than humanitarian concerns.

66. Lyne, Robert Nunez. *Zanzibar in Contemporary Times: A Short History of the Southern East in the Nineteenth Century*. London: Hurst and Blackett, 1905. 328 p.

Written by official in the Zanzibar Government Service. Chapter 15, "The End of Slavery," describes the laws and processes of the transition to free labor, as well as the reactions of slaves and masters. Wages and salaries for different types of work are discussed in chapter 19, and chapter 20 briefly treats the effects of abolition on plantation labor. Includes a bibliography and an index.

67. MacDonald, Duff. *Africana; or, the Heart of Heathen Africa*. 2 vols. London: Simpkin Marshall, 1882.

Written by a minister and member of the Blantyre mission between 1878 and 1881. Volume 1 describes "Native Customs and Beliefs" in East and

Central Africa, including only brief references to slavery. Volume 2 traces the history of mission activity near Lake Nyasa from 1861, with extensive descriptions of mission involvement with slavery. Discusses the mission's fostering of runaway slaves, its resulting alienation from some local chiefs, and its decision to discontinue the practice.

68. Mackenzie, Donald. "Report on Special Mission to Zanzibar and Pemba by Donald Mackenzie, for the British and Foreign Anti-Slavery Society." *Anti-Slavery Reporter* 15 (1895): 69–96.

Mackenzie's article, as with many contributions found in the *Anti-Slavery Reporter*, is revealing about the language and ideology of free-labor advocates in discussing the nature of slavery in a part of Africa, the impact of the recent British takeover, and possible plans for abolition. See entry under Anti-Slavery Society for information on the *Anti-Slavery Reporter*.

69. Martin, Percy F. *The Sudan in Evolution: A Study of the Economic, Financial and Administrative Conditions of the Anglo-Egyptian Sudan.* London: Constable and Company, 1921. 559 p.

Comprehensive history of British colonial rule in Sudan from its establishment in 1898, including brief discussions of the Sudan administration's conditional toleration of slavery and British attempts to halt the slave trade.

70. Mbotela, James Juma. *The Freeing of the Slaves in East Africa.* London: Evans Brothers, 1956. 87 p.

Based on memories of the author's father, who in the late nineteenth century was captured by slavers, set free by British patrols, and brought to Freretown, a settlement of freed slaves near Mombasa. Describes slave caravans and British antislavery activities from the perspective of an African captive. Portrays postemancipation society in Freretown, with references to labor, religion, and marriage. (See John H. Harris, *Recollections of James Juma Mbotela*, also listed in this bibliography.)

71. McDermott, P. L. *British East Africa or IBEA: A History of the Formation and Work of the Imperial British East Africa Company Compiled with the Authority of the Directors from Official Documents and the Records of the Company.* 2d ed. London: Chapman and Hall, 1895. 632 p.

See chapter 23 for discussions of the railroad as an agent of abolition; African and Indian labor in railroad construction; methods for attracting free labor; and processes of abolition. Appendix 18 lists "Decrees, etc. Relating to Slavery and the Slave Trade." Index.

72. Metcalfe, G. E. *Great Britain and Ghana: Documents of Ghana History, 1807–1957*. London: Thomas Nelson and Sons, 1964. 779 p.

Compilation of government documents, primarily from the Colonial Office, *British Parliamentary Papers*, and legislative debates. Organized chronologically, with chapter introductions that provide historical context. Documents contain information on government views and actions regarding the slave trade, domestic slavery in the colony and protectorate, and abolition. Official ambivalence regarding slave emancipation is depicted in several documents in chapter 22. Includes an index.

73. Nevinson, Henry W. *A Modern Slavery*. 1906. Reprint. New York: Schocken Books, 1968. 215 p.

Although this volume focuses on the author's visit to Angola (1904–1905), it is useful for its examination of British antislavery discourse. Particularly in his introduction, Nevinson appraises British efforts towards abolition and "civilization" and suggests that their influence has not been entirely beneficial for Africans.

74. Newbury, C. W. *British Policy towards West Africa: Select Documents, 1786–1874*. Oxford: Clarendon Press, 1965. 656 p.

Documents primarily consist of excerpts from *British Parliamentary Papers* and Colonial Office or Foreign Office dispatches. Materials are divided into the following chapters: "Exploration and Survey," "Legitimate Trade," "Slave Trade," "Relations with African Societies," and "Company and Crown Administration." Introductions to each chapter, as well as short footnotes, place documents in historical context. Contains information on suppression of the slave trade and resettlement of freed slaves. Includes an index.

75. Newbury, C. W. *British Policy Towards West Africa: Select Documents, 1875–1914*. Oxford: Clarendon Press, 1971. 636 p.

As in the first volume, materials are predominantly from the *British Parliamentary Papers* or Colonial Office Confidential Prints to 1916 (C.O. 879). Most entries are excerpts rather than entire documents, with brief notations as to their context. Contains material on slave trading, runaway slaves, and domestic slavery and the colonial government's antislavery policies during the late 1800s. Eleven statistical tables follow, detailing trade and government expenditures for the period between 1800 and 1914. Includes an index.

76. Newman, Henry Stanley. *Banani: The Transition from Slavery to Freedom in Zanzibar and Pemba*. 1898. Reprint. New York: Negro Universities Press, 1969. 216 p.

A description of the Quaker mission station located in Pemba at the time of abolition. The Quaker missionaries managed a clove plantation, which they cited as an example of the virtues of free labor. This account also includes information, from mission sources, about slavery and the process of abolishing it in Zanzibar and Pemba, and gives a good idea of Quaker thinking on the subject.

77. Petherick, Mr. and Mrs. (John). *Travels in Central Africa, and Explorations of the Western Nile Tributaries*. 1869. Reprint. 2 vols. Hants, Eng.: Gregg International, 1968.

British trader who was an agent of the Royal Geographical Society and Consul at Khartoum, and his wife, recount travels in Sudan and Uganda between 1861 and 1863. Appendix A, in volume 2, is Petherick's account of arresting a prominent trader for slave dealing, being accused of slave trading himself, and defending himself against this charge. Illustrates his precarious position as a trader, dependent upon local alliances, and a British official charged with slave trade suppression. See Santi and Hill (in this bibliography) for further information about this incident.

78. Portal, Gerald. *The British Mission to Uganda in 1893*. Edited by Rennell Rodd. London: Edward Arnold, 1894. 351 p.

Travel narrative and diary of H. M. Commissioner to Uganda. See part 2, chapter 1, which refers to abolition and to labor for road construction.

79. Price, W. Salter. *My Third Campaign in East Africa: A Story of Missionary Life in Troublous Times*. London: William Hunt, 1890. 339 p.

Journal and letters of the founder of Freretown and former director of CMS Missions in Eastern Equatorial Africa, written during return to East Africa as temporary mission director between 1888 and 1889. Describes mission activities, relations between the CMS and the British East Africa Company (chapters 8 and 11), runaway slaves, and a ceremony at Rabai in which nine hundred runaways who were ransomed by the IBEAC received their freedom papers. Compares 1888 impressions of Frere Town and Rabai to those of his previous visit thirteen years earlier.

80. Procter, Lovell J. *The Central African Journal of Lovell J. Procter, 1860–1864*. Edited by Norman Robert Bennett and Marguerite Ylvisaker. Boston: African Studies Center, Boston University, 1971. 501 p.

Journal by a member of the first Universities' Mission to Central Africa expedition, who succeeded Bishop Mackenzie as leader of the mission station at Magomero. Editors' introduction describes the origin, purpose, and activities of the UMCA and Proctor's role in it. There are references to slavery and to the mission's antislavery efforts throughout the volume; in particular, chapter 4 depicts missionaries freeing slaves and attaching them to the mission station and describes the UMCA's attempts to defend Mang'anja villagers against slave-raiding.

81. Rankin, Daniel J. *The Zambezi Basin and Nyassaland.* London: William Blackwood and Sons, 1893. 277 p.

Travel account from the 1880s by an employee of British Consul C. E. Foot. The most extensive treatments of British antislavery efforts appear in chapters 9 and 16, which discuss Mombasa and the British administration in Nyasaland. Asserts that diplomacy with Arab slave dealers will be more effective in halting the slave trade than the use of force. Views coastal Arabs as potential allies of the British and Swahilis and other African groups as the slave-trading enemy.

82. Rattray, R. S. *Ashanti Law and Constitution.* 1929. Reprint. Oxford: Clarendon Press, 1969. 420 p.

Ethnography covering family relations, slaves and pawns, and political organizations in the early twentieth century.

83. Rowley, Henry. *The Story of the Universities' Mission to Central Africa, From its Commencement under Bishop Mackenzie, to its Withdrawal from the Zambesi.* 2d ed. 1867. Reprint. New York: Negro Universities Press, 1969. 424 p.

Clerk to Bishop Mackenzie traces the activities of the UMCA between 1860 and 1864. Describes slavery and the slave trade, highlighting the disorder and violence associated with them and the debasement of slave owners and traders. Depicts Mackenzie's encounter with slave traders and emancipation of a group of slaves outside of Magomero, other antislavery activities, and the postemancipation society that developed at the mission station.

84. Santi, Paul, and Richard Hill, trans. and eds. *The Europeans in the Sudan, 1834–1878: Some Manuscripts, mostly unpublished, Written by Traders, Christian Missionaries, Officials, and Others.* Oxford: Clarendon Press, 1980. 250 p.

Documents are primarily from government dispatches and private journals, arranged chronologically, with additional information and commentary by the editors. Chapter 8, on John Petherick, H. B. M. Consul at Khartoum (1849–63), illustrates the links between "legitimate" trade and the slave trade, as well as Petherick's precarious political position as both a British official pledged to oppose slave trading and a merchant heavily involved in Sudanese commerce. Chapter 10 contains excerpts from the journal of Licurgo Santoni between 1877 and 1878, director of posts in Upper Egypt and Nubia, which describes Sudanese slavery, its recent slight decline, and the antislavery activities of Charles Gordon. Contains an index of proper nouns.

85. Slatin, Rudolf C. *Fire and Sword in the Sudan: A Personal Narrative of Fighting and Serving the Dervishes, 1879–1895*. 2d ed. London: Edward Arnold, 1896. 636 p.

Written by an Austrian colonel in the Egyptian army who became governor-general of Darfur, this narrative describes the overthrow of Egyptian government in the Sudan and the author's twelve years (1883–95) as a prisoner of the Khalifa el Mahdi. Contains numerous references to domestic slavery and the slave trade, as well as information on government administration, taxation, labor, religion, and commerce during both Anglo-Egyptian and Mahdi rule. Slatin argued against interfering with slavery on the grounds that Islam justified domestic servitude and that abolition would cause widespread resistance and create a vagrant class of ex-slaves.

86. Smith, M. F. *Baba of Karo: A Woman of the Muslim Hausa*. London: Faber and Faber, 1954. 299 p.

Autobiography covering period between 1890 and 1950 in states of Kano and Zaria. Particularly useful are descriptions of childhood in a prosperous, slave-owning family whose wealth was continually threatened by slave-raiders. Gives details of the slave system, British suppression efforts, and African responses to them. Includes an index.

87. Speke, John Hanning. *Journal of the Discovery of the Source of the Nile*. 1863. Reprint. New York: Greenwood Press, 1969. 658 p.

Account of travel in East Africa between 1859 and 1863. Author's introduction contains discussion of the *wanguana*, men freed from slavery upon the death of the master, many of whom were hired as porters for this expedition. Short discussion of Arab slavers and slave trade in Zanzibar.

88. Stallard, George, and Edward Harrinson Richards. *Ordinances, and Orders and Rules thereunder, in Force in the Colony of Lagos on December 31st, 1893: with an Appendix Containing the Letters Patent Constituting the Colony, and the Instructions Accompanying Them; Various Acts of Parliament; Orders of the Queen in Council; Treaties, and Proclamations*. London: Stevens and Sons, 1894. 1011 p.

Large compendium accessible through both the table of contents (arranged chronologically) and subject index. Particularly useful are laws dealing with slavery, wage labor, criminal procedures, land tenure, public health, marriage, and education. Included in the appendix are texts of the treaties by which Britain gained control of much of the territory of southern Nigeria.

89. Stevenson, James. "The Arabs in Central Africa." *Journal of the Manchester Geographical Society* 4 (1888): 72–86.

Speech given by the chairman of the African Lakes Company at a meeting to consider Britain's interests in Central Africa. Points to devastation and depopulation in the Lake Nyasa region caused by Swahili slave-raiders from Zanzibar. Complains that "Arabs" have blocked the Company's road to Tanganyika and urges British government intervention to protect missionary and commercial enterprises in the region.

90. Stewart, James. *Dawn in the Dark Continent or Africa and its Missions.* The Duff Missionary Lectures for 1902. Edinburgh: Oliphant Anderson and Ferrier, 1903. 400 p.

General history of missionary activities in Africa by a founding member of the Livingstonia mission. Chapter 8 discusses the Blantyre and Livingstonia missions, founded in the 1870s in British Central Africa, which were important early sources of antislavery activity. Also traces the development of the African Lakes Company and its efforts to replace the slave trade with "legitimate" commerce.

91. Stock, Eugene. *The History of the Church Missionary Society: Its Environment, its Men and its Work.* 4 vols. London: Church Missionary Society, 1899–1916.

Describes activities of the CMS inside and outside of England from late 1700s to 1916. Particularly useful are discussions of the settlement of Sierra Leone by freed slaves; African integration into the church and missionary society; native clergy, with special emphasis on Bishop Samuel Adjai Crowther, a freed slave ordained as a minister in 1843; efforts to encourage trade and industry as an alternative to slaving; and the establishment in the 1880s of a society of freed slaves at Frere Town in Mombasa. Contains numerous extracts from speeches, letters, diaries, and newspaper articles. Volume 4 contains an extensive treatment of mission activities in Britain's African colonies.

92. Swan, Charles A. *The Slavery of To-Day: or, the Present Position of the Open Sore of Africa.* New York: D. T. Bass, 1909. 202 p.

British views on Portuguese Africa, especially Angola. Summarizing testimony from laborers and missionaries, author describes the system of contract labor as analogous to slavery and gives evidence of slave trading to coastal islands. Preface expresses hope of the author that book will influence the British government to urge reforms in Portugal's African colonies.

93. Swann, Alfred J. *Fighting the Slave-Hunters in Central Africa: A Record of Twenty-Six Years of Travel and Adventure Round the Great Lakes and of the Overthrow of Tip-Pu-Tib, Rumaliza and Other Great Slave-Traders.* 1910. Reprint. Cass Library of African Studies, Missionary Researches and Travels, No. 8. London: Frank Cass, 1969. 359 p.

Record of the author's experiences from 1882 to 1909 as a member of the London Missionary Society and then a government official. Much discussion of the slave trade, although there is less on the actual process of its suppression than one might infer from the title. Chapter 19, "Wonderful Industrial Development," focuses on changes in technology and labor during the period under study. Includes an index.

94. Thomson, Joseph. *To the Central African Lakes and Back: the Narrative of the Royal Geographical Society's East Central African Expedition, 1878–80.* 1881. Reprint. Cass Library of African Studies, Travels and Narratives, No. 46. 2 vols. London: Frank Cass, 1968.

Includes discussion of the effects on commerce of the end of the slave trade (vol. 1, pp. 138–40); slave caravans (vol. 2, pp. 8–9 and 271–74); the education of Africans by missionary societies (vol. 2, pp. 277–78); and systems of trade and transport (vol. 2, pp. 277–91). Includes an index.

95. Tucker, Alfred R. *Eighteen Years in Uganda and East Africa.* 1911. Reprint. Westport, Conn.: Negro Universities Press, 1970. 362 p.

Written by the Anglican Bishop of Uganda, this account provides useful information on missionary activities in proselytizing and educating Africans. Also of interest is an account of the court proceedings of a suit for freedom by a slave woman who was represented by the author. Includes an index.

96. Young, E. D. *Nyassa; A Journal of Adventures whilst Exploring Lake Nyassa, Central Africa, and Establishing the Settlement of "Livingstonia."* Revised by Horace Waller. London: John Murray, 1877. 239 p.

Account by a British navy officer who headed the expedition to establish the Livingstonia mission and launch its steamer in Lake Nyasa between 1875 and 1876. Provides information on the slave trade (pp. 99–100, 125), Portuguese involvement in slaving (pp. 138, 171–74, 192–203, 211), and the antislavery efforts of the mission party (pp. 162, 215–16). Repeatedly calls for an increased British presence to end the slave trade (e.g., pp. 127–30, 148, 204–206). Contains neither chapter headings nor an index.

BRITISH PARLIAMENTARY PAPERS

97. Great Britain. Parliament. House of Commons. "Coffee: Return to an Order of the Honourable The House of Commons, Dated 23 July 1839 for, A Copy of Correspondence on the Subject of Admitting Coffee, the Produce of Free Labour, from within the British Possessions on the Western Coast of Africa, between Messrs. Forster and Smith and the Treasury." *Parliamentary Papers* 1839 (528), vol. 46. 17 p.

Collection of correspondence between the Treasury and the coffee importing house of Forster and Smith concerning coffee grown at Rio Nunez, a case which provides a good example of the relation of free-labor ideology to the promotion of industry. The importers want the government to grant the "low rate" import tariff on this coffee as it was grown by a Mr. Procter using "Free Labour" in a British Possession. The Treasury refuses, but Forster and Smith call on the support of ex-colonial administrators to argue the necessity of low duties on goods produced by African free laborers in order to keep Africans from returning to the slave trade. In the end, the Treasury investigates Mr. Procter's coffee plantation and finds he does not in fact employ "free labourers."

98. Great Britain. Parliament. House of Commons. "Report from the Select Committee on the West Coast of Africa; Together with the Minutes of Evidence, Appendix, and Index." *Parliamentary Papers* 1842 (551) and (551-II), vols. 11 and 12. 1413 p.

Contains extensive testimony from British and Portuguese merchants, colonial officials, African workers and traders about the possibilities of expanded trade in the three main areas of British influence on the West Coast of Africa: Sierra Leone, the Gold Coast, and the Gambia. The commission recommends the establishment of separate administrations for the British forts in each of these territories. The report and evidence illuminate the status of "Liberated Africans" in these areas; the "desirability" of sending "Liberated Africans" as free laborers to the British West Indies; the potential for increased production of local free laborers; judicial systems for Africans in the territories; and domestic slavery, especially the "pawn system" found in the Gold Coast. Part II has numerous detailed documents on trade and administration, including listings of people arrested for slave trading. Part I: Report and Evidence (776 p.), Part II: Appendix and Index (637 p.).

99. Great Britain. Parliament. House of Commons. "Papers Relative to the Rights of Liberated Africans, and the Prevention of Slave Dealing at Sierra Leone." *Parliamentary Papers* 1852–53 (1680), vol. 65. 34 p.

Begins with a request by Governor Norman MacDonald for approval of his proposed ordinance "to secure and confer upon Liberated Africans the civil and political rights of natural born British subjects." This is followed by a dispatch informing of "Her Majesty's disallowance" of the ordinance. Dispatches summarize many court cases involving the sale of a "Liberated African" into slavery by another "Liberated African"; these cases brought on Governor MacDonald's ordinance. Includes accounts, testimonies, and evidence given by "Liberated Africans" involved in such cases.

100. Great Britain. Parliament. House of Commons. "Papers Relating to the Cultivation of Cotton in Africa." *Parliamentary Papers* 1857 (2257), vol. 38. 11 p.

Two letters from Consul Campbell in Lagos to the Earl of Clarendon; includes Campbell's "Report on the Trade of the Bight of Benin for the year 1856." Campbell gives a detailed account of domestic cotton production, stressing the need to "render some security to life, freedom, property and labour" by ending the export of slaves. Campbell notes the continued reliance on slave labor in cotton production. He offers a comparative discussion of the relative merits and problems slaves encounter between "Mahomedan masters" compared with "Foulah and Yoruba masters." Describes the attempt of a Portuguese slave trader to set up a plantation using slave labor.

101. Great Britain. Parliament. House of Commons. "Return: Copy of the Report of Colonel Ord, the Commissioner Appointed to Inquire into the Condition of the British Settlements on the West Coast of Africa." *Parliamentary Papers* 1865 (170), vol. 37. 64 p.

Commissioner Ord provides separate short summaries for the Gambia, Sierra Leone, the Gold Coast, and Lagos. This polished report gives details about trade and domestic production with brief summary remarks about slavery and the slave trade in the region.

102. Great Britain. Parliament. House of Commons. "Report from the Select Committee Appointed to Consider the State of the British Establishments on the Western Coast of Africa; Together with the Proceedings of the Committee, Minutes of Evidence, and Appendix." *Parliamentary Papers* 1865 (412), vol. 5. 612 p.

Report covers all British territories in West Africa. Minutes of evidence contain 340 pages of interviews. Recommends the return to a centralized administration to be based in Sierra Leone and the cessation of any new extension of territories or treaties "offering protection to native tribes"; and states that the existence of domestic slavery in the newly acquired territory of Lagos "demands the serious attention of the government." The latter is stated differently in an earlier draft: "Possibly English commerce, with less government interference, may gradually effectually eradicate the custom." The index follows immediately in vol. 5, as (C. 412-I) and includes entries under "Domestic Slavery" and "Slave-Trade." Report includes materials on Gambia, Gold Coast, Lagos, Oil Rivers, and Sierra Leone.

103. Great Britain. Parliament. House of Commons. "Despatches on the Subject of Domestic Slavery and Introduction of Slaves by Ashantee Traders into the British Protectorate." *Parliamentary Papers* 1874 (C. 1007), vol. 46. 4 p.

Documents printed to provide historical background to the debate on slavery in the Gold Coast in 1874. Letters to the governor of Lagos, one written in 1866 and the other in 1872, clearly present the problem of slavery as seen from London. The Protectorate's future was seen as threatened by the "embarrassing" presence of domestic slavery and slave trading. The 1866 letter suggests limiting the geographic area of the Protectorate in order to avoid the appearance of slavery within a British-controlled area. See also the two statistical Blue Books that follow in this volume, pp. 1110–19, for revenue data for the period between 1853 and 1872.

104. Great Britain. Parliament. House of Commons. "Slavery on the Gold Coast: Resolution." *Hansard Parliamentary Debates* 1874, 3rd Series, vol. 220, col. 607. 15 p.

Important debate on the refusal to recognize slavery in any form, by the government of the Gold Coast territories. Debate takes place in the context of Governor Strahan's eventual abolition decree of the same year.

105. Great Britain. Parliament. House of Commons. "Correspondence Relating to the Queen's Jurisdiction on the Gold Coast, and the Abolition of Slavery within the Protectorate." *Parliamentary Papers* 1875 (C. 1139), vol. 52. 43 p.

All but one of the twenty-two items are correspondence between the Colonial Ministry under the Earl of Carnarvon and Governor Strahan of the Gold Coast, between August 1874 and January 1875, a crucial period of British acts to abolish slavery and the slave trade on the Gold Coast. Lord Carnarvon's letters present the official view of why the time is right for abolition. Abolition is proclaimed by Governor Strahan (texts of the proclamations and laws are included); his letters express his concern over the efficacy of such edicts and record the responses of "King's and Chief's" to the new proclamation. Some discussion of "debt pawns" is also provided, as well as perceived Ashante and Fante responses.

106. Great Britain. Parliament. House of Commons. "Correspondence Relating to the Affairs of the Gold Coast." *Parliamentary Papers* 1875 (C. 1140), vol. 52. 100 p.

Of 126 items—many of which treat the political economy of the Gold Coast—three relate directly to slavery: no. 39, a letter from Acting Administrator Lee on the "disposal of runaway slaves" (25 May 1874); no. 42, a letter from the Aborigines Protection Society on "Alleged Slave traffic at the Gold Coast"; and no. 89, Governor Strahan's belated response to these charges.

107. Great Britain. Parliament. House of Commons. "Further Correspondence Relating to the Abolition of Slavery on the Gold Coast." *Parliamentary Papers* 1875 (C. 1159), vol. 52. 13 p.

Contains three letters from Governor Strahan to the Home Office, and one letter from the Earl of Carnarvon in response. Strahan includes the text of a petition signed by certain "Kings and Chiefs" opposed to the terms of the emancipation proclamation of November 1874. Strahan and Carnarvon think that the petition is a forgery, attributable to "someone or more of the educated Fantees." Two other petitions, expressing specific African grievances, are included.

108. Great Britain. Parliament. House of Commons. "Papers Relating to Her Majesty's Possessions in West Africa: Sierra Leone and Gold Coast Colony, including Lagos." *Parliamentary Papers* 1875 (C. 1343), vol. 52. 28 p.

A collection of dispatches between London and the colonial governors' offices. For the Gold Coast, for example, there is a letter forwarded from the Reverend T. B. Freeman related to the "pawn" system; a letter from the Aborigines Protection Society; and a notice from the Home Office to Governor Strahan of the Gold Coast asking for more information concerning the "working and results" of the Slave Emancipation Scheme.

109. Great Britain. Parliament. House of Commons. "Convention between the British and Egyptian Governments for the Suppression of the Slave Trade, Signed at Alexandria, August 4, 1877." *Parliamentary Papers* 1878 (C. 1900), vol. 67. 6 p.

Treaty prohibiting the trade of slaves between families and providing penalties for slave dealing. Annex (in French) authorizes the creation of government offices and inspectors charged with resettling freed slaves. Male ex-slaves are to be given employment in the military, agriculture, or domestic service; females are to be placed in "honest homes" for domestic work; and children are to be sent to government schools.

110. Great Britain. Parliament. House of Commons. "Report by Sir David P. Chalmers on the Effect of the Steps Which Have Been Taken by the Colonial Government in Reference to the Abolition of Slavery within the Protectorate." *Parliamentary Papers* 1878 (C. 2148), vol. 55. 4 p.

Chalmers's solicited observations on the migration and settlement of ex-slaves provides information concerning the economic and social effects of emancipation in the Gold Coast. He claims that emancipation did not disrupt the palm-oil trade.

111. Great Britain. Parliament. House of Commons. "Correspondence Respecting the Trial of Certain Persons at Sierra Leone for the Murder of a Slave Girl at the Onitsha on the River Niger." *Parliamentary Papers* 1882 (C. 3430), vol. 46. 59 p.

Papers concerning the 1878 case of a British missionary interpreter who murdered an eleven-year-old girl, whom he had bought out of slavery. Colonial administrators use this case to declare the "good treatment" of ex-slaves in their employment compared to the abuses brought on ex-slaves in the service of missionaries. Includes testimony of African and British witnesses on aspects of daily life of a missionary community.

112. Great Britain. Parliament. House of Commons. "Report on the Soudan by Lieutenant-Colonel Stewart." *Parliamentary Papers* 1883 (C. 3670), vol. 84. 39 p.

This general report contains a section on slavery and the slave trade, asserting that both continue despite Anglo-Egyptian efforts. Recommends railway extension to encourage "legitimate" trade and thereby discourage slaving. Includes an 1883 budget for the suppression of the slave trade, which shows officials' salaries and indicates the level of government commitment to antislavery efforts.

113. Great Britain. Parliament. House of Commons. "Further Correspondence Regarding Affairs of the Gold Coast." *Parliamentary Papers* 1883 (C. 3687), vol. 48. 94 p.

A large collection with detailed descriptions of British administrators' negotiations with African chiefs and other elites. Includes R. La. T. Lonsdale's "Report on Mission to Ashanti and Gyaman (April–July 1881)."

114. Great Britain. Parliament. House of Commons. "Despatch from Sir E. Baring Respecting Slavery in Egypt." *Parliamentary Papers* 1884 (C. 3935), vol. 75. 5 p.

Recommends, for the long term, the abolition of the legal status of slavery in Egypt, but argues that no action should be taken in the short term. Since slavery is sanctioned by Islamic law, its abolition would bring political opposition on religious grounds. Gives numbers of applications for freedom, divided by sex, between 1877 and 1882, and suggests that few slaves are seeking emancipation because of fears that it will lead to starvation.

115. Great Britain. Parliament. House of Commons. "Correspondence Respecting Slavery in Egypt." *Parliamentary Papers* 1887 (C. 4994), vol. 92. 16 p.

Begins with correspondence between Consul-General Evelyn Baring and the Marquis of Salisbury concerning the import of slaves into Egypt by pilgrims returning from Mecca. The report of the Slavery Department for 1885 and 1886 follows and includes the numbers of recorded slave manumissions by province and month. Baring's letter accompanying the report states that slave dealing in Egypt has ended and that the use of free labor is increasing because it is cheaper for employers than slavery.

116. Great Britain. Parliament. House of Commons. "Further Correspondence Respecting the Affairs of the Gold Coast." *Parliamentary Papers* 1888 (C. 5357), vol. 75. 83 p.

Majority of correspondence concerns military and diplomatic issues, but there is some discussion of trade and domestic slavery. Includes detailed accounts of Inspector Dudley's and Captain Lonsdale's mission to the "Denkira and Becquai Districts" during which Lonsdale attempts to free slaves from chiefs and to stop slave trading.

117. Great Britain. Parliament. House of Commons. "Reports on Slave Trade on the East Coast of Africa 1887–88." *Parliamentary Papers* 1888 (C. 5578), vol. 74. 90 p.

Majority of items are short accounts of the "capture and condemnation of dhows by Her Majesty's ships." Covers the Somali Coast, Zanzibar, St. Augustine's Bay and Reunion, Madagascar, and Tajourra, with the majority concerning Zanzibar. Item no. 29 is a detailed general report, including figures on the "Return of Slaves" and "How Disposed Of." Some discussion of the role of missionaries is provided. Also includes "Statement of Muhandu, Slave Fugitive," in item no. 58.

118. Great Britain. Parliament. House of Commons. "Further Correspondence Respecting the Affairs of the Gold Coast." *Parliamentary Papers* 1888 (C. 5615), vol. 75. 190 p.

Largely concerned with the diplomacy involved in the selection of a new Ashanti king. The home government instructs Assistant Inspector Barnett on the need for a strong king for a united Ashanti who can protect traders and "keep his roads open." Some mention of domestic slavery included.

119. Great Britain. Parliament. House of Commons. "Anti-Slavery Decree Issued by the Sultan of Zanzibar, Dated 1st August 1890." *Parliamentary Papers* 1890–91 (C. 6211), vol. 57. 5 p.

Includes the text of the decree of Ali-Bin-Said, Sultan of Zanzibar, and a letter from Colonel C. B. Euan-Smith. Euan-Smith's letter is optimistic that the decree will stop the interference of "well-intentioned humanitarian Societies."

120. Great Britain. Parliament. House of Commons. "Correspondence Respecting the Administration of the Laws Against Slavery in the Gold Coast Colony." *Parliamentary Papers* 1890–91 (C. 6354), vol. 57. 24 p.

Three-way correspondence among the Aborigines' Protection Society, the Home Office, and Governor Brandford Griffith. Begins with a letter from the APS calling attention to the "prevalence of slavery and slave dealing in the Gold Coast Colony." Governor Griffith supplies a lengthy reply, providing evidence from court cases on the regulation and punishment of slave traders and owners. Detailed accounts of each case are provided. Includes excerpts from the 1874 Slave-dealing Abolition ordinance, and material on the questionable status of "pawns." The APS gets the final word in a rebuttal to Governor Griffith's dispatch.

121. Great Britain. Parliament. House of Commons. "Papers Relating to the Suppression of Slave-Raiding in Nyasaland." *Parliamentary Papers* 1892 (C. 6699), vol. 74. 38 p.

Letters written mostly by Commissioner Sir Harry Johnston to the Marquis of Salisbury in London and containing detailed reports of his campaigns against the slave-raiders in Nyasaland. Included are accounts of the campaign against the Yao; Johnston's attempts to persuade Mponda to join the Protectorate's prohibition of slave-raiding; information on the personnel under Johnston's command; discussion of the area's potential mineral and agricultural wealth. There is also a copy of a translated letter from the Sultan of Zanzibar to "Arabs residing in Tanganika," explaining the Sultan's recent decision to cooperate with Britain's suppression of slave trading.

122. Great Britain. Parliament. House of Commons. "Papers Relative to Slave Trade and Slavery in Zanzibar." *Parliamentary Papers* 1892 (C. 6702), vol. 74. 11 p.

Begins with a report from Captain W. H. Henderson on a naval blockade against slave ships in Zanzabar waters for the year 1891. The central document is a letter from British Diplomatic Agent Gerald H. Portal, concerning the labor supply in Zanzibar. He argues that the shortage is due to increased pressure by Europeans to end slavery and by the number of "coolies" and porters hired out by the Imperial British East Africa Company, the Church Missionary Society, and the Congo Free State. In response to this labor demand Portal has the sultan enact a decree against recruitment of Zanzibari laborers. Also includes accusations by the British and Foreign Anti-Slavery Society that British Indian residents and merchants of Zanzibar were promoting the slave trade. A petition from the Indian community and a letter from Portal deny these allegations.

123. Great Britain. Parliament. House of Commons. "Papers Relative to the Suppression of Slave-Raiding in British Central Africa." *Parliamentary Papers* 1893–94 (C. 7031), vol. 85. 11 p.

Two letters from Commissioner Harry H. Johnston to the Foreign Office narrating Johnston's campaigns against slave-raiding and the slave trade. Campaigns center on the "Upper Shire" district, and Johnston mentions the collaboration of the Yao and the difficulties of the African Lakes Company on Lake Malawi, among other details.

124. Great Britain. Parliament. House of Commons. "Paper Respecting the Traffic in Slaves in Zanzibar." *Parliamentary Papers* 1893–94 (C. 7035), vol. 85. 5 p.

Papers on a controversy regarding continued slave trading near Zanzibar after the British had declared a protectorate (1890) and begun to intervene against slavery and the slave trade. The British consul in Zanzibar and the secretary of the British and Foreign Anti-Slavery Society dispute the number of slave dhows evading capture and the involvement of Arabs from the Gulf of Oman and people from the Persian Gulf.

125. Great Britain. Parliament. House of Commons. "Returns of Slaves freed in Zanzibar Waters through Her Majesty's Ships: 1892–93." *Parliamentary Papers* 1893–94 (C. 7247), vol. 85. 8 p.

Short compilation of tables showing the number of slaves captured and "How Disposed Of." During this period, slaves could be "disposed" to one of the following: "In Town, Universities Mission, Zanzibar, French Mission Zanzibar, and Church Missionary Society, Mombasa." Similar reports can be found for other years.

126. Great Britain. Parliament. House of Commons. "Report by Commissioner Johnston of the First Three Years' Administration of the Eastern Portion of British Central Africa, Dated March 31, 1894." *Parliamentary Papers* 1894 (C. 7504), vol. 57. 51 p.

Detailed report includes sections on physical geography, ethnology, the slave trade, taxation, European settlement, missions, trade, and infrastructure. Discusses the progress of slave trade suppression, giving numbers of slaves freed and the circumstances under which they were released. Taxation is described as a means both to support slave trade suppression and to induce settlement of Africans, Arabs, and Europeans in particular areas. The presence of Arabs is deemed incompatible with European civilization, but Indian immigration is encouraged to provide a community positioned between the Africans and Europeans.

127. Great Britain. Parliament. House of Commons. "Correspondence Respecting Slavery in Zanzibar." *Parliamentary Papers* 1895 (C. 7707), vol. 71. 44 p.

Collection begins with a lengthy letter from Charles H. Allen, of the British and Foreign Anti-Slavery Society, to the Earl of Rosebery, petitioning the government to abolish slavery in Zanzibar and Pemba. This letter includes precedent setting proclamations and edicts from other territories, including the Gold Coast. Includes letters from Sir A. Hardinge, Consul S. Smith, and Mr. Rennell Rodd, all of whom argue for gradual abolition.

128. Great Britain. Parliament. House of Commons. "Correspondence Respecting Operations Against Slave-Traders in British Central Africa." *Parliamentary Papers* 1896 (C. 7925–part I and C. 8013–part II), vol. 58. 47 p.

Accounts by Commissioner Harry H. Johnston of his campaigns against slave-trading chiefs and "Arabs" throughout British Central Africa. Mentions slaves to whom Johnston gave freedom papers in 1889 and whom he found in captivity again in 1895. Includes reports on campaigns against chiefs "Mlozi, Matipwiri, Zarah, Mpondo, and Makanjira" and a report by Mr. A. J. Swann on his campaign against "Mwasi Kazungu" in the vicinity of the Blantyre coffee plantations.

129. Great Britain. Parliament. House of Commons. "Convention between Great Britain and Egypt for the Suppression of Slavery and the Slave Trade, Signed at Cairo, November 21, 1895." *Parliamentary Papers* 1896 (C. 7929 and C. 8011), vol. 97. 8p., 19 p.

Abolishes slavery and the slave trade in Egypt and authorizes British cruisers to search ships thought to be engaged in slaving. Authorizes slaves to request "letters of enfranchisement" from the government's Slavery Department, which is charged with administering the Convention and resettling freed slaves. The Egyptian government also is instructed to use its influence to prevent slaving in Central Africa.

130. Great Britain. Parliament. House of Commons. "Report by Commissioner Sir Harry Johnston, K.C.B., on the Trade and the General Condition of the British Central Africa Protectorate, April 1, 1895, to March 31, 1896." *Parliamentary Papers* 1896 (C. 8254), vol. 58. 31 p.

Contains an account of the British Central African Protectorate's political economy, including figures and summaries on population, ethnic groups, health, trade, and postal service. A section entitled "General Condition of the Protectorate," treats in detail the "native labour question" and slave-raiding.

131. Great Britain. Parliament. House of Commons. "Correspondence Respecting Slavery in the Zanzibar Dominions." *Parliamentary Papers* 1896 (C. 8275), vol. 59. 48 p.

Detailed accounts by Sir A. Hardinge explaining the state of slavery in Zanzibar and Pemba. Hardinge elicits letters from members of the Church Missionary Society to support his argument for gradual, rather than "wholesale and hasty," abolition. Includes two letters from women missionaries, Annie J. Grieve and Maggie J. Lockhart, describing the "disastrous" effects abolition would have on women slaves.

132. Great Britain. Parliament. House of Commons. "Instructions to Mr. Hardinge Respecting the Abolition of the Legal Status of Slavery in the Islands of Zanzibar and Pemba." *Parliamentary Papers* 1897 (C. 8394), vol. 62. 8 p.

A letter from the Marquis of Salisbury outlining the provisions and requirements for the abolition declaration to be made by the Sultan of Zanzibar. Gives the history of relations between the sultan and Great Britain; describes Zanzibar's peculiar form of slavery; and addresses issues of compensation and the future legal status of ex-slaves. Mentions negotiations with India to obtain "coolie labour" in order to avert economic difficulties in the Islands. Sir A. Hardinge replies that the sultan agreed to the terms of the decree.

133. Great Britain. Parliament. House of Commons. "Abolition of the Legal Status of Slavery in Zanzibar and Pemba." *Parliamentary Papers* 1897 (C. 8433), vol. 62. 8 p.

Sir A. Hardinge details his negotiations with the sultan over the abolition decree of 7 April 1897. Contains Hardinge's observations of the reception of the decree by the slave population, distinguishing between town and rural slaves. Enclosures include letters between Hardinge and the sultan, and the texts of the two emancipation decrees.

134. Great Britain. Parliament. House of Commons. "Papers Relative to the Liquor Trade in West Africa." *Parliamentary Papers* 1897 (C. 8480), vol. 62. 63 p.

Contains views of the African Trade Section of the Liverpool Chamber of Commerce, the Native Races and Liquor Traffic United Committee, and the Aborigines' Protection Society on the desirability of increasing tariffs on the liquor trade to West Africa. Several references link the liquor and slave trades, indicating that Africans must be prevented from the detrimental effects of both. A report from the Niger Coast Protectorate urges higher tariffs on the grounds that the increased revenue could be used to fight slave dealing and other evils.

135. Great Britain. Parliament. House of Commons. "Report by Sir A. Hardinge on the Condition and Progress of the East Africa Protectorate from Its Establishment to the 20th July, 1897." *Parliamentary Papers* 1898 (C. 8683), vol. 60. 72 p.

Sir A. Hardinge's detailed report offers an account of the political economy of coastal Kenya, Zanzibar, and Pemba. Includes a section on the slave trade and slavery and comments on the difficulties experienced in the transformation to "free labour."

136. Great Britain. Parliament. House of Commons. "Correspondence Respecting the Abolition of the Legal Status of Slavery in Zanzibar and Pemba." *Parliamentary Papers* 1898 (C. 8858), vol. 60. 91 p.

Contains accounts by Sir A. Hardinge concerning the conditions of slaves and ex-slaves on the Islands. Hardinge offers suggestions for the transformation of both rural and town slave-labor to wage labor. He argues for a gradual transformation to wage labor. He discusses the changing status of women slaves and the effects of the abolition decrees on industry, the slave population, the slave trade, missionaries, and concubinage. Contains a report by Commissioner J. P. Farler on the effects of abolition on Pemba. Includes letters from women of the Church Missionary Society protesting the absence of any provision against concubinage in the 1897 abolition decrees and from the British and Foreign Anti-Slavery Society protesting some provisions of the decrees.

137. Great Britain. Parliament. House of Commons. "Report by Sir A. Hardinge on the British East Africa Protectorate for the Year 1897–98." *Parliamentary Papers* 1899 (C. 9125), vol. 63. 33 p.

An extensive and detailed annual report covering the political economy of coastal Kenya, Zanzibar, and Pemba. A section covering the slave trade and slavery discusses the status of female ex-slaves, wives, and concubines. Includes detailed figures and discussion of the increased number of "freedom papers" issued during the period from 1897 to 1898.

138. Great Britain. Parliament. House of Commons. "Report by Her Majesty's Commissioner and Correspondence on the Subject of the Insurrection in the Sierra Leone Protectorate, 1898: Part I—Report and Correspondence; Part II—Evidence and Documents." *Parliamentary Papers* 1899 (C. 9388 and C. 9391), vol. 60. 175 p., 682 p.

In his report, Sir David Chalmers disagrees that African opposition to suppression of the slave trade contributed to the 1898 revolt, which he sees as a tax rebellion. He writes that slavery was dying even before the extension of the British protectorate in 1896, and that the only complaints he received from Africans related to the flight of domestic slaves, not to slave trade suppression. Also disputes the notion that domestic slave desertions would make it more difficult for household heads to pay the hut tax. In separate reports, Governor Frederick Cardew and Administrative Officer J. Chamberlain disagree, arguing that creation of the protectorate caused severe disruptions in the slave trade, which led to discontent and rebellion.

139. Great Britain. Parliament. House of Commons. "Correspondence Respecting the Status of Slavery in East Africa and the Islands of Zanzibar and Pemba." *Parliamentary Papers* 1899 (C. 9502), vol. 63. 63 p.

Mainly consists of letters between Sir A. Hardinge and the Marquis of Salisbury describing the process of liberating slaves. Special attention is given to the case of liberated slaves at Rabai, where some nine hundred runaway slaves were found to be harbored at a Church Missionary Society mission. A letter from Sir Lloyd William Mathews describes the work done to provide for "the destitute, infirm, and sick slaves without masters to assist them." He also includes a paragraph on ex-slave women and prostitution. Contains a lengthy report by Commissioner J. P. Farler on the effects of the abolition decrees on Pemba.

140. Great Britain. Parliament. House of Commons. "Correspondence Respecting Slavery and Slave Trade in East Africa and Islands of Zanzibar and Pemba." *Parliamentary Papers* 1900 (Cd. 96), vol. 56. 25 p.

Deals mainly with the debate over interpretation of the 1897 abolition decrees. The British and Foreign Anti-Slavery Society protests the practice of requiring proof of employment and a place to live before granting freedom papers to slaves. The home government orders this practice stopped and Commissioner J. P. Farler agrees, but worries that this will increase vagrancy. A letter from Sir A. Hardinge describes a trip he made to Pemba in which he praises the progress made there.

141. Great Britain. Parliament. House of Commons. "Correspondence Respecting Slavery and the Slave Trade in East Africa and the Islands of Zanzibar and Pemba." *Parliamentary Papers* 1901 (Cd. 593), vol. 48. 41 p.

This extensive collection begins with an account of the capture of the Sultan of Zanzibar's cousin for slave dealing, interpreted as evidence of both the sultan's loyalty to Britain and the continuing need for antislavery patrols. Next are annual reports for 1900 from the commissioners of Zanzibar and Pemba. Both officials emphasize that slaves find their work preferable to wage labor and have few incentives to file for emancipation. Freed people are reported to be disinclined to work and pose serious problems of vagrancy and drunkenness. Reports also contain demographic data on freed slaves and estimates of the number of inhabitants still enslaved. Also included are discussions of the efficacy of compensating owners of those who are emancipated and divergent views that emancipation has led to moral progress for former owners and slaves, versus argument and evidence of the moral degeneration of ex-slaves.

142. Great Britain. Parliament. House of Commons. "Correspondence Respecting Slavery and the Slave Trade in East Africa and the Islands of Zanzibar and Pemba." *Parliamentary Papers* 1903 (Cd. 1389), vol. 45. 28 p.

Contains information on the numbers and demographic characteristics of slaves freed on the islands from 1897 to 1901, as well as repeated assertions of slaves' reluctance to leave their masters. Several dispatches refer to increases in vagrancy, drunkenness, and prostitution coinciding with slave emancipation and defend labor contracts as a means of preventing idleness and immorality. The 1901 report on slavery from Pemba details planters' methods for acquiring labor on clove plantations in the absence of slavery; reports that ex-slaves are pawning themselves to Indians in exchange for money to buy *shambas*; and notes accusations by Arab planters that the government is undercutting their labor force by sending freed slaves to work at missions. Correspondence between officials of the Friends' Industrial Mission at Pemba and the British consul discusses the case of a woman denied freedom on the basis of being a concubine and illustrates the ambiguity in status of female slaves.

143. Great Britain. Parliament. House of Commons. "Report on Slavery and Free Labour in the British East Africa Protectorate." *Parliamentary Papers* 1903 (Cd. 1631), vol. 45. 9 p.

This short account by W. J. Munson asserts that slavery no longer exists in the protectorate outside of the dominions of the Sultan of Zanzibar and among Somalis. The description of extant slavery divides slaves into three groups—domestics, agricultural laborers, and artisans—and stresses slaves' ability to assimilate into their masters' communities and the lenient treatment they are said to receive. Since slaves have the option to leave their masters and find work on with the Uganda railroad, the report continues, their masters do not abuse them. Slavery is said to be dying naturally. The second half of the report, on free labor, contains information on the labor supply, stereotypes of African laborers, and wage scales and estimates Africans' costs of living. Munson claims current slaves are better off than those freed by the Church Missionary Society.

144. Great Britain. Parliament. House of Commons. "Correspondence Respecting Slavery in the Islands of Zanzibar and Pemba." *Parliamentary Papers* 1905 (Cd. 2330), vol. 56. 6 p.

Contains reports on the status of slavery from Zanzibar and Pemba for 1903. Both attribute low numbers of applications for freedom to the benign nature of slavery and to slaves' contentment with their now improved status. The report from Zanzibar contains statistics on the total number of slaves freed by their owners from 1897 to 1903, and the number of slaves freed in 1903 divided according to sex, ethnicity, place of residence after obtaining freedom, birth place, and occupation.

145. Great Britain. Parliament. House of Commons. "Reports Relating to the Administration of the East Africa Protectorate." *Parliamentary Papers* 1906 (Cd. 2740), vol. 80. 53 p.

The most extensive report in this compilation is from Ukamba Province and includes a discussion of British attempts since 1895 to suppress slave raiding.

146. Great Britain. Parliament. House of Commons. "Memorandum on the Taxation of Natives in Northern Nigeria." *Parliamentary Papers* 1907 (Cd. 3309), vol. 54. 65 p.

Frederick Lugard revises his 1906 memo on taxation contained in *Instructions to Political and Other Officers*. In the section entitled "Effect on Native Labour and Slavery Questions," he writes that taxes on the peasantry will allow the local ruling class to maintain its position without resort to extortion and slave raiding, while inducing landless workers into wage labor. Taxation will prevent the formation of independent communities of ex-slaves. Provision is made for native officials (who are also large landholders) to earn a percentage of the taxes they collect as a salary. A review of taxation in each province follows.

147. Great Britain. Parliament. House of Commons. "Despatch from His Majesty's Agent and Consul-General at Zanzibar, Furnishing a Report on the Administration, Finance, and General Condition of the Zanzibar Protectorate." *Parliamentary Papers* 1909 (Cd. 4816), vol. 59. 53 p.

Lengthy report on administration, finance, economy, commissions, public works, health, justice, education, and slavery. Includes a discussion of the agricultural labor supply and tactics for maintaining it, statistics on various crimes, including vagrancy, and a review of efforts at suppressing the slave trade and domestic slavery from 1868 onward. Argues that, because of the British policy of gradual abolition, slave emancipation has not caused economic disruption and suggests that complete abolition be considered for the near future.

148. Great Britain. Parliament. House of Commons. "Report of the Northern Nigeria Lands Committee and Despatches Relating Thereto; and Minutes of Evidence and Appendices." *Parliamentary Papers* 1910 (Cd. 5102, Cd. 5103), vol. 44.

These documents illustrate a change in government land policy from advocating plantation agriculture to encouraging smallholder production. While Lord Lugard had used land tenure and taxation to force ex-slaves into wage labor and tenancy, the policies of his successor, Percy Girouard, gave peasants access to land but made them subject to increased taxation and state control. Part II of the report, "Land Tenure," describes the existing system of land holding and points out the tension between British notions of private property and indigenous systems of communal access to land. Then it suggests that the British government control all land, but in accordance with local customs; it should guarantee to the occupants that they will be free from disturbance from all parties except the government; and all sales or mortgages should require the government's consent. Part III, "Revenue and Taxation," suggests the implementation of a land tax as well as taxes on trade and livestock.

149. Great Britain. Parliament. House of Commons. "Despatch to the Governor of the East Africa Protectorate Relating to Native Labour, and Papers Connected Therewith." *Parliamentary Papers* 1920 (Cmd. 873), vol. 33. 32 p.

The secretary of state for the colonies reacts to charges of forced labor on government projects and in private employment in British East Africa. Several suggestive appendices are attached: Labour Circular No. 1 of 1919, which instructs District Officers to vigorously recruit native labor; Labour Circular No. 3 of 1920, which cautions against recruitment and labor abuses; the Bishop's Memorandum on Native Labour, which criticizes Labour Circular No. 1 and suggests the existence of forced labor; the Master and Servants Ordinance of 1910, with amendments; and the Native Authority Ordinance of 1912, with amendments.

150. Great Britain. Parliament. House of Commons. "Report on Tanganyika Territory, Covering the Period from the Conclusion of the Armistice to the End of 1920." *Parliamentary Papers* 1921 (Cmd. 1428), vol. 24. 109 p.

See section III, "Administration and Population," which discusses slavery under German rule and illustrates postwar British antislavery discourse. This section also includes information on mission activity and education.

151. Great Britain. Parliament. House of Commons. "Despatch to the Officer Administering the Government of the Kenya Colony and Protectorate Relating to Native Labour." *Parliamentary Papers* 1921 (Cmd. 1509), vol. 24. 5 p.

Colonial Secretary Winston Churchill responds to allegations of forced labor and labor abuses. Issues opinions and new regulations on the following: traditional unpaid labor for the benefit of the reserves; voluntary labor for private employers; compulsory paid labor for the government; and labor from Tanganyika. Instructs district officers to limit their involvement in labor recruitment to providing information to employers and potential employees.

152. Great Britain. Parliament. House of Commons. "Report of a Committee on Trade and Taxation for British West Africa, Appointed by the Secretary of State for the Colonies." *Parliamentary Papers* 1922 (Cmd. 1600), vol. 16. 72 p.

Contains information on forms of taxation, the financial condition of British West African possessions, and the production and sale of selected export items. Most relevant is a section on the tax incentives which induced Africans into government or mine labor and township living.

153. Great Britain. Parliament. House of Commons. "Papers Relating to Native Disturbances in Kenya (March, 1922)." *Parliamentary Papers* 1922 (Cmd. 1691), vol. 16. 22 p.

Concerns the actions, arrest and deportation of Harry Thuku, as well as the riot and bloody suppression that followed. Thuku was detained for instructing Africans not to work for Europeans. Includes a translation of a prayer issued by Thuku and his followers which uses antislavery rhetoric as well as biblical references to call for redress of their grievances.

154. Great Britain. Parliament. House of Commons. "Compulsory Labour for Government Purposes in Kenya." *Parliamentary Papers* 1924–25 (Cmd. 2464), vol. 21. 39 p.

Begins with a summary of regulations on forced labor for government purposes issued in C. 1509 (1921). The rest of the materials deal with the governor of Kenya's request to the secretary of state for permission to conscript railway and dock labor. The correspondence includes information on the labor supply, wages, working conditions, recruitment, and the health of workers. The secretary of state's reasons for discouraging compulsory labor are revealing in terms of both British politics and economic strategies. Includes reports on labor at Kisumu Pier and Docks and statistics on railway workers.

155. Great Britain. Parliament. House of Commons. "International Convention with the Object of Securing the Abolition of Slavery and the Slave Trade." *Parliamentary Papers* 1927 (Cmd. 2910), vol. 26. 24 p.

Contains the text of the International Convention treaty of 25 September 1926. Britain signed and ratified the treaty on 18 June 1927. This convention extended the international community's insistence that colonial powers abolish slavery in their colonies and asked the International Labour Office to consider further extending the ban to forms of forced labor considered analogous to slavery.

156. Great Britain. Parliament. House of Commons. "Correspondence Relating to Domestic Slavery in the Sierra Leone Protectorate." *Parliamentary Papers* 1928 (Cmd. 3020), vol. 18. 78 p.

Compilation of materials illustrating the slow pace of emancipation in the Sierra Leone Protectorate. Begins with reference to the League of Nations' request for information on slavery and the progress of emancipation. The governor's response includes a history of slavery in Sierra Leone since 1896; a comparison of antislavery laws in Sierra Leone and other West African colonies; a recommendation that emancipation be achieved soon, but not immediately; and an ethnic breakdown of the colony's slaves. Includes copies of ordinances relating to slavery, a report of a meeting held with local chiefs, and materials on a Supreme Court case regarding the status of a runaway slave who was forcibly returned to his master.

157. Great Britain. Parliament. House of Commons. "Papers Concerning Affairs in Liberia December 1930–May 1934." *Parliamentary Papers* 1934 (Cmd. 4614), vol. 27. 98 p.

Contains correspondence of Sir John Simon and Mr. Arthur Henderson concerning the Liberia slavery scandal of 1930 and the "Liberian Government's Request for Assistance." Includes a chronological survey and extracts from League of Nations reports on Liberia's petition for assistance.

158. Great Britain. Parliament. House of Commons. "Correspondence Relating to the Welfare of Women in Tropical Africa, 1935–37." *Parliamentary Papers* 1937–38 (Cmd. 5784), vol. 20. 35 p.

Materials relate to the status of women within African marriages and to some administrators' suspicions that the end of slavery did not significantly improve the lives of women. Includes a dispatch from the secretary of state to the administrator of each British African colony requesting information on coerced marriages and the governments' responses to them. The majority of the replies deny any coercion in African marriages but are notable for the ways in which they relate such arrangements to slavery.

SECONDARY SOURCES

159. Afigbo, A. E. "The Eclipse of the Aro Slaving Oligarchy of South-Eastern Nigeria, 1901–1927." *Journal of the Historical Society of Nigeria* 6 (December 1971): 3–24.

160. Ali, Abbas Ibrahim Muhammad. *The British, the Slave Trade and Slavery in the Sudan, 1820–1881*. Khartoum: Khartoum University Press, 1972. 137 p.

    See especially part 3, "The Slave Trade and Slavery: British Ideas and Actions, 1874–1881," which traces the administration of Charles George Gordon, governor-general of the Sudan, and highlights the inconsistencies of British antislavery policy.

161. Allen, Bernard M. *Gordon and the Sudan*. London: Macmillan, 1931. 485 p.

    Extensive treatment of Gordon's antislavery objectives and his expeditions to suppress the slave trade between 1874 and 1885.

162. Armstrong, R. "The Nightwatchmen of Kano." *Middle Eastern Studies* 3 (1967): 269–82.

    Traces the origins of night guards in the early twentieth century to the migration of the Buzu category of Tuareg slaves after emancipation.

163. Asiegbu, J. U. J. "British Slave Emancipation and 'Free' Labour Recruitment from West Africa, 1840–1861." *Sierra Leone Studies* 26 (1970): 37–47.

    Focus is on labor recruitment from Sierra Leone to the West Indies.

164. Austin, Gareth Meredith. "Rural Capitalism and the Growth of Cocoa-Farming in South Ashanti, to 1914." Ph.D. diss., University of Birmingham, 1984. 602 p.

Agricultural transition in Amansie district was implemented largely with servile labor. Discusses the effects of colonial antislavery and antipawning legislation on labor organization and land use.

165. Baer, Gabriel. *Studies in the Social History of Modern Egypt.* Publications of the Center for Middle Eastern Studies, Number 4. Chicago: University of Chicago Press, 1969. 259 p.

See chapter 10, "Slavery and Its Abolition," on nineteenth-century developments in slavery and administrative measures against slavery and the slave trade.

166. Barnes, Bertram Herbert. *Johnson of Nyasaland: A Study of the Life and Work of William Percival Johnson, D.D., Archdeacon of Nyasa, Missionary Pioneer, 1876–1928.* Westminster: Universities' Mission to Central Africa, 1933. 258 p.

Biography of the leader of the first permanent UMCA station in Nyasaland, founded in 1886, and involved in the suppression of slavery as well as efforts to publicize the issue in Great Britain.

167. Berg, Elliot J. "The Development of a Labor Force in Sub-Saharan Africa." *Economic Development and Cultural Change* 8 (July 1965): 394–412.

Contains a general account of forced labor in colonial Africa from 1880 to 1930.

168. Brown, Carolyn A. "Testing the Boundaries of Marginality: Twentieth-Century Slavery and Emancipation Struggles in Nkanu, Northern Igboland, 1920–29." *Journal of African History* 37 (1996): 51–80.

Focuses on the exploitation of forced labor by the colonial state and its repercussions for the process of emancipation in southeastern Nigeria, in the 1920s.

169. Brown, Spencer H. "A History of the People of Lagos, 1852–1886." Ph.D. diss., Northwestern University, 1964. 483 p.

Contains extensive information on the economic activities, home life, and social status of freed slaves from Sierra Leone and Brazil.

170. Case, Glenna L. "Wasipe under the Ngbanya: Polity, Economy and Society in Northern Ghana." Ph.D. diss., Northwestern University, 1979. 865 p.

Chapter 8 addresses the effects of slavery suppression and attributes steep economic decline to it.

171. Cassanelli, Lee V. "Social Construction on the Somali Frontier: Bantu Former Slave Communities in the Nineteenth Century." In *The African Frontier: The Reproduction of Traditional African Societies*, edited by Igor Kopytoff, 214–38. Bloomington: Indiana University Press, 1987.

172. Chanock, Martin. *Law, Custom and Social Order: The Colonial Experience in Malawi and Zambia*. Cambridge: Cambridge University Press, 1985. 286 p.

In chapter 9, "Slaves and Masters," cases brought before the colonial courts reveal the ambiguity that nonrecognition of slavery brought to social and economic relations, especially in regard to marriage and family.

173. Christelow, Alan. "Slavery in Kano, 1913–1914: Evidence from the Judicial Records." *African Economic History* 14 (1985): 57–74.

Highlights the diversity of situations covered by the term "slavery"; the adaptive strategies of traditional rulers and slave owners; the ways in which slaves and the general public understood British antislavery policies; and the practical meanings given to emancipation, particularly for women and children.

174. Clayton, Anthony and Donald C. Savage. *Government and Labour in Kenya, 1895–1963*. London: Frank Cass, 1974. 481 p.

Chapters 1 through 4 treat labor in four categories—slavery, communal labor, compulsory labor, and voluntary contractual labor.

175. Cooper, Frederick. "Contracts, Crime, and Agrarian Conflict: From Slave to Wage Labor on the East African Coast." In *Labour, Law, and Crime: An Historical Perspective*, edited by Francis Snyder and Douglas Hay, 228–52. London: Tavistock Publications, 1987.

176. Cooper, Frederick. *From Slaves to Squatters: Plantation Labor and Agriculture in Zanzibar and Coastal Kenya, 1890–1925*. New Haven: Yale University Press, 1980. 328 p.

Treats slave emancipation in the context of prior British experience with emancipation and changing British conceptions of labor, class, and race. Argues that a conscious program of transforming slaveowners into agrarian capitalists and slaves into wage laborers was subverted by ex-slaves' resistance to work discipline and their tacit renegotiation of older patterns of dependence with their former owners.

177. Coquery-Vidrovitch, Catherine, and Paul E. Lovejoy, eds. *The Workers of African Trade*. Sage Series on African Modernization and Development, vol. 11. Beverly Hills: Sage Publications, 1985. 304 p.

Relevant articles include M. B. Duffill and Paul E. Lovejoy, "Merchants, Porters, and Teamsters in the Nineteenth-Century Central Sudan" (which covers Northern Nigeria, c. 1820–1910); Robert J. Cummings, "Wage Labor in Kenya in the Nineteenth Century" (c. 1840–90); and Allen Isaacman and Elias Mandala, "From Porters to Labor Extractors: The Chikunda and Kololo in the Lake Malawi and Tchiri River Area" (which covers Mozambique and Malawi, c. 1840–80).

178. Coupland, Reginald. *The Exploitation of East Africa, 1856–1890: The Slave Trade and the Scramble.* 1939. Reprint. Evanston: Northwestern University Press, 1967. 507 p.

Focuses principally on Zanzibar and is largely based on dispatches written by Sir John Kirk.

179. Crabitès, Pierre. *Gordon, the Sudan and Slavery.* 1933. Reprint. New York: Negro Universities Press, 1969. 334 p.

Covers Gordon's activities as Anglo-Egyptian administrator of the Sudan from 1874 to 1879 and in 1884 and quotes extensively from his journals, letters, and official correspondence. See chapter 4, "Anti-Slavery 'Prohibition' and 'Regulation'" for his instructions on ending slavery.

180. Daly, M. W. *Empire on the Nile: The Anglo-Egyptian Sudan, 1898–1934.* Cambridge: Cambridge University Press, 1986. 542 p.

Until the 1920s, severe labor shortages motivated administrators to uphold and enforce domestic slavery in the Sudan, while denouncing slavery and the slave trade in official pronouncements.

181. Derrick, Jonathan. *Africa's Slaves Today.* New York: Schocken Books, 1975. 245 p.

Claims that slavery was never completely eradicated in Africa but was transformed into more subtle systems of forced labor, clientage, and pawning.

182. Dike, K. Onwuka. *Trade and Politics in the Niger Delta, 1830–1885: An Introduction to the Economic and Political History of Nigeria.* Oxford: Clarendon Press, 1956. 250 p.

See especially chapters 5 through 9, which trace British involvement in the Niger Delta from antislaving activities in the early 1800s to the parliamentary committee on West Africa of 1865.

183. Duffy, James. *A Question of Slavery.* Cambridge, Mass.: Harvard University Press, 1967. 240 p.

Although book focuses on slavery and forced labor in Portuguese Africa from 1850 to 1920, it provides an important discussion of British official policy and discourse surrounding the African labor issue.

184. Dumett, Raymond E. "Pressure Groups, Bureaucracy, and the Decision-making Process: The Case of Slavery Abolition and Colonial Expansion in the Gold Coast, 1874." *The Journal of Imperial and Commonwealth History* 9 (January 1981): 193–215.

Considers abolition as the unintended result of the end of the sixth Ashanti War, which provided publicity on domestic slavery as well as new military and diplomatic considerations.

185. Ewald, Janet J. *Soldiers, Traders, and Slaves: State Formation and Economic Transformation in the Greater Nile Valley, 1700–1885.* Madison: University of Wisconsin Press, 1990. 270 p.

See chapter 7, "Soldiers, Traders, and Slaves: The Control of Labor during the Turkiyya," which discusses the inefficacy of government antislavery efforts in the 1870s, a consequence of the involvement of local officials in the slave trade. Considers the Madhi rebellion of 1883 as a result of long-term processes that empowered traders at the expense of the state.

186. Falola, Toyin. "Slavery and Pawnship in the Yoruba Economy of the Nineteenth Century." *Slavery and Abolition* 15 (1994): 221–45.

187. Falola, Toyin, and Paul E. Lovejoy, eds. *Pawnship in Africa: Perspectives on Debt Bondage.* Boulder: Westview Press, 1993.

Discusses how pawnship, or debt bondage, existed alongside slavery and acted as a partial alternative to slavery in some regions after the abolition of slavery. Includes chapters on Nigeria, the Gold Coast, and Sierra Leone.

188. Fredriksen, Børge. *Slavery and Its Abolition in Nineteenth-Century Egypt.* Bergen: Universitetet i Bergen, Historisk Institut, 1977. 205 p.

Considers the end of slavery in Egypt as primarily the result of socioeconomic changes only indirectly related to British actions.

189. Gann, Lewis. "The End of the Slave Trade in British Central Africa: 1889–1912." *Rhodes-Livingstone Journal* 16 (1954): 27–51.

Summarizes Britain's suppression efforts, noting the importance of local conditions. Antislavery is seen as a direct precursor of European conquest.

190. Githige, R. M. "The Issue of Slavery: Relations between the CMS and the State on the East African Coast prior to 1895." *Journal of Religion in Africa* 16 (1986): 209–25.

191. Glassman, Jonathon. *Feasts and Riots: Revelry, Rebellion, and Popular Consciousness on the Swahili Coast, 1856–1888*. Portsmouth, N.H.: Heinemann, 1995. 293 p.

Focuses on the 1888 rebellion against the establishment of German colonial authority to critique the conventional analysis of African resistance by stressing the multiplicity of communities. Discusses how plebeian resistance contributed to the failure of the sugar estates despite colonial support for the continuation of slavery. New forms of Islam in the towns challenged patrician patronage by creating alternative relationships of power through popular participation in festivals.

192. Glassman, Jonathon. "The Bondsman's New Clothes: The Contradictory Consciousness of Slave Resistance on the Swahili Coast." *Journal of African History* 32 (1991): 277–312.

193. Grace, John. *Domestic Slavery in West Africa, with Particular Reference to the Sierra Leone Protectorate, 1896–1927*. New York: Barnes and Noble, 1975. 294 p.

This volume attempts to explain why slavery was not abolished in Sierra Leone until 1927 and to put abolition into the context of changing conceptions of Britain's role in West Africa.

194. Grace, John J. "Slavery and Emancipation among the Mende in Sierra Leone, 1896–1928." In *Slavery in Africa: Historical and Anthropological Perspectives*, edited by Suzanne Miers and Igor Kopytoff, 415–431. Madison: University of Wisconsin Press, 1977.

British administrators maintained slavery out of deference to native chiefs, upon whom they relied for local administration, but also provided economic alternatives for escaped slaves. Final emancipation did not provide a radical break, as pawning, forced labor, and polygyny persisted.

195. Gray, Richard. *A History of the Southern Sudan, 1839–1889*. Oxford: Oxford University Press, 1961. 219 p.

For a discussion of the effects of attempts to suppress the slave trade, see especially chapter 6, "British Interests and the Southern Sudan."

196. Haight, Bruce Marvin. "Bole and Gonja: Contributions to the History of Northern Ghana." Ph.D. diss., Northwestern University, 1981. 1307 p.

Examines 1917 anti-British rebellion in the context of changing relations between the British and native inhabitants of Bole, internal British policies, and the region's history. Covers diverse topics including trade, labor, unfree labor, kinship patterns, and Islam.

197. Hargey, Taj. "The Suppression of Slavery in the Sudan, 1898–1939." Ph.D. diss., Oxford University, 1981. 535 p.

Overview of slavery and its suppression under successive administrations in the nineteenth and twentieth centuries. Appendices contain a wealth of statistical information on slave sales, emancipation, and slavery litigation, as well as court judgments and slave petitions for freedom.

198. Harris, Joseph E. *Repatriates and Refugees in a Colonial Society: The Case of Kenya.* Washington, D.C.: Howard University Press, 1987. 201 p.

Concentrates on the community of ex-slaves and repatriated Africans in Freretown and Rabai, Kenya. The return of an educated elite from mostly India, but including diverse places such as Persia and Indian Ocean Islands, allowed for the incorporation of Africans into a community which would later be used by the British to work as "gatekeepers" for the process of African class formation across ethnic and language lines.

199. Hetherwick, Alexander. *The Romance of Blantyre: How Livingstone's Dream Came True.* London: James Clarke, 1931. 260 p.

Discusses the mission's protection of fugitive slaves, which led to intervention in local politics and the disapproval of home authorities, and European trading conflicts with "Arab" slave traders on the northern end of Lake Nyasa. Traces the extension of British governmental authority; the suppression of the slave trade; and labor recruitment in the 1890s and early 1900s, which the author links to forced labor.

200. Hill, Polly. "From Slavery to Freedom: The Case of Farm-Slavery in Nigerian Hausaland." *Comparative Studies in Society and History* 18 (July 1976): 395–426.

201. Hill, Polly. *The Migrant Cocoa-Farmers of Southern Ghana: A Study in Rural Capitalism.* Cambridge: Cambridge University Press, 1963. 265 p.

Many of the early migrant farmers were ex-slaves or former slave dealers, and their adoption of capitalist agriculture represents a little-studied response to slavery abolition.

202. Hill, Richard. *Egypt in the Sudan, 1820–1881*. London: Oxford University Press , 1959. 188 p.

Chapters 11 and 12 contain descriptions of slave trade suppression efforts under Egyptian administration in the 1870s.

203. Hogendorn, Jan, and Paul E. Lovejoy. "Keeping Slaves in Place: The Secret Debate on the Slavery Question in Northern Nigeria, 1900–1904." In *The Atlantic Slave Trade: Effects on Economies, Societies, and Peoples in Africa, the Americas, and Europe*, edited by Joseph Inikori and Stanley Engerman. Durham: Duke University Press, 1992.

204. Hogendorn, Jan, and Paul Lovejoy. "The Development and Execution of Frederick Lugard's Policies Toward Slavery in Northern Nigeria." *Slavery and Abolition* 10 (May 1989): 1–43.

205. Holt, P. M. *The Mahdist State in the Sudan, 1881–1898: A Study of its Origins, Development and Overthrow*. Oxford: Clarendon Press, 1958. 264 p.

See chapter 1, where Holt discusses how the Mahdist revolt was inspired by opposition to Egyptian and British efforts to suppress the Sudanese slave trade.

206. Hopkins, A. G. *An Economic History of West Africa*. New York: Columbia University Press, 1973. 337 p.

Includes discussion of the economic and social effects of emancipation.

207. Hopkins, A. G. "The Lagos Strike of 1897: An Exploration in Nigerian Labour History." *Past and Present* 35 (1966): 133–55.

Places the strike in the context of the transition from slavery to free labor in Nigeria.

208. Ibrahim, Salah el-Din el-Shazali. "The Emergence and Expansion of the Urban Wage-Labor Market in Colonial Khartoum." In *Sudan: State, Capital and Transformation*, edited by Tony Barnett and Abbas Abdelkarim, 181–202. London: Croom Helm, 1988.

Analysis of the rise of urban wage labor in Khartoum during the first half of the twentieth century, with a discussion of efforts by the colonial state to exploit the labor of ex-slaves during the first decade of the century.

209. Igbafe, Philip A. "Slavery and Emancipation in Benin, 1897–1945." *Journal of African History* 16 (1975): 409–29.

Discusses how British abolition efforts coincided with the first entry of troops into Benin. While emancipation was first used to facilitate British occupation, it later became an expression of British commitment to the principles of antislavery.

210. Johnson, Marion. "The Slaves of Salaga." *Journal of African History* 27 (1986): 341–62.

Portrait of one of the leading slave markets in West Africa in the 1870s and 1880s. Notes that runaway Salaga slaves were recruited for the Hausa constabulary by British officials, who paid compensation to the ex-owners.

211. Johnston, Alex. *The Life and Letters of Sir Harry Johnston.* London: Jonathan Cape, 1929. 351 p.

See chapters 4 through 6 for slavery and expeditions against slave traders in East Africa.

212. Kalinga, Owen J. M. *A History of the Ngonde Kingdom of Malawi.* Berlin: Mouton, 1985. 176 p.

Based primarily on oral tradition and covers from c. 1600 to 1894. See chapter 5, "The Alien Intrusion," which describes the activities of Swahili traders, European missionaries, and the African Lakes Company on the northwestern shore of Lake Nyasa. Discusses how fighting between the Europeans and Swahili traders in 1887 focused on terms of trade and political alliances.

213. Kapteijns, Lidwien, and Jay Spaulding. "From Slaves to Coolies: Two Documents from the Nineteenth-Century Somali Coast." *Sudanic Africa* 3 (1992): 1–8.

214. Klein, Martin A. "Slavery, the Slave Trade, and Legitimate Commerce in Late Nineteenth-Century Africa." *Etudes d'Histoire africaine* 2 (1971): 5–28.

Essay based on printed primary and secondary sources on the decline of the Atlantic slave trade, the rise in export-oriented agricultural production, and the accompanying increase in slavery and the slave trade in late nineteenth-century Africa.

215. Klein, Martin A., ed. *Breaking the Chains: Slavery, Bondage, and Emancipation in Modern Africa and Asia.* Madison: University of Wisconsin Press, 1993. 222 p.

See Martin A. Klein's introduction, "Modern European Expansion and Traditional Servitude in Africa and Asia," and William Gervase Clarence-Smith, "Cocoa Plantations and Coerced Labor in the Gulf of Guinea, 1870–1914," which discusses the impact of British abolitionism on slavery under Spanish and Portuguese rule.

216. Kopytoff, Igor, and Suzanne Miers. "African 'Slavery' as an Institution of Marginality." In *Slavery in Africa: Historical and Anthropological*

Perspectives, edited by Suzanne Miers and Igor Kopytoff. Madison: University of Wisconsin Press, 1977.

An interpretation of slavery in Africa that stresses the limbic position of enslaved persons in relation to kinship organization. The authors claim that kinship groups were able to adjust to their inability to recruit new slaves, thus mitigating the disruptive effects of emancipation on colonial regimes.

217. Kopytoff, Jean Herskovits. *A Preface to Modern Nigeria: The "Sierra Leonians" in Yoruba, 1830–1890*. Madison: University of Wisconsin, 1965. 402 p.

In this history of freed slaves and their descendents who migrated from Sierra Leone, the author illustrates the class divisions and tensions evolving in nineteenth-century southern Nigeria.

218. Latham, A. J. H. *Old Calabar, 1600–1891: The Impact of the International Economy upon a Traditional Society*. Oxford: Clarendon Press, 1973. 193 p.

Discusses how local traders switched smoothly from commerce in slaves to that in palm oil, utilizing knowledge and institutions from the former to organize the latter. Points both to a growth in agricultural slave-holding and to the emergence of trading slaves as a result of the palm oil trade.

219. Law, Robin, ed. *From Slave Trade to 'Legitimate' Commerce: The Commercial Transition in Nineteenth-Century West Africa*. Papers from a conference of the Centre of Commonwealth Studies, University of Stirling. Cambridge: Cambridge University Press, 1995. 278 p.

Of special relevance is Kristin Mann's "Owners, Slaves and the Struggle for Labour in the Commercial Transition at Lagos."

220. Lennihan, Louise D. "Rights in Men and Rights in Land: Slavery, Wage Labor, and Smallholder Agriculture in Northern Nigeria." *Slavery and Abolition* 3 (September 1982): 111–39.

221. Lovejoy, Paul E. "Concubinage and the Status of Women Slaves in Early Colonial Northern Nigeria." *Journal of African History* 29 (1988): 245–66.

Based on court records between 1905 and 1906, this study describes the use of the court system to transfer women under the guise of emancipation.

222. Lovejoy, Paul E. *Transformations in Slavery: A History of Slavery in Africa.* Cambridge: Cambridge University Press, 1983. 349 p.

See chapter 8, "Slavery and 'Legitimate Trade' on the West African Coast" (pp. 159–83); chapter 11, "The Abolitionist Impulse" (pp. 246–68); and "Appendix: Chronology of Measures Against Slavery" (pp. 283–87).

223. Lovejoy, Paul E., and Jan S. Hogendorn. *Slow Death for Slavery: The Course of Abolition in Northern Nigeria, 1897–1936.* Cambridge: Cambridge University Press, 1993. 391 p.

Based on extensive oral interviews and research in British and Nigerian archives. Stresses connection of slavery to questions of land, taxation, and the political relationship between British officials and the Hausa-Fulani elite.

224. Macmillan, H. W. "Notes on the Origins of the Arab War." In *The Early History of Malawi,* edited by Bridglal Pachai, 263–282. Evanston: Northwestern University Press, 1972.

The African Lakes Company as well as mission supporters in England derived propaganda value from the war, which played an important role in arousing British interest in Central Africa, later leading to the declaration of the British protectorate.

225. Mahdi, Mandour El. *A Short History of the Sudan.* London: Oxford University Press, 1965. 154 p.

Contains an overview of attempts to suppress slavery and the slave trade from the 1830s into the 1870s.

226. Mandala, Elias. "Capitalism, Kinship and Gender in the Lower Tchiri (Shire) Valley of Malawi, 1860–1960: An Alternative Theoretical Framework." *African Economic History* 13 (1984): 137–69.

Notes that British antislavery efforts in central Africa actually increased women's vulnerability to enslavement, because they benefited ivory traders, who demanded to be paid in female captives. After the British takeover in 1891, the development of cash-crop agriculture and migrant labor contributed to additional shifts in gender relations and the control of resources.

227. Mandala, Elias C. *Work and Control in a Peasant Economy: A History of the Lower Tchiri Valley in Malawi, 1859–1960.* Madison: University of Wisconsin Press, 1990. 402 p.

Describes wage labor as "the real sequel to slavery," and discusses how, after abolition, Africans expanded peasant production as a means of avoiding it. Considers the role of intervention by the colonial government in forcing African labor out of peasant agriculture.

228. Mason, Michael. "Working on the Railway: Forced Labor in Northern Nigeria, 1907–1912." In *African Labor History*, edited by Peter C. W. Gutkind, Robin Cohen, and Jean Copans. Sage Series on African Modernization and Development, vol. 2. Beverly Hills: Sage Publications, 1978.

Coerced "political labor," recruited by European and African political officials, is seen as one of the outcomes of abolition of slavery.

229. McCracken, John. *Politics and Christianity in Malawi, 1875–1940: The Impact of the Livingstonia Mission in the Northern Province.* Cambridge: Cambridge University Press, 1977. 324 p.

Suggests that by the 1890s the mission had effected social and economic transformations that undermined the system of slave-raiding. Traces rise of migrant labor system that replaced slavery.

230. McLoughlin, Peter F. M. "Economic Development and the Heritage of Slavery in the Sudan Republic." *Africa: Journal of the International African Institute* 32 (October 1962): 355–91.

Covers period between 1898 and 1962, outlining nature of indigenous slavery and analyzing the long-term economic effects of abolition in five regions of the Sudan. Discusses the persistence of domestic slavery and serfdom into the mid-twentieth century.

231. McSheffrey, Gerald M. "Slavery, Indentured Servitude, Legitimate Trade and the Impact of Abolition in the Gold Coast, 1874–1901: A Reappraisal." *Journal of African History* 24 (1983): 349–68.

Asserts that the 1874 abolition ordinance provoked a widespread and unanticipated slave response because domestic slavery had become increasingly repressive. In order to preserve commerce, colonial administrations all but nullified the abolition laws, and abolition was not seriously pursued again until after 1900.

232. Miers, Suzanne. "Britain and the Suppression of Slavery in Ethiopia." In *Proceedings of the Eighth International Conference of Ethiopian Studies*, vol. 2, edited by Taddese Beyene, 253–266. Addis Ababa: Institute of Ethiopian Studies, 1989.

Addresses British policy towards slavery in Ethiopia from 1919 to 1936. Stresses the conflict between the Antislavery Society's vocal support of intervention and the Foreign Office's reluctance to attack slavery in an independent country.

233. Miers, Suzanne, and Richard Roberts, eds. *The End of Slavery in Africa*. Madison: University of Wisconsin Press, 1988. 524 p.

Includes the following articles relating to British colonial Africa: Raymond Dumett and Marion Johnson, "Britain and the Suppression of Slavery in the Gold Coast Colony, Ashanti, and the Northern Territories"; Michael Twaddle, "The Ending of Slavery in Buganda"; Suzanne Miers and Michael Crowder, "The Politics of Slavery in Bechuanaland: Power Struggles and the Plight of the Basarwa in the Bamangwato Reserve, 1926–1940"; Thomas J. Herlehy and Rodger F. Morton, "A Coastal Ex-Slave Community in the Regional and Colonial Economy of Kenya: The WaMisheni of Rabai, 1880–1963"; J. S. Hogendorn and Paul E. Lovejoy, "The Reform of Slavery in Early Colonial Northern Nigeria"; and Don Ohadike, "The Decline of Slavery among the Igbo People." The introduction reviews the historiography of slavery and emancipation in Africa. A concluding essay by Igor Kopytoff, "The Cultural Context of African Abolition," gives another interpretation.

234. Morton, Fred. *Children of Ham: Freed Slaves and Fugitive Slaves on the Kenya Coast, 1873 to 1907*. Boulder: Westview Press, 1990. 241 p.

Based on oral testimony and archival sources. Traces the development of organized, self-governing communities of fugitive and freed slaves on the Kenya coast and their relationships with local and foreign officials, CMS missionaries, and the Imperial British East Africa Company.

235. Mowafi, Reda. *Slavery, Slave Trade and Abolition Attempts in Egypt and the Sudan 1820–1882*. Stockholm: Scandinavian University Books/Esselte Studium, 1981. 145 p.

Focuses on the slave trade and its suppression. Extensive bibliography reprints government documents.

236. Nwokeji, G. Ugo. "The Slave Emancipation Problematic: Igbo Society and the Colonial Equation." *Comparative Studies in Society and History* 40 (1998): 328–55.

Examines why the colonial state chose to focus on wage labor formation and control instead of land tenure reform in postemancipation Igboland.

237. Nwulia, Moses D. E. "The Role of Missionaries in the Emancipation of Slaves in Zanzibar." *Journal of Negro History* 60 (1975): 268–87.

238. Nwulia, Moses D. E. *The History of Slavery in Mauritius and the Seychelles, 1810–1875*. East Brunswick, N.J.: Associated University Presses, 1981. 246 p.

See chapter 4, "The Period of 'Amelioration,' 1823–35," chapter 5, "The 'Apprenticeship' System, 1835–39," and chapter 6, "The Post-Emancipation Period, 1839–75."

239. Nwulia, Moses D. E. *Britain and Slavery in East Africa.* Washington, D.C.: Three Continents Press, 1975. 224 p.

Covers period between 1800 and 1908 and primarily focuses on Zanzibar.

240. O'Hear, Ann. "British Intervention and the Slaves and Peasant Farmers of Ilorin, c. 1890–c. 1906." *Paideuma* 40 (1994): 129–48.

Argues that British activities in the 1890s led to the flight of many slaves from Ilorin, but also to a process of reenslavement. The early twentieth century saw increased resistance of underclasses in general.

241. O'Hear, Ann. *Power Relations in Nigeria: Ilorin Slaves and Successors.* Rochester, N.Y.: University of Rochester Press, 1997. 338 p.

Links the decline of slavery in the early twentieth century under British rule with the emergence of a small-scale peasantry as the successor group to slaves. Focuses on resistance and accommodation of freed slaves in their relations with ex-masters and the Ilorin elite.

242. Oliver, Roland. *Sir Harry Johnston and the Scramble for Africa.* London: Chatto and Windus, 1957. 368 p.

Includes a discussion of Johnston's administration of Nyasaland and suppression of the slave trade.

243. Oliver, Roland. *The Missionary Factor in East Africa.* 2d ed. London: Longmans, 1965. 302 p.

Covers period between 1856 and 1949 and contains discussions of missionary efforts to suppress the slave trade and to incorporate freed slaves.

244. Oloruntimehin, B. Olatunji. "The Impact of the Abolition Movement on the Social and Political Development of West Africa in the Nineteenth and Twentieth Centuries." *African Notes* 7 (1971–72): 33–58.

General survey of antislavery activities focused primarily on the slave trade and its abolition. Compares British and French colonies and argues that colonial economic transformations caused slavery to become increasingly irrelevant to West African societies.

245. Olusanya, G. O. "The Freed Slaves' Homes: An Unknown Aspect of Northern Nigerian Social History." *Journal of the Historical Society of Nigeria* 3 (December 1966): 523–38.

Describes homes for freed slave children, run between 1903 and 1925 by the colonial government and the Church Missionary Society.

246. Oroge, E. Adeniyi. "Iwofa: An Historical Survey of the Yoruba Institution of Indenture." *African Economic History* 14 (1985): 75–106.

Argues that Iwofa, a form of pawnship, was distinct from slavery. Examines attempts by colonial administration to transform pawnship into fixed-time labor contracts following abolition.

247. *Paideuma* 14 (1995).

Special edition entitled "Slavery and Slave-Dealing in Cameroon in the Nineteenth and Twentieth Centuries." Introduction by Chem-Langhee and eight articles discuss and compare various slave systems in the region, noting their persistence into colonial era but without focus on emancipation.

248. Phillips, Anne. *The Enigma of Colonialism: British Policy in West Africa.* London: James Currey, 1989. 184 p.

See chapter 3, "Developing the Estates': Slavery and Forced Labour," on the ambivalence of British policy regarding domestic slavery. By the early 1900s, governments were pursuing a variety of methods for creating a wage labor force, but the conflicting demands of maintaining political stability and facilitating capitalist expansion eventually led to an emphasis on peasant production.

249. Porter, Gina. "A Note on Slavery, Seclusion and Agrarian Change in Northern Nigeria." *Journal of African History* 30 (1989): 487–91.

Argues that development issues, particularly modern population density and settlement patterns, need to take on a historical perspective from precolonial slavery.

250. Reynolds, Edward E. "Abolition and Economic Change on the Gold Coast." In *The Abolition of the Atlantic Slave Trade: Origins and Effects in Europe, Africa, and the Americas,* edited by David Eltis and James Walvin. Madison: University of Wisconsin Press, 1981.

Describes the role of Afro-European and African merchants and Basel missionaries in the growth of the cocoa economy from c. 1820 to 1890.

251. Robertson, Claire C. "Post-Proclamation Slavery in Accra: A Female Affair?" In *Women and Slavery in Africa,* edited by Claire C. Robertson and Martin A. Klein. Madison: University of Wisconsin Press, 1983.

Attributes the failure of the 1874 emancipation proclamation in Accra to political and economic structures that frequently made "freedom" unavailable or undesirable for women.

252. Romero, Patricia W. "'Where Have All the Slaves Gone?' Emancipation and Post-Emancipation in Lamu, Kenya." *Journal of African History* 27 (1986): 497–512.

Argues that in spite of legal abolition in 1907, emancipation was a protracted process. Economic decline and stagnation caused ex-slaves to migrate elsewhere or to enter into new relationships of dependency with their former masters.

253. Shaked, Haim. "Charles George Gordon and the Problem of Slavery in the Sudan." *Slavery and Abolition* 1 (December 1980): 276–91.

Based on Gordon's diaries and letters, this article explores his thinking on slavery and its suppression during his tenure as governor of Equatoria from 1874 to 1876, and his first term as governor-general of the Sudan form 1877 to 1879.

254. Shukry, M. F. *The Khedive Ismail and Slavery in the Sudan (1863–1879): A History of the Sudan from the Egyptian Conquest of 1820, to the Outbreak of the Mahdiist Rebellion in 1881, with Special Reference to British Policy and the Work of Sir Samuel Baker and Charles George Gordon.* Cairo: Librairie La Renaissance d'Egypt, 1938. 386 p.

Highlights the mutual reinforcement between Ismail's efforts to extend Egyptian political control into southern Sudan and Uganda and those to combat the slave trade. Argues that discontent among slave traders was responsible for the Mahdist rebellion.

255. Sikainga, Ahmad. "Islamic Courts and the Manumission of Female Slaves in the Sudan, 1898–1939." *International Journal of African Historical Studies* 28 (1995): 1–24.

Discusses how the manumission of slaves in the Sudan had limited effects on women because of their productive and reproductive roles. Shari'a courts played a critical role in denying women access to freedom despite colonial antislavery reforms, which were not effective until the 1930s.

256. Sikainga, Ahmad Alawad. *The Western Bahr al-Ghazal under British Rule, 1898–1956.* Athens, Ohio: Ohio University Center for International Studies, 1991. 183 p.

Includes a brief discussion of manumission and relations between communities of runaway and ex-slaves (known as *Mandala* or *Bandala*), their former masters (the *Baqqara*), and the British colonial state.

257. Sikainga, Ahmad Alawad. *Slaves into Workers: Emancipation and Labor in Colonial Sudan.* Austin: University of Texas Press, 1996. 276 p.

Pays particular attention to the development of Khartoum as both a haven for ex-slaves and a reservoir of wage workers for deployment to agricultural estates.

258. Sikainga, Ahmad Alawad. "The Legacy of Slavery and Slave Trade in the Western Bahr al-Ghazal, 1850–1939." *Northeast African Studies* 11 (1989): 75–95.

Includes a brief discussion of manumission and communities of ex-slaves in the late nineteenth and early twentieth centuries.

259. *Slavery and Abolition* 19 (August 1998).

Special issue entitled "Slavery and Colonial Rule in Africa." Includes introductory overview of the period between 1890 and 1859 by the editors of the series, Suzanne Miers and Martin Klein, and articles focusing on Nigeria, the Gold Coast, Sierra Leone, and Sudan.

260. Smith, M. G. *Government in Zazzau, 1800–1950.* 1960. Reprint. London: Oxford University Press, 1964. 371 p.

On Northern Nigeria. Includes a detailed analysis of a precolonial government where slaves played important administrative and military roles (while other slaves worked on the elite's farms) and how that system changed under colonial rule.

261. Smith, M. G. "Slavery and Emancipation in Two Societies." *Social and Economic Studies* 3 (December 1954): 239–90.

Compares slavery, emancipation, and postemancipation in Jamaica and Zaria, Northern Nigeria (c. 1830–1930).

262. Solá-García, César J. "Slave Emancipation and Colonialism: The British Missionary and Military Campaigns and African Societies in Northern Malawi, 1875–1900." Ph.D. diss., University of Michigan, 1999. 391 p.

263. Strayer, Robert W. *The Making of Mission Communities in East Africa: Anglicans and Africans in Colonial Kenya, 1875–1935.* London: Heinemann, 1978. 174 p.

Particular attention is paid to the development of settlements of freed slaves at Freretown, Rabai, and other locations.

264. Sundiata, I. K. *Black Scandal: America and the Liberian Labor Crisis, 1929–1936.* Philadelphia: Institute for the Study of Human Issues, 1980. 230 p.

Discusses the international controversy over accusations of government involvement in rounding up slaves for plantation labor on islands off West Africa.

265. Sundiata, Ibrahim K. *From Slaving to Neoslavery: The Bight of Biafra and Fernando Po in the Era of Abolition, 1827–1930*. Madison: University of Wisconsin Press, 1996. 250 p.

History of the island of Fernando Po (present-day Bioko) including its role as a British antislaving base in the late 1820s, its colonization by the Spanish in the 1830s, settlement by some five hundred freedpeople from Cuba in the 1860s, the rise of the cocoa economy in the last quarter of the nineteenth century, the official abolition of slavery in the 1880s, and struggles over labor recruitment and forced labor in the late nineteenth and early twentieth centuries.

266. Tamuno, T. N. *The Evolution of the Nigerian State: The Southern Phase, 1898–1914*. Ibadan History Series. London: Longman, 1972. 422 p.

See chapter 11, "Labour and Domestic Slavery."

267. Temu, A. J. *British Protestant Missions*. London: Longman, 1972. 184 p.

Study of British Protestant missions in Kenya and their importance in creating communities of ex-slaves from 1874 to 1929.

268. Thomas, Roger G. "Forced Labour in British West Africa: The Case of the Northern Territories of the Gold Coast, 1906–1927." *Journal of African History* 14 (1973): 79–103.

Argues that labor recruitment for privately owned gold mines was associated with government recruitment for public works, and that distinctions between "communal" and "forced" labor were unclear. Helps to illustrate changes in labor relations necessitated by the abolition of slavery.

269. Twaddle, Michael, ed. *The Wages of Slavery: From Chattel Slavery to Wage Labor in Africa, the Caribbean and England*. London: Cass, 1993.

270. Ubah, C. N. "The Colonial Administration in Northern Nigeria and the Problem of Freed Slave Children." *Slavery and Abolition* 14 (1993): 208–33.

Argues that the administration responded inadequately to the problem of rescuing and rehabilitating freed slave children. Children were hired out as servants instead of being trained for independent wage labor.

271. Ubah, C. N. "Suppression of the Slave Trade in the Nigerian Emirates." *Journal of African History* 32 (1991): 447–70.

Traces different periods in the suppression of slavery in the twentieth century. Considers the role of state intervention in struggles over the enslavement of children.

272. Verger, Pierre. *Trade Relations between the Bight of Benin and Bahia from the 17th to the 19th Century.* Trans. by Evelyn Crawford. Ibadan: Ibadan University Press, 1976. 629 p.

See chapter 15, "The Bight of Benin after 1810: Passing from the 'Guilty Trade' in Slaves to the 'Innocent Commerce' in Palm Oil," and chapter 16, "Formation of a Brazilian Society in the Bight of Benin."

273. Warburg, Gabriel R. "Slavery and Labour in the Anglo-Egyptian Sudan." *Asian and African Studies* 12 (1978): 221–45.

274. Warburg, Gabriel R. "Ideological and Practical Considerations Regarding Slavery in the Mahdist State and the Anglo-Egyptian Sudan: 1881–1918." In *The Ideology of Slavery in Africa*, edited by Paul E. Lovejoy. Beverly Hills: Sage Publications, 1981.

Argues that while the slave trade was eliminated, British administrators tolerated domestic slavery. Domestic slavery only began to disappear after World War I, when immigrants from West Africa provided a cheap free labor force.

275. Willis, Justin. *Mombasa, the Swahili, and the Making of the Mijikenda.* Oxford: Clarendon Press, 1992. 231 p.

Examines social networks and economic options of people living in and around Mombasa. Explores creation and fluidity of Swahili and Mijikenda ethnic identities in the early twentieth century.

276. Willis, Justin, and Suzanne Miers. "Becoming a Child of the House: Incorporation, Authority and Resistance in Giryama Society." *Journal of African History* 38 (1997): 479–96.

Argues that marginal individuals, including slaves, were incorporated through structures of kinship. The Giryama elite was undermined by the abolition of slavery and the imposition of colonial rule that opened up new opportunities for freed people.

277. Wright, Marcia. "Bwanikwa: Consciousness and Protest among Slave Women in Central Africa, 1886–1911." In *Women and Slavery in Africa*, edited by Claire C. Robertson and Martin A. Klein. Madison: University of Wisconsin Press, 1983.

Using the autobiography of a slave woman who eventually became a free member of a mission community, as well as court testimony, Wright illustrates women's circumstances, their attempts to moderate conditions of slavery, and their self-emancipation efforts.

278. Wright, Marcia. "Women in Peril: A Commentary on the Life Stories of Captives in Nineteenth-Century East-Central Africa." *African Social Research* 20 (December 1975): 800–819.

In addition to providing information about the experiences of female slaves, this article suggests a dynamic interpretation of slavery and freedom, with considerable shifts and gradations between the two.

279. Wright, Marcia. *Strategies of Slaves and Women: Life-Stories from East/Central Africa.* New York: Lilian Barber Press, 1993. 238 p.

Uses oral life history narratives combined with written sources to explore the gendered and generational experiences of slavery, emancipation, and conversion to Christianity. Focuses on experiences of women in the period of rapid social and economic transformation from the mid-nineteenth to mid-twentieth centuries.

III South Africa

EDITOR

Frederick Cooper
New York University

COMPILED BY

Frederick Cooper

Lisa Lindsay
University of North Carolina-Chapel Hill

Pamela Scully
Denison College

Kerry Ward
Rice University

INTRODUCTION

To study slavery in South Africa is to look at processes that were deeply rooted in a place and thus linked to the complex history of the southern part of the continent as a whole and at the same time were located elsewhere. In some ways, the slave plantations of the Cape Colony, at least in the western Cape, resembled the West Indies more than Africa, and the abolition of slavery in 1834 and the end of apprenticeship in 1838 followed a schedule set out in relation to the West Indies. British antislavery focused on the sugar islands; that the Cape was included in the abolition acts had little to do with anything that was happening in southern Africa. In this sense, close examination of slavery and emancipation in South Africa puts the focus strongly on the imperial dimension of slave emancipation, on the ways the commercial linkages centered around slaves and the products they created tied together different parts of the world, and on the way in which the attack on "slavery" assumed and in turn promoted a view of the world as bound by a single set of moral standards. Not only was slavery just as wrong in Stellenbosch as in Kingston, but one did not have to know very much about slavery in Stellenbosch to associate it with its other varieties. When officials thought how to regulate the emancipation process, they may well have brought to it conceptions of an ideal social life—for example conceptions of the proper relation between a freed man and a freed woman—that had more to do with idealized images of life at home than the conditions that shaped gender relations in a rural district of South Africa.

At the same time, examining the long and uneven process by which the broad acts against slavery were implemented in the context of South Africa reveals how much of the slave issue was deeply rooted in the particulars of a region and in variations within it. The dichotomy of slavery and freedom that antislavery ideology promoted had to confront more confusing realities. How did efforts to turn slaves into self-motivated individuals differ from policies toward the larger number of Africans who lived just outside the old plantation zone, and whose labor was also sought? Did measures intended to implement the transition to wage labor serve as precedents for the apparatus of control later enacted in relation to Africans who had never been enslaved? Was race given new meaning in the era of reconstruction? When certain long-term Dutch-speaking settlers of South Africa migrated away from the Cape region in the era of abolition (and perhaps because of it), how did the unregulated frontier labor system— where kidnapping and clientage were frequently used by white colonizers—compare to the orderly visions of labor and property being espoused by the Colonial Government? And how did the proximity of African societies, holding onto a considerable degree of autonomy in the 1830s and 1840s, affect the options of ex-slaves in turning the process of emancipation in directions unintended by their "liberators"?

The South African case is peculiar enough: a British colony after 1806, the southern cone of Africa had been inhabited by mixed populations of Africans—hunters and gatherers, pastoralists, farmers, and people combining various forms of subsistence and exchange—into which Dutch colonizers intruded in 1652. At first the settlement was intended to supply Dutch ships as they rounded the Cape on the long voyage to the East Indies—the real source of colonial profits. But many settlers started to assert their autonomy from the Dutch East India Company, eventually to the profit of that company, as South Africa became a producer of wool, grain, and wine. An uneasy frontier pushed outward, and many Africans were displaced into less desirable land to the north of Cape Town, while others were absorbed into the settler economy as their own social units were fatally damaged by land loss and disease. The settlers nonetheless had a severe labor problem, which they solved by following the routes of Dutch imperialism to Asia—the Indies archipelago and South Asia—which allowed settler agriculture to expand. Other slaves came from Africa but mostly via sea routes from territory at a certain distance, notably Madagascar: the displacement of the enslaved person was as usual the foundation of discipline within the slave society.

Much has been written about the extent to which racial boundaries were blurred in the slave era, by intermarriage as well as more opportunistic and oppressive forms of sexual exploitation and by the ambiguities of a frontier situation; the rigid lines of racial division may have been a product of the era of emancipation as much as the era of slavery. A mixed population, with roots in the local African social groups, among Asian slaves, and among whites, became a presence, eventually to be known as "Coloureds." Within this category, the prevalence of Islam—brought by Asian slaves—gave rise to a category known as the Cape Malays, while slaves who became Christian were often referred to as "Cape Coloureds." Many "Coloureds" still speak primarily Afrikaans rather than English; highly differentiated social and cultural patterns remained even in the face of the increasing racial polarization of South Africa over the course of the nineteenth century.

How the Dutch Cape became British South Africa is too convoluted a story to detain us here; suffice it to say that for reasons connected with the Napoleonic wars in Europe—and having nothing to do with South Africa itself—the Cape went from Dutch to British hands in 1795, back to Dutch hands in 1803, and definitively into the British empire in 1806. That was the very eve of the triumph of the antislave trade lobby in England, which would then go on to attack slavery itself in British colonies. So the advent of British rule is, in subsequent histories and quite likely in the minds of slave owners at the time, closely linked with the advent of slave emancipation.

Slavery in South Africa was predominantly a phenomenon of the Cape region, and only part of the Cape at that. But South Africa's frontiers were in 1806 already pushing outward, partly in opposition to the British presence partly because of it. In some instances, that meant the extension of depredations by kidnapping commandos, white and Coloured, and in others it meant the extension of a discourse about the virtues of free labor—and the need for discipline and control to insure that work got done—beyond the slavery zone. The effects of this commando enslavement pattern as well as that of the European slave trade based on Delagoa Bay in nearby Mozambique on conflict among Africans and on African state formation has been much debated in the literature.

The documents in this collection raise fundamental questions about the power and limits of the law in defining and legitimizing new social forms, about conflicting notions of the family in dispute within ex-slave communities as much as between them and their rulers, about the efforts of ex-slaves and their allies to petition authorities as well as to flee or fight oppression, and about how such efforts shifted official discourse. Documents reveal a discourse about a sort of Cape underclass—ambiguously constituted by slaves, Khoi Khoi, and other Africans—rhetoric sometimes used to differentiate the African population and sometimes to homogenize it into a single category, politically dangerous, economically necessary, and culturally inferior. We have tried to include census materials, reports on the state of agriculture in different areas, discussions of marriage laws and practices, discussions of who should and should not receive education, investigations into the ambiguous status of "Coloured" peoples in the postemancipation Cape, discussions of the relationship of race and political rights, and testimony before various commissions about conditions on the uneasy zone where the slavery question ran into the question of how African peasants were to be incorporated into regional market relations. We have included missionary documents and newspapers.

Most of this bibliography was compiled by Pamela Scully while she was doing research in Cape Town on her (now published) doctoral dissertation (see bibliography), and it has been updated most recently by Kerry Ward. Dr. Scully did not include the archival documents she used in her dissertation—the bibliography is limited to published sources only—and we have verified that sources of the type included here are available in U.S. research libraries. We cannot vouch that every document is in a U.S. library. Some may be available in Great Britain; all are available in South Africa. There are some documents from the British Parliamentary Papers, whose particular importance are discussed in the introduction to the British Africa section. As is so often the case in African history—and in some ways is particularly acute in the historiography of nineteenth-century South Africa—getting away from a mission or official centered viewpoint is difficult. The secondary sources we include employ the entire range of sources available, and many of these struggle valiantly to get away from top-down viewpoints, but such scholars—like the users of our bibliography—have to devote much effort to reading official or missionary sources obliquely, often trying to coax information out of the sources, despite the best efforts of the sources themselves. Some of the secondary sources cited here discuss "memory work"—how slavery is represented in museums and other institutions and in rituals and oral histories of communities descended from slaves.

The focus of this bibliography is on regions of the Cape where large-scale agricultural production was important in the late eighteenth and early nineteenth centuries, for that was what defined the "slave" question in South African politics. Studies of African societies in what became South Africa have not dwelled on the salience of enslavement or the slave status. This is much less true of southern Mozambique, where slave trading and slave use was quite significant in and before the nineteenth century, but scholars have emphasized other forms of subordination within Sotho and Nguni societies in South Africa. Although the incorporation of captives was certainly a part of warfare and state expansion in the nineteenth century, the institutionalization of captivity into clearly defined statuses is not often stressed in the historical or ethnographic literature. Hence, we cannot delve into a comparison of the significance of ending slavery in European agriculture in the Cape and African agriculture beyond the colony's effective borders. Our concern is with the consequences of the emancipation of slaves owned by slave owners defined as white. We try to stretch the boundaries by raising questions of how conceptions of labor emerging in the slavery debates played further afield. In South Africa as elsewhere in the British empire of the first half of the nineteenth century, the intensity with which slave emancipation was debated affected the framing of issues concerning race, labor, gender, and culture in a zone of colonization and over a long period of time. At the same time, the consequences of those debates for the lives of people on farms and in cities reflected the complex contexts and struggles in different parts of South Africa.

Frederick Cooper

BIBLIOGRAPHIES, HISTORIOGRAPHICAL ESSAYS, AND INDEXES

1. Henige, David. *A Union List of Africana Archival Materials in Microform.* 2d ed. 1984. 45 p.

   Relevant documents include: the archives of the Church Missionary Society, although no dates are provided; indexes to the correspondence between the Colonial Office and the Cape Colony between 1815 and 1870; miscellaneous correspondence between the Colonial office and the Cape Colony from 1799 to 1835; original correspondence between the Colonial Office and the Cape Colony (no dates); the South African archives of the United Society for the Propagation of the Gospel in Foreign Parts from 1820 to 1900; dispatches from the U.S. Consulate in Cape Town from 1800 to 1906.

2. Miller, Joseph C. *Slavery and Slaving in World History: A Bibliography, 1900–1991.* Milwood, N.Y.: Kraus International, 1993. 556 p.

   For annotation, see bibliography on British Colonial Africa.

3. Miller, Joseph C. *Slavery and Slaving in World History: A Bibliography.* Armonk, N.Y.: M. E. Sharpe, 1999.

   For annotation, see bibliography on British Colonial Africa.

4. Miller, Joseph C. *Slavery: A Worldwide Bibliography, 1900–1982.* White Plains, N.Y.: Kraus International, 1985. 451 p.

   For annotation, see bibliography on British Colonial Africa.

5. Musiker, Naomi. *South African History: A Bibliographical Guide with Special Reference to Territorial Expansion and Colonization.* With the assistance of Reuben Musiker. New York: Garland Publishing, 1984. 297 p.

Mainly references published secondary materials. Includes chapter on travelers' accounts from the seventeenth through the late nineteenth centuries. Precise and extensive annotations.

6. Musiker, R., ed., N. Musiker, comp. *Guide to Cape of Good Hope Official Publications, 1854–1910.* Boston: G. K. Hall, 1976. 466 p.

   Catalogue of annexures and Select Committee reports of the Cape of Good Hope. Listed by subject and chronologically.

7. Stultz, Newell M. *South Africa: An Annotated Bibliography with Analytical Introductions.* Resources on Contemporary Issues. Ann Arbor, Mich.: Pieran Press, 1989. 191 p.

   Has contemporary bias, but two of the earlier chapters on historiography and minority communities have some annotations of interest. Information also on reference works.

8. Westra, P. E. "The Abolition of Slavery at the Cape of Good Hope: Contemporary Publications and Manuscripts in the S. A. Library." *Quarterly Bulletin of the South African Library* 39 (1984): 58–66.

   Essay on primary documents relating to abolition, particularly in the decade before apprenticeship in 1834.

PRIMARY SOURCES

9. Bigge, J. T. "Report upon the Slaves and the State of Slavery at the Cape of Good Hope." In *Records of the Cape Colony from December 1827 to April 1831.* vol. 35. Copied for the Cape Government, from the Manuscript Documents in the Public Record Office, London, by George McCall Theal, Colonial Historiographer. London: William Clowes and Sons, 1905. 27 p.

   Brief history of slavery at the Cape. Includes information on slave registration, manumission, and amelioration of slavery.

10. Cape of Good Hope. *A Handbook to the Marriage Laws of the Cape Colony, the Bechuanaland Protectorate, and Rhodesia. . . . By D. Ward.* Cape Town: J. C. Juta, 1897.

    Accessible compilation of Cape marriage laws, with an appendix containing statutes and proclamations.

11. Cape of Good Hope. *Instructions for the Field Cornets of the Colony of the Cape of Good Hope, 1838.* Cape Town: Albion Press, 1838.

Detailed information on responsibilities and duties of field cornets. Provides insight into local workings of the judicial system, and laws relating to Khoi, ex-slaves, and other free people of "colour."

12. Cape of Good Hope. *Laws Regulating the Relative Rights and Duties of Masters, Servants, and Apprentices in the Cape Colony. . . .* Annotated with decisions under the different sections. Edited by H. Tennant. Cape Town: J. C. Juta, 1906.

Commentary on all laws dealing with labor relations from 1856 to 1905. Legislation covered include 1856 Masters and Servants Act, Act 22 of 1857 regarding employment of "Native Children."

13. Cape of Good Hope. *Records of the Cape Colony from February 1793.* Compiled by George McCall Theal. Printed for the Government of the Cape Colony. 36 vols. London, 1897–1905.

Chronological compilation of official records of the Cape Colony covering the period prior to emancipation that were available in London.

14. Cape of Good Hope. *Statutes of the Cape of Good Hope, 1652–1895.* vol. 1. 2nd ed. Edited by Hercules Tennant and Edgar Michael Jackson. 3 vols. Cape Town: J. C. Juta, 1895.

Volume 1 covers period from 1652 to 1871. Facilitates access to acts such as the Masters and Servants Act which governed labor relations, and the various marriage acts.

15. Cape of Good Hope. Census Office. *Census of the Colony of the Cape of Good Hope, 1865.* G20-'66. Cape Town: Saul Solomon, 1866. 254 p.

Memorandum provides population figures for years 1823 to 1856 and a description of the methods of data collection used in the census. Tables summarizing figures for 1856 and 1865, according to district, on population, occupation, livestock, cultivation, produce, and wool. The body of the census deals with sex and race, mentally and physically handicapped, age, place of birth, education, school attendance, occupation, livestock, land under cultivation, seed sown, and produce. The information in each of the tables is entered at the level of the field cornetcy, thus permitting analysis at the regional, district, or local level.

16. Cape of Good Hope. Legislative Council. "Report of the Committee Appointed on the 27th April, 1855, to Report upon the Papers, Called for and Laid on the Table, Relative to the Case of the Widow Van Eyk, Gerrit Sampson, Hendrik Rooy, Andries Pretorius, Widow Hendriks, Andries Botha, Jacobus Joseph, and Abram July." *Appendix 1 to Votes and Proceedings of Parliament.* Cape Town. 8 p.

Information provided on freedpeople's access to land and on family relationships. Report of a committee appointed to investigate allegations of injustice made predominantly by inhabitants of the Kat River Settlement, arising from events during the 1851 rebellion in the eastern Cape. Report relies on papers submitted by the individuals concerned. Issues of land dispossession are brought out.

17. Cape of Good Hope. Legislative Council. *Master and Servant.*
Documents on the Working of the Order in Council of the 21st July 1846:
Being, Chiefly, Replies to Certain Questions Issued by the Honble the
Legislative Council, to Resident Magistrates, Justices of the Peace,
Ministers of the Gospel, and Others Throughout the Colony. With a
Summary of the Whole. Cape Town: Saul Solomon, 1849. 304 p.

Provides detailed information on contemporary attitudes to social relations in the postemancipation period by employers and members of the judicial establishment. Field cornets, farmers, and others' written replies to questions posed to magistrates about breaches of the law by servants, employers' perceptions of the law and of their servants, magistrates' jurisdiction, employers' attitudes to the passing of a vagrant law. Detailed answers are given by individual magistrates from virtually every district in the Cape Colony. Justices of the peace, field cornets, ministers of religion, missionaries, residents of Cape Town, farmers, and people attending meetings in Clanwilliam, Colesberg, Malmesbury, and New Hantam answer questions regarding servant "misconduct" not covered by the existing law, alternative means of punishment, a vagrancy law, and give information on the numbers of servants they personally employ. Document includes a summary of the answers, arranged by question.

18. Cape of Good Hope. Legislative Council. *Report of the Law of*
Inheritance Commission for the Western Districts, Appointed by His
Excellency the Governor, In Compliance with an Address of the
Legislative Council. G15-'65. Cape Town: Saul Solomon, 1866. 340 p.

The minutes of evidence provide information on status of wives and children under law, attitudes to marriage, and comparison with contemporary legal systems in the United States, Britain, and Europe. One of few documents regarding marriage practice in the colony. Contains resolution of the legislative council, of the commission, instructions from the government, and the final report and proceedings of the commission. The twenty page report relates the findings regarding investigations into both the law of marriage as well as the law of inheritance and includes interviews with sixteen prominent judges, advocates, attorneys, and businessmen. Also includes written replies of the heads of various divisional councils and municipalities to a memorandum issued by the commission. Bills of 1862 and 1864 relating to amendments of the law of inheritance and an act of 1863 to amend the laws of marriage and inheritance in the Colony of Natal are also included. Document is also in *Votes and Proceedings of Parliament*, appendix 2, 1866.

19. Cape of Good Hope. Parliament. House. "Answer to an Address of the House of Assembly to the Lieutenant-governor, dated 20th July, 1854, for the Report of the Commissioners Appointed for Investigating into the Causes of the Kat River Rebellion." *Votes and Proceedings of Parliament.* 1st sess., no. 2. Cape Town. 4 p.

Report on Kat River Rebellion of 1851. Answers questions relating to the extent and causes of the revolt and tries to ascertain which inhabitants participated and which people have legal claim to be recognized as owners of serfs in the settlement. The future of the settlement is considered and recommendations made, which include giving titles of land to serfholders who remained loyal to the colonial government, and declaring forfeiture of titles by those found guilty of rebellion. Role of missionaries is also evaluated.

20. Cape of Good Hope. Parliament. House. "August Vergele et al. The Petition of Householders, and Occupiers of Land of Gendadendal." *Votes and Proceedings of Parliament.* (1854) 1st sess. Cape Town: Saul Solomon. 1 p.

Petition by mission inhabitants, many of whom are probably freedpeople, against proposed conversion of Genadendal lands into freehold tenure. Provides insight into petitioners' views of mission station life. 448 petitioners.

21. Cape of Good Hope. Parliament. House. "Copy of a Communication from the Superintendent-General of Education, Recommending Aid from the Public Revenue to Evening Schools, for the Instruction of the Adult Coloured Population." *Votes and Proceedings of Parliament.* (1857) Appendix 1. G38-'57. Cape Town: Saul Solomon. 1 p.

Illustrates concern regarding the high illiteracy rates among underclass.

22. Cape of Good Hope. Parliament. House. "David Lakey et al. Petition of Householders and Occupants of Land at the Missionary Institution at Groenekloof." *Votes and Proceedings of Parliament.* (1854) 1st sess. Cape Town: Saul Solomon. 1 p.

Petition signed by 212 members of this Moravian mission station. Petitioners probably include some ex-slaves and their children. Written by "coloured" small farmers and householders in response to a proposed division of mission-held land into freehold allotments. Gives insight into their hopes for their children and of their relations with local farmers.

23. Cape of Good Hope. Parliament. House. Select Committee on Granting Land in Freehold to Hottentots. "Report from the Select Committee on Granting Land in Freehold to Hottentots." *Votes and Proceedings of Parliament.* (1854) 1st sess., S.C. 11. Cape Town: Saul Solomon. 51 p.

Minutes provide information on land tenure on the mission stations, the history of the stations as a means of giving Khoi and later emancipated slaves access to land, and the differences in character of these stations. The testimony also illuminates the tension between farmers and inhabitants of the missions. This document is not the actual select committee report but rather minutes of evidence soliciting views of six whites regarding a proposal that land be granted in freehold to the inhabitants of various mission stations run by the United Brethren (Moravian) and the London Missionary Society in the Cape Colony. The interviewees are farmers, missionaries, and traders living near the mission stations of Genadendal, Zuurbraak, Groenekloof, Pacaltsdorp, and Hankey. The document includes the regulations of the Genadendal mission station as well as detailed letters from some of the witnesses.

24. Cape of Good Hope. Parliament. House. Select Committee to Consider and Report on the Master and Servants Ordinance. "Report of a Select Committee, appointed on the 18th July, 1854, to Consider and Report on the Expediency of Repealing or Altering the Master and Servants Ordinance; Consisting of Messrs. J. C. Molteno, Dr. A. J. Trancred, H. H. Loedolff, J. Collett, C. Pote, and J. H. Brand." *Votes and Proceedings of Parliament.* (1854) 1st sess. Cape Town. 2 p.

Provides details on immediate postemancipation context in which the original Masters and Servants Law was framed. The committee members are important farmers and politicians. They recommend changes in existing legislation regarding contracts, punishment, and magisterial jurisdiction, and advocate harsh penalties and stricter control over labor force.

25. Cape of Good Hope. Parliament. House. "The Petition of the Undersigned, Inhabitants of the Town and Division of Worcester." *Annexures to the Votes and Proceedings of the House of Assembly.* (1860) A67-'60. 2 p.

White farmers and townspeople protest the introduction of immigrants exclusively from Britain. Provides details of postemancipation labor relations.

26. Cape of Good Hope. Parliament. House. "Documents in Connection with the Appointment of Missionary of Late Apprentices and Heathen; Also, Correspondence Between the Colonial Government and Minister Consulent of St. Stephen's Church, Cape Town." *Annexures to the Votes and Proceedings of the House of Assembly.* (1859) Vol. 1., A53-'59. 9 p.

Includes memorial from congregation regarding religious education of underclass in Cape Town. Information relating to church schools and missionary activities run by the St. Stephen's congregation.

27. Cape of Good Hope. Parliament. House. "Memorial of J. H. Vanreenen." *Annexures to the Votes and Proceedings of the House of Assembly.* A39-'61. Printed for the House of Assembly by order of Mr. Speaker, 29th May 1861. 2 p.

Memorial of a Dutch-speaking farmer who advocates introduction of Indian laborers to the Cape Colony. Also expresses views on African and white labor.

28. Cape of Good Hope. Parliament. House. "W. C. Botha et al. Petition from Certain Inhabitants of the Field Cornetcy of Fish River, District of Somerset." *Appendix 1 to Votes and Proceedings of Parliament.* vol.2 A26-'59. Cape Town: Saul Solomon, 1859. 2 p.

Petition refers to perceived ineffectuality of Masters and Servants Act in giving employers control over servants.

29. Cape of Good Hope. Parliament. House. *Duties of Field Cornets. Selections From the Ordinances and Acts of Parliament of this Colony Relating to the Duties of Field-Cornets, with a Table of Contents and Index.* Published by Authority. Cape Town: Saul Solomon, 1877. 50 p.

Short and accessible compilation of legislation with regard to local judicial officers. Includes ordinances and acts on crime prevention, the registration of wills, and adjustment of land boundaries and thus gives insight on legal landscape into which slaves were freed.

30. Cape of Good Hope. Parliament. Governor. *General Report of a Commission Appointed by His Excellency the Governor to Inquire into the Claims for Compensation for the Loss of Erven in the Kat River Settlement.* G18.'59. Cape Town: Saul Solomon, 1859. 74 p.

Five-page report by civil commissioners of Graaff Reinet, Cradock, and Alexandria, on investigation held on 1 May 1858 into 134 claims for compensation for land lost during the rebellion of 1850. Twenty schedules attached. Brief history of the Kat River Settlement is included.

31. Cape of Good Hope. Parliament. *Government Publications Relating to the Cape of Good Hope.* Group 2. Statistical Registers 1838–1910. Edited by Shula Marks and Anthony Atmore. African Studies Association of the United Kingdom. East Ardsley, England: EP Microform Limited, 1981. Microform.

 Collection of the annual Blue Books of the Cape Colony. From 1886 called the Statistical Register. Gives breakdown of revenue, educational, military, religious and public expenditure, as well as detailed information on population, imports and exports, agricultural production, wages, prices, manufacturing, land grants, and prisons. Gives district, and often, more local breakdown. Some of the tables are accompanied by a note explaining local practices such as monthly or daily wage payment. Categories of annual entries vary slightly. Later years include summary and report.

32. Cape of Good Hope. Parliament. House. Select Committee on Granting Lands in Freehold to Hottentots. *Minutes of Evidence Taken Before the Select Committee of the House of Assembly on Granting Lands in Freehold to Hottentots.* Printed for the House of Assembly by order of Mr. Speaker, 29th May, 1861. S.C. 13. Cape Town: Saul Solomon, 1856. 67 p.

33. Cape of Good Hope. Parliament. Governor. *Report of an Inquiry as to the Claims of Certain Natives Residing at the Missionary Institutions of Amandelboom and Schietfontein, in the Division of Beaufort, to the Lands on Which They are Located.* G7-'59. Cape Town: Saul Solomon, 1859. 31 p.

 Investigation by the surveyor-general of conflicting land claims between freedpeople, Africans, and white farmers. The first twelve pages concern Amandelboom. Information is given on livestock ownership, available water, and land tenure. Annexure A contains interviews with freed people regarding life on the station and religious affiliations. Also includes interviews with field cornets and white farmers. The second part of report deals with Schietfontein and Africans' land claims. Annexure D is a list of "bastards" from Schietfontein which refers obliquely to former slave status.

34. Cape of Good Hope. Parliament. House. Select Committee on Masters and Servants Act. *Report of the Select Committee on the Masters and Servants Act.* Cape Town: Saul Solomon, 1872. 24 p.

35. Cape of Good Hope. Parliament. House. *Report of the Select Committee Appointed to Consider Mr. T. H. Bowker's Memorial.* Cape Town: Saul Solomon, 1858. 32 p.

Report of a committee formed to investigate complaints of a wealthy farmer, an ex-magistrate of the Kat River Settlement. Bowker asks for adequate reimbursement for services during 1851 war. Witnesses give information on events at Whittlesea, behavior of members of Shiloh mission station, extent of Bowker's land ownership at Kat River, and his residency as magistrate.

36. Cape of Good Hope. Parliament. House. Select Committee On the Missionary Institutions Bill. *Report of the Select Committee appointed to Consider and Report on the Missionary Institutions Bill.* A4-'72. Cape Town: Saul Solomon, 1872. 87 p.

Relates to form of land tenure at mission stations. Includes the report, proceedings, and minutes of evidence of the committee. Interviews with Rev. T. D. Philip and Rev. W. Thompson of the London Missionary Society, and with T. D. Barry and H. W. Pearson, Members of the Legislative Assembly. The missionaries also give their opinions regarding law enforcement on stations and convey the attitudes of mission inhabitants to the bill which proposes the granting of freehold tenure to mission stations. Report includes a copy of the minutes of meetings held by the Commission of the London Missionary Society with the people of Bethelsdorp mission station and list of inhabitants of Zuurbraak Mission Station, minutes of a meeting of mission inhabitants and missionaries at Pacaltsdorp, 23 November 1868, and a letter from the Civil Commissioner Uitenhage to Colonial Secretary, 19 November 1868. Report is also found in *Reports of Select Committees,* 1872.

37. Cape of Good Hope. Parliament. House. *Report of the Superintendent-General of Education For the Year 1866.* G16-'67. Cape Town: Saul Solomon, 1867. 128 p.

Details of the mission schools gives information on people who are probably children of freedpeople. Four-page report summarizes findings contained in accompanying eight tables. All relate to state-funded, private, mission, and industrial schools. Very detailed information on subjects taught, numbers of scholars, and expenditures of individual schools throughout the colony. Includes reports of visits of inspection to sixty-eight schools.

38. Cape of Good Hope. Parliament. House. *Report on Public Education.* Cape Town: Saul Solomon, 1854. 35 p.

Education of freedpeople and other members of the underclass is covered in the report which gives a brief history of public education in the Cape including notes on first class schools, government schools at minor stations like Fort Beaufort, and elementary schools taught by church clerks. Information on attendance, curriculum, language of instruction, standard of teaching, and demand for education as well as information on mission and elementary schools receiving government aid and on those schools connected to public education but not receiving government aid. Excerpts from examination papers for senior pupils are included. This document also appears in the *Votes and Proceedings of Parliament*, 1st sess., 1854.

39. Cape of Good Hope. Parliament. House. *Return of Punishments by Flogging Inflicted at Caledon since the 1st February, 1867.* A18-'67. Cape Town. 3 p.

Table gives names of prisoners flogged in the months April and July 1867. Also states offence, number of lashes and whether under sentence by the circuit or magistrate's court. A warrant of arrest of a convict on a charge of perjury is also included.

40. *The Christian Herald; or, Record of the Progress of Religion and Education in South Africa* 1 (June–November 1838)

A bound volume of a missionary monthly journal published in Cape Town. Topics covered include spread of Islam among urban underclass, discrete roles of mother and father, schooling of freedpeople, and missionary activities in England and South Sea Islands.

41. Fawcett, John. *Account of an Eighteen Months' Residence at the Cape of Good Hope, in 1835–6.* Cape Town: G. J. Pike, 1836.

Brief notes of visits to small villages and mission stations in the western and eastern Cape. Comments on education and religion of mission inhabitants, who probably include freedpeople and Khoi. Section on Cape Town.

42. Great Britain. Parliament. House of Commons. "Applications from the Colonists of the Cape of Good Hope made to the Colonial Office for Representative Government, together with Copies of the Answers Thereto." *Parliamentary Papers.* 1846 (400), vol. 29. 7 p.

Correspondence between the Cape governor and the Colonial Office enclosing resolutions taken by whites in Cape Town asking for representative government. See enclosure number three from Lord Stanley to Governor George Napier, which discusses the relations between

Dutch and English-speaking settlers and the issue of voting rights for Africans and freedpeople.

43. Great Britain. Parliament. House of Commons. "Correspondence Relative to the Establishment of a Representative Assembly at the Cape of Good Hope." *Parliamentary Papers.* 1850 (1137), vol. 38. 108 p.

Includes discussions of Cape franchise and arguments as to implications of having property qualifications which would include the "coloured population." Correspondence provides insight into links between race and class as well as settler attitudes to colonial rule. Attitudes of underclass themselves are not included. Correspondence included between Cape governor, chief justice, attorney general and others. Also dispatches from Earl Grey, the secretary of state, and return showing the population of rural and urban districts and suggested electoral districts as well as details of revenue collected in 1846 and 1847.

44. Great Britain. Parliament. House of Commons. "Correspondence with the Governor of the Cape of Good Hope Relative to the State of the Kafir Tribes, and to the Recent Outbreak on the Eastern Frontier of the Colony." *Parliamentary Papers.* In continuation of Papers presented to Parliament 20 March, 2 May, and June 1851. 1852 (1428), vol. 33. 259 p.

Papers relating to 1851 frontier war. Specific references to revolt at Kat River Settlement and to rumors of revolt amongst rural underclass in the western Cape. Dispatch no. 27, from Governor Harry Smith, encloses report by Mr. Owen on the revolt and the mission stations in Swellendam and Caledon.

45. Great Britain. Parliament. House of Commons. "Correspondence with Governor of the Cape of Good Hope Relative to the State of the Kafir Tribes, and to the Recent Outbreak on the Eastern Frontier." *Parliamentary Papers.* In continuation of Papers presented 14 August 1850. 1851 (1334), vol. 38. 141 p.

Dispatches from colonial officials to the Colonial Office, London, and to government officials within colony. Enclosures include letters from civil commissioners to the secretary to the (Cape) government and testimony by local colonial officials, headmen of African locations and others. Concerns 1851 revolt by ex-slaves and Africans at Kat River Settlement and on borders of Xhosaland. Ex-slaves also served in colonial army sent to quell revolt. Details of tension in Xhosa society, role of the prophet Umlanjeni and actions of Fieldcornet Botha, a leader of resistance at Kat

River. Dispatches of 11 and 31 January c. 1851 from Sir Harry Smith discuss among other topics, the defection of the Cape Corps ('coloured' section of the army) and call-up of men from Moravian Mission stations. Insight also into how families of soldiers provided for in men's absence.

46. Great Britain. Parliament. House of Commons. "Further Papers Relative to the Establishment of a Representative Assembly at the Cape of Good Hope." *Parliamentary Papers.* In continuation of Papers presented to Parliament by Her Majesty's Command, 5 February and 28 June 1850; 19 May 1851; and 3 February and 23 December 1852. 1852–53 (1581), vol. 66. 31 p.

Dispatches from Governor Cathcart and Lieutenant Governor Darling regarding new Cape constitution. Dispatch no. 1, of 15 November 1852 from Governor Cathcart discusses "who are meant by 'Coloured People.'" See also dispatch no. 2 which includes discussion of tranquility of western districts.

47. Great Britain. Parliament. House of Commons. "Further Papers Relative to the Establishment of a Representative Assembly at the Cape of Good Hope." *Parliamentary Papers.* In continuation of Papers presented to Parliament by Her Majesty's Command, 5 February and 28 June 1850; 19 May 1851; and 3 February 1852. 1852–53 (1636), vol. 66. 327 p.

Includes report on withdrawal of squatters ordinance: dispatch no. 4, 12 February 1852. This dispatch contains extensive enclosures such as the minutes of the Legislative Council regarding the squatting ordinance, and memorials of farmers, opinions of ministers of religion, civil commissioners, senior government officials regarding the 1851 unrest in the western Cape. Enclosures to dispatch no. 5 includes discussion of franchise and squatters ordinance in light of revolt.

48. Great Britain. Parliament. House of Commons. "Further Papers Relative to the Establishment of Representative Assembly at the Cape of Good Hope." *Parliamentary Papers.* 1851 (1362), vol. 37. 205 p.

Disparate but important information on attempts to exclude Africans from the franchise, on ongoing resistance at the Kat River settlement, on patterns of landholding there, and on tensions between white farmers and people in the settlement. Direct reference is made to Dutch farmers' sentiments regarding emancipation. Enclosure 5 in no. 8, and enclosures 18 and 20 in no. 12 are particularly pertinent.

49. Great Britain. Parliament. House of Commons. "Further Papers Relative to the Establishment of a Representative Assembly at Cape of Good Hope." *Parliamentary Papers.* 1852 (1427), vol. 33. 106 p.

Includes discussions in Legislative Council, draft ordinance, and memorials regarding the passing of a Squatting Act. Also report of commissioners investigating resistance in western Cape to the proposed act.

50. Great Britain. Parliament. House of Commons. "Report from Governor of Cape of Good Hope . . . relative to the Condition and Treatment of the Children Sent Out by the Children's Friend Society." *Parliamentary Papers.* 1840 (323), vol. 33. 35 p.

Detailed information on number, names and positions of children brought to Cape from Britain under auspices of the Society. Consists of letters between the governor and the colonial secretary and report by the resident magistrate of Cape Town on child labor in western districts, giving information on education, religious instructions, working conditions, and so on in 1839. Additional reports by resident magistrates of Paarl, Caledon, and Malmesbury give personal particulars of each child apprentice living in their districts.

51. Great Britain. Parliament. House of Commons. "Reports of Commissioners of Inquiry into the Condition of the Hottentots . . . and other Native Tribes of South Africa. . . ." *Parliamentary Papers.* 1830 (584), vol. 21. 24 p.

Discussion of labor conditions, wages, illegal adjustment of contracts by fiscals and landdrosts and of workings of Caledon Code of 1809 and later laws pertaining to the Khoi. Role of mission stations is also considered.

52. Great Britain. Parliament. House of Commons. "Return of the White and Coloured Population of the Colony of the Cape of Good Hope, in the Several Districts of the Eastern and Western Divisions, and also of British Kaffraria, According to the Latest Returns Received at the Colonial Office." *Parliamentary Papers.* 1852 (124), vol. 33. 1 p.

Census of May 1849 according to district.

53. Irons, W. *The Settler's Guide to the Cape of Good Hope and Colony of Natal; Compiled from Original and Authentic Materials, Collected by W. Irons, Secretary of the Cape Town Mechanics' Institution. With Some Additional Notices of Those Colonies, and Remarks on the Advantages They Offer to Emigrants.* London: Edward Stanford, 1858.

Discusses rural labor in the context of discussion of agricultural prospects.

54. Krauss, Ferdinand. "A Description of Cape Town and Its Way of Life, 1838–1840." *Quarterly Bulletin of the South African Library* 21 (September 1966): 2–12; (December 1966): 39–50.

Extracts from contemporary travel journal of a German naturalist. The first article describes the layout and architecture of Cape Town, activities at popular market places, and flora and fauna. The second concentrates on the social life of settlers, freedpeople, and Africans.

55. *The Missionary Magazine and Chronicle, Relating Chiefly to the Missions of the London Missionary Society*. London: The Directors of the London Missionary Society, 1836–1866.

Monthly magazine bound in annual set. News from LMS stations across the world. South African focus tends to be on indigenous Africans, not specifically on slaves and freedpeople, but position of the Khoikhoi is considered. South Africa is covered in almost every issue. March 1837 has short article on infant school at Pacaltsdorp. September 1838 contains drawing entitled "The Dying Hottentot Boy" and an account by Pacaltsdorp missionary Anderson. Also minutes of a general meeting of the LMS in England containing statements by Dr. John Philip and African and Khoikhoi leaders on the state of the LMS missions in South Africa. October issue has article on participation of Khoi in commandos in the eastern Cape. Reverend Read describes his arrival at the Kat River Settlement in the December 1838 edition.

56. Philip, John. *Researches in South Africa; Illustrating the Civil, Moral, and Religious Condition of the Native Tribes. . . .* 2 vols. London: James Duncan, 1828.

Gives background to slavery and emancipation, as seen by Superintendent of the London Missionary Society at the Cape, to bring attention to the plight of the Khoi. Volume one deals with Caledon Code of 1809, description of various mission stations. Volume two concentrates on journeys to Griquatown, Bechuanaland, and Namaqualand.

57. Porter, William. *The Porter Speeches*. Speeches Delivered by the Hon. William Porter, During the Years 1839–1845 Inclusive. Cape Town: Trustees Estate Saul Solomon, 1886. 540 p.

A collection of Porter's statements in his first term as attorney-general of the Cape. Topics include colonial labor and immigration as well as concealment of birth by rural women on Moravian mission stations.

58. *The South African Commercial Advertiser*. Cape Town (1824–1869).

News from overseas, articles on education, labor, religion, the law. Coverage of meetings held, memorials sent to the Governor. Reflects opinions of humanitarian lobby at the Cape. Issues in 1837 and 1838 contain articles on slavery in America as well as settler views on coming emancipation in Cape. In general reports on activities of settlers rather than slaves, their descendants, or the African underclass. Does give insights into dominant class perceptions of labor and social relations. Until September 1842 columns repeated in both English and Dutch. Frequent name changes. The Cooperative Africana Microfilm Project (CAMP) at the Center for Research Libraries in Chicago, has microfilm copies of volumes 1 to 38. *The South African Commercial Advertiser* from January 1824 to June 1859: MF 1224, reels 1 to 15; *The South African Commerical Advertiser and Cape Town Mail* July 1853 to July 1860: MF 1224, reels 15 to 19. NUC (Pre-1956 imprints) entry is "*South African Advertiser and Mail.* v. 38–47; Aug. 1, 1860–Sept. 29, 1869. Cape Town 10v. Microfilm ed., positive copy. Frequency varies. Continues as South African Commercial Advertiser. Absorbed by Cape Standard and Mail."

59. Wesleyan-Methodist Missionary Society. *The Report of the Wesleyan-Methodist Missionary Society.* 1830–1860. Annual. London.

Reports of missionary activity around the globe including Southern Africa. Reports for the years 1835 has specific references to apprentices' responses to coming emancipation. Generally good information on freed people's religious activity in Cape Town and in rural western Cape.

SECONDARY SOURCES

---

60. Adhikari, Mohamed. "The Sons of Ham: Slavery and the Making of Coloured Identity." *South African Historical Journal* 27 (1992): 95–112.

Discusses how the heterogeneous Cape slave population was assimilated into a laboring class version of Dutch colonial culture that formed the basis of the category of "coloured" in postemancipation South Africa.

61. Appel, A. "Occupation and ownership of land in Bethelsdorp, 1828–1945." *Contree* 23 (1988): 23–28.

In Afrikaans. Information on landholding policies on LMS Missions in postemancipation era. Discusses lack of clear policies regarding landholding at Bethalsdorp throughout much of the nineteenth century.

62. Atkins, Keletso. *The Moon is Dead! Give Us Our Money! The Cultural Origins of an African Work Ethic, Natal, South Africa, 1843–1900.* Portsmouth, N.H.: Heinemann, 1993. 325 p.

Examines the adaptation of an African work culture to the extension of wage labor in colonial Natal. Explores how indigenous concepts of labor conflicted with those of European colonists.

63. Beinart, William, Peter Delius, and Stanley Trapido, eds. *Putting a Plough to the Ground: Accumulation and Dispossession in Rural South Africa, 1850–1930.* Johannesburg: Ravan Press, 1986. 458 p.

    The first two chapters pertain to the postemancipation era in the Cape: Robert Ross, "The Origins of Capitalist Agriculture in the Cape Colony: A Survey"; Colin Bundy, "Vagabond Hollanders and Runaway Englishmen: White Poverty in the Cape Before Poor Whiteism."

64. Bickford-Smith, Vivian. "The Origins and Early History of District Six to 1910." *The Struggle for District Six: Past and Present*, edited by Shamil Jeppie and Crain Soudien. Cape Town: Bucho Books, 1990.

    Describes the urban history of one of the multiethnic inner-city suburbs of Cape Town from the immediate postemancipation period until the early twentieth century.

65. Bickford-Smith, Vivian. "Slavery, Emancipation and the Question of Coloured Identity." *Collected Seminar Papers on the Societies of Southern Africa in the 19th and 20th Centuries, vol. 19. Collected Seminar Papers.* Vol. 45. London: University of London, Institute of Commonwealth Studies, 1993: 17–25.

66. Boas, Jack. "The Activities of the London Missionary Society in South Africa, 1806–1836. An Assessment." *African Studies Review* 16 (1973): 417–35.

    Examines the role of the London Missionary Society in the antislavery movement in South Africa alongside the extension of missionary activity in the Cape.

67. Bradlow, Edna. "Emancipation and Race Perceptions at the Cape." *South African Historical Journal* 15 (November 1983): 10–33.

    Focuses on Cape Town although it draws information from rural areas.

68. Bradlow, Edna. "The Children's Friend Society at the Cape of Good Hope." *Victorian Studies* 27 (1984): 155–78.

    Discussion a scheme to redress shortage of cheap wage labor in the postemancipation Cape.

69. Bundy, Colin. "The Abolition of the Masters and Servants Act." *South African Labour Bulletin* 2 (May–June 1975): 37–46.

Written the year after the Masters and Servants Act was finally abolished, the article situates the Cape Masters and Servants Act of 1856 in the immediate postemancipation context at the Cape and in the context of earlier legislation in Britain.

70. Cornell, Carohn. "Whatever became of Slavery in Western Cape Museums?" *Kronos* 25 (1988/9): 259–79.

Examines a glaring gap in current western Cape museums. Discusses the reasons for this absence and how it might be remedied.

71. Cory, G. E. *The Rise of South Africa.* 6 vols. 1910–1940. Reprint. Cape Town: Struik, 1965.

Volumes 2 through 6 cover the period from 1820 to 1856. Cory concentrates on relations between settlers and Africans particularly in the eastern Cape, as well as on the policy and practice of the colonial government. Volume 3 covers the period of apprenticeship from 1834 to 1838. Volume 4 also deals with the Transvaal, Orange Free State, and Natal. The work is based on manuscript material in the Cory Library for Historical Research in Grahamstown and consists largely of interviews held in the first two decades of the twentieth century with descendants of Xhosa chiefs and 1820 settlers. Volumes 1 through 3 contain maps of the colony in 1820 and a detailed plan of part of Albany district in 1822 and of Albany, Victoria, Somerset, and the Province of Queen Adelaide in 1851.

72. Crais, Clifton C. "Slavery and Freedom Along a Frontier: The Eastern Cape, South Africa, 1770–1838." *Slavery and Abolition* 11 (September 1990): 190–215.

Discusses the blurring of boundaries between slaves and dependent laborers.

73. Crais, Clifton C. "Gentry and Labour in Three Eastern Cape Districts, 1820–1865." *South African Historical Journal* 18 (November 1986): 125–46.

Districts are Albany, Somerset East, and Fort Beaufort. Also deals with the Kat River Settlement.

74. Crais, Clifton C. *White Supremacy and Black Resistance in Pre-Industrial South Africa. The Making of the Colonial Order in the Eastern Cape, 1770–1865.* African Studies Series, 72. Cambridge: Cambridge University Press, 1991.

Study of slavery, emancipation and the making of a colonial order in the eastern Cape region of the Cape Colony. Chapters cover relations between slaves and dependent laborers, the settlement of and struggles of freedpeople in the Kat River Settlement as well as Dutch and British attitudes to laborers, and the rule of law.

75. Cuthbertson, G. C. "The Impact of the Emancipation of Slaves on St. Andrew's Scottish Church, Cape Town, 1838–1878." *Studies in the History of Cape Town.* Edited by Christopher Saunders and Howard Phillips. 3 (1980): 49–63.

Discusses the Christian missions in Cape Town in the immediate post-emancipation era. Includes a brief demographic description of the free black congregation.

76. Davids, Achmat. "My Religion is Superior to the Law: The Survival of Islam at the Cape of Good Hope." In *Pages from Cape Muslim History*, edited by Yusuf da Costa and Achmat Davids. Pietermaritzburg: Shuter and Shooter, 1994.

Overview of history of Islam at the Cape to the end of the nineteenth century.

77. Delius, Peter, and Stanley Trapido. "Inboekselings and Oorlams: The Creation and Transformation of a Servile Class." *Journal of Southern African Studies* 8 (April 1982): 214–42.

Area of focus is the South African Republic. Analysis of two categories of unfree labor—white servants, formally or informally apprenticed, and Africans performing skilled labor for white settlers. Includes discussion of Khoi's subordinate slave-like status during the slaveholding era in the Cape.

78. Dooling, Wayne. "Agrarian Transformations in the Western Districts of the Cape Colony, 1838–1900." Ph.D. diss., Cambridge University, 1997.

79. Dooling, Wayne. "Cape Settler Society at the Time of Slave Emancipation." *Kleio* 29 (1997): 19–57.

80. Duly, Leslie Clement. *British Land Policy at the Cape, 1795–1844: A Study of Administrative Procedures in the Empire.* Durham, N.C.: Duke University Press, 1968. 226 p.

Provides information on various systems of land tenure at the Cape, such as freehold and quitrent.

81. Du Plessis, J. *A History of Christian Missions in South Africa.* 1911. Reprint. Cape Town: C. Struik, 1965. 494 p.

Rare information on Rhenish missionary activity in western Cape. Terminology and attitudes expressed towards Africans by the author is representative of much white South African thinking at beginning of twentieth century.

82. Du Toit, André, and Hermann Giliomee. *Afrikaner Political Thought: Analysis and Documents*. Vol. One: 1780–1850. Cape Town: David Philip, 1983. 309 p.

    General analysis in broad historical context of slavery, concepts of law and order, frontier debates, the trek, and issues pertaining to self-government.

83. Edwards, Isobel Eirlys. *Towards Emancipation: A Study in South African Slavery*. Cardiff: University of Wales, 1942.

    Concentrates on abolition movement, focusing on the role of the British humanitarians, changes in British imperial policy, and the process of emancipation in the Cape Colony. Includes discussion of emancipation in relation to the West Indies.

84. Elbourne, Elizabeth. "Freedom at Issue: Vagrancy Legislation and the Meaning of Freedom in Britain and the Cape Colony, 1799–1842." *Slavery and Abolition* 15 (1994): 114–50.

    Discusses how the Cape Khoi feared emancipation of slaves would result in their own enslavement through the imposition of proposed vagrancy legislation. Examines speeches made by Khoisan leaders in opposition to vagrancy laws to reveal leaders' interpretations of freedom.

85. Elbourne, Elizabeth, and Robert Ross. "Combating Spiritual and Social Bondage: Early Missions in the Cape Colony." In *Christianity in South Africa: A Political, Social and Cultural History*, edited by Richard Elphick and Rodney Davenport. Oxford: James Currey, 1997.

    Assesses the role of missionary societies, mission communities and conversion to Christianity from slavery through emancipation.

86. Eldredge, Elizabeth A., and Fred Morton, eds. *Slavery in South Africa: Captive Labor on the Dutch Frontier*. Boulder: Westview Press, 1994. 311 p.

    Analyzes slavery on the Dutch frontier of South Africa arguing that slavery persisted beyond formal abolition. Mason covers the process of emancipation in the eastern Cape where freed slaves often remained tied to their ex-masters. Eldredge examines indigenous and Boer slave raiding on the northern Cape frontier and at Delagoa Bay. F. Morton details slave raiding by Boer and African groups in the SAR. Boeyens describes the trade in captive children in the SAR. B. Morton examines the continuation of slavery in the Boer Republics and coerced labor among the BaTswana.

87. Elks, Katherine D. "Crime, Community and Police in Cape Town, 1825–1850." M.A. thesis, University of Cape Town, 1986.

Sources used include records of the Colonial Office, the magistrate of Cape Town, and the Supreme Court. Analysis of social and economic context of crime and law enforcement in Cape Town, from the perspective of a social control argument.

88. Elphick, Richard, and Hermann Giliomee, eds. *The Shaping of South African Society, 1652–1840.* 2d ed. Cape Town: Maskew Miller Longman, 1989. 623 p.

Chapter 3, "The Slaves, 1652–1834," by Nigel Worden and James C. Armstrong, and chapter 8, "The Northern Frontier to c. 1840: The rise and decline of the Griqua People," discuss Cape Slavery.

89. Fredrickson, George M. *White Supremacy: A Comparative Study in American and South African History.* New York: Oxford University Press, 1981. 356 p.

Chapters 2 to 4 are relevant to postemancipation at the Cape. Based mainly on secondary sources.

90. Gordon-Brown, Alfred. *Christopher Webb Smith: An Artist at the Cape of Good Hope, 1837–1839.* Cape Town: Howard Timmins, 1965. 92 p.

Some illustrations of underclass life in Cape Town and Stellenbosch.

91. Harries, Patrick. "Slavery, Social Incorporation and Surplus Extraction; The Nature of Free and Unfree Labour in South-East Africa." *Journal of African History* 22 (1981): 309–30.

Assesses the involvement of the northern Nguni in the slave trade. Considers how the British suppression of slavery shifted the trade towards the Transvaal Boers and domestic slavery particularly among the Gaza of Mozambique.

92. Hengherr, E. "Emancipation and After: A Study of Cape Slavery and the Issues Arising From It, 1830–1843." M.A. thesis, University of Cape Town, 1953.

Deals with apprenticeship, compensation, experience of freed people and immediate concerns of former master class regarding access to labor. Discussion of immigration schemes and representative government.

93. Hunt, Keith S. *Sir Lowry Cole, Governor of Mauritius 1823–1828, Governor of the Cape of Good Hope 1828–1833: A Study in Colonial Administration.* Durban: Butterworths, 1974. 191 p.

Chapter seven covers slave amelioration measures at the Cape from 1823.

94. James, Wilmot G., and Mary Simons, eds. *Class, Caste and Color: A Social and Economic History of the South African Western Cape.* New Brunswick, N.J.: Transaction Publishers, 1992. 258 p.

Re-edition of *The Angry Divide: Social and Economic History of the Western Cape.*

95. James, Wilmot G., and Mary Simons, eds. *The Angry Divide: Social and Economic History of the Western Cape.* Cape Town: David Philip; in association with the Centre for African Studies, University of Cape Town, 1989. 258 p.

Revised papers of a 1986 conference at University of Cape Town treat topics including rural labor in the nineteenth century and urban segregation in the nineteenth and twentieth centuries.

96. Judges, Shirley. "Poverty, Living Conditions and Social Relations: Aspects of Life in Cape Town in the 1830s." M.A. thesis, University of Cape Town, July 1977.

An analysis of poverty and experience of the poor, focusing on housing, social deviance, and drunkenness. Last chapter considers the effects of emancipation on race relations. Uses archival sources and contemporary newspapers, almanacs, and travelers' accounts. Appendices provide estimated living costs and wages, the population of Cape Town in the 1830s, and a map showing racial breakdown of housing.

97. Kirk, Tony. "Progress and Decline in the Kat River Settlement, 1829–1854." *Journal of African History* 14 (1973): 411–28.

Discusses how the relocation of freed colored slaves and ex-mission station residents on the Kat River Settlement helped precipitate an economic crisis leading to rebellion and the dismantling of the community.

98. Krüger, Bernhard. *The Pear Tree Blossoms: A History of the Moravian Mission Stations in South Africa, 1834–1869.* Genadendal, 1966. 335 p.

Detailed narrative of period. Information on customs and lives of freed people on the stations. Uses archival sources located in Moravian Archives, Heideveld, South Africa.

99. Ludlow, Helen. "Groenekloof after the Emancipation of Slaves, 1838–1852: Leavers, Soldiers, and Rebels." In *Missions and Christianity in South African History,* edited by Henry Bredekamp and Robert Ross. Johannesburg: Witwatersrand University Press, 1995.

Examines how mission stations enabled ex-slaves to reconstitute their families after emancipation.

100. Ludlow, Helen. "Missions and Emancipation in the South Western Cape: A Case Study of Groenekloof (Mamre), 1838–1852." M.A. thesis, University of Cape Town, 1992.

Detailed examination of the arrival of ex-slaves at Mamre and their attempts to construct freedom through the reconstitution of family. Examines how ex-slave residents in Mamre selectively entered the wage-labor force in the postemancipation era.

101. Macmillan, W. M. *The Cape Colour Question: A Historical Survey.* 1927. Reprint. New York: Humanities Press, 1969. 304 p.

Based on the papers of John Philip, defender of Khoikhoi rights and leader of London Missionary Society in first half of nineteenth century. Papers were destroyed in fire subsequent to the publication of the book. Chapters on slavery, emancipation, and status of the Khoi.

102. Malherbe, V. C. "Indentured and Unfree Labour in South Africa: Towards an Understanding." *South African Historical Journal* 24 (1991): 3–30.

Attempt to distinguish indentureship/contract labor from serfdom, debt peonage, apprenticeship, and, briefly, wage labor. Looks at emigrant indentures including Moodie's scheme and the Children's Friend Society and at inboekelinge—Khoi children.

103. Marais, J. S. *The Cape Coloured People, 1652–1937.* London: Longmans, 1939. 296 p.

Concentrates primarily on emancipation and its effects on freed slaves and people of "mixed" descent.

104. Marincowitz, John Nicholas Carel. "Rural Production and Labour in the Western Cape, 1838 to 1888, with Special Reference to the Wheat Growing Districts." Ph.D. diss., University of London, 1985.

In addition to looking at agricultural production and labor relations the work also examines the privatization of mission stations in the postemancdescription era and their increasing importance as labor reserves, the beginnings of Afrikaner political mobilization, and the growing diversification of the Western Cape economy in the late nineteenth century.

105. Marks, Shula, and Anthony Atmore, eds. *Economy and Society in Pre-Industrial South Africa.* Harlow, Eng.: Longmans, 1980. 385 p.

Relevant chapters cover Cape liberalism, the frontier, labor markets, and land expropriation.

106. Mason, John Edwin. "'Fit for Freedom': The Slaves, Slavery, and Emancipation in the Cape Colony, South Africa, 1806–1842." Ph.D. diss., Yale University, 1992. 606 p.

Traces the transformation of slavery in the Cape from the end of the slave trade through the period of amelioration, emancipation, and slave apprenticeship that preceded full freedom. Thesis ends with an examination of the immediate postemancipation period. Discusses how slaves and masters struggled throughout the nineteenth century to construct labor and household relationships that best suited their own interests.

107. Miers, Suzanne, and Michael Crowder. "The Politics of Slavery in Bechuanaland: Power Struggles and the Plight of the Baswara in the Bamangwato Reserve, 1926–1940." In *The End of Slavery in Africa*, edited by Suzanne Miers and Richard Roberts, 172–194. Madison: University of Wisconsin Press, 1988.

108. Raum, Johannes William. "The Development of the Coloured Community at Genadendal under the Influence of the Missionaries of the Unitas Fratum, 1792–1892." M.A. thesis, University of Cape Town, 1952.

Detailed history based on mission station archives, much of it originally in German.

109. Rayner, Mary Isabel. "Wine and Slaves: The Failure of an Export Economy and the Ending of Slavery in the Cape Colony, South Africa, 1806–1834." Ph.D. diss., Duke University, 1986.

Analyzes the contradictory policies of the British government that contributed to economic and social tensions and to the boom/slump economy of the wine producing districts in the early nineteenth century. Discussion of slave amelioration leading to emancipation.

110. Ross, Andrew. *John Philip (1775–1851): Missions, Race and Politics in South Africa*. Aberdeen: Aberdeen University Press, 1986. 249 p.

111. Ross, Robert. "The Social and Political Theology of Western Cape Missions, c. 1800–c. 1860." In *Missions and Christianity in South African History*, edited by Henry Bredekamp and Robert Ross. Johannesburg: Witwatersrand University Press, 1995.

Examines aspects of quiescence and opposition to slavery by missionaries. Discusses how conversion to Christianity by ex-slaves was both a form of spiritual freedom and a way to gain access to mission station residence.

112. Ross, Robert. *Adam Kok's Griquas: A Study in the Development of Stratification in South Africa.* Cambridge: Cambridge University Press, 1976. 194 p.

History of Khoikhoi, 'Bastard', and ex-slave society which existed on geographical and social fringes of Cape colonial society.

113. Ross, Robert. *Beyond the Pale: Essays on the History of Colonial South Africa.* Middletown, Conn.: Wesleyan University Press, 1993. 270 p.

Essays examine how the development of capitalism in the Cape Colony in the eighteenth and nineteenth century provided a legacy of colonial class domination based on the control land, labor, and trade.

114. Ross, Robert. "Emancipations and the Economy of the Cape Colony." *Slavery and Abolition* 14 (April 1993): 131–48.

Considers several emancipations—of Khoi, of slaves, and of slave apprentices—which stretched over a decade. Assesses the effects of these emancipations on levels of agricultural production, concluding that productivity increased over all sectors.

115. Russell, Margo. "Slaves or Workers? Relations between Bushmen, Tswana, and Boers in the Kalahari." *Journal of Southern African Studies* 2 (April 1976): 178–97.

116. Sachs, Albie. *Justice in South Africa.* London: Chatto Heinemann for Sussex University Press, 1973. 288 p.

Second chapter on administration and race relations at the Cape from 1806 to 1910 is relevant for studies of postemancipation society.

117. Saunders, Christopher. *Historical Dictionary of South Africa.* African Historical Dictionaries. No. 37. Metuchen, N.J.: Scarecrow Press, 1983. 241 p.

Brief entries on slavery, missions, and Khoikhoi.

118. Saunders, Christopher. "Between Slavery and Freedom: The Importation of Prize Negroes to the Cape in the Aftermath of Emancipation." *Kronos* 9 (1984): 36–43.

Discusses farmers' need for labor after 1838 when many freedpeople migrated to the towns. Information on living conditions of "prize negroes," labor relations under the Masters and Servants Ordinance of 1841, and relations with other members of the Cape underclass.

119. Saunders, Christopher. "Liberated Africans in the Cape Colony in the First Half of the Nineteenth Century." *International Journal of African Historical Studies* 18 (1985): 223–39.

Examines the role of "prize negroes" liberated from slave ships to the Cape after the abolition of the slave trade and slavery. Discusses how the forced apprenticeship of liberated Africans helped alleviate the labor crisis at the Cape following emancipation.

120. Saunders, Christopher, et al., eds. *Studies in the History of Cape Town.* 6 vols. to date. Cape Town: History Department, University of Cape Town, in association with the Centre for African Studies, University of Cape Town, 1979-.

Collected conference papers focusing on history of greater Cape Town in the nineteenth and twentieth centuries. Volume 3 contains a brief bibliographical guide. Volumes 1 through 4 originally published between 1979 and 1983.

121. Sayles, Jane. *Mission Stations and the Coloured Communities of the Eastern Cape, 1800–1852.* Cape Town: A. A. Balkema, 1975. 176 p.

Discusses London Missionary Society and the mission stations of Bethelsdorp, Theopolis, and Hankey, as well as the Kat River Settlement. Appendix A contains a chronology of ecclesiastical and political events from 1652 to 1859, and appendix B contains a list of British governors of the Cape from 1797 to 1861.

122. Scully, Pamela. "Narratives of Infanticide in the Aftermath of Slave Emancipation in the Nineteenth-Century Cape Colony, South Africa." *Canadian Journal of African Studies/Revue Canadienne des Etudes Africaines* 30 (1996): 88–105.

Through a gendered reading of the postemancipation economy, explains the issues of sexuality and labor that pressured unmarried colored women to practice infanticide.

123. Scully, Pamela. "Rape, Race, and Colonial Culture: The Sexual Politics of Identity in the Nineteenth-Century Cape Colony, South Africa." *American Historical Review* (April 1995): 335–59.

Analyzes the legal and social understanding of rape in the aftermath of emancipation. Considers role of racial and sexual categories in the construction of honor.

124. Scully, Pamela. *Liberating the Family? Gender and British Slave Emancipation in the Rural Western Cape, South Africa, 1823–1853.* Portsmouth, N.H.: Heinemann, 1997. 210 p.

Discusses how the abolition of slavery in the Cape Colony initiated an era of contestation over cultural categories and sensibilities which focused primarily on gender and family. Examines how ideologies of gender, race, and sexuality shaped postemancipation colonialism.

125. Scully, Pamela. *The Bouquet of Freedom: Social and Economic Relations in the Stellenbosch District, South Africa, c1870–1900.* Communications no. 17. Cape Town: University of Cape Town, Centre for African Studies, 1990. 130 p.

Examines labor relations on farms of second-largest wine-growing district in the Cape Colony. Considers how industrialization in late nineteenth century helped bring about the first major reformulation of labor relations since emancipation.

126. Shell, Robert Carl-Heinz. *Children of Bondage: A Social History of the Slave Society at the Cape of Good Hope, 1652–1838.* Hanover, N.H.: University Press of New England for Wesleyan University Press, 1994. 501 p.

Examines the social history of slavery at the Cape, including extensive demographic data.

127. Shell, Robert Carl-Heinz. "March of the Mardijckers: The Toleration of Islam at the Cape, 1633–1861." *Kronos* 22 (1995): 3–20.

Discusses how the tolerance of Islam at the Cape was granted in exchange for military duties performed by free black Muslims.

128. Strassberger, Elfriede. *The Rhenish Mission Society in South Africa, 1830–1950.* Cape Town: C. Struik, 1969. 109 p.

Chapter 3 covers stations concerned with preaching to slaves and freedpeople in Stellenbosch, Tulbagh, Worcester, and outstations.

129. Trapido, Stanley. "Aspects in the Transition from Slavery to Serfdom: The South African Republic, 1842–1902." In *The Societies of Southern Africa in the 19th and 20th Centuries*, Vol. 6. Collected Seminar Papers, vol. 20. London: University of London, Institute of Commonwealth Studies, 1976.

Examines the "Boer mode of production" of slavery in the predominantly rural economy of the Afrikaner Republic and its transition to tenancy and finally proletarianization of labor.

130. Van Ryneveld, T. A. "Merchants and Missions: Developments in the Caledon District. 1838–1850." B.A. thesis, Department of History, University of Cape Town, 1983.

Examines changing labor relations in a wheat-growing district near Cape Town.

131. Ward, Kerry. "'Captive Audiences': Remembering and Forgetting the History of Slavery in Cape Town, South Africa." In *Post Colonialism: Culture and Identity in Africa*, edited by Pal Ahluwalia and Paul Nursey-Bray. Commack, N.Y.: Nova Science Publishers, 1997.

Examines how slavery has been represented in three sites: the village of Mamre, the Cape Town Castle, and Robben Island.

132. Ward, Kerry. "Remembering Mamre in the Early Twentieth Century: Life Experiences and the Making of History." In *Missions and Christianity in South African History*, edited by Henry Bredekamp and Robert Ross. Johannesburg: University of Witwatersrand Press, 1995.

Examines the construction of community identity through collective memories of the past that "forget" the slave heritage of the residents.

133. Ward, Kerry, and Nigel Worden. "Commemorating, Suppressing and Invoking Cape Slavery." In *Negotiating the Past: The Making of Memory in South Africa*, edited by Sarah Nuttall and Carli Coetzee. Cape Town: Oxford University Press, 1998.

Discusses how public commemorations of emancipation became increasingly rare in the late nineteenth century but have revived in the era after apartheid.

134. Watson, R. L. "Slavery and Ideology: The South African Case." *International Journal of African Historical Studies* 20 (1987): 24–44.

Discusses weakness of antislavery opinion in Cape, even among liberals, whose concern with property limited movement against slavery. Focuses on English (i.e., nonslaveholding) population.

135. Watson, R. L. *The Slave Question: Liberty and Property in South Africa*. Middletown, Conn.: Wesleyan University Press, 1990. 274 p.

136. Whiteside, J. Rev. *History of the Wesleyan Methodist Church of South Africa*. London: Elliot Stock, 1906.

Chapter seven on Methodism at the Cape refers to emancipation, the actions of freedpeople and the attitudes of former slaveowners.

137. Worden, Nigel. "Slavery and Amnesia: Towards a Recovery of Malagasy Heritage Representations of Cape Slavery." In *Fanandevozana ou esclavage*, coordinated by Rajaoson Francois. Proceedings of Colloque international sur l'esclavage à Antananarivo Musée d'Art et d'Archeologie de l'Université o' Antanarivo, 1995.

Examines the shifting proportion of Malagasy slaves at the cape and suggests that they became subsumed under the broader category of "African" slaves. Consequently, Malagasy heritage has been neglected in the current representations of Cape slavery.

138. Worden, Nigel. "Diverging Histories: Slavery and its Aftermath in the Cape Colony and Mauritius." *South African Historical Journal* 27 (1992): 3–25.

Discusses how emancipation did not break down a racially structured society in either place. Whereas plantation slaves in Mauritius were replaced by Indian indentured workers, freedpeople at the Cape and their descendants remained in the agrarian labor force.

139. Worden, Nigel, and Clifton Crais, eds. *Breaking the Chains: Slavery and its Legacy in the Nineteenth-Century Cape Colony.* Johannesburg: Witwatersrand University Press, 1994. 346 p.

Introduction by Worden and Crais situates slavery and emancipation over the "long nineteenth century." Chapters cover apprenticeship, the rural economy, the significance of compensation, family issues, labor control legislation, and segregation.

IV Cuba

Rebecca J. Scott
University of Michigan

COMPILED BY

Rebecca J. Scott

Alejandra Bronfman
Yale University

Ada Ferrer
New York University

Kathleen Lopez
University of Michigan

Aims McGuinness
University of Wisconsin-Milwaukee

Javier Morillo-Alicea
Macalester College

The construction of a postemancipation society in Cuba, as elsewhere, was a gradual process. But in Cuba even the moment of emancipation was itself long and drawn out: beginning in 1868 with rebel decrees for limited abolition, continuing in 1870 with colonial policies for the freeing of children and the elderly, and culminating in 1880 with the establishment of an apprenticeship system *(patronato)* which lasted until 1886. In this bibliography we have therefore incorporated numerous sources on the process of emancipation itself, including legislative, administrative, and statistical documents which shed light on how slaves won their freedom—whether through legal decrees, participation in armed insurgency, individual rulings by the new *juntas* which oversaw the transition out of slavery, or self-purchase. We have also included abolitionist tracts when they contain information on the conditions of slaves freed by one or another act in the gradual process of emancipation or when they elaborate a detailed vision of postemancipation society.

After final legal abolition in 1886, the nature of available historical sources changes significantly. Before abolition, slaves and apprentices were almost invariably identified as such in historical documents, for both slaveowners and the state were very much interested in keeping track of legal property. After freedom was achieved, sources rarely identified former slaves. Even in manuscript plantation records, for example, former slaves often become indistinguishable from other workers long free. This poses a particular challenge for historians, and some have responded by simply folding the history of former slaves into that of the Cuban rural working class. In doing so, however, one risks losing the specificity of the experiences of those who had been born into the world of slavery.

The transition away from slavery in Cuba has also been embedded in two powerful national narratives: the development of a modern sugar industry and the achievement of political independence. The shift from slave to free labor is often seen as caused by, or at least inseparable from, the transition from the *ingenio* (plantation/mill complex) to the *central* (a centralized sugar mill, grinding cane from multiple suppliers). And the period from 1868 to 1898, which encompasses slave emancipation and the initial construction of a postemancipation society, also marks the thirty years of struggle for independence from Spain.

This bibliography thus necessarily contains much material relevant to the study of the centralization of sugar production and the achievement of national independence. Slaves and former slaves were, after all, important protagonists in both processes. A few years before the beginning of emancipation, 47 percent of the island's slave population worked on sugar estates. After final abolition in 1886, the sugar industry still relied heavily on the labor of former slaves, though they were now accompanied by large numbers of Spanish immigrants and long-free Cubans. We have thus included and annotated representative statistical reports, compilations of laws, and secondary works on sugar production and immigration.

During the three major anticolonial insurgencies of the late nineteenth century, many slaves, former slaves, and free children of slave mothers found their way to rebel and Spanish lines. They both influenced and were influenced by the process of seeking independence. Sources on the Ten Years' War, the Guerra Chiquita, and the final War of Independence often cast light on the experience of emancipation in the context of military conflict, the evolving commitment of the rebels to full emancipation, and the process of recruitment to rebel ranks. Recent microhistorical work on war in specific locales has also made it possible to begin to probe the motives of former slaves who participated in these conflicts and to trace the importance of achieving veteran status, with its concomitant claim to respect and citizenship.

However, while we have included many items relevant to the sugar industry and to political independence, we have also tried to work a bit against the grain of the two national narratives of sugar and of nation-building. In studying the sugar sector itself, we have paid special attention to sources that may permit regional studies, so that the story of local adaptations is not lost in the powerful overall trend toward foreign investment and the concentration of sugar processing. We have also sought out less well-known evidence on the coffee and tobacco sectors and gathered every scrap we could find on small-scale subsistence and market farming. For many former slaves, emancipation involved *diminishing* one's ties to the sugar estates. To explore the experience of freedom, then, one must examine the question of alternatives to wage labor in sugar.

The outbreak of a vast anticolonial insurgency just nine years after final abolition powerfully framed the question of the meaning of freedom within a dramatic saga of multiracial alliance in pursuit of Cuban independence. The conviction that abolition was an achievement of the earlier anticolonial wars, and an integral part of national liberation, constituted an important element in the formation of an inclusive ideal of nationhood. A near-consensus emerged that Cuban nationality was by definition transracial and that the question of race had been superseded by the achievement of national independence. Some Afro-Cuban activists, including veterans of the independence wars, challenged the complacency of the Cuban elite on this question, and a few authors raised questions in the 1940s, 1950s, and early 1960s about the self-congratulatory tone of the dominant scholarship. But only recently have scholars effectively probed the role of racial ideologies within the separatist movement, and noted the ways in which a partial "silencing" of race has impeded the study of the lived experiences of freed persons, and of the dynamics of racial identification in the late nineteenth and early twentieth century.[1]

In our selection of sources on the struggle for independence we have therefore been sparing with the classic—and stirring—texts invoking national unity. We have concentrated instead on memoirs, campaign diaries, and local narratives that convey something of the quotidian experiences of recruitment to or flight from the insurgencies, imprisonment by the Spanish, enclosure in the "reconcentration" camps, labor on "vegetable prefectures," and contacts with maroon communities. For many of these phenomena, the printed sources are simply inadequate, and one must turn to archival records. But where printed sources do exist that can point the way, we have included them and provided detailed annotations.

With the end of Spanish sovereignty and the beginning of formal United States occupation in 1899, the nature of the written record changes again. Although postemancipation documents generated by Cubans often avoided any reference to racial identifications, North American administrators and officers in Cuba generally utilized racial categories of one kind or another in drafting their reports. Beginning with the indispensable censuses of 1899 and 1907, local and national-level reports for the periods of U.S. occupation (1899–1902 and 1906–

1. Ada Ferrer, in *Insurgent Cuba: Race, Nation, and Revolution, 1868–1898* (Chapel Hill: University of North Carolina Press, 1999), surveys this literature and proposes a new synthesis based on research in archival and printed sources. See also Aline Helg, *Our Rightful Share: The Afro-Cuban Struggle for Equality, 1886–1912* (Chapel Hill: University of North Carolina Press, 1995); Tomás Fernández Robaina, *El negro en Cuba, 1902–1958: Apuntes para la historia de la lucha contra la discriminación racial* (Havana: Editorial de Ciencias Sociales, 1994); and Alejandro de la Fuente, *A Nation for All: Race, Inequality and Politics in Twentieth-Century Cuba* (Chapel Hill: University of North Carolina Press, 2001).

1909) contain statistical information which makes frequent correlations between racial classifications and recorded evidence on employment, literacy, education, marital status, and land tenure. We have inventoried and annotated the richest of these occupation reports, along with the censuses, in a separate subsection, while remaining painfully aware of their biases and frequently quite explicit ethnocentrism, as well as their tendency to treat "race" as a powerful determinant of behavior.

At the same time, local authorities, particularly in the province of Las Villas (Santa Clara), hastened to create published records of their initiatives and progress. With the new phase of expansion in the sugar industry, copious statistical reports, as well as nominal lists of estates and their output, were published, both during and after the United States occupations. Due to limitations of space, we have not been able to include all of these, nor are all of them available outside of Cuba itself, but we have provided a selection, with some suggestions for their use.

While excavating materials on race in the early republic, we have tried not to prejudge the question of whether racial, class, or national affiliations were in any sense "more important" for former slaves and their descendants. We have found that the salience of different identifications tended to shift under different circumstances. Thus we have compiled primary materials reflecting on the early workers' movement in the sugar industry, on the alternately muted and volatile discussions of race and discrimination, and on the evolution of patron-client relations in the countryside, as well as basic evidence on housing, wages, and migration.

The early republic also saw the publication of extensive materials on what was often identified as Afro-Cuban culture, sometimes framed within the ambiguous rubrics of criminology, ethnography, and folklore. This literature constitutes a subject of study in itself, as revealing of elite preoccupations as it is of the lives of people of African descent.[2] We have not attempted to incorporate all of these materials. Instead, we have selected studies whose evidence is grounded in identifiable times and places, facilitating their use as historical sources. Thus, for example, we have included some of the works of Fernando Ortiz on slavery and African *cabildos*, but we have not attempted to identify the full range of works that deal more generally with religious and symbolic aspects of *santería* or *ñañiguismo*.

A few additional notes on procedure: We have fully annotated all bibliographical and primary sources, providing for the latter a descrip-

2. See Alejandra Bronfman, "Reforming Race in Cuba, 1902–1940," Ph.D. diss., Princeton University, 2000.

tion of their contents and, when possible, suggesting ways in which they might be used to explore particular aspects of postemancipation society. For most secondary sources in English, we have composed brief annotations that simply indicate the geographical and temporal scope of the work, though in the case of early or rare works we have provided some indication of the contents. For secondary sources in Spanish, often more difficult for North American readers to obtain, we have gone a step further to indicate some of the topics covered and the kinds of sources used. We do not, however, try to summarize fully the authors' arguments; that judgmental task we leave to the individual researcher.

We have of necessity been selective in our inclusion of government reports and literature from contemporary periodicals. We have incorporated and annotated the richest of the publications of the United States government on Cuba, but the researcher may well wish to retrace our steps through the usual guides to government publications in order to pick up items of special interest for particular topics. We have included a dozen or so key articles on sugar, emancipation, and the social world of the countryside published in nineteenth- and early-twentieth-century periodicals, but again, the researcher should consult the comprehensive finding aids and indices to Cuban periodical literature for further references.

Because of limitations of space, we have had to exclude certain categories of secondary works. Though we have included certain particularly rich autobiographies, we have generally not included biographies. Many of the prominent figures of this period were involved in the struggle for independence, and readers can find relevant materials listed and annotated in the thorough bibliographies of the independence movement published by the Biblioteca Nacional "José Martí" in Havana, cited below.

Finally, we have occasionally stretched the boundaries of this bibliography to include guides to unpublished sources in Cuba. A thorough guide to archives in Cuba would greatly exceed the scope of this project; we are collaborating in once facet of that task under other auspices.[3] In the meantime, however, we are cognizant of the exceptional difficulties of preparing for research on the island, and so we have slipped in a few items that enable the researcher to envision and anticipate what he or she may find in the Archivo Nacional de Cuba and the Biblioteca Nacional

3. A guide to provincial and local archives in Cuba, coordinated by Louis A. Pérez, Jr., Marel García, and Rebecca Scott, is scheduled for publication in 2002 by Ediciones Unión in Havana and by the University of Pittsburgh Press.

"José Martí," repositories of vast wealth for the study of postemancipation society in Cuba. A recently published volume of essays gives a hint of the kinds of microhistorical work that can be carried out using material available in regional archives.[4] Together, these may whet the appetite for primary research in Cuba.

REBECCA J. SCOTT

ADA FERRER

4. Fernando Martínez Heredia, Rebecca J. Scott and Orlando F. García Martínez, eds., *Espacios, silencios y los sentidos de la libertad: Cuba entre 1878 y 1912* (Havana: Ediciones Unión, 2001).

BIBLIOGRAPHIES, HISTORIOGRAPHICAL ESSAYS, AND INDEXES

1. Cuba. Archivo Nacional. *Catálogo de los fondos del Consejo de Administración de la Isla de Cuba.* 3 vols. Havana: Archivo Nacional, 1948–1950.

   Catalogue of documents in the Fondo Consejo de Administración of the Archivo Nacional, dating from 1862 through 1898. The Consejo functioned as both an appellate and a consultative body. Documents are listed alphabetically, sometimes by topic or person involved, sometimes by first word in document title, or by type of document. The latter appears to be most common, and thus many entries are listed under such headings as: *demanda, queja, reclamación, sentencia, título, renuncia, consulta, autorización, contrato, carta,* and many others. *Legajo* (bundle) and *expediente* (file) numbers are provided for each document. Researchers can use this catalogue to identify relevant materials available in the archives prior to making research trips to Cuba. In some cases the titles of individual files are themselves useful for analyzing the types of appeals handled by the Consejo. Appeals by slaves and *patrocinados* appear in the listing, as do other cases related to the process of emancipation.

2. Deschamps Chapeaux, Pedro. *El negro en el periodismo cubano en el siglo xix.* Havana: Ediciones R., 1963. 110 p.

   Guide to over one hundred Afro-Cuban newspapers of the nineteenth century, most of which were published between 1879 and 1899. Entries are arranged alphabetically by title of newspaper and list years and place of publication, names of editors, and type of newspaper (e.g. political, literary). In addition, many entries contain brief histories of the paper and excerpts from articles and editorials on subjects such as independence and Afro-Cuban civil rights. Includes Afro-Cuban newspapers published in exile.

3. Fermoselle-López, Rafael. "The Blacks in Cuba: A Bibliography." *Caribbean Studies* 12 (October 1972): 103–12.

   A short bibliography of primary and secondary works divided into categories: general, slavery and abolition, race relations, folklore, and language. Contains 191 items, many of which are available in the U.S. Not annotated.

4. Fernández Robaina, Tomás, ed. *Bibliografía sobre temas afrocubanos*. Havana: Biblioteca Nacional "José Martí." Depto. de Investigaciones Bibliográficas, 1986. 581 p.

   Comprehensive bibliography of sources on Afro-Cuban history. Includes references to individual articles in the Afro-Cuban press; often quotes fragments from them. Covers nineteenth and twentieth centuries. Also lists books, and some scattered archival evidence. Main body of volume is organized chronologically, but also contains topical sections on Afro-Cuban belief systems, art and literature, women, music and dance, poetry, publications, societies, and major Afro-Cuban figures. Detailed index. Most useful as a finding aid for identifying materials located in Cuba, but also cites numerous published materials available in the U.S.

5. García Carranza, Araceli. *Bibliografía de la guerra de independencia, 1895–1898*. Havana: Editorial Orbe, 1976. 746 p.

   Annotated bibliography of printed primary and secondary materials on the Cuban War of Independence. Annotations generally provide a brief description and/or a review of the item's table of contents. Relevant sources include materials on social and economic conditions of the late 1890s and numerous war diaries which can be used to examine issues of black participation in the insurrection, race relations in the insurgent army, and relations of workers and property holders with Spanish and Cuban forces.

6. García, Gloria, Violeta Serrano, Irma Tamayo, and Alejandrino Borroto. *Fuentes estadísticas para la historia económica y social de Cuba (1760–1900)*. Vol. I. *Población*. Havana: Editorial Academia, 1987. 231 p.

   First volume of results of a bibliographic search by a team from the Instituto de Ciencias Sociales of the Academia de Ciencias. Consists of a sequential listing of reference number and title of individual files located in various record groups of the Archivo Nacional de Cuba (ANC). Organized chronologically. Concentrates on files containing statistical material of one kind or another. Includes references to numerous slave lists and population counts. Designed to be used as a finding aid when conducting research in the archives, it can also provide a sense of available documentation to the researcher planning a project. Should be used in conjunction with the guides to specific record groups published by the ANC.

7. García, Gloria, Violeta Serrano, Irma Tamayo, and Alejandrino Borroto. *Fuentes estadísticas para la historia económica y social de Cuba (1760–1900)*. Vol. II. *Agricultura, ganadería y minería*. Havana: Editorial Academia, 1987. 178 p.

Second volume of index to documents, following format of first. Concentrates on documents relating to agriculture, ranching, and mining during the colonial period. Agricultural censuses cited often contain figures on slave and free labor. Contains a very detailed index of place names and subjects.

8. Griffin, A. P. C. *List of books relating to Cuba, with Bibliography of Maps by P. Lee Phillips*. Washington, D.C.: Government Printing Office, 1898. 61 p.

Extensive bibliography of materials relating to Cuba found in the Library of Congress, divided into sections on books, magazine articles, government documents, maps, and manuscript sources. Books are arranged alphabetically by author. The articles (1825–98), government documents (1822–96), maps (1492–1876), and manuscripts (1710–94) are arranged chronologically. Some entries contain brief annotations. Items cover a wide range of topics, including slavery, the struggle for independence, sugar, and agriculture in general.

9. Pariseau, Earl J., ed. *Cuban Acquisitions and Bibliography: Proceedings and Working Papers of an International Conference held at the Library of Congress, April 13, 1970*. Washington, D.C.: Library of Congress, 1970. 164 p.

Collection of essays on Cuban materials available in the United States, England, Spain, and Germany. David Burks's essay reviews printed primary and bibliographic sources on Cuba to 1933 available at the Library of Congress. Georgette M. Dorn's essay reviews manuscript sources available in the Library of Congress. Papers by Bernard Naylor, Juan Martínez-Alier and José Ramón Barraca de Ramos, and Hans Pohl review archival, manuscript, and printed primary sources on Cuba after 1868 available in libraries and archives in England, Spain, and Germany, respectively.

10. Pérez, Lisandro. "The Holdings of the Library of Congress on the Population of Cuba." *Cuban Studies/Estudios Cubanos* 13 (winter 1983): 69–76.

    Review of printed primary sources on Cuban demography at the Library of Congress. Most of the holdings listed are general sources such as census reports, nongovernmental statistical compendia, and reports of U.S. governments of occupation. The author also includes documents with statistical data on education, marriage, and sanitation. Sources are divided into three sections: the colonial period; 1899–1958; and the socialist period.

11. Pérez, Louis A. *Cuba: An Annotated Bibliography*. New York: Greenwood Press, 1988. 301 p.

    Annotated bibliography of printed primary and secondary sources on Cuba, historical and current. Includes sections on travel accounts, slavery and race, population, colonial Cuba, and struggles for independence. Also contains sections on the economy, agriculture, industry, and labor, with an emphasis on revolutionary Cuba.

12. Pérez, Louis A., Jr. "Cuba Materials in the Bureau of Insular Affairs Library." *Latin American Research Review* 13 (1978): 182–88.

    List of materials available in the papers of the Bureau of Insular Affairs held at the U.S. National Archives in Washington, D.C. Most of the sources listed are U.S. and Cuban government publications for the early twentieth century. Includes references to available annual reports by Cuban government agencies for agriculture, public education, and the Rural Guard. These annual reports are useful for the study of Afro-Cuban social, economic, and political life in the early republic.

13. Pérez, Louis A., Jr. "Record Collections at the Cuban National Archives: A Descriptive Survey." *Latin American Research Review* 19 (1984): 142–56.

    List of document collections at the Cuban national archives. Each collection is given a brief description, with information on its chronological focus and the type of documents catalogued. A general indication is given about the types of subjects treated in each collection. Many of the collections described are of potential relevance to the study of postemancipation society. Among these are documents generated by anticolonial rebellions in which slaves and former slaves participated. These documents are housed in the *fondos* Roloff, Calixto García, Máximo Gómez, Academia de la Historia de Cuba, and others. Also relevant are collections of colonial government records regarding rents, taxes, land use, slavery, and political surveillance, in such holdings as Consejo de Administración, Gobierno General, Miscelánea, Bienes Embargados, and Realengos. This guide also contains references for other guides located in the ANC which describe holdings in local archives and collections in smaller cities such as Bayamo and Sanctí Spíritus.

14. Pérez, Luis Marino. *Bibliografía de la revolución de Yara. Folletos y libros impresos de 1868 a 1908.* Havana: Imp. Avisadora Comercial, 1908. 73 p.

   List of books and pamphlets relating to the Ten Years' War published between 1868 and 1908. Arranged chronologically by year of publication. Some entries contain annotations with information on the author and/or contents of the source.

15. Plasencia, Aleida, ed. *Bibliografía de la guerra de los diez años.* Havana: Biblioteca Nacional "José Martí," 1968. 388 p.

   An annotated bibliography of printed primary and secondary sources on the Ten Years' War. Some manuscript sources available at the Biblioteca Nacional "José Martí" are also listed. Annotations generally provide brief descriptions and/or a table of contents. Includes useful section on diaries and memoirs written by Cuban, Spanish, and foreign participants in the war which can provide insight into relationship between slaves and insurgents, and, more generally, between the insurrection and the breakdown of slavery.

16. Pomrenze, Seymour. *Materials in the National Archives Relating to Cuba.* Washington, D.C., 1948. 13 p.

   Briefly discusses collections in the U. S. National Archives, dividing them into three categories: records relating to the period before the 1895 revolution, records of the period of revolution, war, and military government (1895–1902), and records from 1902 until 1939. For the first two periods the material discussed is mostly military, while for the last period collections containing information on agriculture and sugar production are emphasized.

17. Ruiz Santovenia, Ernesto. "Manuscritos Existentes en la Biblioteca Nacional 'José Martí' acerca de la Esclavitud." In *Temas acerca de la esclavitud,* edited by members of the Departmento de Historia de Cuba, Academia de Ciencias. Havana: Editorial de Ciencias Sociales, 1988.

An eighty-three-page listing of the item number and title of individual documents located in the Biblioteca Nacional "José Martí" in Havana. Several of the items listed date from the last years of slavery and can provide evidence on the flight of slaves, self-purchase, and conflict on plantations.

18. Santamaría García, Antonio, and Consuelo Naranjo Orovio. "La historia social de Cuba, 1868–1914. Aportaciones recientes y perspectivas." *Historia Social* 33 (1999): 133–58.

Review of recent historiography of Cuba between 1868 and 1914, with a focus on works of social and economic history published in the 1990s. Includes a bibliography with works by more than one hundred historians related to themes such as slave emancipation, racial ideology, European immigration, and changes in the sugar economy.

19. Santos Quilez, Aleida de los. *El campesinado cubano. Breve bibliografía*. Havana: Editora Política, 1980. 148 p.

Extensive listing of printed primary and secondary sources relating to the Cuban peasantry. Includes some archival sources, but does not contain a systematic listing of relevant archival materials. Contains references to some late-nineteenth- and many early-twentieth-century materials useful for examining the incorporation of former slaves into rural society. Final section lists relevant periodicals, with a twentieth-century focus.

20. Trelles y Govín, Carlos M., ed. *Bibliografía cubana del siglo XIX*. 8 vols. Matanzas: Imp. de Quirós y Estrada, 1911–1915.

Bibliography of sources written in the nineteenth century. Arranged alphabetically by author. Entries sometimes contain excerpts or annotations with information on the author and book. Volumes most useful for postemancipation studies are 5 (1869–78); 6 (1879–85); 7 (1886–93); and 8 (1894–99).

21. Trelles y Govín, Carlos M., ed. *Bibliografía cubana del siglo XX*. Matanzas, 1916–1917.

Lists books and pamphlets published in Cuba between 1900 and 1916, providing place and date of publication and page numbers. Arranged by year, within which alphabetically by author. Entries sometimes contain excerpts or annotations. An appendix includes some biographical information on authors (place and date of birth, date of death), and the index lists authors alphabetically.

22. Trelles y Govín, Carlos Manuel. *Bibliografía social cubana*. Havana: Biblioteca Nacional "José Martí," 1969. 106 p.

A 1924 bibliography of five hundred books and articles dealing with Cuban social history from the eighteenth century through the early 1920s. Most of the items listed are from the late nineteenth and early twentieth centuries and touch on topics related to the process of emancipation, including the living and working conditions of laborers, slavery and abolition, education, trade unionism, and women. Some of the entries are annotated. The bibliography also contains a very useful listing of about two hundred newspapers published by trade guilds, unions, and socialist and anarchist organizations. This list provides the place of publication and date in which the newspaper was founded.

23. Trelles y Govín, Carlos M. *Biblioteca histórica cubana*. 3 vols. Matanzas and Havana: Imp. de Juan Oliver, Imp. de Andrés Estrada, and Dorrbecker, 1922–1926.

Three-volume bibliography on Cuban history from settlement through the early twentieth century. The organization is thematic and chronological. Of particular interest for the study of postemancipation societies are sections on slavery, abolition, immigration, the Rural Guard and Liberation Army, education, and *ñañiguismo*. A section on campaign diaries for the final war of 1895 includes diaries which appeared in Cuban newspapers in the twentieth century and which do not necessarily appear in other bibliographies of the war. Among these are the campaign diaries of several leaders of color, including Quintín Bandera and Pedro Díaz. Many of the entries are annotated to provide information on the author and/or contents of the item. In addition the author periodically includes relevant statistical information. For example, in the section on education, he provides tables of school attendance broken down by year and race. All three volumes contain useful name and subject indices.

24. Trelles y Govín, Carlos M. "Bibliografía de autores de la raza de color en Cuba." *Cuba Contemporánea* 43 (1927): 30–78.

List of books written by Cubans whom Trelles judged to be people of color, from the early nineteenth through the early twentieth century. Divided into two sections: "During the Age of Slavery" and "After Slavery." Each section is then arranged alphabetically by author. Includes works in drama, literature, education, history, politics, and medicine, among others.

25. Tro, Rodolfo. *Cuba, viajes y descripciones, 1493–1949*. Havana, 1950. 188 p.

Bibliography of travel literature which includes diaries, journals, and travel guides written by tourists, journalists, soldiers, economists, agronomists, and others who traveled to Cuba, generally from the United States, Spain, Germany, France, and England, from the early colonial period through the late 1940s. The majority are nineteenth- and twentieth-century sources. Entries are arranged alphabetically. Besides standard bibliographic data, most entries include the date of the authors' visits to Cuba and the location of the book. Some entries include information on the background of the visitor and a summary of the contents. The materials are mostly from major Cuban libraries, the U.S. Library of Congress, the New York Public Library, the national libraries of Spain and France, and the British Museum.

26. Zanetti, Oscar. "La historiografía de temática social (1959–1984)." *Revista de la Biblioteca Nacional "José Martí"* 27 (1985): 5–17.

Surveys work on slave trade, labor, immigration, Chinese indentured laborers, population, and class. Reviews the monographic work of major working scholars.

PRIMARY SOURCES

27. Acosta y Albear, Francisco de. *Memoria sobre el estado actual de Cuba.* Havana: A. Pegó, 1874. 28 p.

General discussion of potential strategies Spanish authorities could pursue to preserve Cuba as a colony. Discusses possibility of abolition in the context of the Ten Years' War. Author briefly describes labor and agricultural conditions, dividing the island into the peaceful zones of the west and the eastern zones dominated by anticolonial rebellion. The author, a Spanish officer and landowner, details his own personal losses due to the war and increased taxes. He claims that Afro-Cubans constitute 90 percent of the insurgent army. Discussion of the process of emancipation in the period between 1868 and 1873 cites the importance of the Moret Law, as well as slave initiatives in buying their own (or their family members') freedom as the principal reasons for the decline of the slave population in those years.

28. Acosta y Albear, Francisco. *Compendio histórico del pasado y presente de Cuba y de su guerra insurreccional.* Madrid: Imp. a cargo de Juan José de las Heras, 1875. 160 p.

Brief account of the Ten Years' War from its outbreak in 1868 to 1875, written by a brigadier in the Spanish army. Discusses largely unsuccessful attempts by the Spanish to create black loyalist companies, referring to rapid armed desertion to insurrectionist camps. Labels black participation in the insurgency as "dominant" and refers to the insurrection as "virtually a race war." Makes suggestions for political and military reforms, including the use of blacks as soldiers but in racially and regionally integrated companies. Also briefly discusses economic conditions on the island in 1875. Perceives large-scale labor shortages in agriculture and makes suggestions for multiracial labor importation programs.

29. Aguilera, Francisco Vicente. *Notes about Cuba.* New York, 1872. 54 p.

Written by member of the Cuban Revolutionary Party in New York to help persuade the U.S. Congress to grant recognition to Cuban insurgents during the Ten Years' War. Divided into two sections, one titled "slavery," the other "revolution." The brief slavery section emphasizes Spain's delay in abolishing the slave trade and argues that the insurgents are fighting Spain partly to abolish slavery. The second section on the war reviews conditions and resources of both the Cuban and Spanish armies. Uses excerpts from official documents of the Cuban revolutionary government describing military campaigns. Also uses Cuban newspaper excerpts and letters allegedly captured from Spaniards, which describe extensive damage in coffee regions of Oriente. Contains occasional references to the presence of Afro-Cubans and Chinese among insurgent ranks.

30. Alfonso y García, Ramón María. *Viviendas del campesino pobre en Cuba.* Havana: La Moderna Poesía, 1904. 31 p.

Examination of the housing conditions of the rural poor in Cuba. Discusses problems of hygiene, overcrowding, water access, and ventilation. Lists and describes different types of housing common among *campesinos* of different social levels. Though some of the material is technical, it can be used as evidence of the standard of living of rural workers in the early years of the twentieth century.

31. Alonso y Sanjurjo, Eugenio. *Apuntes sobre los proyectos de abolición de la esclavitud en las islas de Cuba y Puerto Rico.* Madrid: Imp. de la Biblioteca de Instrucción y Recreo, 1874. 68 p.

Brief review of Spanish and Cuban abolition proposals through 1873. Since most of the proposals are post-1868, this collection serves as a useful introduction to the effects of the Ten Years' War on the movement to abolish slavery.

32. Arbelo, Manuel. *Recuerdos de la última guerra de independencia de Cuba.* Havana: Imp. Tipografía Moderna, 1918. 335 p.

War memoir written by a small-scale landholder in Matanzas who joined the local rebel movement in early 1896. The author concentrates on daily life within insurgent ranks and identifies specific troops as composed of former slaves and/or sugar workers, among these the troops commanded by Eduardo García. Arbelo also served for some time alongside Afro-Cuban officer Enrique Fournier and provides details on his troops and activities. The memoir is unique in its attempt to raise issues regarding black discontent with the independence process. Because many of the events described by Arbelo occur in sugar regions, the memoir can also be used to explore relations between insurgents and sugar planters and workers, as well as the condition of the local sugar industry in the midst of war.

33. Armas y Céspedes, José de. *El trabajo libre.* Havana: La Propaganda Literaria, 1880. 65 p.

Political discussion of economic reforms guiding the transition from slave to free labor, in the form of a letter to Antonio Cánovas del Castillo, president of the Council of Ministers. Discusses such issues as the *patronato* and indemnification of slaveowners.

34. Arredondo y Miranda, Francisco de. *Recuerdos de la guerra de Cuba (Diario de campaña, 1868–1871).* 1878. Reprint. Havana: Biblioteca Nacional "José Martí," 1962. 192 p.

War diary written by owner of medium-sized farm in Camagüey who participated in insurrection from 1868 to 1871. Can be used to examine the ways in which preexisting patron-client relations between landowners and workers affected patterns of participation and recruitment in the insurrection. Illuminates the ways in which the relationship between sectors of the leadership and the institution of slavery affected their participation. Also provides some evidence on the participation of slaves.

35. Asociación de Colonos de Cuba. *Informe del comité ejecutivo nacional.* Havana: Montalvo y Cárdenas, 1935.

Summaries of meetings of the Asociación de Colonos de Cuba which took place between May 1934 and February 1935. Refers to discussions of such topics as moratorium on *colono* debt; repeal of consumption tax on sugar; fixed minimum rates to be paid by mills receiving *colono* cane; and reciprocity treaties with the U.S. Can be used to explore relationship between *colonos* and the national state and between *colonos* and mill owners.

36. Atkins, Edwin F. *Sixty Years in Cuba: Reminiscences of Edwin F. Atkins.* 1926. Reprint. New York: Arno Press, 1980. 362 p.

Memoir by major North American landowner and sugar planter in Cuba. Atkins acquired the Soledad estate, located near Cienfuegos in Santa Clara province, and developed it into a central sugar mill. Contains descriptions of his encounters with specific former slaves and rebels, as well as discussions of politics, race, and the development of the sugar industry. Can be used in conjunction with the voluminous manuscript material on the Atkins properties available in the records of the U.S.-Spanish Treaty Claims Commission, located in the U.S. National Archives; with the Atkins Family Papers in the Massachusetts Historical Society in Boston; and with Soledad plantation materials in archives in Havana and Cienfuegos.

37. Bacardí y Moreau, Emilio, comp. *Crónicas de Santiago de Cuba*. Reprint. 9 vols. Madrid: Gráficas Breogán, 1973.

An extensive compilation of fragments of evidence on the history of the city of Santiago de Cuba and, to a lesser extent, its surrounding region, from its founding in the sixteenth century to the late nineteenth century. Sources quoted include newspapers, official documents, and municipal records. Is organized chronologically, year by year, and has a name and subject index. Different volumes were originally published at different dates beginning in 1908, and there are multiple editions. Vol. IV of this reprint edition, for example, covers the period from 1868 to 1870, early years of the Ten Years' War, and provides evidence of links between war and the breakdown of slavery.

38. Ballou, Maturin M. *Due South or Cuba Past and Present*. 1885. Reprint. New York: Negro Universities Press, 1969. 316 p.

Travel account written the year before the end of the *patronato*. Contains discussions of the conditions and uses of free, contract, and "apprenticed" labor on the island.

39. Barnet, Miguel, ed. *Biografía de un cimarrón*. Havana: Instituto de Etnología y Folklore, Academia de Ciencias de Cuba, 1966. 220 p.

Interview-based account of the life of Esteban Montejo, apparently born in the 1860s. First sections describe his life as a runaway. Book deals in detail with his years as a free worker on two sugar plantations in Santa Clara province. Includes descriptions of working conditions, gender relations, Afro-Cuban religious practices, recreation, diet, and other aspects of black social life after emancipation. Short section on Montejo's participation in the War for Independence is useful for examining the role played by former slaves in that struggle; should be read in conjunction with recent archive-based work on Montejo by Michael Zeuske, cited in the section on secondary sources.

40. Batrell Oviedo, Ricardo. *Para la historia. Apuntes autobiográficos de la vida de Ricardo Batrell Oviedo.* Havana: Seoane y Álvarez, 1912. 181 p.

Military memoir of black participant in final war of independence. Author was born on a sugar estate in Matanzas in 1880 and joined the insurrection in 1895 at the age of fifteen. Provides substantial evidence of social conditions in Matanzas countryside during the war and of relations between Afro-Cuban and white insurgents, between insurgents and Spanish military, and between insurgents and peasant families who resisted Spanish reconcentration. Especially useful for examining Afro-Cuban insurgents' views on the independence struggle. Conveys sense of betrayal following marginalization of Afro-Cubans in postindependence politics.

41. Boza, Bernabé. *Mi diario de la guerra, desde Baire hasta la intervención americana.* 2 vols. Havana: La Propagandista, 1900–1904.

The author of this memoir/diary identifies himself as an officer serving with General Máximo Gómez. First volume focuses on events from the perspective of the troops accompanying Gómez in Camagüey and then across the *trocha* into Las Villas (Santa Clara). Includes description of rebel efforts to halt the operation of sugar plantations and of responses of *pacíficos* to the arrival of rebel troops. Second volume deals with politics and discipline within the rebel ranks.

42. Bullard, Lieutenant Colonel R. L. "The Cuban Negro." *The North American Review* 184 (15 March 1907): 623–30.

A U.S. colonel's observations on the social status of Afro-Cubans, including his impressions of Afro-Cuban culture, occupational opportunities, and relations with Cuban whites. His goal is to answer the question of whether demands for greater participation in government are justified.

43. Cabrera, Francisco de A. *Episodios de la Guardia Civil. Cuba.* Valencia, 1897.

Each chapter in this book describes a particular incident involving the Spanish Civil Guard in Cuba. Most of the episodes recounted date from the Ten Years' War through the beginning of the final independence war, with many dating from the period of peace between 1880 to 1895. The book is an excellent source for the study of rural banditry and can also be used to explore relations between colonial authorities and rural people and the extent of reconstruction following the Ten Years' War. The author occasionally identifies towns or neighborhoods inhabited primarily by former slaves after emancipation.

44. *Campaña de Cuba. Recopilación de documentos y ordenes dictadas con motivo del movimiento insurreccional que tuvo lugar la noche del 26 de agosto de 1879 en la ciudad de Santiago de Cuba siendo comandante general de la provincia el excmo. Señor General D. Camilo Polavieja y Castillo.* Cuba: Sección Tipográfica del E. M. de la Comandancia General, 1880. 758 p.

Collection of telegrams, letters, and reports written by or to Camilo Polavieja, Spanish commander of the province of Santiago de Cuba. Documents provide references to slave flight, slave uprisings on plantations, and general modes of slave resistance during the period of the Guerra Chiquita. Orders passed as emergency measures also provide insights into ways in which slaves were challenging Spanish rule. The end of the volume contains lists of insurgents arrested. Individuals are usually identified by name and color; occupation and residence are noted irregularly.

45. Cano, Bienvenido, and Federico Zalba. *El libro de los Síndicos de Ayuntamiento y de las Juntas Protectoras de Libertos.* Havana: Imprenta del Gobierno y Capitanía General, 1875. 347 p.

Compilation of rulings by the Síndicos de Ayuntamiento and by the Juntas Protectoras de Libertos. (*Síndicos* were individuals appointed to represent slaves in legal proceedings; Juntas were boards formed to administer the Moret Law of 1870.) The book is divided into three parts. The first contains rulings concerning the *síndicos* from 1836 to 1875, dealing with such issues as the organization of the *sindicaturas,* appeals for freedom by specific slaves, and restrictions governing the process of *coartación* (gradual self-purchase). The enactments vary in scope, some addressing island-wide questions of organization, others specific situations of individual slaves and owners. The second part contains rulings concerning the Juntas Protectoras addressing issues such as the proper identification of sexagenarians, the baptism of freed infants, and salaries of Junta officials. Enactments attempt to regulate the process of gradual abolition, defining the responsibilities and rights of slaves, owners, and Juntas. This section contains a chart listing the number of slaves freed under each provision of the Moret Law through mid-1875. The third section of the book compiles decrees regarding the control of the slave population from the sixteenth century through 1874.

46. Céspedes Casado, Emilio. *La cuestión social cubana.* Havana: La Propagandista, 1906. 15 p.

Paper presented by the director of the Booker T. Washington Institute of Popular Education in Havana, a group dedicated to workers' education and particularly to the education of Afro-Cuban workers. The paper discusses the history of Afro-Cuban participation in the formation of the Cuban nation, the transition from slave to citizen, the effects of U.S. intervention on the political life of Afro-Cubans, current problems in Cuban race relations, and suggestions for "racial elevation." Can be used to examine forms of Afro-Cuban social organization and political activity, as well as discourses of racial and national identity in the early republic.

47. China. Tsung li ko kuo shih wu ya men. *Report of the Commission sent by China to Ascertain the Condition of Chinese Coolies in Cuba.* 1876. Reprint. Taipei: Ch'eng Wen Publishing, 1970. 236 p.

Detailed report by a commission of enquiry sent to Cuba in 1874 to investigate the condition of indentured and free Chinese workers, and to report to the Chinese government. Investigators visited plantations in Havana (Las Cañas), Matanzas (San Cayetano, Concepción, Armonía), Cárdenas (Esperanza, Recreo, San Antonio), Colón (España, Flor de Cuba), Sagua la Grande (Santa Anna, Santa Isabella, Capitolis), Cienfuegos (Juniata, Candelaria), and sugar warehouses in Catalina, as well as jails and depots in Guanajay and in the plantation regions listed above. Report quotes extensively from depositions taken from Chinese workers. Although collected in the presence of overseers and administrators, the workers' depositions describe in detail the conditions of their recruitment and sale, working conditions on plantations and in work gangs (*cuadrillas*), and the abuses to which they were subject. Their testimony also touches upon social status, diet, health, and other aspects of daily life, including initiatives taken by the Chinese to attempt to enforce their legal rights. The report offers useful evidence about forms of nominally free labor used before abolition and about relations between black slaves and another group of ethnically distinct rural workers. A facsimile edition of the English-language portion of the report has been published, with a new introduction by Denise Helly, as *The Cuba Commission Report: A Hidden History of the Chinese in Cuba* (Baltimore: Johns Hopkins University Press, 1993).

48. Clark, Victor. "Labor Conditions in Cuba." *Bulletin of the Department of Labor* 41 (July 1902): 663–793.

Account of working conditions by North American investigator. Is imprecise on early history, but contains detailed description of the labor force during period of first U.S. occupation. Discusses racial and ethnic divisions within the labor force, the origins of labor unions, and the overall labor supply. Notes that "women are paid the same wages as men in the cane fields" (p. 697). Useful for series of wages and prices, and for scattered observations on the nature of relations between employers and employees in both rural and urban settings.

49. Clark, William, J. *Commercial Cuba: A Book for Business Men.* New York: Charles Scribner's Sons, 1898. 514 p.

A guide to social, economic, and political conditions in Cuba designed to serve potential U.S. investors. Sections on each province review agricultural conditions, transportation, and population of municipalities within the provinces. Contains overview of conditions in the sugar industry. A section on population discusses labor problems, including what the author sees as laborers' preference for work on independent plots over wage work on plantations.

50. Comité por los Derechos del Negro. *Informe de la comisión investigadora de los sucesos de Trinidad y otros trabajos del comité por los derechos del negro.* Havana, 1934. 22 p.

Rare published work on the killing of an Afro-Cuban activist in the town of Trinidad.

51. Commission on Cuban Affairs. *Problems of the New Cuba. Report of the Commission on Cuban Affairs.* New York: Foreign Policy Association, 1935. 523 p.

Report written in 1934 by a special commission formed by the Foreign Policy Association soon after the revolution of 1933. Commission members included several professors of economics, sociology, education, and public health, some members of the Foreign Policy Association (a nongovernmental body). Leland Jenks, author of *Our Cuban Colony* (see below), also served on the commission. Contains information on, among other things, population distribution by race, living conditions of black Cubans, and to a lesser extent, of Chinese residents, and on political participation among Cubans of color. Includes figures for income, expenditures, and size of typical Cuban families, including figures for some Haitian immigrant families. Examines labor unrest in the early 1930s, with special attention to conflicts on sugar estates. Also discusses topics such as land tenure, crop yields, and social welfare. Contains no bibliography.

52. *Conspiración de la raza de color descubierta en Santiago de Cuba el 10 de diciembre de 1880 siendo comandante general de la provincia el Exmo. Sr. Teniente General Don Camilo Polavieja y Castillo.* Santiago de Cuba: Sección Tipográfica del Estado Mayor, 1880. 207 p.

Collection of telegrams and letters by and to Santiago commander General Camilo Polavieja concerning a proindependence conspiracy less than six months after the end of the Guerra Chiquita. Reprints several insurgent letters purportedly captured and deciphered by the Spaniards. The letters lay out plans for the insurrection and provide details on the movement's organizational strengths and bases of support. Contains list of 265 individuals arrested in connection with the conspiracy. The column next to their names that is labeled "class" bears classifications such as *moreno, pardo*, woman, child, or peasant. A sizeable percentage appear to have been people of color. Because Polavieja purposely refrained from punishing whites, however, the list may be misleading.

53. Consuegra y Guzmán, Israel. *Mambiserías*. Havana: Imp. del Ejército, 1930. 214 p.

War memoir written by the aide-de-camp to General Gerardo Machado in the final war of independence. Consuegra was active in the province of Las Villas. His memoir is an excellent source for the study of daily life in the insurgency and contains material on social relations between officers and soldiers and between black and white insurgents.

54. Conte, Rafael, and José M. Capmany. *Guerra de razas: Negros contra blancos*. Havana: Imprenta Militar de Antonio Pérez, 1912. 196 p.

Narrative account of the uprising of 1912 in Guantánamo. Contains descriptions of military campaigns of Cuban army and briefly describes situation in rebel zones. Characterizes conflict as a race war. Contains brief discussion of black political activity and reproduces documents allegedly written by rebel forces.

55. Cruz, Manuel de la. *Episodios de la revolución cubana*. 1890. Reprint. Havana: Instituto del Libro, 1967.

Anecdotal, dramatized recollections of the Ten Years' War based on writings of participants. Some of the episodes involve people identified as former slaves. Contains information on conditions in the countryside, insurgent relations to farms and estates, and Afro-Cuban participation. Uses published memoirs of war experiences by Francisco de Acosta y Albear, James O'Kelly, and others who remain unspecified. Since sources are not listed many of the anecdotes cannot be verified. Written between the major wars of independence, it does, however, provide evidence of how separatists portrayed the first struggle for independence and the Afro-Cuban role within it.

56. Cruz, Manuel de la. *La revolución cubana y la raza de color*. Key West, Fla.: Imprenta "La Propaganda," 1895. 24 p

Proindependence pamphlet written two months after the outbreak of the war for independence in February 1895. Counters claims that the insurrection was a race war with a discussion of black participation and the future of postindependence Cuba.

57. Cuba. Academia de Ciencias. *Indice histórico de la provincia de Camagüey, 1899–1952.* Havana: Instituto del Libro, 1970. 316 p.

A compilation of individual items, chronologically organized, concerning the province of Camagüey. Includes information on workers' organizations, political groups, elections, officeholders, and demonstrations. Transcribes some documents in detail and reproduces several photographs. A bibliography indicates that the items are from newspapers, the provincial archives, published sources, interviews, and depositions. Individual items are not footnoted, however.

58. Cuba. Archivo Nacional. *Documentos para servir a la historia de la Guerra Chiquita (Archivo Leandro Rodríguez).* 3 vols. Havana: Archivo Nacional de Cuba, 1949–1950.

Collection of primary documents relating to the Guerra Chiquita of 1879 through 1880. Includes letters between civilian leaders of the separatist movement in New York and officers of revolutionary clubs both within and outside Cuba, as well as letters between the civilian leadership in New York and military leaders in Cuba. Includes reports of specific campaigns in Cuba, which provide some evidence of rural conditions during the war. Among the subjects treated in the correspondence are Afro-Cuban participation in the insurgency, debates over Afro-Cuban leadership, and connections between the insurrection and slavery and emancipation. Of particular interest are letters from Carolina Rodriguez, conveying her perception of the behavior of the *gente de color* in Santa Clara. Letters are generally organized chronologically. Index may be used to find letters to, by, or about particular Afro-Cuban insurgents or about particular locations where one knows slaves or *convenidos* (those slaves freed by the Convenio de Zanjón in 1878) to have been active in the insurrection.

59. Cuba. Comisión Consultiva Agraria. *Memoria de sus trabajos.* Havana: Imp. M. Ruiz, 1908. 112 p.

Report on work accomplished by the Comisión Consultiva Agraria from its creation in 1907 through 1908. The group was founded by prominent agriculturalists to represent their interests before the state. Includes proposals made by the group regarding such areas as immigration, labor codes, financing, transportation, and agricultural education.

60. Cuba. Comisión de Higiene Especial. *La prostitución en Cuba y especialmente en la Habana.* 2 vols. Havana: Imp. P. Fernández, 1902. 186 p.

Study of prostitution in Cuba following the war and U.S. occupation. Contains statistics on the social background of prostitutes. The 585 Cuban-born prostitutes are divided by provinces and broken down into racial categories: white, *mestiza*, and black. Contains further information on literacy, also divided by race. Emphasizes the high percentage of white prostitutes relative to the population and the low representation of Afro-Cuban women. This trend is contrasted to that of post–Ten Years' War period during which, according to Benjamín Céspedes, the majority of prostitutes were said to be women of color. More generally, the author attributes the rise in prostitution to the war, Spanish reconcentration policy, and the high rates of orphaned children.

61. Cuba. Comité Estatal de Estadísticas. *Memorias inéditas del censo de 1931.* Havana: Editorial de Ciencias Sociales, 1978. 356 p.

Compilation of data from the 1931 census, including materials that were not published at the time of the count itself. Includes general population counts, divided by "etnia" (*blancos, negros, mestizos,* and *amarillos*). Also includes information on immigration, occupation, and instruction. Should be used, when possible, in conjunction with earlier publications of preliminary results from this census.

62. Cuba. Dirección del Censo. *Census of the Republic of Cuba. 1919.* Havana: Maza, Arroyo y Caso, 1922. 968 p.

This volume, published in English, contains the full report of the 1919 census, and expands upon the preliminary report published in Spanish (see following item in this bibliography). Introduction explains link to electoral reform and the issuance of voting cards in conjunction with enumeration of the population. Text includes discussion of history, geography, climate, politics, and immigration. Electorate is analyzed by color, education, and birthplace, divided by province, as are data on literacy and occupations. Population tables are extensive, providing local level data on education, occupation, family status, and birthplace, further divided into categories native whites, foreign whites, and colored.

63. Cuba. Dirección General del Censo. *Estados que comprenden el número de habitantes y electores de la República, segun la enumeración practicada en 15 de septiembre de 1919.* Havana: Imp. de Rambla, Bouza y Ca., 1920. 99 p.

A brief preliminary summary of the results of the 1919 census, giving population totals and number of *electores* by province, *término municipal*, and *barrio*. For full results of the census, published later, see previous item in this bibliography.

64. Cuba. Secretaría de Agricultura, Comercio y Trabajo. *Industria Azucarera, Zafra de 1925 a 1926*. Havana: Imp. Montalvo y Cárdenas, 1926. 128 p.

Figures on sugar production during harvest of 1925-1926. There is an entry for each *central* (sugar mill), which lists total *arrobas* of cane ground at the mill, distinguishing between *caña de administración* (cane grown by farmers on land belonging to the estate) and cane grown by independent *colonos*. These figures appear to vary widely from case to case, with some *centrales* grinding a majority of estate cane and others relying almost entirely on cane grown by independent *colonos*. Combined with data collected for other years, these figures can help one explore the relative strength or weakness of *colonos* in a particular area over a period of time. The *centrales* are arranged by province. A brief introduction lists new *centrales* which began grinding cane that year and old *centrales* which did not grind cane any cane for the period. Note: Similar volumes exist with the same corporate author for earlier harvests during the Republican period, though the information and format vary from year to year (see item below).

65. Cuba. Secretaría de Agricultura, Comercio y Trabajo. *Industria Azucarera. Memoria de la zafra realizada en el año de 1917 a 1918*. Havana: Rambla, Bouza y Ca., 1919.

A summary of production figures for the sugar harvest of 1917–18. Each *central* has a one page entry with the names of the owners, administrators, and other supervisors, dates of grinding, amount and quality of cane ground by the mill. Unfortunately, this report does not distinguish between *caña de administración* (cane grown by farmers on land belonging to the estate) and cane grown by independent *colonos*. However, the information provided here can be used to assess the situation of particular sugar mills or of particular regions during the postwar sugar boom. (The parallel report for 1915–16 has a similar title. Volumes exist for the harvest of 1918–19, 1919–20, and 1925–26, with the same author and varying titles.)

66. Cuba. Secretaría de Agricultura, Comercio y Trabajo. *Legislación obrera de la República de Cuba*. Havana: Rambla, Bouza y Ca., 1919. 290 p.

Publication of labor laws in effect as of 1919. These include laws regarding registration of workers, wages, and work hours for state laborers; prohibition of payment with scrip; days off on Sundays; workplace accidents; workers' housing; and immigration. Also includes proposed labor laws pending Congressional approval as of 1919, and laws regarding women's and children's labor, strike legislation, arbitration, and immigration.

67. Cuba. Secretaría de Agricultura, Industria y Comercio. *Memoria de los trabajos y servicios de este departamento correspondiente al periodo de tiempo transcurrido desde el 10 de mayo de 1902 hasta el 31 de diciembre de 1903.* Havana: Imp. P. Fernández, 1904.

Annual report of the secretary of agriculture for 1902 and 1903. Contains brief summaries of conditions of selected industries, principally livestock, tobacco, and mining. Includes tables of production figures of sugar mills, tobacco, coffee, and cacao farms for harvests between 1901 and 1902 and between 1902 and 1903. Sugar tables are arranged by province and figures are provided for each *central* within the province. Tobacco, coffee, and cacao figures are also arranged by province and *término municipal.* These tables list the number of farms of each kind and give production figures by *término municipal,* though not by individual farm.

68. Curbelo, José. *Proyecto de inmigración nacional para la isla de Cuba y de la más fácil realización.* Havana: La Propaganda Literaria, 1882. 26 p.

Essay proposes replacement of *patronato* labor with Spanish immigrant workers, citing Cuba's need for a new social and economic order after Ten Years' War. Advocates granting free transportation and plots of land to immigrant families, and contains charts predicting increased productivity if plan is carried out.

69. Dabán y Ramírez, Luis. *Situación política del departamento oriental de la isla de Cuba desde el 9 de julio de 1878 al 22 de junio de 1879, siendo comandante general el excmo. Sr. Mariscal de Campo Don Luis Dabán y Ramírez de Arellano.* Santiago de Cuba: Sección Tipográfica del Estado Mayor, 1881. 123 p.

Collection of telegrams and letters by and to Luis Dabán regarding conditions in Santiago between the end of the Ten Years' War in 1878 and the outbreak of the Guerra Chiquita in 1879. The letters address questions of slave resistance, including the refusal to work and continued flight from plantations. Can be used to explore ways in which slaves used the nationalist insurrection and its aftermath to further their own goals of freedom.

70. Deerr, Noel. *Memorandum. Condiciones de la industria azucarera en Cuba.* Havana: El Iris, 1915. 30 p.

Examination of Cuban sugar industry based on observation of following mills: Toledo, El Pilar, Rosario, Soledad (Cienfuegos), Trinidad, Constancia, Santa Gertrudis, Alava, Soledad (Guantánamo), Rio Cauto, Tingüaro, Nueva Luisa, Armonía, Morón (Ciego de Avila), and Santa María. Cuban conditions are compared to those in Hawaii and Java. While much of the discussion is technical, Deerr addresses labor issues, arguing that the relative backwardness of the Cuban sugar industry was caused by low prices and the high cost of scarce labor.

71. Descamps, Gastón. *La crisis azucarera y la isla de Cuba.* Havana: La Propaganda Literaria, 1885. 187 p.

Comparative discussion of sugar production in Cuba, Puerto Rico, the British and French Caribbean, and Louisiana. The second half of the book is devoted to the Cuban sugar industry. Discusses the process of gradual abolition, the effects of anticolonial insurrections, free labor and vagrancy, and technological advances in production. Consists largely of extended quotations from other sources, such as Ibañez, *Observaciones sobre la utilidad.* . . . (see below), British Foreign Office records, *Memoria sobre un ingenio central en Puerto-Príncipe*, and others.

72. Edo y Llop, Enrique. *Memoria histórica de Cienfuegos y su jurisdicción.* 2nd ed. Cienfuegos: J. Andreu, 1888. 1067 p.

Detailed, voluminous history of Cienfuegos and outlying area. Arranged chronologically by year. Contains information on Ten Years' War in the area. Provides details on local events, such as the founding of a school for children of color in 1883, and reproduces useful statistical data, such as the number of *patrocinados* in 1883. Note: a later edition of the volume was published in 1943.

73. Espinosa y Ramos, Serafín. *Al trote y sin estribos (Recuerdos de la Guerra de Independencia).* Havana: Jesús Montero, 1946. 286 p.

War memoir from the final war of independence in Las Villas. Describes rebel attacks on local *ingenios* and provides evidence of racial and class tensions within the insurrection.

74. Ferrara, Orestes, ed. *Anuario estadístico de la República de Cuba.* Cleveland: Arthur H. Clark Company, 1915. 191 p.

Compilation of statistics, including information on population, immigration, births, and the sugar and tobacco industries. Collects data from censuses and documents from various branches of government, including the Secretaría de Hacienda, Secretaría de Gobernación, Secretaría de Sanidad y Beneficiencia, and the Secretaría de Agricultura, as well as from issues of *La Gaceta* and *El Tabaco*. Some information goes back to the sixteenth century, although the collection is strongest on the early twentieth century. Charts include estimates of numbers of slaves entering Cuba, racial breakdowns of the population through time, and total population numbers, as well as levels of immigration by nationality. The section on deaths includes a yearly list of causes of death, with detailed references to specific diseases.

75. Ferrer, Horacio. *Con el rifle al hombro*. Havana: Imp. "El Siglo XX," 1950. 403 p.

Broad overview of author's participation in insurrection and in political life in Cuba, through the period of the dictatorship of Gerardo Machado. Ferrer, who grew up in Matanzas, joined the anticolonial conspiracy in 1893 as a medical student, and participated in the 1895–98 conflict. An unusual aspect of this memoir, one useful for the study of society after slavery, is its account of the events of 1912 in Oriente, which the author characterizes as an "alzamiento racista."

76. Figueras, Francisco. *Cuba y su evolución colonial*. Havana: Imprenta Avisador Comercial, 1907. 441 p.

Account of Cuban colonial history based on theory of cultural degeneration through racial intermixture. Explains political corruption as a consequence of characteristics of the Latin race, which is described as inferior to Anglo-Saxon race and further tainted morally and physically through its involvement with slavery. Advocates the furthering of civilization in Cuba through presence and influence of Anglo-Saxon cultures. Does not cite sources but does cite work of degeneration theorist Max Nordau.

77. Flint, Grover. *Marching with Gomez: A War Correspondent's Field Note-Book Kept during Four Months with the Cuban Army*. Boston: Lamson, Wolffe, 1898. 294 p.

Diary of U.S. newspaper correspondent who spent four months in early 1896 with the Cuban insurgent army during the War of Independence. Flint spent much of his time with Gómez's troops, traditionally viewed as substantially Afro-Cuban. Can be used to examine racial and social composition of Cuban army, roles played by Afro-Cubans, and organization of Cuban army.

78. Forbes Lindsay, Charles. *Cuba and her People of To-Day*. Boston: L. C. Page, 1911. 329 p.

Designed to aid potential investors in Cuba. Contains advice on Cuban labor relations. Section devoted to sugar industry contains figures on costs and profits of planters and mill operators. Includes general information on other industries. Reflects one version of North American perceptions of "national character" of Cubans, both black and white, and of Cuban race relations.

79. Gallego García, Tesifonte. *Cuba por fuera*. Havana: La Propaganda Literaria, 1890. 254 p.

Travel account written by a Spanish lawyer. Describes his travels through the countryside, devoting particular attention to effects of the Ten Years' War in the provinces of Oriente and Camagüey. Visits sites important during that war, such as the *trocha*, Guáimaro, and Zanjón. Talks to several local rural people who had participated in the insurgency. Can be used to examine the level of reconstruction approximately ten years after the end of the war. Also discusses the state of Cuban education, journalism, literature, and other related fields.

80. Gallenga, A. *The Pearl of the Antilles*. 1873. Reprint. New York: Negro Universities Press, 1970. 202 p.

Travel account written in 1873 to describe conditions created by the Ten Years' War. Contains sections on slaves, slave owners, and emancipation, exploring question of how free labor could be substituted for slave labor without undermining production. Author interviews two prominent sugar planters on their opinions on emancipation and free labor. Discusses conditions of work on plantations, effects of Moret law of 1870, and the Ten Years' War.

81. García Morales, Francisco. *Guía de gobierno y policía de la isla de Cuba. Compendio de las atribuciones gubernativas de los alcaldes ... con un prontuario alfabético de la legislación vigente sobre policía y ordén público*. Havana: La Propaganda Literaria, 1881. 258 p.

Guide to colonial administration that summarizes the responsibilities of local colonial officials: *alcaldes, tenientes de alcalde*, and *alcaldes de barrio*. Contains alphabetical listing of legislation current in 1880, including laws on such topics as black *cabildos*, Chinese residents in Cuba, vagrancy, *patrocinados*, banditry, *ñáñigos*, farm fences, cane fires, and riots.

82. Gómez, Fernando. *La insurrección por dentro*. 2nd ed. Madrid: Biblioteca de La Irradiación, 1900. 512 p.

A study of the Cuban insurgency of 1895 designed to provide a Spanish audience with a glimpse of the organization and day-to-day life within the Cuban ranks. The author's discussions are based partly on documents recovered from insurgents themselves, including unpublished war diaries, rebel proclamations and handbills. Based on these documents, the author discusses activities of several leaders of color, including Antonio Maceo during the Western invasion and his stay in Pinar del Río, and Quintín Bandera and José González in Las Villas.

83. Gómez, Juan Gualberto. *La cuestión de Cuba en 1884. Historia y soluciones de los partidos cubanos.* Madrid: Imp. de Aurelio J. Alaria, 1885. 105 p.

Reviews history and social composition of Cuban political parties following the Pact of Zanjón of 1878. Summarizes the political, economic, and social programs of each, including their positions on slavery, emancipation, and immigration. Censures Spanish resistance to reforms in the post-Zanjón period. Useful review of political and ideological currents surrounding the struggles for independence and emancipation written by a prominent Afro-Cuban journalist, activist, and participant in the Cuban independence movement.

84. Gómez, Juan Gualberto. *Por Cuba libre.* Edited with an introduction by Emilio Roig de Leuchsenring. Havana: Editorial de Ciencias Sociales, 1974. 513 p.

A compilation of newspaper articles, essays, and letters by Juan Gualberto Gómez. Among the pieces anthologized are articles from the Afro-Cuban newspaper *La Fraternidad*, essays on such topics as political, social and economic conditions in the 1880s, conspiratorial activities in preparation for the final war of independence, and public statements regarding the role of United States in Cuba. Also included is Gómez's brief autobiography. The introductory essay by Emilio Roig de Leuchsenring is a biographical essay on the life of the author.

85. Gómez, Máximo. *Diario de campaña, 1868–1899.* Havana: Biblioteca Nacional "José Martí," 1986. 409 p.

War diary of Dominican-born rebel officer who became a general in the Ten Years' War and who held the highest rank in the Liberation Army during the final war of independence. The diary covers Gómez's participation in both wars, as well as his activities outside Cuba during the period of peace between 1880 and 1895. During the final war in 1895, Gómez, together with Antonio Maceo, led Cuban forces in the invasion of the western half of the island. The diary can therefore be used to explore questions of the rebellion's impact on sugar estates in the western provinces. A thirty-six-page appendix reproduces the war diary of José Martí, kept between 9 April and 17 May 1895.

86. Gómez, Máximo. *El viejo Eduá o mi último asistente.* Havana: Instituto Cubano del Libro, 1972. 112 p.

Collection of six essays and letters by Máximo Gómez, one of the principal leaders of the Cuba's independence movement. The title essay "El viejo Eduá" centers around his relationship with several runaway slaves who served as assistants and guides during the Ten Years' War. Provides insight into roles played by slaves and ex-slaves during insurrection as well as subsequent portrayals of those roles.

87. Gonzales, Narciso G. *In Darkest Cuba: Two Months' Service under Gómez Along the Trocha from the Caribbean to the Bahama Canal.* Columbia, S.C.: State, 1922. 455 p.

Memoir of a Cuban-American journalist, raised on a South Carolina plantation, who traveled to Cuba in 1898 to fight in the War of Independence under Máximo Gómez. Describes conditions of insurgent army and Cuban countryside, particularly in Camagüey province. Describes his journey through *potreros* (stock-raising farms) run by the insurgents and provides evidence of racial and class hierarchies within the insurgent army. Discusses conditions of *reconcentrados* and describes various military engagements.

88. Goodman, Walter. *The Pearl of the Antilles, or an Artist in Cuba.* London: Henry S. King, 1873. 304 p.

Travel account written by artist who lived in Cuba from 1864 to 1869. Account includes descriptions of visits to sugar and coffee estates in eastern Cuba. Several chapters deal with the Ten Years' War and contain descriptions of encounters between Spanish troops and runaway slaves, as well as black participation as *bomberos* (firemen).

89. Guerra y Sánchez, Ramiro. *La industria azucarera de Cuba.* Havana: Cultural, 1940. 304 p.

Analysis of conditions of Cuban sugar industry. Though the emphasis is on conditions in the 1930s, author traces historical development of specific features of the industry in the republic. Contains useful sections on the emergence of land concentration, the development of the *colonato*, on divisions within the *colono* class, and on non-*colono* labor in the sugar industry, including material on wages and labor activism.

90. Guiteras, John, ed. *Free Cuba*. Publishers Union, 1897. 617 p.

Collection of several book-length and shorter writings on the Cuban War of Independence, prepared for a U.S. audience during the war. The contents are Part I: Historical and Descriptive by Guiteras; Part II: Causes and Justification of the Present War by Rafael Merchán; Part III: The Prosperity of Cuba by F. G. Pierra; Part IV: In Rebel Camp and Spanish Prison by Captain Ricardo Navarro; and Part V: The Cuban Revolution of 1895 by Gonzalo Quesada. Merchán's contribution is particularly useful for its attention to economic aspects of the insurrection, such as the effect on property, and for its discussion of race relations within the movement. Includes numerous illustrations, including several ones of rebel forces and plantations in rebel zones.

91. Gutiérrez y Salazar, Pedro. *Reformas de Cuba. Cuestión social*. Madrid: Imp. de Manuel G. Hernández, 1879. 85 p.

Proposal for the abolition of slavery in Cuba (1879) outlining conditions for a six year *patronato* and the indemnification of slave owners and detailing plans for the reorganization of Cuban labor through education and immigration.

92. Hazard, Samuel. *Cuba with Pen and Pencil*. Hartford, Conn., 1871. 584 p.

Travel account which describes journey across the island. Author visits several large sugar estates in Matanzas and Cienfuegos and coffee farms in eastern Cuba.

93. Herrera, José Isabel. *Impresiones de la guerra de independencia (narrado por el soldado del Ejército Libertador)*. Havana: Editorial Nuevos Rumbos, 1948. 160 p.

One of the few memoirs published by a black soldier in the war of independence. The author, known also as Mangoché, was a fifteen-year-old sugar worker near San Felipe in Havana province when he joined the insurgents during the western invasion of December 1895–January 1896. He participated mostly in the sugar regions of Havana province and served for part of the war as an assistant (servant) to a rebel officer. The memoir is a valuable source because (along with Ricardo Batrell's *Para la historia*, above) it is one of the few descriptions of daily life in the insurgency from the perspective of a young black worker. It can be used to study social relations within the insurgent ranks, the responses of local rural people to the insurgent invasion from the east, and the relationship between insurgents and sugar workers. It can also be used to explore the sense of betrayal prevalent among some Afro-Cuban veterans in the early republic. Herrera, still unable to write in 1948, narrated the memoir.

94. Hinton, Richard J. "Cuban Reconstruction." *North American Review* 168 (January 1899): 92–102.

A North American's interpretation of Cuba's "reconstruction," focusing on opportunities for investment and on race relations on the island. The author points to perceived differences of race and racial attitudes between Cuba and the United States. He describes white Cubans as "more intelligent" than their peninsular counterparts in other former Spanish colonies and black Cubans as "more industrious" than their U.S. or Haitian counterparts.

95. Hyatt, Pulaski F., and John T. Hyatt. *Cuba: Its Resources and Opportunities*. New York: J. S. Ogilvie, 1898. 211 p.

Appraisal of business opportunities in Cuba written by former U.S. consul and vice-consul in Santiago de Cuba. Contains sections on Cuban social customs ("from a business man's point of view"), rural life, agricultural industries, annexation, and labor. The section on labor conditions includes excerpts from reports by Otto E. Rimer, U.S. consul in Santiago in 1886.

96. Imbernó, Pedro José. *Guía geográfica y administrativa de la isla de Cuba*. Havana: La Lucha, 1891. 312 p.

Dictionary of Cuban place names. Includes detailed descriptions of locations, including very small rural towns. Sometimes includes population figures for small towns. There are entries for different types of small landholdings, and the entry for *ingenio* supplies a list of sugar estates on the island. Includes information on the location of railroad lines and stations.

97. Instituto de Historia del Movimiento Comunista y la Revolución Socialista de Cuba. *El movimiento obrero cubano: Documentos y artículos*. Havana: Editorial de Ciencias Sociales, 1975. 457 p.

Vol. 1 is a compilation of documents focused on ideology, strikes, and union organization during the period from 1865 to 1925. Includes rural materials as well as urban, such as documents on the strikes of sugar workers in Cruces (Santa Clara) in 1902.

98. Jiménez Castellanos, Adolfo. *Sistema para combatir las insurrecciones en Cuba*. Madrid: Establecimiento Tipográfico, 1883. 230 p.

A study of the Ten Years' War written by a Spanish officer. Discusses conditions within the insurgent camp and Spanish plans and offensives against the Cuban insurgents. The author devotes some attention to the participation of slaves in the rebellion.

99. Jiménez, Juan Bautista. *La colonia.* Havana: Imp. de A. Alvarez, 1894.

Author was an industrial engineer affiliated with the Círculo de Hacendados y Agricultores de Cuba. Argues that the sugar industry became more efficient with the end of slavery, the increased division of labor, and the rise of the *colonato.* Much of the book is highly technical, with discussions of varieties of cane, optimal planting cycles, machinery, and so on. Gives costs of cultivating cane by *caballería* for *colonos* using varying techniques of cultivation. Workers' salaries are specified in the cost calculations.

100. Jiménez, Juan Bautista. *Los esclavos blancos, por un colono de Las Villas.* Havana: Imp. de A. Alvarez y Comp., 1893. 112 p.

A polemical account of the exploitation of *colonos* (cane farmers), authored by a grower. Describes conditions in the 1890s in the central province of Santa Clara, enumerating the methods used by mill owners to reduce the payments made to farmers supplying the mills. Calls for *colonos* to unite and demand an increased minimum payment from central mills. Useful both for the description of working conditions and for imagery of cane farmers as "white slaves." Important for understanding the structural position of *colonos* during a period of rapid expansion in sugar production.

101. López Tuero, Fernando. *Estado moral de los factores de la producción en Cuba y Puerto Rico.* Madrid: Lib. de D. Fe, 1896. 57 p.

A study of labor, economic, and commercial conditions in Cuba and Puerto Rico published in Spain during Cuba's final war of independence. It advocates the establishment of strong commercial ties between the metropole and the two islands so as to diminish the colonies' need to search for other external markets. The study gives a general sense of economic conditions in the countryside and includes some generalizations about rural wages and the value and productivity of rural land.

102. Labra y Cadrana, Rafael María de. *La brutalidad de los negros.* 1876. Reprint. Havana: Imp. de la Universidad de la Habana, 1961. 45 p.

Spanish abolitionist pamphlet published in 1876 to counter antiabolitionist arguments about "the natural condition of the slave race." Contains figures on crime rates, occupations, literacy, and so on among free blacks, particularly for the 1870s. Includes comparisons of these figures with similar ones for Puerto Rico immediately following emancipation there in 1873. Short section reprints slaveowners' advertisements for the sale or rental of their slaves in 1875 and 1876. Author was a major abolitionist figure and prolific author. (We have included only a small selection of Labra's many pamphlets in *Societies after Slavery*.)

103. Labra y Cadrana, Rafael María de. *La raza de color en Cuba*. Madrid: Establecimiento Tipográfico de Fortanet, 1894. 36 p.

Epistolary pamphlet containing letters written on the occasion of the dedication of a monument to Labra by the Directorio Central de las Sociedades de la Raza de Color in honor of Labra's commitment to the abolition of Cuban slavery. Among most interesting letters are those from Labra to the head of the Directorio, his close friend and associate Juan Gualberto Gómez, and the Directorio's response printed in the newspaper *La Igualdad*. The collection reflects abolitionist attitudes toward emancipation and former slaves. Also sheds light on postemancipation political order and efforts by some Spanish and Cuban reformers to militate for broader political and civil rights after slavery.

104. Labra y Cadrana, Rafael María de. *Mi campaña en las Córtes Españolas de 1881 a 1883*. Madrid: Imp. de Aurelio J. Alaria, 1885. 365 p.

Collection of Labra's speeches and motions in the Spanish Cortes between 1881 and 1883. Most have to do with autonomy and colonial administration, electoral laws, budgets, military service, and so on. Contains Labra's 1882 motion for the abolition of the *patronato*, which gives some insight into the abolitionist cause in Cuba, the stance of planters regarding final abolition, conditions in sugar mills, and the relationship between abolition and Spanish-Cuban relations.

105. Lagardere, Rodolfo. *La cuestión social de Cuba*. Havana: La Universal de Ruíz y Hermano, 1887.

Controversial tract written by a pro-Spanish journalist of color. Published one year after final legal emancipation, the book rejects any political alternative to Spanish rule as the onset of racial war. At the same time, however, he condemns Cuban autonomism for its lack of commitment to racial equality.

106. Leyva y Aguilera, Herminio. *La Guerra Chiquita. El movimiento insurreccional de 1879 en la provincia de Santiago de Cuba*. Havana: La Universal, 1893. 90 p.

A book published in response to assertions made in 1893 by Camilo Polavieja, former captain-general of the island and former governer of Santiago province, about his central role in bringing about the end of the proindependence rebellion known as the Guerra Chiquita (1879–1880). Leyva's response emphasizes the important role played by Cuban autonomists in defeating the independence effort of 1879. Polavieja's original assertions, reprinted at the beginning of the book, stress the black character of rebellion in Oriente, the importance of black political leadership, and alleged efforts at transnational black activism in the Liga Antillana.

107. Llorens y Maceo, José S. *Con Maceo en la invasión.* Havana, 1928. 205 p.

War memoir of rebel officer who accompanied Maceo's troops during the western invasion of 1895 through 1896. Though the focus is on narrating military encounters, the author also provides evidence relevant for examining relations between insurgents and local peasants in areas newly occupied by rebel forces. Describes relations between rebels and sugar producers especially in the provinces of Matanzas and Santa Clara. Author discusses rebel orders to burn sugar estates and rebel exactions of "tribute" payments from estate owners and administrators anxious to prevent the torching of sugar cane.

108. McHatton-Ripley, Eliza. *From Flag to Flag: A Woman's Adventures and Experiences in the South during the War, in Mexico, and in Cuba.* New York: Appleton, 1889. 296 p.

Memoir of U.S. owner of sugar estate Desengaño outside the city of Matanzas. Briefly discusses relations between the sugar estate and neighboring, Cuban-owned coffee plantation. Describes working and living conditions of slaves and Chinese contract laborers. Includes a description of a small Chinese "rebellion" about plantation food which occurred during the Ten Years' War. Can be used to explore effects of that war on sugar estates.

109. Martí, Carlos. *El país de la riqueza.* Madrid, 1918. 263 p.

Travel guide written by a Spaniard resident in Cuba for twenty years and active in education, journalism, and Cuban immigration policy. Contains brief section on immigrant labor in sugar and on the Asociación de Fomento de Inmigración, which is seen by the author as a protector of immigrant workers' rights.

110. Martí, José. *La cuestión racial.* Habana: Editorial Lex, 1959. 144 p.

Collection of essays by José Martí on race, drawn from the edition of his *Obras Completas* published in 1946. Includes the newspaper articles "Basta," "Pobres y Ricos," "Mi raza," "El plato de lentejas," "Sobre negros y blancos," and others. Useful for exploring the character of Martí's opposition to racism, the concept of slave emancipation as redemptive of white guilt, and the ideal of a transracial Cuban national identity.

111. Martínez-Fortún y Foyo, José A. *Anales y efemérides de San Juan de los Remedios y su jurisdicción.* Vol. 12. Remedios: Imp. Eduardo J. Roque, 1941.

Part of a larger, multivolume, antiquarian work with varying place and date of publication. This volume deals with 1936 and contains references to organizations, meetings, deaths, bombings, elections, kidnapping, sugar harvest, suicides, sugar prices, cane burning, poverty, dances, epidemics, sermons, comets, earthquakes, and the weather. The deaths of several elderly African are announced. Appendix 4, in this volume, includes a description of the 1895–98 rebel campaign of Máximo Gómez in Las Villas (Santa Clara), as well as other events from 1895 to 1898.

112. Matanzas, Provincia de. Exma. Diputación Provincial. *Censo agrícola. Fincas azucareras. Año de 1881.* Matanzas: Imp. Aurora del Yumurí, 1883. 11 p.

Short agricultural census on sugar production in Matanzas in 1881, broken down by municipality. Information provided includes number of farms, acreage under cultivation, amounts of sugar and sugar by-products produced. No information specifically dealing with labor is provided. A table with comparable information is provided for the period from 1792 to 1862.

113. Montalvo, José R. "El problema de la inmigración en Cuba." *Revista Cubana* 8 (December 1888): 524–38.

A discussion of means to encourage European migration to Cuba immediately following the emancipation of slaves. Useful for understanding racial ideology and the idea of *blanqueamiento* embraced by some members of the Creole elite in the aftermath of abolition and again following independence.

114. Morehouse, Henry L. *Ten Years in Eastern Cuba: An Account of Baptist Missions therein under the Auspices of the American Baptist Home Mission Society.* New York: American Baptist Home Mission Society, 1910. 56 p.

General description of the educational and spiritual work of Baptist missionaries in eastern Cuba from approximately 1899 to 1909. Includes summaries of work accomplished in towns in the districts of Santiago, Manzanillo, Camagüey, Bayamo, Las Tunas, Guantánamo, Nipe Bay, and Baracoa. Contains occasional references to conditions of residents in these towns, many of which were found along the lines of the Cuba Company railway.

115. Núñez Machín, Ana. *Memoria amarga del azúcar.* Havana: Editorial de Ciencias Sociales, 1981. 213 p.

Compilation of testimonies on experience of work in the sugar sector in Cuba in the first half of the twentieth century. The editor/author provides no indication of how these documents were collected and provides only the name of each speaker. Texts themselves in some cases specify the region. Provides some evidence on the links between subsistence activities and wage labor.

116. "Noticia de las fincas azucareras en producción que existían en toda la isla de Cuba a comenzar el presupuesto de 1877–78. . . ." *Revista Económica* (7 June 1878): 7–24.

List of plantations, owners, output, labor force. Figures on labor need to be used with caution, as the category "libres y alquilados" at times encompassed former slaves freed by the Moret law, who were not necessarily part of the active work force.

117. O'Kelly, James. *The Mambi-Land or, Adventures of a Herald Correspondent in Cuba.* Philadelphia: J. B. Lippincott, 1874. 359 p.

Memoir of *New York Herald* correspondent who lived and traveled with insurgent troops during the Ten Years' War. Particularly useful for examining the roles played by slaves in the insurrection, the organization of runaway slave communities tied to the insurrection, and the social organization of rebel forces.

118. Olivares, José de. *Our Islands and their People as Seen with Camera and Pencil.* Vol. 1. St. Louis: N. D. Thompson Publishing, 1899. 384 p.

First of a two-volume series designed to give the U.S. public a glimpse of everyday life in Cuba, Puerto Rico, the Philippines, and Hawaii. Most of the first volume deals with Cuba. It is generally divided into chapters on the island's provinces, containing hundreds of photographs and descriptions of conditions in each region. Some photographs, however, appear to have been substantially retouched. Contains introduction by Major-General Joseph Wheeler of the U.S. Army.

119. Pérez, Louis A., Jr., ed. *Slaves, Sugar, and Colonial Society: Travel Accounts of Cuba, 1801–1899.* Wilmington, Del.: Scholarly Resources, 1992. 239 p.

Selections from nineteenth-century travelers' accounts of Cuba, arranged thematically by chapter and chronologically within chapters.

Includes several descriptions of daily life on sugar plantations and detailed accounts of the organization of slavery on the island. Contains chapters on crime, religion, rural life, education, and health. The collection can serve as a preliminary bibliography of sources for travel literature for the island. The book ends with a bibliographical essay by the editor that surveys secondary literature on Cuba in the nineteenth century.

120. Pepper, Charles. *To-Morrow in Cuba*. 1899. Reprint. New York: Young People's Missionary Movement of the United States and Canada, 1910. 316 p.

Written by U.S. newspaper correspondent to provide overview of social, economic, and political conditions in Cuba on the eve of U.S. occupation. Reviews conditions in agricultural industries, with information on the organization of labor in sugar. A section on race briefly discusses black political participation, civil rights, and labor practices, including what the author perceives as a preference for cultivating independent plots over wage work on plantations.

121. Perpiña y Pibernat, Antonio. *El Camagüey. Viajes pintorescos por el interior de Cuba*. Barcelona: Libreria de J. A. Bastinos, 1889.

Written by a Spanish priest who traveled through Camagüey around 1866. Though his trip itself predates the beginning of emancipation, the author contrasts conditions preceding the insurrection of 1868 with those after the termination of the war in 1878. He provides detailed descriptions of the towns he visits, often including the difference in the number of people, houses, stores, and churches in 1867 and the late 1880s. He describes "popular diversions" in many small towns and comments on the level of racial and gender integration at these activities. Also included are descriptions of his visits to local *ingenios* and to slave *conucos* on those estates.

122. Pichardo, Hortensia, ed. *Documentos para la historia de Cuba*. 2 vols. Havana: Editorial de Ciencias Sociales, 1976–77.

A two-part collection of documents, the first of which covers the period from the arrival of Europeans to 1898, and the second from 1898 to the 1920s. Contains many fundamental texts, including the law abolishing slavery and establishing the *patronato* in 1880, texts by José Martí, and decrees issued by the intervention governments.

123. Piedra Martel, Manuel. *Mis primeros treinta años*. 2nd ed. Havana: Editorial Minerva, 1944. 510 p.

Memoir of author's childhood, adolescence, and participation in insurgent forces from 1895 onward. Account centers on his time as field assistant to Antonio Maceo, detailing recollections of various battles. Includes sections on the early insurrection in Oriente, on the invasion of the western sugar regions in late 1895 and early 1896, and on Maceo's final months in Pinar del Río province. The author provides a sense of social relations within the insurgency, arguing that there existed little racial or regional tension among soldiers or officers. Material from the author's participation in the war also appears in his *Campañas de Maceo en la última Guerra de Independencia* (Havana: Editorial Lex, 1946).

124. Pla, José. *La raza de color. Necesidad de instruir y moralizar a los individuos de color y de fomentar el matrimonio entre los patrocinados.* Matanzas: Imp. "El Ferro-Carril," 1881. 79 p.

Written by a Spanish cleric, this book advocates moral and civic instruction for newly freed slaves. It commends the colonial state for implementing legislation to facilitate the transition to freedom and calls on Cuban slaveowners to comply with new measures. Contains brief section on what the author sees as Afro-Cuban support for continued Spanish rule on the island.

125. Polavieja y del Castillo, Camilo García. *Relación documentada de mi política en Cuba.* Madrid: Imp. de Emilio Minuesa, 1898. 356 p.

First-hand account by Spanish governor of the provinces of Puerto Príncipe and Santiago de Cuba, and later of the island. Quotes extensively from his correspondence with and reports to other Spanish officials. Useful discussions of black participation in the Ten Years' War, the Guerra Chiquita of 1879, and the preparations for the final war of independence. An extensive section on banditry in the 1880s and 1890s includes details on his own antibanditry measures and a discussion of connections between bandit Manuel García and insurgent leader Antonio Maceo. Describes agricultural conditions during the wars, and briefly discusses his role in the Junta Protectora del Trabajo Agrícola e Industrial in Puerto Príncipe, which made small loans to landowners for the reconstruction of their farms following the Ten Years' War.

126. Ponvert, Katherine S. *Cuban Chronicle: The Story of Central Hormiguero in the Province of Las Villas, Cuba.* Fredericksburg, Va.: Holly Hill Press, 1961. 100 p.

Memoir of Katherine Ponvert, wife of owner Anthony Ponvert, who lived on the Hormiguero estate near Cienfuegos from 1929 to 1954. Relying on records of the plantation manager and her mother-in-law's stories, she discusses mill operations dating back to 1880. She refers briefly to the conditions of some ex-slaves following emancipation, to the impact of the 1895 War of Independence on the grinding of cane, and to the boom period following World War I. For the period after her arrival in 1929, she examines relations between *colonos* and mill owners and the impact of political tensions during the 1930s on estate workers. Contains detailed descriptions of style of life of American estate owners for the period between 1900 and 1950. The memoir can be used to complement materials on Hormiguero in the U.S./Spanish Treaty Claims Commission collection in the U.S. National Archives.

127. Porter, Robert P. *Industrial Cuba.* New York: G. P. Putnam's Sons, 1899. 415 p.

Description of the financial, commercial, and industrial condition of Cuba between 1898 and 1899 written by a U.S. special commissioner to Cuba and Puerto Rico. Deals mostly with problems faced by U.S. occupation government. Contains sections on sugar, tobacco, mining, and other industries, on railroads, sanitation, political parties, taxation, population, and so on. Short chapter on payment of insurgent soldiers gives salary figures for officers and privates. Chapter dealing with labor problems contains extracts from notes taken during interviews with overseers and planters. Provides information on the racial composition of the labor force on an unspecified cane farm, monthly salaries for each position at the farm, diet, and rules and regulations of the *barracones* (living quarters of workers).

128. Primelles, León. *Crónica cubana, 1915–1918.* Havana: Editorial Lex, 1955. 659 p.

Addresses following topics, each of which occupies a section of the book: politics, administration of justice, economy, communications, proletariat, historical studies, education, literature and art, sports, society notes, religion, penal law, delinquency and immorality, medicine and sanitation, natural sciences, diplomacy and international affairs. Each subsection contains a summary of events and lists relevant books and articles published in Cuba each year from 1915 to 1918. Also has useful name index, subject index, and a list of Cuban periodicals and publishing companies. Draws on literature mentioned in summaries, government documents, and newspapers. Subsequent volumes by same author exist.

129. Quesada, Gonzalo de. *Cuba.* Washington, D.C.: Government Printing Office, 1905. 541 p.

General introduction to Cuba's political structure, economy, and laws, by minister of Cuba to the United States. Includes chapters on immigration and education. Discussions of agriculture and landholding are the most extensive. Includes detailed information on different agricultural products on the island, including sugar, tobacco, coffee, rice, and many minor fruits and vegetables. For each crop the author provides a sense of the cost of the production process from planting to harvesting and/or figures on yield per *caballería* and crop's market price. The section on sugar provides figures on sugar production from the 1890s through the early years of the republic. Emphasis is placed on the declining cost of sugar production, which the author attributes to improvements in technology and the labor market and to the elimination of colonial taxes and tariffs and of strikes and civil strife. The discussion of landholding includes information on how to purchase land, especially public and commonly held lands (*haciendas comuneras*) in Oriente and Camagüey. The final portion of the book reprints A. P. C. Griffin's extensive bibliography *Books Relating to Cuba* (above).

130. Roa, Ramón Mauricio. *Con la pluma y el machete.* 3 vols. Havana: Academia de Historia, 1950.

Collection of author's writings from his early days in the independence movement to his death. Includes memories of revolt and tributes to leaders. Provides evidence on daily life in the rebellion, on relations between peasants and insurgents and between insurgents and runaway slave communities (*palenques*). One chapter discusses the participation of two freed slaves named José Antonio Legón and Joaquín Júa. Provides detailed description of the signing of the Pact of Zanjón, and rationale for decision to end hostilities.

131. Robinson, Alfred G. *Facts and Figures on the Cuban Situation, Prepared at the Request of the Cuban Planters' Association.* Washington, D.C.: Press of B. S. Adams, 1902. 27 p.

Brief report published at the request of the Cuban Planters' Association and designed to encourage liberal trade concessions for Cuban agricultural industries. Argues that labor scarcity and high agricultural wages resulted in part from the fact that workers who would normally be employed in sugar had been drawn away to labor in railroad industry and the Rural Guard.

132. Roloff y Mialofsky, Carlos. *Indice alfabético y defunciones del Ejército Libertador de Cuba, Guerra de Independencia.* Havana: Imp. de Rambla y Bouza, 1901. 263 p.

List of surviving members of the Cuban Liberation Army during the last
War of Independence (1895–98). Roster is organized alphabetically and
by military unit. Most entries provide parents' names, date joined, and
rank. A final section contains incomplete lists of members killed during
the war. Information provided on date of incorporation can be used to
explore waves of recruitment and, together with data on rank, can also
be used to explore questions about mobility within the ranks of the rebel
army. Can be used in conjunction with manuscript materials in the collections Roloff and Ejército Libertador in the Cuban national archives
to obtain additional information on occupations, literacy, national and
regional origin of army members. Used together with lists of slaves and
former slaves, the roster can be used to identify army members who were
former slaves. The roster contains no direct information on racial
identifications of soldiers.

133. Rosal y Vázquez, Antonio. *En la manigua, diario de mi cautiverio.*
Madrid, 1876. 293 p.

Diary of Spanish officer captured by Cuban troops near Holguin and held
for fifty-six days in 1873. Describes organization of Cuban forces in an
attempt to aid Spanish military efforts. Can be used to examine racial and
social composition of Cuban army, rebel discipline, conditions in the
countryside, and race relations in the Cuban forces.

134. Rosell y Malpica, Eduardo. *Diario del teniente coronel Eduardo Rosell
y Malpica, 1895–1897.* 2 vols. Edited by Benigno Souza. Havana:
Academia de la Historia de Cuba, 1949–50.

A diary kept by the administrator of a sugar *ingenio* in Matanzas after
he joined the independence movement. The first volume covers the period between August 1895 and March 1896, during Rosell's exile in New
York and Nassau, where he had contact with a group of Cuban ex-slaves
who had participated in the Guerra Chiquita and settled in Nassau as
small property owners. The second volume begins with his arrival in
Cuba as an insurgent and ends with his death on a battlefield in 1897.
Rosell landed in eastern Cuba and made his way west to Matanzas. The
second volume provides evidence of the effects of the war on the countryside, daily life in the rebellion, and tensions between different groups
of insurgents.

135. Rosillo y Alquier, Fermín. *Noticia de dos ingenios y datos sobre la
producción azucarera de la isla de Cuba.* Havana: Imp. "El Iris," 1873.
49 p.

Description of two large *ingenios* in Matanzas province in the early
1870s. Information is provided on production techniques, acreage under

cultivation, and production figures. The author also provides information on the number of laborers employed. For white laborers, specific occupations within the estate are provided. The lists do not distinguish occupations for nonwhite laborers, nor do they distinguish between free and unfree black labor. The author makes general observations on the state of the Cuban sugar industry, pointing to a rise in free black labor and an increasing division of labor between *centrales* and *colonos*.

136. Ruiz Suarez, Bernardo. *The Color Question in the Two Americas.* Translated by John Crosby Gordon. New York: Hunt Publishing, 1922. 111 p.

An essay written by an Afro-Cuban lawyer residing in New York. Draws comparisons between U.S. and Cuban race relations in specific arenas including the church, the status of women, and political and cultural organizations. Includes his analysis of the conflict of 1912 in Cuba.

137. Secretaría de Agricultura, Comercio y Trabajo. *Portfolio azucarero, Industria azucarera de Cuba 1912–1914.* Havana: Imp. "La Moderna Poesía," 1915. 424 p.

A compilation of basic statistics for *centrales* and *ingenios*, organized by province. Each entry gives the names of owners at time of publication, size, output for the 1913 season, and also some information on the use of *colonos*. Contains photographs of each estate. Ends with a general collection of statistics that includes numbers of *colonos* per estate.

138. Serra, Rafael. *Para blancos y negros: ensayos políticos, sociales y económicos.* Havana: Imprenta "El Score," 1907. 215 p.

Collection of essays and reprinted newspaper articles, many of them authored by Rafael Serra y Montalvo, the prominent black newspaper editor, politician, and advocate of racial equality. Includes discussions of past and future role of people of African descent in electoral politics in Cuba and the United States, different aspects of racial discrimination, and the importance of education as a remedy for social injustice. Reprints images of numerous well-known Cubans of color, including figures such as Quintín Bandera, Evaristo Estenoz, and Eulogia Pérez de la Rosa.

139. Serrano y Díez, Nicolás María. *Situación económica de la isla de Cuba al advenimiento del Ministerio Cánovas en enero de 1884.* Havana: Tip. de Ruiz y Hermano, 1884. 64 p.

Analysis of Cuban economy in 1884 with special emphasis on sugar and tobacco production. Calls for economic reform under continued Spanish rule. Blames troubled state of commercial agriculture on factors including war, costly free labor, and poor management. Decries injustice of slavery while warning of the dangers of African-led racial war. Laments that *raza de color* lacks culture and enlightenment to become good *colonos.* Calls for increased European immigration as well as education and evangelization of slaves in preparation for coming emancipation.

140. Spain. Cortes, 1879–1880. *Discursos de la ley de abolición de la esclavitud en la isla de Cuba.* Madrid, 1879–1880.

Compilation of Spanish parliamentary debates concerning abolition. Delegates from Cuba invoke their observations of conditions on the island, as well as recommendations for action.

141. Spain. Instituto Geográfico y Estadístico. *Censo de la población de España, según el empadronamiento hecho en 31 diciembre de 1887.* 2 vols. Madrid, 1891–92.

Conveys population census of Spain and overseas possessions. Section on Spain divided by province. Data classified by sex, civil status, education level, birthplace, and nationality. Section on Cuba divided by province and contains two forms of classification: 1) persons present, transient, and absent, subdivided into "Spanish" and "Foreign" categories; and 2) sex and education level, with two subcategories for race, "white" and "of color."

142. Spain. Ministerio de Ultramar. *Spanish Rule in Cuba. Laws Governing the Island. Review Published by the Colonial Office in Madrid, with Data and Statistics Compiled from Official Records.* New York, 1896. 67 p.

Review of Spanish laws related to Cuba, including the legal framework of abolition.

143. Spain. Ministerio de Ultramar. *Cuba desde 1850 a 1873.* Madrid: Imp. Nacional, 1873. 301 p.

Collection of official documents reproduces reports from the Captains General to the Ministerio de Gobierno and the Ministerio de Guerra, decrees concerning institutions of governance in Cuba, and 1870 census materials including data on slavery. Reports of the Captains General are useful for information on public education, conspiracies, and proposals for police, tax and constitutional reform. Appendix contains memoirs of the Conferencia de la Junta Informativa de Ultramar, held in Madrid in 1866 and 1867, which addressed questions of reforms in Puerto Rico and Cuba.

144. Steele, James W. *Cuban Sketches.* New York: G. P. Putnam's Sons, 1881. 220 p.

Travel account written by former U.S. consul in Cuba. Contains chapters on the Ten Years' War, black and Chinese labor, and conditions on sugar estates.

145. Suárez Argudín, José. *Cuestión social.* Havana, 1870. 121 p.

Essay takes as its starting point the imminent demise of slavery. Author compares Cuban, French, and English slavery, emphasizing what he perceives as the relatively benevolent aspects of Cuban slavery. Examines legal and social issues raised by the eventual transition to wage labor, such as family structure, market relations, immigration, and education.

146. Suzarte, José Quintín. *Estudios sobre la cuestión económica de la isla de Cuba.* Havana: Miguel de Villa, 1881. 68 p.

Rare collection of essays on economic condition of the island.

147. Taybo, Antonio C. y Ca. *Indice general de fundos y haciendas de la isla de Cuba.* Havana: Imp. Militar, 1915. 88 p.

A guide to property in Cuba with an introduction on law, history, and geography. Includes useful lists of terminology for the measurement of land. The first volume published covers Camagüey, listing properties and location of notarial records pertaining to them. Useful as a reference work for regional or municipal studies. Could provide background information and leads, for example, for a study of emancipation in insurgent-occupied territory of Sibanicú and Porcayo in 1869. The author's prologue refers to his study as a multivolume work, including a volume for each province and another on *realengos* throughout the island. It is not clear, however, how many of the subsequent volumes were printed.

148. Torres Lasqueti, Juan. *Colección de datos históricos-geográficos y estádisticos de Puerto del Príncipe y su jurisdicción.* Havana: Imp. "El Retiro," 1888. 370 p.

A local history of the province of Puerto Príncipe (or Camagüey) from its first settlement in the early sixteenth century to 1879. The first part of the book is a chronological log of events, the third section of which covers the period between 1869 and 1879. This section provides a sense of the progress of the Ten Years' War in the region and offers statistical evidence of economic decline as a result of insurgency and counterinsurgency. For example, it lists figures for population, houses, farms, and livestock in 1868 and 1879, reflecting the effects of war on the local countryside. The second part of the book is a general overview of the region's geography and political and administrative organization from the sixteenth century through 1879. It includes descriptions of rural roads and lists of local office holders.

149. Townshend, Frederick Trench. *Wild Life in Florida, with a Visit to Cuba.* London: Hurst and Blackett, 1875. 319 p.

Travel account which includes a visit to a Cuban sugar estate in Marianao, outside Havana. Describes conditions for Chinese contract workers and slaves. Briefly discusses conditions for black children technically freed by the Moret Law of 1870 but who continued to work on the estates.

150. U.S. Department of Commerce. *The Cane Sugar Industry: Agricultural, Manufacturing, and Marketing Costs in Hawaii, Porto Rico, Louisiana, and Cuba.* Washington, D.C.: Government Printing Office, 1917. 462 p.

Report on the sugar industries of Hawaii, Puerto Rico, Cuba, and Louisiana, with emphasis on the comparative costs of sugar production. Section on Cuban industry is based on visits to Cuban sugar estates in early 1916 and examination of estate record books. The *colonato* system is discussed, and distinctions are made between independent *colonos, colonos* who cultivate estate lands, and *colonos* who cultivate land owned by third parties. Average prices paid by the estates for cane cultivated by each type of *colono* are calculated. Figures are provided for the number of Cuban- and foreign-born *colonos* and average acreage under cultivation by *colonos* during the 1912–13 harvest, broken down by province. Rates of pay for field labor are also provided, and broken down into cultivating (plowing, planting, weeding), cutting, and hauling labor costs. Some cost comparisons between the eastern and western Cuban sugar estates are also provided.

151. U.S. Spanish Treaty Claims Commission. *Final Report of William Wallace Brown, Assistant Attorney-General.* Washington, D.C.: Government Printing Office, 1910. 200 p.

Can function as a partial index to the collection in the U.S. National Archives of original case files of this commission, established to adjudicate claims of U.S. citizens following the conclusion in 1898 of the U.S. war with Spain.

152. U.S. Spanish Treaty Claims Commission. *Table of Cases, Index-Digests of Briefs, Awards, etc.* (Volume 24. Published for the Department of Justice.) Washington, D.C.: Government Printing Office, 1910. 205 p.

Accompanies the 23 other bound volumes of briefs presented in cases before the U.S. Spanish Treaty Claims Commission, and printed for the Department of Justice. This volume contains a table of cases briefed with a cross-reference to the printed volume in which the briefs appear, and a schedule of claims filed with the commission and their disposition. These lists can serve as a guide to the printed briefs, which contain extensive evidence on agriculture, labor, and the insurgency (1895–98). In conjunction with the final report of the commission, it can also be used as a guide to the extensive manuscript depositions and exhibits filed before the commission and located in the U.S. National Archives.

153. U.S. Spanish Treaty Claims Commission. *Briefs of the Claimants and the Government before the Spanish Treaty Claims Commission.* 24 vols. Washington, D.C.: Government Printing Office, 1901.

Contain printed pleadings before the U.S. Spanish Treaty Claims Commission. Individuals and corporations alleging U.S. citizenship were able to file for damages resulting from events of the conflict (1895–98). These volumes represent only a fraction of the total documentation generated by the commission, which is deposited in the U.S. National Archives. However, the printed pleadings provide an entrée into the manuscript materials, and can be of use in themselves for the study of social and economic conditions in the late 1890s and for evidence of the conduct and impact of the war. The volumes are organized by topic and are carefully indexed. Copies can be found in some law libraries.

Volumes 2 and 3 include claimants' briefs on liability for damages by insurgents; volume 4 includes claimants' briefs on war damages, reconcentration and the Treaty of 1795; volume 5 includes government briefs on war damages, reconcentration, and the Treaty of 1795; volume 6 includes briefs of claimants and government on right to recover under mortgages, crop liens, and so on. Volume 6 is thus of particular interest for the study of the *colonato* (contract cane farming) and the character of *colono* contracts. (See immediately preceding entry for index.)

154. Urrutia y Blanco, Carlos de. *Los criminales de Cuba y D. José Trujillo.* Barcelona: Fidel Giró, 1882. 471 p.

Memoir of Havana police chief that claims to list and describe the cases of every individual he arrested or detained between 1867 and 1881. The cases are arranged chronologically by date of initial arrest. Entries generally provide name, age, marital status, parents' names, race, and birthplace of suspect. Circumstances of arrest, prior criminal record, and outcome of case are also provided. Cases vary widely and include such charges as vagrancy, homicide, theft, lack of proper documentation, flight, bearing arms, and threatening whites. Contains a section on individuals associated with the *ñáñigo* cults. Although the focus is urban, one can trace the migration of some rural workers to the city, and also the use of forced labor on rural estates as punishment.

155. Usategui y Lezama, Angel. *El colono cubano: Ensayo de derecho agrario.* Havana: Jesus Montero, 1938. 284 p.

A work of legal reference and legal history, written after the promulgation, in the 1930s, of legislation to defend and protect Cuban cane farmers. Volume traces the legal history of the *colonato*, beginning with Spanish colonial legislation. Attends to definitional questions, and the imprecision of usage of the term *colono*. Discusses the Law of 2 March 1922, which formalized some aspects of *colono* contracts. Examines in detail questions concerning agricultural loans, milling contracts, registration of contracts, and sugar prices, as well as the history of state intervention in the sugar industry and of formal organization among cane farmers.

156. Valdés-Domínguez, Fermín. *Diario de soldado.* 4 vols. Havana: Universidad de la Habana, Centro de Información Científica y Técnica, 1972–1975.

Diary of a rebel officer who served part of the final war of independence as General Máximo Gómez's secretary. Because of his official capacity, the diary includes correspondence between Gómez and other insurgents, as well as documents relating to the courts-martial of insurgent officers. The originals of many of the documents which appear in Valdés-Domínguez's diary are preserved in the collections Máximo Gómez and Revolución de 1895 in the Cuban National Archives. Written during the war, the diary is a valuable source for the study of ideological and social tensions within insurgent ranks. Transcribed and edited by Hiram Dupotey Fideaux.

157. Varela Zequeira, Eduardo and Arturo Mora y Varona. *Los bandidos de Cuba.* Havana: La Lucha, 1891. 213 p.

A study of rural banditry that describes relations between bandits and landholders. Includes descriptions of several kidnappings of landowners by bandits, providing names and racial labels for bandits. Also describes Spanish offensives against bandit forces and describes the members of colonial militia engaged in antibanditry campaigns as blacks and mulattos (*pardos* and *morenos*). Authors are journalists for the newspaper *La Lucha*.

158. Varona, Enrique José. "El Bandolerismo." *Revista Cubana* 7 (June 1888): 481–501.

Article on banditry contains some references to general situation of rural population.

159. Velasco, Carlos de. "El problema negro." *Cuba Contemporánea* 1 (February 1913): 73–79.

Article advocating legislation to restrict nonwhite immigration to the island. Argues that interests of landowners in search of cheap labor conflicted with maintenance of social order. Useful for understanding tensions between landowners and the state, as well as for exploring the relationship between public policy and racial ideology in the period following the "race war" of 1912.

160. Villanova, Manuel. *Economía y civismo*. Havana: Ministerio de Educación, 1945. 402 p.

Reprints two important articles related to emancipation. "Estadística de la abolición de la esclavitud en Cuba" contains statistical charts accounting for different ways slaves obtained their freedom, with figures from all six provinces. "Censo de población de la provincia de Matanzas" uses the 1887 Matanzas census to compare population density with that of 1877 and to examine and compare literacy rates of blacks and whites, measured within municipalities.

161. Zaragoza, Justo. *Las insurrecciones en Cuba*. 2 vols. Madrid: M. G. Hernández, 1872–73.

Two-volume political history of Cuba, focusing on rebellions and movements for political reform. The second volume begins with 1854. Especially useful for the study of the Ten Years' War. The author reproduces insurgent decrees and proclamations and offers an extensive analysis of the process of confiscation of rebel-owned property by Spanish authorities.

U.S.-SUPERVISED CENSUSES AND U.S. GOVERNMENTAL RECORDS

162. U.S. War Department. Cuban Census Office. *Report on the Census of Cuba, 1899*. Washington: Government Printing Office, 1900. 786 p.

Results of the census carried out in the final months of 1899, under the supervision of the U.S. government. Population tables cross-tabulate various characteristics including occupation, sex, age, literacy, citizenship, conjugal condition, and birthplace. The tables of agriculture contain data on land tenure and crops planted. Population figures of municipalities are divided by "general nativity" and "color" using the categories Native white, Foreign white, Negro, Mixed, and Chinese. Other tables are divided by "race" and "nativity" using the categories Native white, Foreign white, and Colored, while the figures on land tenure, apparently taken from a separate agricultural schedule, are simply divided into White owners, White renters, Colored owners, and Colored renters. Also contains maps, photographs, and discussion of census findings, plus a brief overview of Cuban population statistics for earlier periods. Particularly useful for developing regional profiles of the population and of landholding in the postemancipation period. Also intriguing as a document reflecting various schemata for the classification of racial identifications.

163. Cuba. Military Governor. (John R. Brooke). *Civil Report of Major-General John R. Brooke, U.S. Army, Military Governor, Island of Cuba.* Washington: Government Printing Office, 1900. 476 p.

Covers the period from 27 December 1898 through December 1899. In addition to General Brooke's report, it contains those of other officers, including the reports of the secretaries of agriculture, commerce, industries, and public works, as well as the reports of the military commanders in the departments of Matanzas, Santa Clara, Havana, Pinar del Río, Santiago, and Puerto Príncipe. Includes Brooke's "Final Report." Contains orders issued by Brooke's office, with intriguing detail on such items as rebel veterans' right to keep their horses as well as fierce debates over the provision of assistance to small-scale farmers. (Another edition of this report consisting of three volumes, published in Havana in 1899, also exists. Much of the same material, and the regional reports, appear in vol. I, part 6, of the 1899 *Annual Reports* of the U.S. War Department.)

164. Cuba. Military Governor. (Leonard Wood). *Civil Report of Major General Leonard Wood, Military Governor of Cuba, for the Period from December 20, 1899, to December 31, 1900.* 12 vols. Havana, 1901.

Annual report of the U.S. military governor of Cuba, Major General Leonard Wood. Vol. I contains Wood's personal report, including discussions of resistance to the U.S. occupation, the formation of the Rural Guard, and educational reform. Vol. II contains civil orders and circulars issued during 1900. Vol. III contains the reports of the secretary of state and government and reports of the civil governors. Vol. IV includes information on sanitation, yellow fever, and charities. Vol. V contains a report from the secretary of finance. Vol. VI includes a report from the secretary of justice. Vol. VII contains the report of the secretary of agriculture, commerce, and industry, including discussions of immigration and labor shortages as well as statistics related to the sugar industry and other agricultural products organized by province. Includes a chart for each province that gives the names of *ingenios* existing at the end of 1899, their size in *caballerías*, and their condition (*"no destruido," "reconstruido,"* or *"destruido"*). An additional chart for each province gives the name of the proprietor or *encargado* of each active *ingenio* and its sugar and molasses production (in *sacos* and *bocoyes*) for the *zafra* of 1899–1900. Vol. VIII is dedicated to education. Vols. IX and X contain reports from the secretary of public works. Vols. XI and XII contain information produced by the chief engineer.

Beyond their obvious importance for studying the U.S. occupation itself, these reports can be used to examine questions of particular importance to former slaves in the countryside, such as the establishment of the Rural Guard and its role in maintaining security on estates, the recovery of production in the sugar sector, and patterns of public education.

165. Cuba. Military Governor. (Leonard Wood). *Civil Report of the Military Governor, 1901.* 15 vols. Havana, 1903.

Annual report of the U.S. Military Government of Cuba. Vol. I contains the report of Military Governor Leonard Wood, and his correspondence with members of the Constitutional Convention concerning the Platt Amendment. Also contains charts of fiscal data such as the allotment of funds to "fiscal zones" and customs revenue. A geological report includes a geological analysis of the island, topographical descriptions, photos, and drawings of geological formations. Vol. II contains the civil orders and circulars issued by the military government and ends with an index of subjects and names for the reprinted documents. Vol. III is a report by the secretary of state and government. Electoral statistics include tabulations of electors registered and lists of expenses accrued for the municipal elections of 1901. Also contains reports by the Bureau of Sanitation, the Vaccination Bureau, and the Division of Penal Institutions, which includes charts of inmates listed by crime committed, race, and occupation. Vol. IV includes a report from the chief sanitary officer. Vol. V contains the report of the superintendent of the department of charities, including reports on and photographs of hospitals, nursing training schools, and orphanages. Vol. VI contains the reports of the captain of the Port of Havana, the supervisor of police, and the Rural Guard. Vol.

VII contains the reports of the chief quartermaster pertaining to insular affairs, the auditor, the treasurer, the secretary of finance, among others. Vol. VIII is a "statement of all merchandise imported." Vol. IX contains the report of the secretary of public instruction, which includes tables of school employees, teachers, and student enrollment figures by province. Vols. X and XI cover the first and second halves of 1901, respectively, and contain reports from the secretary of justice. They also include reports from the president of the Audiencia in Havana to the secretary of justice, as well as reports from all provincial Audiencias. Statistical data include charts on property transactions and real estate, charts of misdemeanors, crimes, and trials (most of which are categorized by race, literacy and civil status), and information pertaining to administration of the Supreme Court and Audiencias. Vol. XII contains the report of the Department of Agriculture, Commerce, and Industries, including tables on livestock and agricultural production, with lists of output by province and, in some cases, by plantation. Vol. XIII is the report of the chief engineer, Department of Cuba. Includes descriptions of public works projects such as street paving, waste collection, and park construction and rehabilitation. Contains information on personnel working on projects, including some pictures. Also contains detailed maps and photographs of Havana. Vols. XIV and XV contain reports from the Corps of Engineers.

166. Cuba. Military Governor. (Leonard Wood). *Civil Report of the Military Governor, 1902.* 6 vols. Havana, 1903.

Brigadier General Leonard Wood's third report as military governor. Vol. I contains General Wood's personal report, which includes his thoughts on the recent elections. Expresses frustration at how it "continues to be difficult to interest . . . the property-holding elements in the conduct of the island's political affairs." Also notes that "there has been almost an absence of any indication of race feeling." Part two of this volume gives output statistics for various agricultural industries, as well as a detailed chart of registered active mines. Part three of the volume is the final report of the Sanitary Department. The descriptions of on-site inspections describe working conditions in factories and urban living conditions. Volumes II and III reprint civil orders and circulars for the period, as well as the report of the Central Vaccination Bureau. Volume IV contains reports of the secretary of justice and the chief justice of the Supreme Court. Accompanying documents give statistics on crimes, convictions, and so on. Statistics on attempted suicides are categorized by sex, race ("White," "Negro," and "Mixed" or *mestizo*), method used and causes (e.g., "family troubles"). Volume V contains the report of the engineering officer of Havana, report on the mineral resources of Cuba, and the report of the captain of the Port of Havana. Includes detailed maps of Havana highlighting roads in the city. Volume VI contains the report of the chief engineer of the island. Contains many photographs and drawings of buildings recently built or under construction.

167. Cuba. Oficina del censo. *Censo de la República de Cuba bajo la administración provisional de los Estados Unidos. 1907.* Washington, D.C.: U.S. Census Office, 1908. 707 p.

Spanish-language publication of the results of the 1907 census, carried out during the second U.S. occupation of the island. Begins with general essays on subjects such as public works, trade, and criminality, followed by a detailed analysis of the findings of this census. Contains almost three hundred pages of tables on the population of Cuba's eighty-two *términos municipales*. Unlike the 1899 census, this one does not contain detailed statistics on landholding or acreage in particular crops. It does, however, cross-tabulate many characteristics of the population including literacy, birthplace, citizenship, marital status, age, sex, and race. The categories employed are the parallel to those of the 1899 census: *blancos nativos, blancos extranjeros, negros, mestizos, amarillos.* For certain purposes, including the compilation of data on occupations, the last three groups are combined under the heading *de color.* In the data on marital status, a distinction is made between *casados* and *consentimiento mútuo.* Letters contained in appendices provide some insight into the selection of enumerators and the process of enumeration.

168. Cuba. Oficina del censo. *Cuba: Population, History and Resources, 1907.* Washington, D.C.: United States Bureau of the Census, 1909.

Compendium of information from the U.S.-supervised Cuban census of 1907 (see above), and, to a lesser extent, from the 1899 census (see above) and Gonzalo de Quesada's 1905 *Cuba* (see above). Contains data on immigration, race, literacy, occupations, marital status, age, landholding, and so on. Includes numerous photographs, maps, and explanations of census data.

169. Cuba. Provisional Governor (C. E. Magoon). *Report of Provisional Adminstration from October 13th, 1906 to December 1st, 1907, by Charles E. Magoon, Provisional Governor.* Havana: Rambla and Bouza, 1908. 557 p.

In addition to the governor's report, this volume includes in the appendix reports of the Departments of State and Justice, Government, Treasury (*Hacienda*), Public Instruction, Public Works, Agriculture, Commerce, and Industry, Sanitation, and the report of the commanding general of the Armed Forces in Cuba. (Also published in Spanish.)

170. Cuba. Provisional Governor, 1906–1909 (C. E. Magoon). *Report of Provisional Administration from December 1st, 1907 to December 1st, 1908, by Charles E. Magoon, Provisional Governor.* Havana: Rambla and Bouza, 1909.

171. U.S. War Department. Office of the Chief of Staff. *Military Notes on Cuba. 1909.* Washington: Government Printing Office, 1909. 757 p.

Provides detailed information on villages and townships throughout the island, divided by province, with the Ciénaga de Zapata accorded a separate section. Based on the work of the Military Information Division of the Army of Cuban Pacification in 1906, 1907, and 1908. Includes local maps, tables indicating administrative structure of provinces, and reports of terrain, water supply, and buildings in each locale. Can be used to frame regional studies, to locate individual sugar plantations, and to explore linkages between town and countryside. Can also help to orient work in the archival records of the Military Information Division, located in the U.S. National Archives. Complements the 1907 census.

SECONDARY SOURCES

172. Aimes, Hubert H. S. "The Transition from Slave to Free Labor in Cuba." *The Yale Review* 15 (May 1906): 68–84.

General description of transition to free labor in Cuba, emphasizing the lack of social and economic disruption accompanying the change. Uses published U.S. congressional and consular records, and can thus serve as a guide to some important contemporary U.S. printed sources on the subject.

173. Álvarez Estévez, Rolando. *Azúcar e inmigración, 1900–1940.* Havana: Editorial de Ciencias Sociales, 1988. 290 p.

Study, based on secondary sources, newspapers, and archival materials from Cuba, of Antillean immigration to Cuba in the twentieth century. Provides an index of relevant governmental decrees in the appendix.

174. Álvarez Mola, Martha Verónica, and Pedro Martínez Pírez. "Algo acerca del problema negro en Cuba hasta 1912." *Universidad de la Habana* 179 (May–June 1966): 79–93.

A brief survey of Afro-Cuban political mobilization after abolition. Focuses on the 1908 formation of the *Partido Independiente de Color* and general resistance of Afro-Cubans to discrimination.

175. Anuario de Estudios Cubanos. Vol. 1. *La república neocolonial.* Havana: Editorial de Ciencias Sociales, 1973. 430 p.

Collection of essays, most based on primary sources, and including significant amounts of statistical data. Of particular interest for the study of postemancipation social relations are Juan Pérez de la Riva, "Los recursos humanos de Cuba al comenzar el siglo: inmigración, economía y nacionalidad (1899–1906)" and the collection of over one hundred pages of documents at the end of the volume. The latter includes transcriptions of documents from the Archivo Nacional de Cuba on the 1917 uprising in Oriente known as "La Chambelona."

176. Anuario de Estudios Cubanos. Vol. 2. *La república neocolonial.* Havana: Editorial de Ciencias Sociales, 1979. 478 p.

Collection of essays on migration, labor movement, political parties, sugar industry, covering period 1900 through 1930s. Includes Juan Pérez de la Riva, "Cuba y la migración antillana, 1900–1931"; Carlos del Toro González, "La fundación de la primera central sindical nacional de los trabajadores cubanos (Los Congresos Obreros de 1892 a 1934)"; Francisco López Segrera, "Algunos aspectos de la industria azucarera cubana (1925–1937)"; among others. The essay by Pérez de la Riva contains extensive statistics on migration, and a discussion of racism. The essay by del Toro includes a compilation of raw material on meetings of national workers' organizations.

177. Arredondo, Alberto. *El negro en Cuba.* Havana: Editorial Alfa, 1939. 174 p.

An early effort to write a history of Cuba focused on the influence of Cubans of "pigmentación negra," whom he contrasts with those "de epidermis blanca, prieta o mestiza." Drawing on printed sources, the author constructs a generally heroic portrait of black Cubans. Emphasizes multiple goals of those who fought in between 1895 and 1898, and estimates proportion of insurgents of color at 75 percent of the fighting force. Engages contemporary debates on solutions to problems of discrimination.

178. Baltar Rodríguez, José. *Los chinos de Cuba: Apuntes etnográficos.* Havana: Fundación Fernando Ortiz, 1997. 231 p.

Building on oral, periodical, archival, and visual sources, the author (trained as an art historian) examines the history of the Chinese in Cuba, with an emphasis on Havana. Provides evidence on organizations and societies formed among immigrants and contains a chapter on theaters. Calls attention, for example, to a Chinese theater opened in 1875 in Cienfuegos, whose performances were attended by Chinese workers from the surrounding sugar towns.

179. Barcia, María del Carmen. *Burguesía esclavista y abolición.* Havana: Editorial de Ciencias Sociales, 1987. 229 p.

Analysis of process of gradual abolition in Cuba based on extensive research in the Cuban National Archives, in manuscript collections at the Biblioteca Nacional "José Martí," and in printed primary sources. Contains useful statistical appendices on slave prices, sugar production, fluctuations in sugar prices through 1887, and slave population and its distribution across different agricultural industries. Lists of *ingenios* provide details on level of mechanization, and a list of *ingenio* owners traces changes in the number of *ingenios* each owner owned in 1860 and 1878.

180. Beck, Earl R. "The Martínez Campos Government of 1879: Spain's Last Chance in Cuba." *Hispanic American Historical Review* 56 (May 1976): 268–89.

Examines the effects of Spain's internal politics on Cuban political and economic reforms, including abolition, following the Pact of Zanjón in 1879. Uses Spanish, British, and German consular records and Spanish legislative documents and newspapers.

181. Bergad, Laird. *Cuban Rural Society in the Nineteenth Century: The Social and Economic History of Monoculture in Matanzas.* Princeton: Princeton University Press, 1990. 425 p.

History of province of Matanzas from 1800 to 1900 that focuses on the growth of sugar monoculture and associated transformations in demography, technology, land use, commerce and credit, and labor. Includes discussion of free blacks, Spanish immigrants, poor white and mulatto smallholders, and Chinese contract laborers. Makes extensive use of archival materials and statistical information located in Spain and Cuba.

182. Betancourt, Juan René. *Doctrina negra: la única teoria certera contra la discriminación racial en Cuba.* Havana: P. Hernández y Cia., 1955. 80 p.

Critique of racial discrimination in Cuba with proposals for furthering racial equality. Includes a brief discussion of the history of race and party politics as well as the activities of "sociedades negras" following independence.

183. Betancourt, Juan René. *El Negro: Ciudadano del futuro.* Havana: Cárdenas y Cia., 1959. 248 p.

Includes essays on Juan Gualberto Gómez, Evaristo Estenoz, *sociedades negras,* racial discrimination, and other topics relevant to the study of race in Cuban society in the republican period.

184. Brass, Tom, and Marcel van der Linden, eds. *Free and Unfree Labour: The Debate Continues.* Bern: Lang, 1997. 602 p.

Collection of essays treating the nuances of free and unfree labor over a wide chronological and geographical range. Part I addresses theoretical issues surrounding the debate; part II consists of case studies from the United States, Caribbean, Latin America, Russia, India, and Australia, including Joan Casanovas, "Slavery, the Labour Movement and Spanish Colonialism in Cuba (1850–1898)." Part III is a concluding essay on the origins, spread, and normalization of free wage labor.

185. Brock, Lisa and Digna Castañeda Fuertes, eds. *Between Race and Empire: African-Americans and Cubans before the Cuban Revolution.* Philadelphia: Temple University Press, 1998. 298 p.

Collection of essays on interaction between people of African descent from the United States and Cuba, with a focus on the late nineteenth and the early twentieth century.

186. Carbonell, Walterio. *Crítica: Cómo surgió la cultura nacional.* Havana: Ediciones Yaka, 1961. 131 p.

An early post-revolutionary analysis of the sources of Cuban national culture. The author emphasizes African components of Cuban culture and criticizes other revolutionary writers for interpreting white elite nationalists as the fathers of Cuban identity. Argues that conflicts between slaves and slaveholders provided the fundamental dynamic of Cuban history. This is an interpretive essay rather than a documented work of history, but its perspective was nearly unique at the time and the essay is useful in contextualizing other secondary works produced in this period.

187. Carr, Barry. "'Omnipotent and Omnipresent?' Labor Shortages, Worker Mobility, and Employer Control in the Cuban Sugar Industry, 1910–1934." In *Identity and Struggle at the Margins of the*

Nation-State: The Laboring Peoples of Central America and the Hispanic Caribbean, edited by Aviva Chomsky and Aldo Lauria-Santiago. Durham: Duke University Press, 1998.

Examines how patterns of worker resistance, accommodation, and strategies for maximizing autonomy during the expansion of the sugar industry were influenced by the structure of sugar mill complexes, crop cycles, high levels of worker mobility, and cultivation of subsistence plots. Compares western and eastern Cuba, with emphasis on the new mills of the provinces of Camagüey and Oriente.

188. Carr, Barry. "Mill Occupations and Soviets: The Mobilisation of Sugar Workers in Cuba, 1917–1933." *Journal of Latin American Studies* 28 (1996): 129–58.

Analysis of growth of unionization of sugar workers, with focus on role of the Cuban Communist Party. Draws on newspaper accounts, private papers, and U.S. diplomatic reports.

189. Carreras, Julio Angel. *Esclavitud, abolición y racismo*. Havana: Editorial de Ciencias Sociales, 1985. 148 p.

General history of Cuban slavery, abolition, and racism from sixteenth century to 1961. Analyzes abolitionism in Camagüey and Las Villas. Account of Republican years covers the Platt Amendment, West Indian immigration, violence of 1912, and Constitution of 1940.

190. Casanovas, Joan. *Bread, or Bullets! Urban Labor and Spanish Colonialism in Cuba, 1850–1898*. Pittsburgh: University of Pittsburgh Press, 1998. 320 p.

Examines organizing strategies and ideological tendencies of workers in urban Cuba, including the formation of alliances among workers of different origins. Focuses on western Cuba (especially Havana), Las Villas, and Puerto Príncipe. Based on archival sources in Cuba, Spain, and the United States as well as newspapers.

191. Centro de Estudios del Caribe. *Anales del Caribe 6*. Havana: Casa de las Américas, 1986. 363 p.

Collection of essays on the occasion of the centennial of the abolition of slavery in Cuba. Includes essays by Jorge Ibarra on political implication of class and race dynamics in the eastern and central provinces in 1868 and by Argeliers León on African culture in America. Introduction is in Spanish, English, and French.

192. Cepero Bonilla, Raúl. *Azúcar y abolición: Apuntes para una historia crítica del abolicionismo*. Havana: Editorial Cenit, 1948. 196 p.

Classic study of the relation between the Cuban sugar industry and the process of emancipation. Discusses the connections between slavery and different movements for reform, annexation, and independence and examines the role played by different groups in these movements. Examines racism, the lack of philosophical antecedents for abolitionism in Cuba, and the decline of slavery in the face of new economic structures. Argues that most of the liberal reformers remained committed to white supremacy. Sources include numerous Cuban newspapers, as well as the writings of Cuban intellectuals on race, slavery, abolition, labor, and nationalism.

193. Corbitt, Duvon C. *A Study of the Chinese in Cuba, 1847–1947.* Wilmore, Ky.: Asbury College, 1971. 142 p.

A study of Chinese immigrants in Cuba, relying on such sources as the reports by "masters" of Chinese laborers filed with the Junta de Fomento and on publications of supporters and opponents of the "Coolie" trade. Useful for examining planters' perceptions of different forms of labor. Contains 1874 figures on relative cost of indentured and free labor. Contains Chinese immigration figures, 1903 to 1924.

194. Corbitt, Duvon C. "Immigration in Cuba." *Hispanic American Historical Review* 22 (May 1942): 280–308.

General overview of immigration policies from colonial period through 1942. Some attention is given to different plans for the promotion of immigration after emancipation, including the importation, at different times, of workers from the Canary Islands, China, and the British West Indies.

195. Corwin, Arthur F. *Spain and the Abolition of Slavery in Cuba, 1817–1886.* Austin: University of Texas Press, 1967. 373 p.

Chronological study of the diplomatic and political aspects of abolition in Cuba, from Spain's first treaty with Great Britain to final abolition in 1886. Emphasis is on Spanish policy. Relies primarily on Spanish, British, and U.S. diplomatic documents, on debates in the Spanish Cortes, and on anti- and proabolitionist literature.

196. de la Fuente, Alejandro. *A Nation for All: Race, Inequality, and Politics in Twentieth-Century Cuba.* Chapel Hill: University of North Carolina Press, 2001. 449 p.

Study of the role of race in nationalist ideologies, government politics, and political mobilization in Cuba from the First Republic through the 1990s. Discusses black participation in labor markets, education, and politics. Based on archival and newspaper research in Cuba and the United States.

197. de la Fuente, Alejandro. "Race and Inequality in Cuba, 1899–1981." *Journal of Contemporary History* 30 (1995): 131–68.

Uses census data on fertility rates, infant mortality, literacy and occupational status to examine the dynamics of racial inequality.

198. de la Fuente, Alejandro. "Myths of Racial Democracy: Cuba, 1900–1912." *Latin American Research Review* 34 (1999): 39–73.

Discussion of racial ideology and political mobilization in Cuba in the early twentieth century. Includes a review of recent scholarship on ideologies of racial inclusiveness in Cuba and Brazil.

199. Denslow, David Albert, Jr. "Sugar Production in Northeastern Brazil and Cuba, 1858–1908." Ph.D. diss., Yale University, 1974. 172 p.

Analyzes differences in sugar production between Northeastern Brazil and Cuba in terms of technology, land supply, availability of capital, and labor costs.

200. Diembicz, Andrés. "Poblamiento post-azucarero en Cuba: Perduración y funciones socio-económicas actuales." *Economía y desarrollo* 34 (March–April 1976): 99–115.

Discussion of evolution of settlements around sugar plantations. See next item in this bibliography for more extensive treatment.

201. Diembicz, Andrzej. *Plantaciones cañeras y poblamiento en Cuba.* Havana: Editorial de Ciencias Sociales, 1989. 134 p.

Using censuses, aerial photos, field research data, and secondary sources, the author generates a series of maps and graphs plotting population densities of sugar-growing regions and spatial distribution of sugar plantations between 1860 and 1970.

202. Duke, Cathy. "The Idea of Races: The Cultural Impact of the American Intervention in Cuba, 1898–1912." In *Politics, Society, and Culture in the Caribbean,* edited by Blanca Silvestrini. San Juan: Universidad de Puerto Rico, 1983.

Examines racial ideologies that informed U.S. policy in Cuba during the occupations between 1898 and 1902 and between 1906 and 1909, and the consequences for public health, education, and electoral politics. Sources include Cuban newspapers and papers of Leonard Wood and Elihu Root.

203. Dumoulin, John. *Azúcar y lucha de clases: 1917.* Havana: Editorial de Ciencias Sociales, 1980. 284 p.

Uses newspaper and government sources to examine the crisis and strikes in the Cuban sugar industry in 1917. Emphasizes growth of workers' organizations and position of the Cuban bourgeoisie. The appendix includes transcription of pamphlets from workers' organizations.

204. Dumoulin, John. *El movimiento obrero en Cruces, 1902–1925. Corrientes ideológicas y formas de organización en la industria azucarera.* A volume of Sonia Aragón García, ed., *Las clases y la lucha de clases en la sociedad neocolonial cubana.* Havana: Editorial de Ciencias Sociales, 1981. 65 p.

A continuation of Dumoulin's essay on the formation of the proletariat in the sugar zone of Cruces (see below).

205. Dumoulin, John. "El primer desarrollo del movimiento obrero y la formación del proletariado en el sector azucarero. Cruces, 1886–1902." *Islas* 48 (May–August 1974): 3–66.

Analysis of transformations in Cruces, a sugar-producing region near Cienfuegos, Cuba, in the province of Santa Clara (Las Villas). Discusses technology, work force, early labor organizations. Describes intersection between Afro-Cuban organizations and workers' groups. Traces development of anarcho-syndicalist sentiment and the general strike of 1902. Includes transcriptions of pamphlets by and aimed at workers.

206. Dye, Alan. *Cuban Sugar in the Age of Mass Production: Technology and the Economics of the Sugar "Central," 1899–1929.* Stanford: Stanford University Press, 1998. 343 p.

History of technological change in the sugar industry, including discussion of the *colonato* and the rise of the sugar latifundium.

207. Ely, Roland T. *Cuando reinaba su majestad el azúcar.* Buenos Aires: Editorial Sudamericana, 1963. 875 p.

Voluminous study of Cuban sugar industry in the nineteenth century, mostly through the late 1860s. Briefly discusses decline of slavery due to the ending of the slave trade but does not deal with process of abolition or with effects of emancipation. Discusses functioning of sugar plantations, including such topics as technology, transportation, and organization of labor. Final sections treat the social life of "sugar nobles," their marriage patterns, education, pastimes, and so on. Extensive bibliography lists printed, archival, and manuscript sources; contains detailed lists of contents of Moses Taylor papers, including lists of Taylor's correspondents and their positions.

208. Entralgo, Elías. *La liberación étnica cubana.* Havana: Universidad de la Habana, 1953. 272 p.

Interpretation of Cuban history centered on the idea of race and racial mixture. Three sections examine the conditions of slavery and acts of resistance and rebellion; antislavery and reformist ideas of Cuban intellectuals including Saco and Arango y Parreno and "liberationist" ideas of Martí, Sanguily, and Enrique José Varona; the phenomenon of *mulatez* and its implications for the future of Cuba.

209. Epstein, Erwin H. "Social Structure, Race Relations, and Political Stability in Cuba under U.S. Administration." *Revista/Review Interamericana* 8 (Summer 1978): 192–203.

General overview of social and economic conditions of Afro-Cubans during U.S. occupations (1898–1902 and 1906–1909) based primarily on census data. Contains brief discussions of Afro-Cuban resistance to U.S. intervention, black political participation, and race relations.

210. Estevez y Romero, Luis. *Desde el Zanjón hasta Baire. Datos para la historia política de Cuba.* Havana: La Propaganda Literaria, 1899. 686 p.

A study of Cuban political history in the period between 1878 and 1895. Focuses primarily on the question of colonial reform. Discusses electoral policy and provides evidence on landholders excluded from voting in colonial elections. Contains discussions of banditry and Spanish attempts at defeating bandits. Useful for understanding the political context in which gradual emancipation unfolded.

211. Fermoselle, Rafael. *Política y color en Cuba: La guerrita de 1912.* Montevideo, Uruguay: Ediciones Geminis, 1974. 244 p.

Study of the political background to the "Race War" of 1912, beginning with the Ten Years War but concentrating on events after the uprising of 1906. Summarizes the political platform of the Independent Party of Color (PIC) formed in 1908 and explores the relationship between established black political leaders in mainstream political parties and PIC leaders. Also summarizes allegations of links between PIC and other political interest groups.

212. Fernández Robaina, Tomás. *El negro en Cuba, 1902–1958. Apuntes para la historia de la lucha contra la discriminación racial en la neocolonia.* Havana: Editorial de Ciencias Sociales, 1990. 225 p.

Overview of history of Afro-Cubans with a primary focus on the struggle for civil rights. First half of the book covers the period between emancipation and the 1930s. Outlines the history of civic associations and political organizations including the Directorio Central de Sociedades de la Raza de Color, the Comité de Veteranos y de Sociedades de la Raza de Color, and the Partido Independiente de Color.

213. Ferrer, Ada. "Esclavitud, ciudadanía y los límites de la nacionalidad cubana: La Guerra de los Diez Años, 1868–1878." *Historia Social.* (Valencia) 22 (1995): 101–25.

Examines concepts of citizenship and participation of Afro-Cubans in the Ten Years' War. Uses archival material from Cuba and Spain.

214. Ferrer, Ada. *Insurgent Cuba: Race, Nation, and Revolution, 1868–1898.* Chapel Hill: University of North Carolina Press, 1999. 273 p.

Close study of race and formation of ideology of nationality, and of role of Afro-Cubans in insurgency. Pays particular attention to the provinces of Matanzas, Puerto Príncipe, and Santiago de Cuba. Draws on extensive archival evidence from Spain and Cuba.

215. Ferrer, Ada. "Cuba, 1898: Rethinking Race, Nation, and Empire." *Radical History Review* 73 (1999): 22–46.

Overview of the author's research on the history of struggles over race and nationalism in Cuba from 1868 through U.S. intervention in Cuba in 1898.

216. Goizueta-Mimó, Felix. *Bitter Cuban Sugar: Monoculture and Economic Dependence from 1825–1899.* New York: Garland Publishing, 1987. 287 p.

Economic history of Cuban sugar in the nineteenth century. Deals with economic characteristics of monoculture, market conditions, capital formation, and sugar technology. Brief section on effects of emancipation on demand, supply, and wages of laborers. Cites examples of strikes, development of workers' cooperatives, guilds, newspapers around the time of emancipation. Contains numerous appendices and tables, with information on investments, revenues, operating expenses, and profits at a "typical" sugar mill (1863), on railroads used by sugar mills founded between 1806 and 1899, on the type of equipment used in the crystallization process in sixty-five sugar mills in the 1860s.

217. Grillo, David. *El problema del Negro cubano.* 2d ed. Havana: Impresora Vega y Cia., 1953. 169 p.

Discussion of racial discrimination by a member of the Club Atenas, an Afro-Cuban society. Focuses on the post-1933 period.

218. Guerra y Sánchez, Ramiro. *La industria azucarera de Cuba*. Havana: La Moderna Poesía, 1940. 304 p.

A general survey of the sugar industry on the island, concentrating on the early twentieth century, up to 1939. Includes separate chapters for different spheres of sugar production: agricultural sector (*colonias*), labor, *hacendados* and *ingenios*, and sugar markets. Tables include information on imports and exports from the *Secretaría de Hacienda*, lists of refineries from *Instituto Cubano de Estabilización del Azúcar*, and minimum wages from the *Comisión Nacional de Salarios Mínimos*. Provides lists of labor unions for each province.

219. Guerra y Sánchez, Ramiro. *Azúcar y población en las Antillas*. 1944. Reprint. Havana: Editorial de Ciencias Sociales, 1976. 299 p.

Account of the rise of cane-farming in Cuba in late nineteenth and twentieth centuries, emphasizing destructive effect of large holdings and foreign investment. For English translation with an introduction by Sidney Mintz, see Ramiro Guerra y Sánchez, *Sugar and Society in the Caribbean: An Economic History of Cuban Agriculture* (New Haven: Yale University Press, 1964).

220. Helg, Aline. *Our Rightful Share: The Afro-Cuban Struggle for Equality, 1886–1912*. Chapel Hill: University of North Carolina Press, 1995. 361 p.

Study of racial ideology and Afro-Cuban resistance in Cuba from the end of slavery to the events of 1912. Analyzes composition of the Partido Independiente de Color and repression of the movement.

221. Helly, Denise. *Idéologie et ethnicité: Les Chinois Macao à Cuba, 1847–1886*. Montreal: Les Presses de l'Université de Montréal, 1979. 345 p.

Detailed study of Chinese immigrants in Cuba. Extensive bibliography of primary and secondary sources. Analyzes contradictory elements in the status of an ethnically distinct group of indentured workers in a slave society, and the challenge this posed to concepts of "racial" dominance. Relevant to understanding of variety of forms of free labor predating and accompanying abolition.

222. *Hispanic American Historical Review* 78 (November 1998).

Special issue marking centennial of 1898. Addresses questions regarding empire, nationality, race, class, and citizenship during the transition in Cuba and Puerto Rico from Spanish to U.S. rule. Contributions include an introduction by Arcadio Díaz-Quiñones; Francisco A. Scarano, "Liberal Pacts and Hierarchies of Rule: Approaching the Imperial Transition in Cuba and Puerto Rico"; Christopher Schmidt-Nowara, "National Economy and Atlantic Slavery: Protectionism and Resistance to Abolitionism in Spain and the Antilles, 1854–1874"; Astrid Cubano-Iguina, "Political Culture and Male Mass-Party Formation in Late-Nineteenth-Century Puerto Rico"; Ada Ferrer, "Rustic Men, Civilized Nation: Race, Culture, and Contention on the Eve of Cuban Independence"; Rebecca J. Scott, "Race, Labor, and Citizenship in Cuba: A View from the Sugar District of Cienfuegos, 1886–1909"; and Carmen Diana Deere, "Here Come the Yankees! The Rise and Decline of United States Colonies in Cuba, 1898–1930."

223. Hoernel, Robert B. "A Comparison of Sugar and Social Change in Puerto Rico and Oriente, Cuba, 1898–1959." Ph.D. diss., Johns Hopkins University, 1977.

224. Hoernel, Robert B. "Sugar and Social Change in Oriente, Cuba, 1898–1946." *Journal of Latin American Studies* 8 (November 1976): 215–49.

Study of demographic, social, and economic changes in Oriente from the beginning of the first American occupation to about the end of World War II. Sources include Cuban censuses, U.S. War Department records for the occupation period, U.S. and Cuban Department of Agriculture records, and U.S. trade bulletins.

225. Howard, Philip A. *Changing History: Afro-Cuban Cabildos and Societies of Color in the Nineteenth Century.* Baton Rouge: Louisiana State University Press, 1998. 227 p.

Uses Spanish colonial archival material including correspondence of governors general and population records to trace origins of nineteenth-century urban Afro-Cuban mutual aid societies. Analyzes changing cultural and political practices and role of societies in Ten Years' War and postemancipation society until 1895.

226. Ibarra, Jorge. *Ideología mambisa.* Havana: Instituto Cubano del Libro, 1967. 215 p.

The first part of the book discusses slavery, emancipation, the sugar industry, annexationism, and Afro-Cuban culture in the formation of Cuban national identity. The second part is a compilation of essays published earlier in Cuban journals on the Pact of Zanjón, the Guerra Chiquita, Antonio Maceo, José Martí, Carlos Manuel de Céspedes, Ignacio Agramonte, the Platt Amendment, and early anti-imperialism.

227. *Ibero-Amerikanisches Archiv* 24 (1998).

Special collection of articles on race, society, and culture among people of African descent in Latin America. Of interest for the study of post-emancipation society are Reinhard Liehr, Matthias Röhrig Assunção and Michael Zeuske, "Afro-Latin America's Legacy. Introduction"; Consuelo Naranjo Orovio, "Immigration, 'Race' and Nation in Cuba in the Second Half of the 19th Century"; Stephan Palmié, "Fernando Ortiz and the Cooking of History"; and Matthias Röhrig Assunção and Michael Zeuske, "'Race,' Ethnicity and Social Structure in 19th Century Brazil and Cuba."

228. Iglesias García, Fe. *Del ingenio al central*. Havana: Editorial de Ciencias Sociales, 1999. 203 p.

History of sugar production in Cuba from 1880 through the end of the War of Independence in 1898. Based primarily on research in the National Archive of Cuba, the Provincial Archive of Matanzas, and printed sources. Analyzes the effects of emancipation on sugar production and discusses the importance of *patrocinados* in the labor force until final abolition in 1886.

229. Iglesias García, Fe. "Algunos aspectos de la distribución de la tierra en 1899." *Santiago* 40 (December 1980): 119–78.

Analysis of patterns of landholding and land use in Cuba, based on the statistics of the U.S.-supervised census of 1899 and complementary data from the *Gaceta de la Habana* and the reports of the U.S. occupation governments. Analyzes aggregate data and specific municipalities. Emphasizes the existence of smallholdings along with ranches and plantations. Important work for understanding different patterns of evolution of land use and of land ownership.

230. *Illes i Imperis* 2 (spring 1999).

This issue of a new multilingual journal published at the Facultat d'Humanitats of the Universitat Pompeu Fabra in Barcelona collects many of the papers delivered at a November 1998 conference entitled "Después de 1898: Identidad nacional, racial y social en Cuba, España, Filipinas y Puerto Rico." Of particular interest for the study of postemancipation Cuba are: Rebecca J. Scott, "Reclamando la mula de Gregoria Quesada: El significado de la libertad en los valles del Arimao y del Caunao, Cienfuegos, Cuba"; Sergio López Rivero y Francisco Ibarra, "Sobre transigentes e intransigentes en la Cuba ocupada, 1898–1902"; Michael Zeuske, "Clientelas regionales, alianzas interraciales y poder nacional en torno a la 'Guerrita de Agosto'" (on the 1906 conflict); Jorge Ibarra Cuesta, "Caciquismo, racismo y actitudes ante el status político futuro de la isla en las provincias occidentales de Cuba, 1906–09"; and Christopher Schmidt-Nowara, "From Slaves to Spaniards: The Failure of Revolutionary Emancipationism in Spain and Cuba, 1868–1895."

231. Jenks, Leland Hamilton. *Our Cuban Colony: A Study in Sugar.* New York: Vanguard Press, 1928. 341 p.

Drawing on U.S. governmental documents, traces the development of U.S. economic interests (including investment in sugar, tobacco, railroad, and mining industries) and U.S. diplomacy with respect to Cuba from the early nineteenth century through the first quarter of the twentieth century.

232. Jiménez Pastrana, Juan. *Los chinos en la historia de Cuba: 1847–1930.* Havana: Editorial de las Ciencias Sociales, 1983. 225 p.

A general history of Chinese labor immigration to Cuba, concentrating on changes in government policies toward immigration throughout the period. Details the participation of Chinese in the Ten Years War and the War of Independence, using Spanish government documents and newspaper articles. This expanded version of the author's 1963 work titled *Los chinos en las luchas por la liberación cubana (1847–1930)* includes an examination of Chinese immigration policy in the early republic. Appendix reproduces Spanish government decrees concerning Chinese immigration from 1849 to 1877.

233. Kiple, Kenneth F. *Blacks in Colonial Cuba, 1774–1899.* Gainesville: University Presses of Florida, 1976. 115 p.

Summary of printed census data from 1774 to 1899 and unofficial population estimates which have taken on "the authority of censuses." Is especially useful in pointing out the shortcomings, contradictions, and omissions found in many of the statistical sources on Cuba's black population.

234. Klein, Herbert S. "Consideraciones sobre la viabilidad de la esclavitud y las causas de la abolición en la Cuba del siglo diecinueve." *La Torre* 21 (July–December 1973): 307–18.

Examines competing explanations for the end of slavery.

235. Knight, Franklin. *Slave Society in Cuba during the Nineteenth Century.* Madison: University of Wisconsin Press, 1970. 228 p.

Analysis of Cuban slavery, based largely on archival materials located in Spain and on printed primary sources. Chapter on Ten Years' War addresses dynamics of abolition.

236. López Valdés, Rafael. "La inmigración indostana a Cuba y sus antecedentes en las Antillas." *Santiago* 25 (March 1977): 161–92.

Essay by anthropologist on Indian migrants to Cuba.

237. Le Riverend, Julio, et al. *Temas acerca de la esclavitud.* Havana: Editorial de Ciencias Sociales, 1988. 288 p.

Collection of articles related to the history of slavery, with a focus on the late eighteenth and on the nineteenth century. Essays of particular interest for postemancipation studies include Julio Le Riverend, "El esclavismo en Cuba. Perspectivas del tema," which gives an overview of the historiography of slavery in Cuba from the mid-nineteenth century to 1988; Ernesto Ruiz Santovenia, "Manuscritos existentes en la Biblioteca Nacional 'José Martí,'" which gives over three hundred annotated citations to manuscripts related to the history of slavery in the Cuban national library, including many from the 1880s; and Doria González, "El mercado mundial azucarero y su incidencia en la crisis definitiva esclavista," which examines the role of changes in the international sugar market in the abolition of slavery.

238. Losada Álvarez, Abel F. "The Cuban Labor Market and Immigration from Spain, 1900–1930." *Cuban Studies* 25 (1995): 147–64.

Uses census data, principally 1907 and 1919 censuses, to examine participation of Spanish immigrants in different economic sectors, stressing proportional increase of foreign white workers in the agricultural sector and proportional decrease of those workers in the commercial sector.

239. Lundahl, Mats. "A Note on Haitian Migration to Cuba, 1890–1934." *Cuban Studies/Estudios Cubanos* 12 (July 1982): 21–36.

Analysis of Haitian migration to Cuba from 1890 to 1931, concentrating on the period between World War I and 1931. Provides statistics on numbers of Haitian migrants and briefly discusses labor conditions for the migrants, the majority of whom were cane cutters in eastern Cuba.

240. Maluquer de Motes, Jordi. *Nación e inmigración: los españoles en Cuba (ss. XIX y XX).* Gijón: Ediciones Jucar, 1992. 190 p.

Detailed study of Spanish immigration to Cuba in the nineteenth and early twentieth centuries. Uses published census data and counts of passengers; makes careful adjustments to raw data. Provides statistical estimates and discussion of role of Spaniards in the Cuban economy.

241. Marrero, Levi. *Cuba: Economía y sociedad.* Vol 9. *Azúcar, ilustración y conciencia (1763–1868).* Madrid: Editorial Playor, 1983. 318 p.

One of a multivolume set, richly illustrated, which draws on primary materials. This volume and others in the series reproduce documents, statistics, and images related to slavery and abolition.

242. Martínez Furé, Rogelio. *Diálogos imaginarios.* Havana: Editorial Arte y Literatura, 1979. 283 p.

Series of essays on Africa and Cuba by Cuban anthropologist/ethnomusicologist. Contains some essays that are specifically historical, including one on the work of Fernando Ortiz, and several on the African origins of Cuban slaves. Discusses the *cabildos de nación*, important Afro-Cuban institutions, particularly in the colonial period.

243. Martínez Heredia, Fernando, Rebecca J. Scott, and Orlando F. García Martínez, eds. *Espacios, silencios y los sentidos de la libertad: Cuba entre 1878 y 1912.* Havana: Ediciones Unión, 2001.

Collection of essays from a conference held in Cienfuegos in March of 1998, with an introduction by Fernando Martínez Heredia. Essays include Rebecca J. Scott, "Reclamando la mula de Gregoria Quesada: el significado de la libertad en los valles del Arimao y del Caunao, Cienfuegos, Cuba (1880–1899)"; Carlos Venegas Fornias, "La arquitectura de la intervención"; Hernán Venegas Delgado, "Formación regional y economía en el centro de Cuba"; Fe Iglesias García, "La concentración azucarera y la comarca de Cienfuegos"; David Sartorius, "Conucos y subsistencia: el caso del ingenio Santa Rosalía"; Irán Millán Cuétara and Orlando García Martínez, "Testimonios de construcciones industriales azucareras en Cienfuegos entre 1819 y 1920"; Ada Ferrer, "Raza, region y género en la Cuba rebelde: Quintín Bandera y la cuestión del liderazgo político"; Orlando García Martínez, "La Brigada de Cienfuegos: un análisis social de su formación"; Michael Zeuske, "'Los negros hicimos la independencia': aspectos de la movilización afrocubana en un hinterland cubano. Cienfuegos entre colonia y República"; Alejandro de la Fuente, "Mitos de "democracia racial": Cuba, 1900–1912"; Jorge Ibarra Cuesta, "Caciquismo, racismo y actitudes en relación con el status político en la Isla en la provincia de Santa Clara (1906–1909)"; Alejandra Bronfman, "Más allá del color: clientelismo y conflicto en Cienfuegos, 1912"; Fernando Martínez Heredia, "Ricardo Batrell empuña la pluma"; Blancamar Rosabal León, "Ricardo Batrell, un expediente inconcluso";

Fernando Coronil, "Poblar la historia"; Jorge Ibarra Cuesta, "Comentarios acerca de 'Mitos de "democracia racial": Cuba, 1900–1912'"; John H. Coatsworth, "La independencia de Cuba en la historia de América Latina"; and Tomás Fernández Robaina, "Recordando una experiencia enriquecedora."

244. Moreno Fraginals, Manuel. *La historia como arma y otros estudios sobre esclavos, ingenios, y plantaciones*. Barcelona: Editorial Crítica, 1983. 178 p.

A collection of essays by a major economic historian, some of which address the question of the causes of abolition.

245. Moreno Fraginals, Manuel, Frank Moya Pons, and Stanley L. Engerman, eds. *Between Slavery and Free Labor: The Spanish-Speaking Caribbean in the Nineteenth Century*. Baltimore. The Johns Hopkins University Press: 1985. 292 p.

Collection of essays on transition from slavery to free labor. Includes work on plantations in the Caribbean by Manuel Moreno Fraginals; on Cuba by Rebecca J. Scott, Fe Iglesias García, Francisco López Segrera, and Franklin W. Knight; on Puerto Rico by José Curet, Benjamin Nistal-Moret, Andrés A. Ramos Mattei; on the Dominican Republic by Frank Moya Pons, José del Castillo, and Patrick Bryan. Also includes notes on a theoretical economic model by Herbert S. Klein and Stanley Engerman and an epilogue by Sidney W. Mintz.

246. Moreno Fraginals, Manuel. *El ingenio. Complejo económico social cubano del azúcar*. 3 vols. Havana: Editorial de Ciencias Sociales, 1978.

Detailed, classic study of Cuban sugar industry in eighteenth and nineteenth centuries. Discusses labor, technology, ideology, and strategies of "sacarocracy." Uses plantation account books, government correspondence, contemporary accounts. Although the text concentrates on the pre-emancipation period, the statistical appendices include extensive production and export data for the late nineteenth and twentieth century as well. Vol. III includes a detailed glossary and a one hundred-page annotated bibliography of sources on sugar.

247. Naranjo Orovio, Consuelo and Tomás Mallo Gutiérrez, eds. *Cuba, la perla de las Antillas*. Actas de las Ia Jornadas sobre Cuba y su Historia. Aranjuez: Doce Calles, 1994. 344 p.

Collection of essays on nineteenth- and twentieth-century Cuban history. Categorized under the rubrics of culture, population and society, politics and economy, many are based on primary materials, both Cuban and Spanish. Of particular interest for the study of postemancipation social relations are essays on Spanish immigration by Jordi Maluquer de Motes and Consuelo Naranjo Orovio.

248. Naranjo, Consuelo, Miguel A. Puig-Samper, Luis Miguel García Mora, eds. *La nación soñada: Cuba, Puerto Rico y Filipinas ante el 98.* Aranjuez: Doce Calles, 1996. 893 p.

Proceedings of a conference held in Aranjuez, Spain, in April 1995. Focus is generally on period from 1870 to 1914, with particular attention to the transformations surrounding the year 1898. Of particular interest for the study of former slaves and questions of race are: Consuelo Naranjo Orovio, "En búsqueda de lo nacional: migraciones y racismo en Cuba (1880–1910)"; Alejandro de la Fuente, "Negros y electores: desigualdad y políticas raciales en Cuba, 1900–1930"; Rebecca J. Scott, "'The Lower Class of Whites' and 'The Negro Element': Race, Social Identity and Politics in Central Cuba"; Antonio Santamaría García, "Caña de azúcar y producción de azúcar en Cuba. Crecimiento y organización de la industria azucarera cubana desde mediados del siglo XIX hasta la finalización de la Primero Guerra Mundial"; Joan Casanovas Codina, "El movimiento obrero y la política colonial española en la Cuba de finales del XIX."

249. Nelson, Lowry. *Rural Cuba.* 1950. Reprint. New York: Octagon Books, 1970. 285 p.

Contains results of field research by North American rural sociologist in 1945 and 1946. Community studies were done, with Cuban collaboration, in two regions of Pinar del Río province and in Cabaiguán (Santa Clara), Cienfuegos/Trinidad area (Santa Clara), Alto Songo (Oriente), Florida (Camagüey), Sancti Spíritus (Santa Clara Province), Bayamo (Oriente), San Antonio de las Vegas (Havana), Florencia, and Güines (Havana). Covers a wide range of crop regions, including tobacco, coffee, sugar, cattle, and mixed farming. Although the main focus is on the period of the study itself, volume contains discussions on topics that have an important historical dimension, such as squatters and their expulsion, patterns of tenantry, settlement patterns, and seasonal work rhythms in specific crop regions.

250. Ortiz, Fernando. *La secta conga de los matiabos de Cuba.* Mexico City: UNAM, 1956. 325 p.

A study of maroon communities composed of African slaves. Contains detailed descriptions of relations between insurgent forces and maroons during the Ten Years' War. Describes maroon ceremonies held to aid the insurgent cause and gives glimpse of insurgent reactions to these ceremonies. Descriptions are based on war memoirs and diaries such as Roa's (see above) and others published in Cuban newspapers in the early republic.

251. Ortiz, Fernando. *Los negros brujos*. Reprint. 1906. Havana: Editorial de Ciencias Sociales, 1995. 238p .

Reprint of study of Afro-Cuban religion, by major Cuban anthropologist, examining different cults, gods, rituals, and superstitions. Concentrates on *brujería* (witchcraft) and *brujos* (witches). Offers sketches of "typical" Cuban witches. Gives examples of incidents of *brujería* taken from Cuban newspapers (1902–04). Discusses affinities between African religions and Catholicism in Cuba and the "de-Africanization" of Afro-Cuban witchcraft.

252. Ortiz, Fernando. *Los negros esclavos: Estudio sociológico y de derecho público*. 1916. Reprint. Havana: Editorial de Ciencias Sociales, 1996. 478 p.

Broad study of Cuban slavery, including discussions of the institution's history, the slave trade to Cuba, slaves' working conditions in farms and cities, slave rebellions, and freedpeople. Contains sections on the specific African origins of Cuban slaves and on "psychology of Afro-Cubans." The final section of the book reprints Spanish documents dealing with slavery, including, for example: Ley de vientres libres (1870), Reglamento del patronato de esclavos (1872), Ley de abolición de la esclavitud (1880), and Reglamento de la ley de 1880 aboliendo la esclavitud en Cuba (1880).

253. Ortiz, Fernando. "Las rebeliones de los afro-cubanos." *Revista Bimestre Cubana* 4 (March–April 1910): 97–112.

An essay exploring Afro-Cuban resistance to slavery. Cites suicide and crime as examples of subversion and asks why slave resistance was not as successful in Cuba as in other countries. Useful for looking at Ortiz's definitions of race, racism, and resistance.

254. Ortiz, Fernando. "Los cabildos afro-cubanos." *Revista Bimestre Cubana* 16 (January–February 1921): 5–39.

An essay on *cabildos*, organizations that grouped together individuals of African birth. Describes ceremonies, group leadership, and hierarchies. Lists groups registered in 1909 with the provincial government of Havana that were derived directly or indirectly from *cabildos*.

255. Orum, Thomas T. "The Politics of Color: The Racial Dimension of Cuban Politics during the Early Republican Years, 1900–1912." Ph.D. diss., New York University, 1975. 320 p.

Discusses Afro-Cuban participation in the wars for independence, especially in the war between 1895 and 1898. Contains detailed examination of black participation in formal politics of early republic, with information on their membership in political parties, in local and national offices, police forces, the army, and the Rural Guard, leading up to the formation of the Partido Independiente de Color and the "race war" of 1912.

256. Page, Charles A. "The Development of Organized Labor in Cuba" Ph.D. diss., University of California, 1952. 367 p.

History of organized labor in Cuba focusing on western portion of the island from 1850 to 1950.

257. Pérez de la Riva y Pons, Francisco. *El café: Historia de su cultivo y explotación en Cuba*. Havana: Jesús Montero, 1944. 383 p.

Study of the rise and decline of coffee cultivation in Cuba. Discusses process of production, the work of slaves and Chinese contract laborers, and the influence of French and Haitian coffee growers in eastern Cuba. Covers the period from the late eighteenth century to roughly 1940. Though it contains statistical data on wages of coffee workers, residents on coffee farms, and the value of land, most of these figures are from before or after the postemancipation period.

258. Pérez de la Riva y Pons, Francisco. *El negro y la tierra, el conuco y el palenque*. Havana, n.d.

Rare pamphlet that examines forms of access to land by black Cubans.

259. Pérez de la Riva, Francisco. *La habitación rural en Cuba*. Havana: Editorial Lex, 1952. 99 p.

General essay that examines five types of rural dwelling: the *quinta*, the *bohío*, the *barracón*, and the *casa de vivienda*. Also describes the genesis of the *batey*, or mill yard of the sugar plantation, and the role of the *conuco* (provision ground) and *palenque* (runaway slave community) in establishing dispersed patterns of habitation. Contrasts building patterns in central mills owned by Cubans and those developed by North Americans, associating the latter with residential segregation by occupation. Discussion of different forms of habitat provides evidence for a portrait of the material conditions of life for former slaves and other rural dwellers. No footnotes or bibliography. Apparently based on research and observation by author, a specialist in Cuban rural history.

260. Pérez de la Riva, Juan. "La inmigración antillana en Cuba durante el primer tercio del siglo XX." *Revista de la Biblioteca Nacional "José Martí"* 42 (May–Aug. 1975): 74–88.

On West Indian immigrants to Cuba in the early twentieth century.

261. Pérez de la Riva, Juan. *Para la historia de las gentes sin historia.* Barcelona: Editorial Ariel, 1976. 200 p.

Collection of essays by major Cuban historian including two articles on indentured Chinese workers and an essay on the return of freedpeople to Africa.

262. Pérez de la Riva, Juan. "La contradicción fundamental de la sociedad colonial cubana: trabajo esclavo contra trabajo libre." *Economía y Desarrollo* 2 (April–June 1970): 167–78.

Theoretical essay.

263. Pérez de la Riva, Juan. *El barracón y otros ensayos.* Havana: Editorial de Ciencias Sociales, 1975. 529 p.

A collection of essays including studies on Chinese indentured workers, slaves' housing, and aspects of the slave trade. Contains numerous demographic studies of particular regions and estates.

264. Pérez Guzmán, Francisco. *Herida profunda.* Havana: Ediciones Unión, 1998. 259 p.

History of the military strategy of "reconcentración" and relations between the Spanish military, Cuban rebels, and the civilian population of Cuba from 1896 to 1898.

265. Pérez, Louis A., Jr. "Insurrection, Intervention, and the Transformation of Land Tenure Systems in Cuba, 1898–1902." *Hispanic American Historical Review* 65 (May 1985): 229–54.

Essay on the period of the first U.S. intervention on the island, focusing on the relationship between the occupation government's actions and Cuban and U.S. landowning interests. Includes a partial list of U.S. land companies operating on the island.

266. Pérez, Louis A., Jr. "Politics, Peasants, and People of Color: The 1912 'Race War' in Cuba Reconsidered." *Hispanic American Historical Review* 66 (August 1986): 509–39.

Analysis of socioeconomic roots of the 1912 "race war" in southeastern Oriente. Examines targets of protest during the uprising. Bulk of the article surveys economic, social, and demographic changes in the region from 1899 to the outbreak of the uprising. For the background to the uprising, Pérez's sources include census data, U.S. War Department records, Santiago provincial report for 1904–05, and transcripts of cases involving the eviction of Cuban peasants by sugar and railroad companies. For accounts of the uprising itself, Pérez uses U.S. consular records and Cuban newspapers.

267. Pérez, Louis A., Jr. "Toward Dependency and Revolution: The Political Economy of Cuba Between Wars, 1878–1895." *Latin American Research Review* 18 (spring 1983): 127–42.

Discussion of broad economic changes in Cuba between the wars for independence, with particular attention to changes in the sugar industry and in relations with the United States.

268. Pérez, Louis A., Jr. *Lords of the Mountain: Social Banditry and Peasant Protest in Cuba, 1878–1918*. Pittsburgh: University of Pittsburgh Press, 1989. 267 p.

A study of banditry in eastern Cuba based on analysis of social and economic conditions of the peasantry. Includes discussion of events of 1912 in Oriente.

269. Pérez, Louis A., Jr. *Cuba between Empires, 1878–1902*. Pittsburgh: University of Pittsburgh Press, 1983.

Detailed analysis of the politics and economics of the island across the period during which emancipation took place and postemancipation society emerged.

270. Pérez-Cisneros, Enrique. *La abolición de la esclavitud en Cuba*. Costa Rica: Litografía e Imp. LIL, S. A., 1987. 177 p.

Contains brief, narrative essay on abolitionism in Cuba and Spain. Book consists mostly of reproductions of nineteen documents relating to abolition. These include: treaties between Spain and England regarding the Cuban slave trade; the Reglamento of slavery (1842); penal codes for slave traders; the Moret Law, the Pact of Zanjón; the *patronato* law; and the law ending the *patronato* in 1886.

271. Pirala, Antonio. *Anales de la guerra de Cuba*. 3 vols. Madrid: F. González Rojas, 1895–1898.

History of the Ten Years' War written by Spanish historian. The work is unique in its extensive use and reproduction of unpublished Spanish and Cuban documents, including rebel memoirs, confidential Spanish military and administrative reports, circulars of both Spanish and Cuban armies, and handbills and proclamations written by rebel leaders. Explores the links between slavery and insurrection, the participation of slaves, and relations between insurgents and rural society. Volume three includes discussion of the Guerra Chiquita (1879–80) and the postwar period through 1885.

272. Pollitt, Brian. "Some Problems of Enumerating the 'Peasantry' in Cuba." *Journal of Peasant Studies* 4 (January 1977): 162–80.

Review of some of the available sources regarding the rural population, pointing out the flaws in them. The author looks specifically at the censuses of 1899, 1943, 1946, and 1953, as well as the surveys gathered by Lowry Nelson in his *Rural Cuba*, among others.

273. Portuondo Linares, Serafín. *Los Independientes de Color: Historia del Partido Independiente de Color.* 2nd ed. Havana: Editorial Librería Selecta, 1950. 281 p.

Documents the history of the Partido Independiente de Color from its formation in 1908 to the armed uprising of 1912. Using the press as its principal source, the book provides details about the party's leadership and platform as well as a close account of the congressional debates concerning the law that ruled the party illegal.

274. Poumier, María. *Apuntes sobre la vida cotidiana en Cuba en 1898.* Havana: Editorial de Ciencias Sociales, 1975. 239 p.

History of different aspects of Cuban society in the late 1890s, including discussions of the effects of the War of Independence on rural and urban society and soldiers' experiences in the Ejército Libertador. Based largely on printed primary and secondary sources.

275. Poumier-Taquechel, María. *Contribution à l'étude du banditisme social à Cuba: L'histoire et le mythe de Manuel García "Rey de los Campos de Cuba" (1851–1895).* Paris: L'Harmattan, 1986. 459 p.

A study of rural banditry in Cuba, focusing on popular perceptions of the bandit Manuel García. Links literary sources with archival and newspaper evidence. Draws connection between anticolonial sentiment and bandits' resistance to authority.

276. Risquet, Juan F. *Rectificaciones, la cuestión político-social en la isla de Cuba.* Havana: Tipografía América, 1900. 205 p.

A critique of Spanish colonialism written in the 1890s by Afro-Cuban exile in Florida. Contains sections on slavery, the slave trade, and abolition. The section on slavery includes a table which provides figures by province for the number of *patrocinados* freed for different reasons (including self-purchase) between 1880 and 1884. Author uses abolitionist literature and contemporary newspaper articles to address the topic of slave discipline during the period of apprenticeship. A chapter on the struggle for black civil rights in the postemancipation period discusses legislative aspects of struggles over black access to public places and links racism and discrimination against Afro-Cubans to Spanish colonial rule. This chapter also contains a long section on Juan Gualberto Gómez and the Directorio Central de las Sociedades de la Raza de Color. Two chapters on black cultural and intellectual production provide brief biographical sketches of individual figures. Two appendices reproduce articles from the Afro-Cuban newspaper *La Igualdad* which were written to counter claims made in the *Diario de la Marina* about similarities between Haiti and Cuba. Useful for examining black political activity in the 1890s and for exploring links between this activity and anticolonial mobilization.

277. Rivero Muñiz, José. *El movimiento laboral cubano durante el período 1906–1911: Apuntes para la historia del proletariado en Cuba.* Santa Clara: Universidad Central de las Villas, 1962. 177 p.

Overview of labor organization between 1906 and 1911, primarily of cigar makers in Havana, with some information on railroad labor organization. Appendix includes a 1907 letter from Samuel Gompers to Emilio Sánchez and Domingo Salazar, president and secretary of the Comité Ejecutivo de los Tabaqueros de la Habana, a 1907 letter from Charles Magoon to the president of the Unión de Fabricantes de Tabacos y Cigarros de la Isla de Cuba, and regulations of the Partido Obrero Socialista de la Isla de Cuba.

278. Rivero Muñiz, José. *El movimiento obrero durante la primera intervención.* Santa Clara: Universidad Central de las Villas, 1961. 223 p.

Includes information on return of insurgents to the countryside after the war.

279. Rojas, Ursinio. *Las luchas obreras en el Central Tacajó.* Havana, 1979.

A firsthand account of labor mobilization in this *central*, written by one of the organizers of the strike of 1933. Traces the history of Tacajó from 1916, when it was founded by the United Fruit Company. In addition to personal anecdotes, it reprints documents from strikes of the Sindicato Nacional de Obreros de la Industria Azucarera in Santa Clara, Camagüey, and Oriente. Provides postrevolutionary names of *centrales* in Occidente, Matanzas, Las Villas, Camagüey, and Oriente, alongside their earlier names.

280. Rousset, Ricardo V. *Historial de Cuba*. 3 vols. Havana: Librería Cervantes, 1918.

Historical survey of rural Cuba. Each of the three volumes deals with two provinces: volume 1 with Pinar del Río and Havana, volume 2 with Matanzas and Santa Clara, and volume 3 with Camagüey and Oriente. Provides historical and geographical overview of each of the provinces, including lists of roads and maps of *hatos* and *corrales* with corresponding list of names and dates of founding. The bulk of each of the volumes is the breakdown of the province into *términos municipales*. For each *término* the author provides descriptions of their establishment and history, and divides the *término* into neighborhoods, providing information on population, agriculture, and history. Provides details at a very local level. For example, in his description of the *término municipal* of Alto Songo the author provides information on the percentage of the population said to have taken part in various anticolonial rebellions, along with information on changes in local agricultural industries.

281. Rushing, Fannie T. *"Cabildos de Nación and Sociedades de la Raza de Color*: Afrocuban Participation in Slave Emancipation and Cuban Independence, 1865–1895." Ph.D. diss., University of Chicago, 1992. 378 p.

282. Sarracino, Rodolfo and Francisco Pérez Guzmán. *La Guerra Chiquita: Una experiencia necesaria*. Havana: Editorial Letras Cubanas, 1982. 380 p.

Examination of social and political aspects of the Guerra Chiquita (1879–80). Provides detailed accounts of relative strength of insurrection both within and outside Santiago province.

283. Schmidt-Nowara, Christopher. *Empire and Antislavery: Spain, Cuba, and Puerto Rico, 1833–1874*. Pittsburgh: University of Pittsburgh Press, 1999. 239 p.

Intellectual history of links between colonial ideology and slavery, with a focus on the Spanish Abolitionist Society. Based on archival research in Spain, Cuba, Puerto Rico, and the United States.

284. Schroeder, Susan. *Cuba: A Handbook of Historical Statistics*. Boston, 1982. 589 p.

A compilation of statistical data on demography, labor, production, foreign trade, government, and other topics. Drawn from printed sources. Main focus is first half of the twentieth century.

285. Schwartz, Rosalie. "The Displaced and the Disappointed: Cultural Nationalists and Black Activists in Cuba in the 1920s." Ph.D. diss., University of California, San Diego, 1977. 271 p.

Examination of cultural nationalism and debates over race in the 1920s.

286. Schwartz, Rosalie. *Lawless Liberators: Political Banditry and Cuban Independence*. Durham, N.C.: Duke University Press, 1989. 297 p.

An analysis of the social and political dimensions of banditry, focused on the provinces of Havana and Matanzas in the late nineteenth century.

287. Scott, Rebecca. "Relaciones de clase e ideologías raciales: acción rural colectiva en Louisiana y Cuba, 1865–1912." *Historia Social* 22 (1995): 127–49.

Comparative essay focused on dynamics of cross-racial alliance and politicization of race.

288. Scott, Rebecca J. *Slave Emancipation in Cuba: The Transition to Free Labor, 1860–1899*. Princeton, N.J.: Princeton University Press, 1985. 319 p.

Draws on archival materials in Cuba and Spain to analyze the dynamics of emancipation and the formation of a postemancipation society. Uses comparative regional/provincial analysis to examine hypotheses on the breakdown of slavery. (A reprint edition, with a new afterword by the author, appeared from the University of Pittsburgh Press in 2000).

289. Scott, Rebecca J. "Fault Lines, Color Lines, and Party Lines: Race, Labor, and Collective Action in Louisiana and Cuba, 1862–1912." In Frederick Cooper, Thomas C. Holt, and Rebecca J. Scott, *Beyond Slavery: Explorations of Race, Labor, and Citizenship in Postemancipation Societies*. Chapel Hill: University of North Carolina Press, 2000.

Cuban portion of this comparative analysis is focused on the province of Santa Clara.

290. Scott, Rebecca J. "Raza, clase y acción colectiva en Cuba, 1895–1912: Formación de alianzas interraciales en el mundo de la caña." In Arcadio Díaz Quiñones, ed., *El caribe entre imperios (Coloquio de Princeton)*, a special number of *Op. Cit.: Revista del Centro de Investigaciones Históricas* (Río Piedras, Puerto Rico) 9 (1997): 131–63.

Analysis of the possibilities and limits of interracial alliances in the military, labor movements, and party politics from the onset of the War of

Independence of 1895 to the violent suppression of the Partido Independiente de Color in 1912. Focuses primarily on the region of Cienfuegos.

291. Scott, Rebecca J. "Reclaiming Gregoria's Mule: The Meanings of Freedom in the Arimao and Caunao Valleys, Cienfuegos, Cuba, 1880–1899." *Past and Present* 170 (February 2001): 181–216.

Uses plantation records and notarial documents to trace claims to productive resources.

292. Serviat, Pedro. *El problema negro en Cuba y su solución definitiva.* Havana: Editora Política, 1986. 197 p.

Considers the history of racial discrimination in Cuba from the colonial period to the onset of the Cuban Revolution. Appendices include citations to archival documents related to *cabildos* and *sociedades negras*, the texts of the 1886 law for the abolition of slavery and the royal order for the suppression of the *patronato*, a list of black generals in the War of Independence, and a table with the Cuban population broken down by racial category for censuses between 1899 and 1981.

293. Stolcke, Verena (Martinez-Alier). *Marriage, Class and Colour in Nineteenth-Century Cuba: A Study of Racial Attitudes and Sexual Values in a Slave Society.* 1974. Reprint. Ann Arbor: University of Michigan Press, 1989. 202 p.

Examination of practices and regulations concerning race and sexuality in Cuba up to 1881, when a governmental decree eliminated legal restrictions on interracial marriage. Based chiefly on Cuban archival records and parish baptism and marriage registers. Introduction to reprint edition discusses the implications of Stolcke's analysis for recent scholarship on the social construction of gender and kinship relationships, the possibilities of family organization under slavery, and matrifocal family units.

294. Toro, Carlos del. *El movimiento obrero cubano en 1914.* Havana: Instituto Cubano del Libro, 1969. 201 p.

Institutional history of Cuban labor organization leading up to the National Workers' Conference in 1914. One chapter addresses the Conference itself, with detailed accounts of sessions, persons attending, and topics discussed. Appendices list 1914 strikes, meetings, and protests; labor journals and publications; and unions and organizations in Havana, including names of union officers.

295. Torres-Cuevas, Eduardo, and Eusebio Reyes. *Esclavitud y sociedad: Notas y documentos para la historia de la esclavitud negra en Cuba.* Havana: Editorial de Ciencias Sociales, 1986. 280 p.

Overview of Cuban slavery from sixteenth century to 1886. Final section includes Spanish laws and decrees concerning slavery, the *patronato*, and abolition. Contains Juan Pérez de la Riva's figures on the number of slaves brought to Cuba each year from 1762 to 1863.

296. Turner, Mary. "Chinese Contract Labour in Cuba, 1847–1874." *Caribbean Studies* 14 (July 1974): 66–81.

A survey of Chinese immigration to Cuba, focused on the use of Chinese workers to solve labor problems after the 1840s.

297. Vázquez, Ricardo. *Triunvirato: Historia de un rincón azucarero de Cuba.* Havana: Comité Central del Partido Comunista de Cuba, 1976. 67 p.

Brief history of the *ingenio* Triunvirato in the *término municipal* of Santa Ana in Matanzas province. Includes discussions of slavery and the *patronato*. Discusses the growth of the *colonato* in the early twentieth century. Includes a list of all the *colonos* on Triunvirato's lands in 1922, with names, amount of land rented, and price paid.

298. Venegas Delgado, Hernán, and Armando Armas García. *Acerca de la historia del Central "Trinidad" (F.N.T.A.), 1893–1960.* Santa Clara: Universidad Central de las Villas, 1988.

Case study of a major central sugar mill that was developed by U.S. investor Edwin Atkins in the 1890s. Analyzes labor force, land use, and production. Carefully documented, using published sources and property registers along with interviews and other archival sources. Useful for analyzing transformations in what had been slave-based sugar plantations.

299. Venegas Delgado, Hernán. "Acerca del proceso de concentración y centralización de la industria azucarera en la región remediana a fines del siglo XIX." *Islas* 73 (1982): 63–121.

A concise history of sugar in the region of Remedios (in Santa Clara province) in the nineteenth century, focused on technological and labor innovations. The article's appendix presents figures for *ingenio* production in 1887–88 and 1889–90, advertisements for machinery taken from the *Revista de Agricultura*, and maps of Remedios and the *ingenio* "Narcisa."

300. Venegas Delgado, Hernán. "Apuntes sobre la decadencia trinitaria en el siglo xix." *Islas* 46 (September–December 1973): 159–251.

Examines the decay of the sugar-producing region of Trinidad, in Santa Clara province, in the latter part of the nineteenth century. Analyzes the effects of the Ten Years' War and provides detailed information on local conditions drawn from national and regional archives. Discusses process of concentration of sugar holdings in the late nineteenth century.

301. Wolf, Donna M. "The Cuban 'Gente de Color' and the Independence Movement, 1879–1895." *Revista/Review Interamericana* 5 (fall 1975): 403–21.

Examines social conditions of Afro-Cubans during period from 1879 to 1895. Discusses briefly the Afro-Cuban press and mutual aid societies, Afro-Cuban participation in the preparations for the final war of independence, and the political leadership of Afro-Cubans including Juan Gualberto Gómez, Martín Morúa Delgado, and Antonio Maceo.

302. Wolf, Donna Marie. "The Caribbean People of Color and the Cuban Independence Movement." Ph.D. diss., University of Pittsburgh, 1973. 464 p.

First part uses secondary sources and published Cuban and Spanish primary documents to look at role and participation of people of color in wars in 1868–78, 1879–80, and 1895–98. Second part describes responses of government officials in Jamaica, Haiti and Santo Domingo to the Cuban Independence Movement between 1868 and 1898, relying mainly on diplomatic correspondence and newspapers.

303. Zanetti, Oscar and Alejandro García, eds. *United Fruit Company: Un caso del dominio imperialista en Cuba.* Havana: Editorial de Ciencias Sociales, 1976. 450 p.

A collaborative project carried out by students at the University of Havana using company records to analyze the role of the United Fruit Company, which was active in Cuba from 1901 to 1959. Volume aims to examine company strategies, social consequences of plantations, and role of the company in encouraging migrant labor from elsewhere in the Caribbean. Most of the material comes from the central mills "Preston" and "Boston," in eastern Cuba, and from the company administrative headquarters on the island. Includes detailed information on salary levels for company employees.

304. Zeuske, Michael. "Die diskrete Macht der Sklaven. Zur politischen Partizipation von Afrokubanern während des kubanischen

Unabhängigkeitskrieges und der ersten Jahren der Republik (1895–
1908)—eine regionale Perspektive." *Comparativ* 7 (1997): 32–98.

Detailed presentation of the author's study of the incorporation of former
slaves into the anticolonial struggle and into Cuban political life. Uses
enlistment registers, pension claims, and notarial records from the central region to estimate proportion of the Cuban fighting force likely to
have been composed of former slaves and descendants of slaves. An updated essay on this subject by the same author appears in Martínez,
Scott, and García, eds., *Espacios, silencios* (see above).

305. Zeuske, Michael. "The Real Esteban Montejo?: A Re-reading of
Miguel Barnet's *Cimarrón.*" *New West Indian Guide/Nieuwe West-
Indische Gids* 71 (1997): 265–79.

Discussion of the best-known life history of a Cuban born into slavery,
Esteban Montejo, whose memoir was based on oral interviews compiled
by Miguel Barnet (see above). Zeuske juxtaposes passages from the
memoir with newly-uncovered archival material about Montejo's life as
an agriculturalist in the central province of Santa Clara (Las Villas) after the 1895–98 war. (Same issue includes reply by Barnet.)

V Brazil

EDITOR

Rebecca J. Scott
University of Michigan

COMPILED BY

Rebecca J. Scott

Judith Allen
Independent Scholar

Aims McGuinness
University of Wisconsin-Milwaukee

Karl Monsma
Federal University of São Carlos, Brazil

Lara Putnam
University of Costa Rica

João José Reis
Federal University of Bahia, Brazil

INTRODUCTION

There is a long tradition of interpretive writing in Brazil on the aftermath of abolition. The earliest of these writings often addressed both historical and sociological questions, seeking evidence from the late nineteenth and early twentieth centuries that could explain contemporary social patterns, including the continued disproportionate impoverishment of Afro-Brazilians. Later scholars built on these literatures, and on the impressive body of scholarship on slavery itself, and began to address new questions concerning labor relations, family structures, cultural patterns, and gender relations. Often working with notarial and judicial archives, they profiled a wide range of historical actors, including small farmers as well as masters and slaves, and opened the way to a new generation of postslavery studies.

Several Brazilian historians have recently published major works on the strategies and aspirations of slaves and *libertos* (former slaves), emphasizing the interaction between the agency of Afro-Brazilians and the constraints imposed by continuing structures of domination. Scholars are examining the ways in which former slaves sought access to land, at times through networks of clientelism and at times through a variety of forms of informal property rights. Maria Helena Machado has written of a "peasant project" within emancipation, and Hebe Mattos has looked at the development of new social identities among the long-free and the recently-freed. These and other scholars have re-examined rural protest within the early Brazilian republic. Sidney Chalhoub, meanwhile, has studied processes of reform in urban areas and their implications for Afro-Brazilians, particularly in the realms of public health and housing.[1]

Several pioneering compilations have drawn on oral historical materials, and work now in progress promises to take this line of inquiry further. Moreover, recent legislation based on the 1988 Brazilian constitution established mechanisms for recognizing land rights of "the remanescentes das comunidades dos quilombos" and has thus stimulated collaboration between historians, anthropologists, and activists to explore the emergence of different forms of land use within and alongside formerly slave-based plantations, as well as to trace the history of more

1. Maria Helena Machado, *O plano e o pânico: os movimentos sociais na década da abolição* (Rio de Janeiro: Editora Universidade Federal do Rio de Janeiro, 1994), Hebe Maria Mattos, *Das cores do silêncio: os significados da liberdade no sudeste escravista, Brasil Século XIX* (Rio de Janeiro: Nova Fronteira, 1998), and Sidney Chalhoub, *Cidade febril: cortiços e epidemias na Corte imperial* (São Paulo: Companhia das Letras, 1996).

isolated *quilombos*. Recent masters' and doctoral theses, most of them written within Brazil itself, have also begun to mark out an agenda for yet another wave of studies, often focused on very close study of individual microregions.[2]

Our compilation of secondary works from these multiple generations of scholarship aims among other things to encourage specialists of other regions to attend to the extraordinary recent scholarship emerging from Brazil, continuing the tradition of fruitful comparative debate. Most books and many articles have been given English-language annotations, which we hope will make these works more easily accessible to those for whom Portuguese is not their major language of research.

Our section on printed primary sources has a somewhat different goal. The best of the recent secondary work rests on ground-level manuscript archival materials and oral histories. But in our examination of *printed* primary sources we have also been struck by the survival of local-level data of various kinds in government-issued sources and personal memoirs, as well as in the immense volume of statistical compilations. The memoir literature, for example, often portrays from a planter's point of view interactions and challenges that can then be sought out and examined in judicial records to try to develop multiple perspectives. Printed primary sources of these kinds can also help to identify important regions and questions for further study and assist in the examination of the larger structures within which microhistories need to be situated.

We have defined the boundaries of the Brazil section roughly as 1871 to 1930, thus encompassing the process of gradual emancipation and the transformations in agriculture that followed final abolition. In selecting items for inclusion, we have annotated a large number of materials focusing on export crops (including sugar, coffee, and cacao) and as many as possible on the mixed-farming regions in which plantations were often embedded. We have incorporated travel literature only sparingly, in part because other bibliographies can serve as guides to that body of work, but we have tried to locate as many rural memoirs as possible.

We have been selective in our citing of statistical materials. Two existing bibliographic volumes, *Processo de modernização do Brasil, 1850–1930*, and Roberto Córtes Conde and Stanley Stein, *Latin America: A Guide to Economic History, 1830–1930*, contain comprehensive annotated

2. See, in addition to the works cited in the entries below, the ongoing project "Memórias do Cativeiro" at the Laboratório de História Oral e Iconografia of the Universidade Federal Fluminense, coordinated by Hebe Maria Mattos and Mariza de Carvalho Soares.

lists of statistical and demographic compilations on Brazil. We have therefore concentrated our efforts on those sources that have a particular focus on rural labor or that have direct implications for the study of rural labor, such as discussions of landholding, wages, and output. We have also included several published census volumes and highlighted their shifting usage of terminology on color. But for a full guide to statistical and economic data, as well as census publications, the researcher should consult the two volumes mentioned above.[3]

We have been highly selective in our citing of sources on folklore and Afro-Brazilian religion. There is a rich Brazilian literature on folklore from both rural and urban areas, and some scholarship on Afro-Brazilian religion was conceived by its authors as an extension of the study of folklore. In *Societies after Slavery* we have incorporated only a small fraction of this work, concentrating on those studies that are based on fieldwork carried out before 1930 and that specify the time and place of the material compiled, and we have passed over the more general or the more recent discussions of customs and ritual practices. Two very extensive bibliographies, Alves, *Bibliografia Afro-Brasileira*, and Porter, *Afro-Braziliana: A Working Bibliography*, provide a wealth of additional citations.

The study of society after slavery in Brazil has also drawn on an extensive and sophisticated body of scholarship on racial identity and "race relations," as well as on close ethnographic and ethnohistorical work on Afro-Brazilian culture. When selecting from among works on race relations and rural sociology, we have concentrated on works that were actually written *during* the period covered by the bibliography (1871–1930) and on later works that draw on primary historical materials. We have generally not included the rich ethnographic and interpretive literature from the 1950s onward on questions of racial identity and social relations, except in cases where it is explicitly grounded in new historical data.

In a few instances, we have included recent works of rural sociology

3. When compiling this bibliography, it has been our practice to locate each item and examine it directly to verify the citation and the contents as we prepare the annotation. Original orthography, with all its inconsistencies, has been retained in order to facilitate library searches. In the final months of preparing the Brazil section, however, we found that some potentially useful statistical compilations were now unavailable on interlibrary loan within the United States. Rather than follow our own rule mechanically, and exclude these last items from our bibliography, we decided to leave them in, indicating the source of our reference. We hope that by pointing the way to these sources, we will make it easier for researchers to locate and make good use of them.

that provide rigorous explorations of the terminology of labor relations and land tenure (such as the concept of *morador*) that may be of particular use to historians. We realize that recent anthropological work, such as that of Eliane Cantarino O'Dwyer, Neuza Mendes Gusmão, and Robin Sherriff, is also opening up new modes of analysis of racial categories and ideology. Though compiling a bibliography of such ethnographic sources is beyond the scope of the current project, we do anticipate that these and other ongoing works will lead to a new dialogue between anthropology and history in the Brazilian context. A collaborative project recently undertaken at the Universidade Federal Fluminense, for example, promises to yield rigorous and carefully-documented studies of the process of settlement of former slaves on the land in rural Rio de Janeiro.[4]

We have not included general histories of Brazil, even when they contain chapters on abolition and the transition to free labor, on the grounds that such items are relatively easy to locate through conventional means. We would note, however, that these works can be extremely useful. For instance, the magisterial work edited by Sérgio Buarque de Holanda and Pedro Moacyr Campos contains a chapter by Emilia Viotti da Costa on the subject of export agriculture that is an important point of reference for subsequent study.[5]

As we acknowledged in the general introduction, this section is the fruit of lively international collaboration, and we look forward eagerly to the appearance of an expanded Portuguese-language edition of this portion of the bibliography. Brazilian scholars are at the forefront of the effort to combine close social and economic history with searching examinations of racial categories, racial identification, and the complexities of social interactions in contexts of clientelism. The frameworks developed by scholars such as Hebe Mattos and Sidney Chalhoub can thus enrich work on postemancipation society in other parts of the world, while adding to the complexity of our understanding of Brazil itself.

REBECCA J. SCOTT

4. This work is tentatively entitled "Terras de Quilombo no Estado do Rio de Janeiro: diálogos entre antropologia e história," coordinated by Hebe Maria Mattos and Eliane Cantarino O'Dywer.

5. See Emília Viotti da Costa, "O escravo na grande lavoura," in Sérgio Buarque de Holanda and Pedro Moacyr Campos, eds., *História geral da civilização brasileira*, Tomo II, *O Brasil monárquico*, Vol. IV, *Declínio e queda do império* (São Paulo: Difel, 1974), 85–137.

1. Abrahão, Fernando Antônio. *As ações de liberdade de escravos do Tribunal de Campinas.* Campinas: Universidade Estadual de Campinas/Centro de Memória, 1992. 105 p.

   Catalogue for collection of 157 judicial cases related to manumission of slaves (*ações de liberdade*) located in the Arquivo do Tribunal de Justiça de Campinas at the Centro de Memória of the Universidade Estadual de Campinas (UNICAMP). Cases date from 1803 to 1888, with majority from years between 1871 and 1885. Catalogue summarizes each case, noting legal method of manumission or other judicial process (e.g., manumission in exchange for *pecúlio* or slave's savings); slave's name, age, and name of master; name of solicitor (*solicitador*); name of sponsor (*curador*); estimated value of slave, *pecúlio*, or deposit for Fundo de Emancipação; judicial action taken; total number of folios pertaining to case; and archival finding aid. Introduction and conclusion to catalogue provide historical background for the collection and review legislation and judicial apparatus related to emancipation. Includes helpful index to themes, names, and places encountered in the cases.

2. Alves, Henrique L. *Bibliografia Afro-Brasileira: estudos sobre o negro.* 2d ed. Rio de Janeiro: Livraria Editora Cátedra, 1979. 181 p.

   An unannotated bibliography of published primary and secondary sources concerning the African presence in Brazil. Contains 2,283 items in English and Portuguese, many of them articles found in Brazilian journals. Entries cover a wide range of subjects, including folklore, published legislative acts regarding slavery and abolition, and "popular" articles from the first half of the twentieth century.

3. Arquivo Nacional. *Guia brasileiro de fontes para a história da África, da escravidão negra e do negro na sociedade atual.* 2 vols. Rio de Janeiro: Arquivo Nacional, 1988.

   Guide to repositories of historical documentation in Brazil relevant to the history of Africa and Africans in Brazil, slavery, and Afro-Brazilians in contemporary society. Focuses on governmental and ecclesiastical archives. Entries are organized geographically according to state and typically include the name and address of the repository, general description of the repository's contents, and information about accessibility for researchers.

4. Arquivo Público Estadual (Espírito Santo). *Fontes para a história da escravidão negra no Espírito Santo.* Vitória: Arquivo Público Estadual, 1988. 130 p.

   List of sources in the Arquivo Público Estadual of Espírito Santo relating to slavery including manuscripts and other documents dating from 1770 to 1921. Includes descriptions of archival document groups entitled "Governadoria" and "Polícia" as well as printed sources located in the Biblioteca do Arquivo Público Estadual. Valuable for research on topics such as agricultural practices of slaves; slave flight; criminal records; abolitionist activity; process of emancipation; and the baptism, birth, death, and marriage of slaves. Also includes a list of other relevant archival holdings in Espírito Santo.

5. Bahia. Arquivo Público do Estado da Bahia. *Guia de fontes para a história da escravidão negra na Bahia.* Salvador, Bahia: Arquivo Público do Estado da Bahia, 1988. 218 p.

6. Bahia. Secretaria da Cultura. Departamento de Bibliotecas. *Documentação jurídica sobre o negro no Brasil, 1800–1888.* Salvador, Bahia: Empresa Gráfica da Bahia, 1989. 270 p.

   Index of legal and juridical documents related to black people in Brazil from 1800 through 1888, including laws, decrees, *cartas régias*, and resolutions. Grouped according to type of document and then listed chronologically. Based on reference works located in the Biblioteca Pública do Estado da Bahia, aspires to cover entirety of Brazil. Includes subject index, glossary, and bibliography.

7. Bailly, Gustavo Adolpho, comp. *Índice alphabético da legislação brasileira sobre agricultura, indústria e commércio no período de 15 nov. 1889 a 31 dez. 1924.* Rio de Janeiro: Officina Industrial Gráphica, 1925. 190 p.

   Index of national decrees and laws regarding agriculture, industry, and commerce for the period from the beginning of the republic through 1924. Arranged alphabetically by topic. Each entry gives the date, number, and a brief description of the law. Contains entries for different agricultural products, including about 150 entries under *"Assucar."* Other categories include *Trabalho, Terras e Colonisação*, and *Rural (Salário)*.

8. Bandeira, Pedro Silveira, and Marli M. Mertz, eds. *Manual bibliográfico de história econômica do Rio Grande do Sul e temas afins.* 2 vols. Porto Alegre: Secretaria de Coordenação e Planejamento/ Fundação de Economia e Estatística, 1986.

Comprehensive annotated bibliography of books on economic and social history of Rio Grande do Sul, alphabetized by last name of author. Includes subject index.

9. Barcelos, Luiz Claudio, Olivia Maria Gomes da Cunha, and Tereza Cristina Nascimento Araújo. *Escravidão e relações raciais no Brasil: cadastro da produção intelectual (1970–1990)*. Rio de Janeiro: Centro de Estudos Afro-Asiáticos, 1991. 259 p.

Catalogue of theses, dissertations, articles, and books related to slavery and race relations produced in Brazil between 1970 and 1990, with more limited coverage of non-Brazilian works. Includes sections with the following headings: Production from Master's and Doctorate Courses; Production by Authors; Publications from Meetings, Seminars, and Symposia; List of Consulted Works, Libraries, and Graduate Courses. Citations for scholarly works include name of author, title, and publishing information or institution where produced. All entries coded numerically according to topic, with topics and their respective codes as follows: 1) bibliographies, printed sources, and general studies; 2) slavery and abolition; 3) race relations and inequality; 4) political participation, culture, and identity; 5) religion. Heading of "Slavery and Abolition" includes works that deal with transition from slave to free labor.

10. Barman, Roderick. "Brazil and its Historians in North America: The Last Forty Years." *The Americas* 46 (January 1990): 373–99.

Bibliographical essay that includes a discussion of the trends in research topics on Brazilian history and a complete list of related doctoral dissertations produced at U.S. universities since 1950. (Theses that can be located through this essay are generally omitted from *Societies After Slavery*.)

11. Berger, Paulo. *Bibliografia do Rio de Janeiro de viajantes e autores estrangeiros (1531–1900)*. 2nd ed. Rio de Janeiro: Secretaria de Estado de Educação e Cultura, 1980. 478 p.

Lists more than fifteen hundred published works by foreigners who visited the city of Rio de Janeiro between 1531 and 1900. Includes sources located in libraries in Austria, Brazil, Denmark, Great Britain, the Netherlands, the former Soviet Union, Sweden, and the United States. Each entry consists of a citation of the work in question, the name of a library where it may be consulted, the lifespan of the author, and the pages of the book that relate to Rio de Janeiro. Bibliography not annotated. Majority of works published before emancipation.

12. Conrad, Robert. *Brazilian Slavery: An Annotated Research Bibliography.* Boston: G. K. Hall, 1977. 163 p.

A selectively annotated bibliography of published works on slavery in Brazil comprising approximately 990 entries. Organized in four sections: bibliographies and research aids, the slave trade and its suppression, slavery, and abolition. The first section includes general reference works on Afro-Brazilians and on aspects of nineteenth-century Brazil, and thus in many cases encompasses society after slavery. A few of the works in the section on abolition also deal with the postemancipation period. In some cases the compiler provides description of contents, in other cases the citation. There is an author index.

13. Cortés Conde, Roberto, and Stanley J. Stein, eds. *Latin America: A Guide to Economic History, 1830–1930.* Berkeley: University of California Press, 1977. 685 p.

This major bibliography of primary and secondary sources contains an extensive section on Brazil compiled by Nícia Villela Luz. The section begins with an introductory essay on Brazilian historiography and then provides approximately 650 annotated entries. It lists works of reference and statistical compilations, and is an excellent guide to censuses, travelers' accounts, periodicals, and government publications as well as studies on economics and finance. Contains, among others, sections on: slavery, including some works on abolition; regional economy, including studies of specific states and provinces; agriculture, with statistical works, general works, and studies of specific crops. (Note: Only a fraction of the census publications annotated in Cortés Conde and Stein have been included in *Societies After Slavery.*)

14. Ferrara, Miriam Nicolau. *A imprensa negra paulista (1915–1963).* São Paulo: Faculdade de Filosofia, Letras e Ciências Humanas/ Universidade de São Paulo, 1986. 279 p.

History of black newspapers in city of São Paulo. Provides a bibliography and list of relevant newspapers including name of newspaper, place and dates of publication, and editor or editors.

15. Gaspar, Lúcia, coord. *O negro no Brasil: uma contribuição bibliográfica.* Recife: Fundação Joaquim Nabuco/Editora Massangana, 1994. 197 p.

Annotated bibliography of works in the library of the Fundação Joaquim Nabuco related to Afro-Brazilians in the present and the past, including books, pamphlets, newspaper articles, and theses. Organized thematically. Includes indexes organized by personal name, title of work, and place.

16. Graham, Ann Hartness. *Subject Guide to Statistics in the Presidential Reports of the Brazilian Provinces, 1830–1889.* Austin: Institute of Latin American Studies, University of Texas at Austin, 1977. 454 p.

Statistics are indexed by subject, province, and year. In some cases they are indexed by city or area within province. Includes sections on agricultural products, births and baptisms, cacao, cattle, cholera, coffee, crime, deaths and burials, fazendas, indigents, land, manufacturing and artisanry, marriages, military forces, military registration and recruits, night schools, orphans, police, population, primary education, prisons and prisoners, secondary education, slavery, smallpox, sugar, teachers, vaccinations, and yellow fever, as well as other subjects. Also includes a bibliography of 1,085 *relatórios* and one location where each may be found, including some available only as manuscripts. (Note: researchers should see the website established by the author, which may be reached through the website of the Center for Research Libraries: http://www.crl.uchicago.edu/.)

17. Gutiérrez, Horacio and John Monteiro. *A escravidão na América Latina e no Caribe.* São Paulo: Centro de Estudos Latino-Americanos/ Universidade Estadual de São Paulo, 1990. 141 p.

Bibliography on slavery in Brazil and the Caribbean. Out of 1647 titles, 79 are works published in Brazil and elsewhere on the decline of slavery, abolition, and transition to free labor. Concentrates on secondary sources published in the 1970s and especially the 1980s. Not annotated. Includes an index of authors.

18. Leite, Miriam Lifchitz Moreira, Maria Lúcia de Barros Mott and Bertha Kauffmann Appenzeller. *A mulher no Rio de Janeiro no século XIX. Um índice de referências em livros de viajantes estrangeiros.* São Paulo: Fundação Carlos Chagas, 1982. 167 p.

Index of 153 published works by foreign travelers that discuss women in the city of Rio de Janeiro in the nineteenth century. Entries divided into three broad categories: family, race and class, and religion. Relevant subheadings within these categories include miscegenation, labor and black women, black women's clothing, and race relations. Each entry includes name of author, year of author's visit to the city, a short annotation, and a listing of the most relevant pages of the book. Index concludes with a bibliography with full citations of all works appearing in the book, alphabetized by author. Majority of works precede emancipation.

19. Levine, Robert. *Brazil, 1822–1930: An Annotated Bibliography for Social Historians*. New York: Garland Publishing, 1983. 487 p.

Annotated bibliography of books, articles, dissertations, and unpublished papers relevant to the study of Brazilian social history from independence to 1930. Almost all cited works date from before 1982. Approximately half are published in English, the remainder in Portuguese or other languages. Citations include author, title, publishing information or institution where produced, and a brief annotation. Citations are generally categorized by topic. Among those topics of special interest for postemancipation studies are labor; demography; slavery, including a subcategory entitled "Abolition and After"; sex roles and the family; and ethnic and race relations.

20. Loureiro, Ilka Cavalcanti, comp. *Memória da abolição: catálogo de artigos de jornais do Arquivo Joaquim Nabuco, 1871–1901*. Recife: Fundação Joaquim Nabuco/Editora Massangana, 1988. 246 p.

Unannotated catalogue of 622 articles related to abolition located in the Arquivo Joaquim Nabuco. Articles listed in chronological order. Includes indexes organized by title of newspaper, subject, and name.

21. Mertz, Marli Marlene, and Pedro Silveira Bandeira, eds. *Guia de artigos de história econômica do Rio Grande do Sul*. Vol. 1. Porto Alegre: Fundação de Economia e Estatística, 1991. 274 p.

Annotated bibliography of articles appearing in several journals and magazines published in Rio Grande do Sul, some of them historical journals and others nonacademic publications oriented especially toward rural producers (e.g., *Estância, O Progresso, Revista Rural Gaúcha, O Sol Rural*). Includes many articles published in the early 20th century that could serve as primary sources. Especially good for the organization and technology of agriculture and ranching. Includes subject index and information about library holdings of cited publications.

22. Pôrto, Angela, Lilian de A. Fritsch, and Sylvia F. Padilha, comps. *Processo de modernização do Brasil, 1850 -1930: economia e sociedade, uma bibliografia*. Rio de Janeiro: Fundação Casa de Rui Barbosa, Centro de Estudos Históricos, 1985. 364 p.

Major annotated bibliography of 2,053 books on Brazilian economy and society between 1850 and 1930. Includes sections on published statistics, compilations of laws, published collections of documents, published correspondence, *relatórios*, and travelers' accounts. Other entries are classified by subject, including land, agricultural credit and cooperatives, coffee, sugar, slave labor, free labor, quality of life (*condições de vida*), urbanization, urban marginality, social movements, abolitionism, class-based associations, and social stratification. A large number of the books included were published during the period between 1850 and 1930. Each entry includes bibliographic information, a reference to one library in Brazil where the work may be found, and a description of the contents of the book. Includes author index, title index, and a brief subject index. According to the introduction, it does not include books with a regional focus, except those that are of national interest.

23. Porter, Dorothy B. *Afro-Braziliana: A Working Bibliography*. Boston: G. K. Hall, 1978. 294 p.

Cites approximately five thousand primary and secondary works with some bearing on the African experience in Brazil. Not all entries are annotated, and not all are available in the United States. The author has provided locations and, where possible, Library of Congress call number classifications. The work is divided into two parts: the first contains lists of travelers' accounts, historical works, and writings on race relations, African influence on language, the arts, religion, sports, and cooking; the second provides an alphabetically organized list of authors (and their respective writings) who are of Afro-Brazilian heritage or who have written about Afro-Brazilian subjects. Works by authors such as Jorge Amado, Manuel Querino, Gregório de Matos, and Edison Carneiro are included. Introduced with a historical discussion both of the African contribution to Brazil and of the scholarship related to that contribution.

24. Queiroz, Suely Robles Reis de. *Historiografia do Nordeste*. São Paulo: Secretaria da Cultura, Divisão de Arquivos do Estado, 1979. 73 p.

An extensive historiographical essay discussing writings on the Brazilian Northeast from early colonial times to the present. Contains full footnotes with references both to primary and secondary works. Suggests lines of future research, including interpretive questions and categories of primary documentation such as newspapers and governors' reports. Concludes with a detailed discussion of various explanations for the stagnation of the sugar industry in the Brazilian Northeast at the end of the nineteenth and beginning of the twentieth century and raises the question of the consequences of abolition for the Northeast.

25. Rio Grande do Sul. Arquivo Histórico. *Abolição e República: acervos do Arquivo Histórico do Rio Grande do Sul*. Porto Alegre: Escola Superior de Teologia e Espiritualidade Franciscana, 1989. 106 p.

Partial inventory of sources in the Arquivo Histórico do Rio Grande do Sul concerning abolition and the proclamation of the republic. Section on abolition lists the extensive collection of *relatórios, falas,* and *mensagens* of presidents and governors of Rio Grande do Sul between 1835 and 1907, along with annotations of explicit references to slavery, abolition, *quilombos,* and blacks, whether free or enslaved *(pretos, pardos, africanos, negros, crioulos,* and *libertos).* Provides specific locations of cited documents. Archive also contains *relatórios* and *mensagens* from later periods, but they are not included in this guide.

26. Rodrigues, José Honório. "A literatura brasileira sobre açúcar no século XIX." *Brasil açucareiro* 19 (May 1942): 16–38.

    Review essay of publications related to sugar in Brazil, focusing on the literature from the nineteenth century on questions such as technological advances in sugar production, tariffs, the slave trade, abolition, and immigration. Followed by a chronologically organized bibliography of relevant works published between 1816 and 1897.

27. Samara, Eni de Mesquita, and Iraci del Nero da Costa. *Demografia histórica: bibliografia brasileira.* São Paulo: Instituto de Pesquisas Econômicas, 1984. 75 p.

    Bibliography on historical demography. Some works listed deal with postemancipation period. Includes works in progress and M.A. and Ph.D. theses. Thesis entries are annotated; others are not. Includes an index of authors and researchers.

28. Santos, Edilma Coutinho dos. *Memória editorial da Fundação Joaquim Nabuco, 1952–1989.* Recife: Fundação Joaquim Nabuco, Editora Massangana, 1992. 172 p.

    Lists all books and journals published by the Fundação Joaquim Nabuco over the past four decades. Majority of works deal with society and culture in the North and Northeast. Includes indexes organized by author and contributor, title, topic, institution, symposium, and series. Two series, *Abolição* and *República,* have reprinted a variety of important publications from the era of emancipation. (This listing does not, however, give the original publication dates for reprinted materials.)

29. Szwed, John F. and Roger D. Abrahams. *Afro-American Folk Culture: An Annotated Bibliography of Materials from North, Central and South America and the West Indies.* Philadelphia: Institute for the Study of Human Issues, 1978. 814 p.

    Part II includes a section on Brazil which lists 526 items published in Brazil and elsewhere. Each entry includes author, title, place of publication, and brief annotation.

30. *O abolicionista.* 1880–1881. Reprint. Recife: Fundação Joaquim
    Nabuco/Editora Massangana, 1988. 158 p.

    Facsimile reprint of fourteen issues of *O abolicionista*, organ of the
    Sociedade Brasileira contra a Escravidão, published from 1 November
    1880 through 1 December 1881, while newspaper was under direction
    of Joaquim Nabuco. Introductory essay by Leonardo Dantas Silva
    sketches Nabuco's biography and abolitionist activities.

31. Abreu, S. Fróes. *Alguns aspectos da Bahia.* Rio de Janeiro: Typ. do
    Jornal do Commercio, 1926. 133 p.

    Seven sketches of different regions of Bahia by an official of the
    Ministério da Agricultura who traveled through the state in late 1925
    and early 1926. Regions discussed include the Recôncavo, Maraú,
    Salobro, Juazeiro, and the southern coast. Treats the current state of
    agriculture, labor conditions, transportation, flora and fauna, and pos-
    sibilities for economic development. Chapter on sugar region sketches
    the history of sugar production in Bahia from colonial period to present.
    Discusses division of labor on sugar *engenhos* between *moradores*, who are
    described as descendants of slaves, and seasonal workers from the *sertão*
    known as *catingueiros*.

32. Alves, Isaías. *Matas do sertão de baixo.* Salvador: Edições Reper, 1967.
    310 p.

    Regional history and memoir of the town of Santo Antônio de Jesus and
    surrounding area in the Bahian Recôncavo. Told chronologically begin-
    ning with the colonial period and ending with the first decades of the
    twentieth century. Author's family had ties to the Bahian tobacco
    economy. Portrayal of postemancipation period addresses such topics as
    the local reception of the final abolition of slavery, settlement patterns
    of freedpeople, market fairs, free labor, and a tobacco workers' strike in
    1901.

33. Andrews, C. C. *Brazil, Its Condition and Prospects.* 3rd ed. New York:
    D. Appleton, 1891. 352 p.

    Author was U.S. consul-general to Brazil from 1882 to 1885. Makes
    observations about issues including the organization of public education
    and government. Contains a brief description of the coffee plantations of
    the south-central region, as well as an account of a visit to the Fazenda
    Ibicaba of Senator Nicolau de Campos Vergueiro, famous for its use of

free German *colonos* since the middle of the century. Includes brief references to the wages of free agricultural laborers. Contains chapters on the state of agriculture and on the debates regarding the emancipation of slaves.

34. Bailly, Gustavo Adolpho, comp. *Legislação agrícola brasileira*. Rio de Janeiro: Officina Industrial Gráphica, 1930.

    Consists of multiple volumes, the first of which was published in 1930. Includes laws and regulations, as well as relevant contracts and agreements entered into by the federal government. In 1930, volumes on a variety of topics were planned, including sugar, coffee, agricultural credit, *fazendas*, labor, housing, and pensions (*montepio*).

35. Barbosa, Rui. *Emancipação dos escravos. O Projeto Dantas (dos sexagenários) e o parecer que o justifica*. 1884. Reprint. Rio de Janeiro: Fundação Casa de Rui Barbosa, 1988. 372 p.

    Reprint of Rui Barbosa's report advocating passage of the Dantas Project, a bill proposed to the General Assembly in 1884 that called for the liberation of slaves who reached the age of sixty, the end of the slave trade between provinces, and the enlargement of the imperial emancipation fund. Barbosa's discussion of the organization of former slaves' labor after abolition is of special interest, especially his approving discussion of the stipulation that *libertos* be required to remain consistently employed in the *município* where they were emancipated for five years after attaining their freedom. This edition is accompanied by four appendices which present the original Dantas Project and three subsequent drafts, a chronology of the Project's proposal and defeat, a historical inquiry into the reasons for the dissolution of the Chamber of Deputies in 1884, and a circular distributed by Barbosa to voters announcing his candidacy for the General Assembly, also from 1884.

36. Bello, Júlio Celso de Albuquerque. *Memórias de um senhor de engenho*. Recife: Fundação do Patrimônio Histórico e Artístico de Pernambuco/Diretoria de Assuntos Culturais, 1985. 229 p.

    Memoir of sugar plantation owner in Pernambuco. Author was born in 1873 on the Engenho Tentugal and lived on the Engenho Queimadas. Describes physical environment, popular festivals, and abolition of slavery. Representative of landholders who remained within the tradition of the *banguê* rather than becoming suppliers to the *usinas*. Text has a preface by Gilberto Freyre, and another by José Lins do Rego.

37. Bittencourt, Anna Ribeiro de Goes. *Longos serões do campo*. 2 vols. Rio de Janeiro: Nova Fronteira, 1992.

Memoirs of a minor novelist (1843–1930) born and raised on a Bahian *engenho*. Volume 1, *O major Pedro Ribeiro*, is a biography of the author's maternal grandfather. Volume 2, *Infância e juventude*, was written in the 1920s and relates events of her youth. Includes telling anecdotes of the rural social world of *fazendeiros*, slaves, and *agregados*. While the narrative ends with Bittencourt's marriage in 1865, occasional comments make reference to later years, as when the author reminisces with ex-slaves (who remained in the family's service) about her beloved mother.

38. Bomfim, Manoel. *A América Latina: males de origem. Estudo de parasitismo social.* Rio de Janeiro: H. Garnier, 1905. 432 p.

A passionate critique of Latin America's Iberian heritage. Blames the problems of the region on the "parasitism" of European colonizers. Attributes the lack of agricultural vigor in places such as Brazil to the former reliance on slaves. Vehemently opposes the Social Darwinists' views regarding the natural inferiority of indigenous and African peoples and the detrimental impact of widespread *mestiçagem*. Attributes the "indolence" of the labor force to lack of education, deemed a legacy of colonialism.

39. Bomilcar, Álvaro. *O preconceito de raça no Brasil.* Rio de Janeiro, 1916. 105 p.

Written in 1911 and published five years later, this study represents a forceful attack on racism in Brazil. First half focuses on the causes of the 1910 naval mutiny in the Bay of Guanabara (without describing the event itself), seeing it as a result of enormous disparities between white officers and black, mulatto, and *caboclo* sailors. Criticizes scientific racism and positivist belief in the inherent intelligence of whites. Attempts to show the deficiencies of people of Portuguese descent, who, he suggests, have not benefited Brazil nearly as much as other European immigrants. Argues that racism barred people of color from business and industry. Calls for serious rather than sentimental studies of African and Indian contributions to the development of the nation.

40. Brazil. Senado Federal. Subsecretaria de Arquivo. *A abolição no parlamento: 65 anos de luta, 1823–1888.* 2 vols. Brasília: Senado Federal/Subsecretaria de Arquivo, 1988.

This collection reproduces documentation from the Brazilian parliament related to slavery from 1823 through 1888, including speeches, laws, decrees, and projects for laws. Focuses on the Lei do Ventre-Livre of 1871, Lei do Sexagenário of 1885, and the Lei Aúrea of 1888. Documents are drawn from the Secção de Arquivo Histórico da Subsecretaria de

Arquivo do Senado. Bibliography includes works related to slavery and abolition contained in the Biblioteca do Senado.

41. Brazil. Sociedade Nacional de Agricultura. *Impressões do nordeste brasileiro. Conferências do Dr. Paulo de Moraes Barros, realisadas sob os auspícios da Sociedade Nacional de Agricultura, no Rio de Janeiro, e da Sociedade Rural Brasileira, em São Paulo, em 1923.* Buenos Aires: Editorial Universitaria, 1924. 158 p.

Account of a thirty-two-day fact-finding tour of the northeastern states of Ceará, Rio Grande do Norte, and Paraíba by members of the Sociedade Nacional de Agricultura at the request of the president. Describes settlements encountered as the commission traveled north from Bahia, including accounts of architecture, local agriculture and industry, ethnic characteristics of the population, and conversations with local personages. Cities and towns visited include Paraíba, Itabaiana, Borborema, Campina Grande, Cajazeiras, Icó, Orós, Poço dos Paus, Barbalha, Crato, Juazeiro do Ceará, Quixeramobim, Fortaleza, Uruburetama, Sobral, Viçosa, Ipú, Ibiupina, Guaramiranga, Aracaty, Mossoró, Natal, Parelhas, Gargalheira, and Cruzeta. Concludes with a summary of progress achieved in public works and transportation as well as recommendations for future government investment in transportation, irrigation, and colonization.

42. Bulhões Carvalho, José Luiz Sayão Lobato de. *Progrès de l'immigration italienne au Brésil. Conférence faite à Rome, le 17 Octobre 1925, au Palais Sciarra, siège de la Cassa Nazionale per le Assicurazione Sociali, sous les auspices de l'Istituto Cristoforo Colombo.* Rio de Janeiro: Imp. de la Statistique, 1925. 21 p.

Responding to criticisms in the Italian press and parliament of the conditions faced by Italian immigrants on São Paulo coffee plantations, Bulhões Carvalho stresses the legal and administrative protection immigrants enjoy and draws on statistics from the 1920 census to demonstrate high levels of Italian property ownership within the province.

43. Calmon, Francisco, Marques de Góes. *Vida econômico-financeira da Bahia de 1808 a 1899. (Elementos para a história de 1808 a 1899).* Bahia: Imprensa Official do Estado, 1925. 124 p.

A chronologically organized economic and political history of nineteenth-century Bahia written by a member of one of the region's elite families. Focus is divided between the agrarian and urban sectors, with more detailed information regarding commerce and exports. Contains brief discussion of Bahia's central sugar factories but virtually nothing on the postemancipation labor market. Describes protests of shortages of foodstuffs. Lists export figures for major products between 1886 and 1891. Includes an appendix of the legislative measures mentioned in the main body of the text.

44. Campos, João da Silva. *Procissões tradicionais da Bahia.* Publicações do Museu da Bahia no. 1. Salvador: Secretaria da Educação e Saúde da Bahia, 1941. 265 p.

Description of religious processions and festivals, including those in which the black lay Catholic brotherhoods participated. Divided into discussions of "extinct" and ongoing practices. Focuses on the processions of the city of Salvador, although chapters of the same brotherhoods existed in the countryside. Makes occasional references to other parts of Brazil.

45. Congresso Agrícola, Pernambuco, 1878. *Trabalhos do Congresso Agrícola. Outubro de 1878.* 1878. Reprint. Recife: Fundação Estadual de Planejamento Agrícola de Pernambuco, 1978. 465 p.

Facsimile reproduction of proceedings of the Agricultural Congress of Recife in 1878. Includes speeches, reports, and other documents related to the state of agriculture in the Northeast, particularly sugar cultivation. Works address themes such as availability of capital, technological innovations, the future of slavery, and the suitability of native and immigrant free labor for agricultural work.

46. Conrad, Robert Edgar. *Children of God's Fire: A Documentary History of Black Slaves in Brazil.* Princeton: Princeton University Press, 1983. 515 p.

Includes twelve documents on the struggle for abolition.

47. Couty, Louis. *O Brasil em 1884: esboços sociológicos.* Translated by Ligia Vassalo. Rio de Janeiro: Fundacão Casa de Rui Barbosa; Brasília: Senado Federal, 1984. 258 p.

Portuguese translation of collection of essays published in 1884 by a French émigré professor of industrial biology at the Polytechnic School of Rio de Janeiro. Author, who came to Brazil in 1879, saw slave labor as the main obstacle to progress, but did not believe that abolition would solve the problem. He argued that the *liberto* would be a poor agricultural worker and supported European immigration. Volume contains chapters on colonization, technology, sharecropping, and slave emancipation, among other topics. Useful both as a reflection of a specific modernizing ideology, and because author visited coffee plantations in Rio de Janeiro and São Paulo and advised on their development.

48. Carli, Gileno Dé. *Aspectos açucareiros de Pernambuco*. Rio de Janeiro, 1940. 73 p.

Report on contemporary state of sugar production in Pernambuco. Focuses on social aspects of the *usina*, including composition of rural workforce, medical care and education available to workers, workers' diet and migration patterns. Discusses implications of emancipation for workers' housing, the impact of rise of *usina* on urban and rural society, and irrigation and cultivation techniques. Includes contemporary photographs of workers and *usina* architecture. Reprints sugar production statistics for Pernambuco from 1925 through 1939.

49. Dafert, F. W. "A falta de trabalhadores agrícolas em São Paulo." *Relatório annual do Instituto Agronômico do Estado de São Paulo (Brazil) em Campinas. 1892.* São Paulo: Typographia da Companhia Industrial de S. Paulo, 1893. Pp. 201–9.

Beginning with a description of the agricultural labor market in Prussia, the author calculates hectares cultivated per worker and agricultural production per worker in that country. Calculating corresponding statistics for São Paulo (from 1887 data), he concludes that there is no lack of laborers in São Paulo, only a lack of efficient laborers due in part to the lack of a work ethic among *fazendeiros*. He argues that falling wages after 1890 drove "good workers" (both Italians and *libertos*) away from the plantations, while "bad workers" or vagabonds still found salaries high enough to make do with part-time labor.

50. Dalla Vecchia, Agostinho Mario. *Vozes do silêncio: depoimentos de descendentes de escravos do Meridião Gaúcho*. 2 vols. Pelotas: Editora Universitária/Universidade Federal de Pelotas, 1994.

Transcripts of thirty-two interviews conducted by author with descendants of slaves in southern Rio Grande do Sul. Companion volumes for author's *Os filhos da escravidão: memórias de descendentes de escravos da região meridional do Rio Grande do Sul* (see separate listing in this bibliography under "Secondary Sources"). Interviews touch on themes such as work, leisure, family, and religion before and after emancipation, as well as migration and political participation of former slaves.

51. Silva, Leonardo Dantas, comp. *A imprensa e a abolição*. Recife: Fundação Joaquim Nabuco/Editora Massangana, 1988.

Facsimile reprints of single editions of twenty-four newspapers published in Pernambuco in the 1870s and 1880s. Abolition is a prominent theme of all the selections, each of which is preceded by a short history of the publication in question, including its position on slavery and other background information, such as the newspaper's relation to people of color or its role in party politics.

52. Denis, Pierre. *Le Brésil au xxᵉ siècle*. 4th ed. Paris: Librairie Armand Colin, 1911. 312 p.

General description of Brazil (including geography and politics) at the beginning of the twentieth century. Contains four chapters that explore the development of coffee and settlement patterns in São Paulo. Some of author's observations based on farm account books to which he had access and interviews with European coffee laborers. Includes a chapter on the state of black and mulatto workers (especially those in Minas Gerais and in the sugar-producing regions) twenty years after emancipation. Author offers familiar argument that ex-slaves were indolent and unreliable as free laborers. Attributes part of this irregularity to the alleged failure of female ex-slaves to work after abolition.

53. Dunlop, Charles J., comp. *Legislação brasileira do trabalho*. 3d ed. Rio de Janeiro: Empreza Almanak Laemmert, 1939.

Contains the text of laws and decrees concerning labor in force in 1939. Indexed by subject and date. Includes sections on work-related accidents, retirement and pensions, worker identification papers (*carteira profissional*), hours and conditions of work, minimum wage, unionization, rural labor, labor of minors, and female labor. Most laws included were passed in the 1930s.

54. Dunn, Ballard S. *Brazil, the Home for Southerners: Or, a Practical Account of What the Author and Others, who Visited that Country, for the Same Objects, Saw and Did while in that Empire*. New Orleans: Bloomfield and Steel, 1866. 272 p.

Report by Louisiana minister on the potential of Brazil as a future settlement site for U.S. farmers. Author purchased land in São Paulo, where he claimed the conditions for cotton-growing were far superior to those of the U.S. South. Includes description of the Brazilian "labor question" and suggests that a future North American colony would rely on wage labor.

55. *Estudos afro-brasileiros. Trabalhos apresentados ao 1º Congresso Afro-Brasilerio reunido no Recife em 1934*. Vol. I. Facsimile edition introduced by José Antônio Gonsalves de Mello. Recife: Fundação Joaquim Nabuco. Editora Massangana, 1988. 275 p.

First volume of the proceedings of the First Afro-Brazilian Conference, held in Recife in 1934. The twenty-four presentations reprinted here reflect dominant trends in Afro-Brazilian studies in the early 1930s and also provide information on Afro-Brazilian society in the first decades after abolition. Authors in this volume include Melville Herskovits, Edison Carneiro, and Arthur Ramos. Topics addressed include Afro-Brazilian religion, folklore, health, and labor conditions. (See also below entry for *Novos estudos afro-brasileiros.*)

56. Falcão, Theophilo Borges. *Actividade commercial da Bahia. Da colônia aos nossos dias; estudo synthético do Dr. Theophilo Borges Falcão, Secretario da Fazenda e Thesouro do Estado.* Bahia: Imprensa Official do Estado, 1927. 21 p.

Brief summary of a century of Bahian economic activity, emphasizing exports of sugar, cotton, tobacco, coffee, and cacao. Notes crisis of production following "abandonment" of rural properties in wake of abolition. Offers statistics on total imports and exports for some years and exports of specific products for others.

57. Ferreira, Desembargador Vieira. "Cachoeira e Porangaba. (A concessão de sesmarias no Brasil e a lavoura de café nas montanhas de Valença)." *Revista do Instituto Histórico e Geográfico Brasileiro* 213 (October–December 1951): 202–328.

Author's history and recollections of the parish of Santa Tereza de Valença in Rio de Janeiro. Emphasizes the early acquisition by his family of the lands that would become a coffee *fazenda* in the middle decades of the nineteenth century. Contains boyhood observations of the *senzalas*, which housed skilled and unskilled slave labor, and of the slave population on the eve of emancipation. Author claims that the majority of slaves remained on the *fazenda* after abolition.

58. Ferreira, Felix. *A província do Rio de Janeiro. Notícias para o emigrante.* Rio de Janeiro: H. Lombaerts, 1888. 80 p.

Description of the city and province of Rio de Janeiro, intended for distribution abroad. Section on the city of Rio de Janeiro describes state buildings, transportation, public utilities, and cultural life. Short descriptions of each municipality, including geography, principal crops, railroad access, and number and type of *engenhos.* Emphasis on the opportunities for small agriculturalists. Statistics on the number of agricultural, commercial, and industrial establishments in each municipality as well as the public school enrollment (by sex) in each municipality. There is no mention of slavery or abolition. Concludes with offer of free passage for immigrants. Illustrated. Includes fold-out map of the province.

59. Ferrez, Gilberto. *Bahia: velhas fotografias, 1858–1900.* Rio de Janeiro: Kosmos/Banco da Bahia Investimentos, 1988. 199 p.

Rural and urban photographs primarily of Salvador and nearby towns, including an *engenho* in the countryside. Mainly photos of landscape and buildings. Introduced by historian Katia Mattoso.

60. Ferrez, Gilberto. *Pioneer Photographers of Brazil: 1840–1920*. Center for Inter-American Relations, 1976. 143 p.

    Exhibition catalogue reprints works by fifteen early photographers, each introduced by a brief historical discussion. Panoramas and upper-class portraits predominate but collection also offers glimpses of street vendors, gold miners, and slaves on a coffee plantation.

61. Ferrez, Gilberto. *Velhas fotografias pernambucanas, 1851–1890*. Rio de Janeiro: Campo Visual, 1988. 90 p.

    Includes photographs of Recife, Olinda, Iguaçu, Goiana, Cabo, Vila do Una (Palmares), and the cape of Santo Agostinho. Emphasis on landscapes and architecture.

62. Fonseca, Luís Anselmo da. *A escravidão, o clero e o abolicionismo*. 1887. Reprint. Recife: Fundação Joaquim Nabuco/Editora Massangana, 1988. 686 p.

    Facsimile reprint edition of antislavery tract by Luís Anselmo da Fonseca that is highly critical of church's role in maintenance of slavery. Author was Bahian man of color and professor of medicine. Part I consists of general reflections on the Brazilian clergy and relationship between slavery and Christianity, philosophy, and law. Part II focuses on the abolitionist movement in Bahia, including transition from slave to free labor in the Bahian capital, activities of emancipation societies and abolitionism in the Bahian interior. Part III critiques positions of different members of church hierarchy regarding slavery. Part IV examines current state of slavery, criticizes the practice of conditional manumission, and discusses the future of antislavery legislation. Reproduction of original text accompanied by short biographical note on author by Renato Berbert de Castro.

63. Fragoso, Arlindo. *Notas econômicas e financeiras*. Bahia: Imprensa Oficial do Estado, 1916. 572 p.

    One hundred and one brief essays written while the author was Secretary General of the State of Bahia. Most essays focus on the underlying economic problems to which Fragoso attributes the crisis of 1913 and 1914: the conditions of the international commodity market, state fiscal imbalances, burdensome foreign loans, and tight credit. Statistics include state government budgets, agricultural and industrial production, exports, tax collection, exchange rates, and debt payments. While some pieces are national in scope, many focus on Bahia or, less frequently, on São Paulo.

64. Freitas, Affonso de. *Tradições e reminiscências paulistanas.* 1921. Reprint. São Paulo: Livraria Martins Editôra, 1955. 225 p.

This work, first published in 1921, combines writings on folklore and tales of São Paulo's past by a prominent Paulista historian and intellectual. Quotes extensively from songs, sayings, poems, and children's games, mainly from the nineteenth century, including some with origins in slave society and others from the heyday of abolitionism. Particular attention given to Tupi-Guarani and African influences in language, music, dance, and popular festivals.

65. Lacombe, Américo Jacobina, Eduardo Silva, and Francisco de Assis Barbosa, eds. *Rui Barbosa e a queima dos arquivos.* Rio de Janeiro: Fundação Casa de Rui Barbosa, 1988. 142 p.

Compilation of historical documents related to the activities of abolitionist and Ministro da Fazenda Rui Barbosa in the late 1880s and early 1890s, including Barbosa's 1890 order for the burning of documents in the Ministério da Fazenda in order to prevent indemnification of ex-slaveowners. Includes reproductions of newspaper articles, proposed legislation, and correspondence related to the question of indemnification and the destruction of the records. Preceded by three essays, one by each of the editors, which seek to understand Barbosa's decision to destroy the records and reflect on its implications for subsequent historiography.

66. Lalière, A. *Le café dans l'état de Saint Paul, Brésil.* Paris: Augustin Challamel, 1909. 417 p.

Account of coffee production in São Paulo. Includes statistics on yearly exports from the state from 1880 to 1906 and on production by municipality in 1904, as well as lengthy technical descriptions of the stages of coffee cultivation and processing. Detailed description of operations on the Fazenda Boa Vista São Manoel and the Central Carrecedo in Piracicaba. Quotes letters from various planters regarding labor arrangements. Discussion of contracts established with Italian immigrants includes sample *carnet* for laborer showing cash advances and payments for specific tasks and for harvested coffee. Many photographs of laborers in fields and mills.

67. Lehmann, Ernst. "Relatório sobre a fazenda de São João de Montanha em Piracicaba." *Relatório annual do Instituto Agronômico do Estado de*

São Paulo (Brazil) em Campinas, 1892. São Paulo: Typographia da Companhia Industrial de S. Paulo, 1893. 77-81.

Description of conditions and activities on *fazenda* established as an agricultural school and model farm. Notable for concluding paragraph on "The question of the workers," which describes how workers' complaints about the communal kitchen led to its abolition and to concessions of both increased foodstuffs for home preparation and additional land for vegetable cultivation.

68. Leite, Miriam Moreira, org. *A condição feminina no Rio de Janeiro, século XIX: antologia de textos de viajantes estrangeiros.* São Paulo: HUCITEC, 1993. 223 p.

Anthology of travelers' accounts.

69. Limongi, J. Papaterra. "O trabalhador nacional." *Boletim do Departamento do Trabalho* 5 (1916): 349–71.

Describes the author's visit to a Trappist plantation in the municipality of Tremembé, in São Paulo, that employed *caboclos* in the cultivation of rice and coffee. Argues against "irrational" prejudices that hold that *caboclos* are poor workers and inferior to immigrants. Advocates the creation of *colônias* composed of *caboclos* and suggests that small properties owned by Brazilian nationals may prove superior to large landholdings.

70. Limongi, J. Papaterra. "O trabalho agrícola no Brasil." *Boletim do Departamento Estadual do Trabalho* 6 (1917): 453–64.

Discusses different proposals for the stabilization of labor for export agriculture, including the sale of plots located near plantations to *colonos*. Asserts that foreign immigration has had a beneficial influence on the habits and aspirations of Brazilian workers and argues for the incorporation of a greater number of native workers in coffee production, with special attention to the situation of São Paulo.

71. Maestri Filho, Mário José, ed. *Depoimentos de escravos brasileiros.* São Paulo: Editora Ícone, 1988. 88 p.

Includes interviews with two very old ex-slaves conducted in 1981 and 1982 in Curitiba and Rio de Janeiro, as well as a court deposition made in 1861 by a free black man from Uruguay who was illegally enslaved in Rio Grande do Sul and sued to regain freedom.

72. Marc, Alfred. *Le Brésil: Excursion à travers ses 20 provinces.* 2 vols. Paris: Charaire et Fils, 1890.

Based on travels of the author, a geographer and editor of the journal *Le Brésil.* Concentrates on the economic conditions of the country in the

1880s. Contains detailed geographical descriptions, export figures for individual ports and provinces, municipal expenditures, and discussions of colonization, railways, rubber collecting, agriculture, and local manufacturing. Comments on the renewed vigor of agriculture in Maranhão after abolition; describes sugar centrals in Paraíba and Pernambuco; analyzes disruptive effects of emancipation in Bahia; discusses immigration in São Paulo and southern provinces; examines Indian population in the interior. Particularly useful for the minute descriptions of specific regions and for the author's advocacy for free labor and immigration.

73. Martins, Francisco Dias. *A producção das nossas terras*. Brazil. Serviço de Agricultura Prática. Rio de Janeiro: Typographia da Directoria de Estatística, 1915. 215 p.

Contains information on planting, techniques of cultivation, productivity, and costs of production for a wide variety of specific crops by state. In some cases this information is given for specific *municípios*. Contains almost no information about labor or wages. Based on questionnaires sent to estate owners, farmers, and agricultural inspectors in the early 1910s.

74. Martins, Francisco Dias. *ABC do Agricultor*. 4th ed. Rio de Janeiro: Imp. Nacional, 1921. 466 p.

Intended for popular education in agricultural techniques and rural health, this book was used as a primary school textbook. Contains information on principal crops (including tree crops) of Brazil, including techniques of cultivation, timing of planting and harvest in different regions of the country, and instructions for the projection of costs and profits for each crop. Also includes information on soils, agricultural tools, how to choose land, weights and measures, parasites and illnesses of both humans and animals, and a chapter on how to teach with this book.

75. Matos, Odilon Nogueira de. "O Visconde de Indaiatuba e o trabalho livre em São Paulo." *Anais do VI Simpósio Nacional dos Professores Universitários de História* 6 (1973): 761–79.

Memoir of Joaquim Bonifácio do Amaral, the Visconde of Indaiatuba (1815–84), an early promoter of immigrant labor on the coffee farms of nineteenth-century São Paulo. Owner of the farm Sete Quedas in Campinas, the Visconde recorded his observations of thirty years' experience (1852 to 1882 approximately) with European labor. His was one of the few colonies where the share system *(parceria)* endured with some success. Rather than blame the individual laborers for the failure of the system elsewhere, the Visconde argued that the interference of foreign consuls as well as strong planter support for slave labor were responsible for the apparent failure of free labor. Editor introduces the document with a brief description of the reaction of travelers and modern-day scholars to the colony of Sete Quedas.

76. Mello, Félix Cavalcanti de Albuquerque. *Memórias de um Cavalcanti.* São Paulo: Companhia Editora Nacional, 1940. 193 p.

Selections from the journals of a member of one of Pernambuco's most powerful families, introduced by a lengthy biographical and sociological essay by Gilberto Freyre. Most journal entries mark the births, deaths, comings, and goings of Mello's family members, and occasionally those of the slaves and free *pardos* and *mulatos* associated with the household. A dedicated monarchist and conservative, Mello describes bitterly the riots of "o povo" in the streets of Recife in the 1880s.

77. Mello, José Antônio Gonsalves de. *O Diário de Pernambuco e a história social do Nordeste (1840–1889).* 2 vols. Recife, 1975.

Selections from the northeastern newspaper include articles, editorials, readers' contributions, statistics, and poems. Selections organized under the headings of economy, society, culture, demography, history of Pernambuco and of Recife, and biographies. Most relevant are the readings about the economy in the 1880s, which include editorials and letters arguing over how to incorporate new technology and adapt labor systems to prepare for the impending end of slavery. Other items of interest include a summary (by municipality) of slaves and *libertos* legally registered in Pernambuco in 1887, their ages and value; a first person account of an 1866 colonization project by immigrants from the U.S. Confederacy; and a detailed 1857 demographic profile of the parish of Jaboatão, including the name, age, race, and civil status of every inhabitant (slave and free) of each *engenho* within the parish.

78. Milet, Henrique Augusto. *Miscelânea econômica.* 1879. Reprint. Recife: CEPE, 1991. 110 p.

First published in Recife in 1879, this collection comprises essays that appeared in the pages of the *Jornal do Recife* between 1876 and 1879. Criticizing the prevailing wisdom of laissez-faire, Milet calls for government action (in the form of reduced export taxes, increased credit, and technical assistance) to revive the ailing sugar industry of Pernambuco, Alagoas, and Paraíba. Compared to other works by Milet this collection is didactic and theoretical, offering fewer details and less specific analysis of the northeastern context.

79. Milet, Henrique Augusto. *Os quebra-quilos e a crise da lavoura*. 1876. Reprint. São Paulo: Global, 1987. 136 p.

A series of articles written in 1875 for the *Jornal do Recife*, accompanied by additional explanatory notes. Author was a planter. Discusses the *quebra-quilos* movement and the general situation of agriculture, particularly cane and cotton in period prior to abolition. Includes essay on moral and economic advantages of abolition of slavery.

80. Nabuco, Joaquim. *Campanha abolicionista no Recife (Eleições 1884). Discursos de Joaquim Nabuco*. 1885. Reprint. Recife: Fundação Joaquim Nabuco, 1988. 205 p.

Facsimile edition of collection of speeches given by Joaquim Nabuco during his victorious 1884 campaign to represent the first district of Pernambuco (including city of Recife) as a Liberal in the Câmara dos Deputados. Speeches address themes such as adverse moral, political, and economic effects of slavery; abolitionism; and importance of voting by free people of color. Original edition includes preface with brief account of campaign by Aníbal Falcão. Reprint edition preceded by scholarly introduction by Fernando da Cruz Gouvêa.

81. Nabuco, Joaquim. *O Abolicionismo*. 1883. Reprint. 4th ed. Petrópolis: Editora Vozes, 1977. 204 p.

Seventeen short essays advocating the abolition of slavery written in 1883 while the author was in Great Britain. Begins with a definition of abolitionism and a history of abolitionist activity in Brazil. Criticizes the Rio Branco law and demands total emancipation through parliamentary means. Author stresses that his call to action is directed towards the free, not to the slaves themselves. Laments negative effects of slavery on national character and economy and praises free labor and European immigration. Envisions abolition as a starting point for a more profound renovation of the Brazilian government and people. Includes introductory essays by Gilberto Freyre, Graça Aranha, and Gilberto Amado as well as a chronology of Nabuco's life and a short bibliography of works by and about the author.

82. *Novos estudos afro-brasileiros. Trabalhos apresentados ao 1° Congresso Afro-Brasileiro do Recife*. Vol. II. Rio de Janeiro: Civilização Brasileira, 1937. 352 p.

Second volume of the proceedings of the First Afro-Brazilian Conference in Recife, 1934. Authors of papers in this volume include Gilberto Freyre, Jorge Amado, Luís da Câmara Cascudo, and Edison Carneiro. Includes articles on the African influence on Brazilian society, folklore,

Afro-Brazilian religion, black music, racial "bio-types," racial mixture, blacks and education, popular literature, and the consumption of marijuana. (See also above entry for *Estudos afro-brasileiros.*)

83. Pang, Eul-Soo. *O engenho central do Bom Jardim na economia baiana: alguns aspectos de sua história, 1874–1891.* Rio de Janeiro: Arquivo Nacional/Instituto Histórico e Geográfico Brasileiro, 1979. 318 p.

    Brief profile (57 p.) of short-lived project by the Costa Pinto family to develop a central sugar mill in Santo Amaro, Bahia, followed by extensive appendix (160 p.) of transcribed documents. Primary emphasis is on elite family and the economic development of the central mill, with some discussion of the labor force and the consequences of abolition. Appendices and footnotes to archival sources also provide a point of entry for the study of other aspects of labor and landholding in the sugar region of Bahia.

84. Patrocínio, José do. *Campanha abolicionista: coletânea de artigos.* Rio de Janeiro: Fundação Biblioteca Nacional, Departamento Nacional do Livro, 1996. 283 p.

    Collection of articles related to slavery and emancipation written by abolitionist José do Patrocínio and published in three newspapers from Rio de Janeiro between 1880 and 1889, including the *Gazeta de Notícias*, *Gazeta da Tarde*, and the *Cidade do Rio*. Introductory essay by José Murilo de Carvalho.

85. Pinheiro, Paulo Sérgio and Michael M. Hall. *A classe operária no Brasil, 1889–1930. Documentos.* 2 vols. São Paulo, 1979–1981.

    A two-volume collection of primary documents relating to labor history during the first republic: *Vol. 1: O movimento operário* (São Paulo: Editora Alfa Omega, 1979) and *Vol. 2: Condições de vida e de trabalho, relações com os Empresários e o Estado* (São Paulo: Brasiliense, 1981). Each volume is prefaced by a short bibliographical or contextual note. Most common sources are articles from radical and/or Italian-language newspapers. Overall the collection has a strong urban and industrial focus, with special attention to the conditions and actions of Italian immigrants. Southern coffee labor receives some coverage; northern sugar receives less. Volume 1 focuses on the nascent workers' movement: strikes and unions; anarchists; anarcho-sindicalists; and communists. The first section of volume 2, on living and working conditions, contains several essays which compare conditions of *fazenda* labor before and after abolition.

86. Poliano, L. Marques. *A Sociedade Nacional de Agricultura: resumo histórico.* Rio de Janeiro, 1945. 179 p.

Sympathetic history of the association through which large landowners worked for the advancement of Brazilian agriculture. Includes detailed, year-by-year account of the society's activities (congresses, publications, experimental and educational projects, etc.) from 1897 to 1945. Of interest for the various programs and proposals aimed at "the problem of national agricultural labor" in the years following abolition.

87. Querino, Manuel. *A Bahia de outrora.* 3d ed. Reprint. Bahia: Livraria Progresso Editora, 1955. 348 p.

Collection of writings on Afro-Brazilian topics pertaining to the history and culture of Salvador, Bahia, in the nineteenth and early twentieth centuries. The author, who lived from 1851 to 1923, was a teacher, labor organizer, abolitionist, and one of Brazil's first historians of color. Divided into approximately fifty short and often unrelated sections, this collection places greatest emphasis on African-Catholic religious syncretism; popular culture including song, dance, and festivals; military participation of people of color; and the meaning of certain historical events for Afro-Brazilians.

88. Querino, Manuel. *A raça africana e os seus costumes.* 1916. Reprint. Salvador: Livraria Progresso Editora, 1955. 174 p.

Collection of the author's writings, many of which appear elsewhere (see other entries for this author). In addition to title essay, volume contains "O africano como colonisador" and "Os homens de côr preta na história." Last section provides very short sketches of thirty-eight Brazilians of color (educators, priests, military figures, musicians, etc.) who lived in the nineteenth and early twentieth centuries.

89. Querino, Manuel. *As artes na Bahia. (Escôrço de uma contribuição histórica).* 2d ed. Bahia: Officinas do "Diário da Bahia," 1913. 241 p.

Exploration of the arts of Bahia by one of the individuals closest to the subject at the turn of the twentieth century. Demonstrates author's expertise on the region's architecture, sculpture, and theater, among other art forms. Pays close attention to the artistic contribution of the artisanal worker and of individuals involved the "building trades." Describes the beginning of Salvador's labor movement in the 1870s and provides a good description of working class conditions in that city during the last decades of the nineteenth century. The majority of the book is dedicated to brief biographical sketches of approximately seventy figures (both Brazilian and foreign) who worked in a wide variety of artistic fields in Salvador.

90. Querino, Manuel. *Costumes africanos no Brasil*. Rio de Janeiro:
Civilização Brasileira, 1938. 351 p.

Volume republishes author's writings on the impact of African culture
in Bahia, especially in the city of Salvador. Book is divided into four parts:
"A raça africana e seus costumes na Bahia," originally published in 1916;
"O colono preto como factor da civilização brasileira," first published in
1918, and later published under the title *O Africano como colonisador*; "A
arte culinária na Bahia," published in 1928; and "Notas de folk-lore
negro," which includes nine of the discussions on Afro-Brazilian religion
and culture found in *A Bahia de outrora* (see above). "A raça africana" discusses various practices and beliefs of *Candomblé* as author witnessed
them around the turn of the twentieth century. "O colono preto" provides
a historical sketch of various measures slaves took to free themselves.

91. Querino, Manuel. *O africano como colonisador*. 1918. Reprint.
Salvador, Bahia: Livraria Progresso Editora, 1954. 43 p.

Originally published as *O colono preto como factor da civilização brasileira*,
and also available in English under the title *The African Contribution to
Brazilian Civilization* (translation and introduction by E. Bradford
Burns). Very brief review of various forms of resistance to slavery, ranging from the *quilombo* of Palmares to the mutual aid societies of a later
period.

92. Rancourt, Etienne de. *Fazendas e estâncias: Notes de voyage sur le
Brésil et la République Argentine*. Paris: Plon-Nourrit et Cie, 1901.
286 p.

French traveler's observations of urban and rural life in the Brazilian
states of Rio de Janeiro, São Paulo, and Paraná in 1899. Final chapter
based on author's visit to a number of Argentine ranches (*estâncias*).
Describes decline of coffee in Rio de Janeiro and transition to other crops,
especially manioc, for which he includes a cost/benefit analysis. Assesses
economic liabilities associated with coffee farming in São Paulo and describes a brief journey to the Paulista frontier of the coffee region. Includes a passage on a rural religious procession made up of people of
color in the Paulista countryside.

93. Rebouças, André. *Agricultura nacional: estudos econômicos.
Propaganda abolicionista e democrática, setembro de 1874 a setembro de
1883*. Reprint. 1883. Recife: Fundação Joaquim Nabuco, 1988. 409 p.

Assembles writings published by the abolitionist leader between 1874
and 1883. Illustrates the breadth of Rebouças's political concerns, including abolition, the treatment of immigrants, the organization of agricul-

tural production, and land reform. Of particular interest for postemancipation studies is Rebouças's call for the "democratization" of land (redistribution to former slaves, immigrants, and other smallholders) as a necessary complement to abolition.

94. Rebouças, André. *Diário e notas autobiográficas.* Rio de Janeiro: Livraria José Olympio Editora, 1938. 457 p.

Annotated, edited collection of selections from the diary of André Rebouças and autobiographical notes by the same. Chapters I through IV cover Rebouças's education and work as an engineer, different voyages, and participation in the Paraguayan War. Chapter VI focuses on abolitionist politics. Brief diary entries provide information on plans for an emancipation law and the creation of the Associação Central Protetora dos Emancipados in 1870, the foundation of the Sociedade Brasileira contra a Escravidão in 1880, Rebouças's work for *O Abolicionista* and the *Gazeta da Tarde*, and a detailed account of the passage of the Golden Law in 1888 in which Rebouças describes his dealings with figures such as José do Patrocínio, Joaquim Nabuco, and Dom Pedro II. Chapter VII focuses on the immediate aftermath of abolition. Entries briefly discuss Rebouças's involvement in the Sociedade Central de Imigração and register his concern for land distribution to *libertos* and conflicts between *liberto* squatters and the military. Chapter VIII concludes the volume with diary entries and letters written by Rebouças during his exile from Brazil after the fall of the monarchy.

95. Rodrigues, Raimundo Nina. *L'animisme fétichiste des nègres de Bahia.* Bahia: Reis e Companhia, 1900. 158 p.

Early study by the Bahian physician and anthropologist based on five years of observation of *Candomblé* as practiced in the *terreiros* of Salvador. Contains occasional references to the belief systems of the surrounding countryside. Illustrates the widespread influence of Yoruba-inspired beliefs among the last generation of Africans, as well as among Brazilian-born people of color. Describes in detail festivals, physical design, and rites of passage for the religious hierarchy of Gantois, one of Salvador's oldest and best-known *terreiros*. Explains syncretic "exchange" between African and Catholic saints, African magic, the symbolic significance of plant life and other natural objects, and concludes that syncretism existed not only between Catholic and African belief systems, but between the latter and spiritist as well as Cardicist practices. Briefly discusses official attempts to curtail *Candomblé* and the attendant use of powerful patrons as a means of protecting the *terreiros*.

96. Rodrigues, Raimundo Nina. *Os africanos no Brasil.* Brasiliana vol. 9, 3d ed. São Paulo: Companhia Editôra Nacional, 1945.

The first ethnographic study of the Afro-Brazilian population, this work was published posthumously in 1932, though an incomplete version appeared in 1905 under the title *O problema da raça negra na América portuguesa.* Much of this work focuses upon the Yoruba-Jeje (or "Sudanese") presence in Bahia, as travelers' accounts and the early chronicles had led to the mistaken impression that only subequatorial (or "Bantu") Africans had populated Brazil. Related to this is a chapter on the Islam-inspired rebellions carried out by the Yoruba-Jeje, as well as a chapter on Africans still living in Salvador, many of whom supplied information to the author. The remaining chapters are dedicated to African language and art, popular festivals and folklore, and Afro-Brazilian religious beliefs. In all of these the author traces the dominance of the Yoruba presence. Though informed by contemporary notions of scientific racism, this book influenced virtually every subsequent study of this nature.

97. Romero, Sílvio. *Folclore brasileiro.* vol. 2: *Contos populares do Brasil.* Annotated by Luís da Câmara Cascudo. Rio de Janeiro: José Olympio, 1954.

Collection of popular short stories originally published at the end of the nineteenth century, organized by author. Part 3 of this work presents sixteen stories of African and *mestiço* origin. While some tales mention slavery, none deals explicitly with emancipation.

98. Smith, Herbert Huntington. *Brazil: The Amazons and the Coast.* New York: Charles Scribner's Sons, 1879. 644 p.

North American naturalist describes his travels in Brazil between 1874 and 1878. Areas covered include the Amazon, Paraíba, Pernambuco, Bahia, and Rio de Janeiro. Long chapter describes drought in Ceará and wretched conditions of refugees in Fortaleza. Chapter on social life in Rio de Janeiro examines upper classes, mechanics and small shopkeepers, free laborers, and slaves. Description of coffee plantation at Entre Rios decries the overworking of young slaves which author attributes to owner's knowledge of their upcoming emancipation.

99. Sociedade Nacional de Agricultura. *Legislação agrícola do Brasil.* 3 vols. Rio de Janeiro: Imp. Nacional, 1910.

Consists of three volumes: *Volume I. Primeiro Período: Império (1808–1889). Primeira Parte: Agricultura; Volume II. Primeiro Período: Império (1808–1889). Segunda Parte: Indústrias Ruraes; Volume III. Fim do Primeiro*

Período: Império (1808–1889). Volume I includes laws related to the regulation of agriculture, including the final abolition of slavery (Lei de 13 de maio de 1888). Volume II consists almost entirely of documents relating to the establishment of specific *engenhos centrais* between 1875 and 1889. Volume III contains documents concerning the importation of immigrants and the foundation of *colônias*, as well as a burst of legislation dating from 1889 regarding the extension of credit for agriculture.

100. Sociedade Nacional de Agricultura. *Legislação agrícola do Brasil.* Rio de Janeiro, 1960–.

New edition of a collection published by the Sociedade Nacional de Agricultura in 1910. This edition is arranged chronologically, whereas the original was arranged by topic. Contains the text of laws related to agriculture, as well as a chronological list of laws. The first two volumes also contain indexes.

101. Sociedade Nacional de Agricultura, Rio de Janeiro. *Atlas do Brasil.* São Paulo: Weiszflog Irmãos, 1908. 50 leaves of plates.

Contains national maps of geology, soil types, climate, population density, agricultural schools and institutions, as well as maps showing where different crops are produced (including coffee, sugar, cotton, tobacco, rubber, and cacao). Contains state maps showing location of different agricultural and extractive activities and soil types. Also includes diagrams of exports of various agricultural products from different states.

102. Souza, Jonas Soares de. "Uma empresa pioneira em São Paulo: O engenho central de Porto Feliz." *Coleção Museu Paulista (Série de História)* 7 (1978): xi–159.

Commemorates the centennial of the Usina Porto Feliz in São Paulo, which was founded in 1878 and was the third central sugar mill in Brazil. Provides historical introduction which describes the evolution of the central mills and of the *engenho central* of Porto Feliz in particular. Reproduces the enabling legislation for the concession of central mills in Brazil as well as all legal actions pertaining to Porto Feliz for the period from 1875 to 1907. Notes lack of sufficient laborers and reluctance on the part of cane growers to sign contracts with the mill but does not discuss labor relations at length.

103. Tschudi, Johann Jakob von. *Viagem às províncias do Rio de Janeiro e S. Paulo.* São Paulo: Publicações comemorativas sob o alto patrocínio da Comissão do IV Centenário da Cidade de São Paulo, 1953. 209 p.

Translation of two sections of a five-volume work by Swiss diplomat and naturalist J. J. Tschudi (1818–87). Describes Tschudi's travels in Rio de

Janeiro and São Paulo between 1860 and 1866, while he served as Swiss ambassador to Brazil. Describes Tschudi's visits to *fazendas* and *colônias de parceria*. Pays special attention to labor conditions of Swiss immigrants. Discusses impact of abolition of slave trade and speculates on future impact of emancipation.

104. Vasconcellos, Alfredo de. *Dos contractos agrícolas e pecuários; locação de serviços agrícolas e pecuários. Empreitada e parceria. Arrendamento de prédios rústicos. Accidentes no trabalho agrícola. Jurisprudência e legislação. Formulário.* São Paulo: Saraiva, 1922. 260 p.

Juridical treatise describing variants of agricultural contracts. Covers different kinds of labor contracts, including *locação de serviços* (contracting by day or month), *empreitada* (contracting by job), and *parceria* (sharecropping). Describes conditions under which work accidents must be indemnified and factors which determine compensation. Includes sample contracts for: agricultural colonist, administrator of rural property, *empreitada*, *parceria*, and agricultural property rental. Throughout, cites scholars' commentaries as well as relevant law, decree, or article of Civil Code.

CENSUSES AND RELATED COMPILATIONS

105. Bahia. Directoria de Estatística. *Notícia histórica e informações estatísticas do Estado da Bahia.* Bahia: Imp. Oficial do Estado, 1932. 43 p.

Pamphlet containing statistical information from Bahia as well as a historical essay about the state. Statistics include the total population in 1932 organized by *município* and changes in population and population density from 1822 to 1932, as well as contemporary statistics on male and female enrollment in educational institutions, exports and imports, major foreign trading partners, cacao production for 1931–32 *safra* organized by *município*, tobacco exportation, and financial situation of state government.

106. Brazil. Conselho Nacional de Estatística. *A população do Brasil. Dados censitários, 1872–1950.* Rio de Janeiro: Serviço Gráfico IBGE, 1958. 36 p.

Synopsis of statistical information from censuses of 1872, 1890, 1900, 1920, 1940, and 1950. Includes information on total population organized by sex, age, color, marital status, religion, nationality, and literacy. Presents information for nation as a whole as well as by state, including the Distrito Federal. Useful as a guide to individual census compilations.

107. Brazil. Directoria Geral de Estatística. *Recenseamento geral da República dos Estados Unidos do Brazil em 31 de dezembro de 1890. Districto Federal (Cidade do Rio de Janeiro) Capital da República dos Estados Unidos do Brazil.* Rio de Janeiro: Typ. Leuzinger, 1895. 454 p.

Includes many types of statistics not found in the national censuses for this and later years, with focus on city of Rio de Janeiro. Particularly helpful for the study of family structure. Divides population totals for each parish by sex, race, marital status, and age (not cross-tabulated). Tabulations include transient populations (maritime and land-based); country of origin of foreigners who have adopted Brazilian nationality; religion; physical defects; literacy; and possession of scientific, literary, or artistic titles. Tables on family composition compile information on parents' nationality, age at marriage, degree of kinship, number of children living and dead, physical defects of children, and length of marriage. Many tables cross-tabulated with race (*branca, preta, cabocla, mestiça*). Includes list (by parish) of all inhabitants over ninety years of age, including their names, ages, place of birth, race, sex, marital status, occupation, and residence. As the vast majority of those listed are *pretos*, most born in Africa, the list provides a rich source of information on the lives of elderly freedmen and women.

108. Brazil. Directoria Geral de Estatística. *Relatorio apresentado ao Dr. Miguel Calmon du Pin e Almeida, Ministro da Industria, Viação e Obras Públicas pelo Dr. José Luiz S. de Bulhões Carvalho (Director Geral de Estatística).* Rio de Janeiro: Typ. da Estatística, 1908. 205 p.

Summary of Brazilian census of 1900. Includes nine statistical charts for the nation as a whole as well as for twenty individual states. Charts include information on the following: 1) total population, number of residences of one and two or more persons, and number of various types of buildings; 2) nationality and number of illiterates organized by sex; 3) adherents of principal religions organized by sex, age, and number of illiterates; 4) age of inhabitants organized by sex; 5) principal nationalities of inhabitants organized by sex, age, number of illiterates and religion; 6) age of inhabitants organized by marital status and sex; 7) paternity (legitimate, illegitimate, legitimated, foundlings, and unknown), physical defects, and residences of inhabitants organized by nationality and sex; 8) religion and nationality of inhabitants organized by sex; 9) professions of inhabitants organized by nationality and sex. No mention is made of race or previous state of servitude of inhabitants.

109. Brazil. Directoria Geral de Estatística. *Annuário estatístico do Brazil.* 4 vols. Rio de Janeiro: Typ. de Estatística, 1908–12, 1936, 1937, 1939–40.

Serial publication contains statistical tables on a great variety of topics. Volume 3 for 1908 through 1912 focuses on religion, public health, the penal system, and education. Most statistics are for the city of Rio de Janeiro and are divided by sex and municipal district. Tables on prisoners jailed and prisoners released over the course of the year are the only statistics cross-tabulated by race (*brancos, amarelos, negros,* and *mestiços*). Volumes for later years have broader topical and geographical coverage and cover population movements, agricultural and industrial production, railroad construction, real estate values, imports and exports, hospital occupancy, insurance, unionization, social and cultural facilities and associations, and public administration and fiscal balances. Also included is information on rural wages for each state, divided by job. Some tables report men's, women's, and children's wages separately. Almost all tables are divided by state and some are further subdivided by municipality. Many statistics are cross-tabulated by race, nationality, marital status, age, sex, and occasionally by level of education and profession.

110. Brazil. Directoria Geral de Estatística. *Valor das terras no Brazil segundo o censo agrícola realizado em 1 de setembro de 1920.* Rio de Janeiro: Typ. da Estatística, 1924. 51 p.

Reports land values in each state by municipality, listing area of rural establishments included in census; value with and without improvements; and relation between area included in census and total surface of municipality.

111. Brazil. Directoria Geral de Estatística. *Recenseamento do Brazil realizado em 1 de Setembro de 1920.* 5 vols. Rio de Janeiro: Typ. da Estatística, 1922–1930.

The official 1920 census volumes. Vol. 1 contains an essay on the "evolution of race" in Brazil which could be useful for studying racial ideology in the 1920s. Vol. 1 also includes a history of Brazilian censuses, including those conducted by states or provinces, as well as general information about how the 1920 census was carried out, including sources of error. Part 1 of vol. 3 contains extensive statistics on agriculture, including nationality of proprietors, value of rural property, and livestock organized by state and in some cases by *município*. Part 5 of vol. 4 includes information on sex, nationality, age, and professions organized by state and *município*. Part 2 of vol. 5 contains information on wages for various rural occupations, such as cane cutters, agricultural laborers (*trabalhadores a enxada*), and cattle herders, by *município*. Part 3 of vol. 5 contains a list of every sugar mill in Brazil, along with information for each one on capacity and technology.

112. Brazil. Directoria Geral de Saúde Publica. *Annuário de Estatística Demographo–Sanitária*. 10 vols. Rio de Janeiro: Imp. Nacional, 1909, 1910, 1922–28.

Annual publications of the Department of Public Health present a massive array of statistics on births, marriages, specific illnesses, deaths, infant mortality, and so on. Many of these are cross-tabulated with race (*branca, parda, preta*, and *côr ignorada*), as well as profession, marital status, age, and parish. Almost all tables list male and female totals separately. Most tables only cover the city of Rio de Janeiro, although the final section of each volume contains assorted data from other cities.

113. Brazil. Ministério da Agricultura, Indústria e Commércio. Diretoria do Serviço de Inspecção e Fomento Agrícolas. *Aspectos da economia rural brasileira*. Rio de Janeiro: Officinas Graphicas Villas Boas, 1922. 988 p.

A compilation of data on Brazilian agriculture. Main focus of the statistical data is the period from approximately 1911 to 1921. Volume is divided by state, with descriptions of agricultural zones, individual cultigens, yield per hectare, and the agricultural calendar. Contains detailed discussion of rural wages and land prices in each state. The section "Salário dos trabalhadores ruraes" for each state (except Maranhão) is particularly useful for information about hours of work, regional variations in the level and forms of payment, and patterns of intrastate migration. These essays also discuss the division of labor by age and sex, and make some suggestions about employers' strategies and workers' own choices and preferences.

114. Brazil. Ministério da Agricultura, Comércio e Obras Públicas. *Relatório apresentado à Assembléia Geral na primeira sessão da décima oitava legislatura*. 18 vols. Rio de Janeiro: Typ. Nacional, 1861, 1864, 1866, 1868, 1870, 1873, 1877, 1882, 1890, 1892, 1910–15, 1922, 1924.

Each of the eighteen volumes describes the activities sponsored by the Ministry of Agriculture, Commerce, and Public Works over the course of the year: botanical and veterinary research projects; schools; museums;

public works; railroad construction; etc. The 1882 volume contains tables on the number of manumissions (private and reimbursed) in each province for that year. Volumes for 1882, 1890, and 1892 list concessions given in each province for the establishment of *engenhos centrais*. Volumes for 1910 through 1914, under the heading of "Serviço de Protecção aos Índios e Localisação de Trabalhadores Nacionaes," give general descriptions of the situation of former slaves and call for their reincorporation into the agricultural labor force.

115. Brazil. Ministério da Agricultura, Indústria e Comércio. Directoria Geral de Estatística. *Indústria assucareira no Brasil*. Rio de Janeiro: Typ. da Estatística, 1919. 102 p.

First section summarizes the results of a questionnaire sent by Directoria Geral de Estatística to all *usinas* nationwide (215, or about three-fourths, responded). Resulting statistics on capacity, type, sugar yield, and annual production from 1912 to 1918 are broken down by state and specific *usina*. Other sections offer data from 1902 to 1917 on yearly sugar exports (broken down by state, sugar quality, and importing nation) and on sugar production, consumption, and prices within Brazil (broken down by state and, in the case of prices, by month). Commentary stresses continuing importance of "antiquated" *banguê* production, not included in all statistics. Concludes with statistics on world production of cane and beet sugar, yields per hectare in various countries, and per capita consumption from 1906 to 1916.

116. Brazil. Ministério da Agricultura, Indústria e Commércio. Diretoria Geral de Estatística. *Resumo de várias estatísticas econômico-financeiras*. Rio de Janeiro: Typ. da Estatística, 1924. 175 p.

Compilation of aggregate population statistics based on 1920 and earlier censuses. Table 5 shows number of farms in each state classified by tenure and size; other tables summarize characteristics of owners, animals on farms, crops cultivated, detailed information on sugar centrals, coffee and other exports. Contains statistics on wages in the Federal District, rural wages by state in 1911 and 1921. Also has sections on finance and transportation. Particularly useful for comparative data on tenure and wages.

117. Brazil. Ministério da Agricultura, Indústria e Commércio. Directoria Geral de Estatística. *Recenseamento do Brasil realizado em 1 de setembro de 1920: relação dos proprietários dos estabelecimentos ruraes recenseados no Estado da Bahia*. Rio de Janeiro: Typ. da Estatística, 1928.

Census of rural landholdings in Bahia. (Editors were unable to locate a copy in the United States. For an article based in part on this work, see Mary Ann Mahony, "Afro-Brazilians, Land Reform, and the Question of Social Mobility in Southern Bahia, 1880–1920," cited below.)

118. Brazil. Ministério da Fazenda. Directoria Geral da Contabilidade. *Informações sobre o estado da lavoura.* Rio de Janeiro: Typ. Nacional, 1874. 245 p.

Report on the state of agriculture in individual provinces and Brazil as a whole based on results of questionnaire sent by Ministerio da Fazenda to provincial presidents. Summary of results for Brazil as a whole lists causes for economic stagnation including lack of technical knowledge, scarcity of capital, labor shortage, lack of roads, high taxation, and tariffs. Treatment of labor shortage includes discussion of effects of Rio Branco Law of 1871, including effects on work habits of freedpeople and relations between free and slave laborers. Includes reports from thirteen provinces: Bahia, Paraíba, Espírito Santo, Alagoas, Rio Grande do Sul, Paraná, Rio Grande do Norte, Pernambuco, Goiás, Minas Gerais, São Paulo, Piauí and Amazonas. Provincial reports vary in quantity and type of information. Report from Bahia is most complete, with a discussion of effects of Rio Branco Law, a list of registered *engenhos*, and a chart based on information collected in 1873 and 1874 that lists numbers of slaves and children of slave women in Bahia divided by sex. Volume includes appendix compiled by the Directoria Geral da Contabilidade with further information on the state of agriculture in Bahia, Maranhão, Pará, and Paraná. Concludes with report on the mortgage debt (*"divida hypothecaria"*), with a table detailing the total mortgage debt for Brazil organized by province and year, followed by fifteen tables for individual provinces organized by *comarca* and year. Provinces included are Rio de Janeiro, Espírito Santo, Bahia, Sergipe, Pernambuco, Alagoas, Paraíba, Rio Grande do Norte, Maranhão, Pará, Amazonas, Santa Catarina, Rio Grande do Sul, Minas Gerais, and Goiás.

119. Brazil. Ministério da Indústria, Viação e Obras Públicas. Directoria Geral de Estatística. *Sexo, raça e estado civil, nacionalidade, filiação, culto e analfabetismo da população recenseada em 31 de dezembro de 1890.* Rio de Janeiro: Officina da Estatística, 1898. 446 p.

A series of tables based on data from the 1890 census. Data presented for nation as a whole as well as broken down by state, municipality, district, and parish. Separate sections summarize race (*branco, prêto, caboclo,* and *mestiço*) organized by sex and marital status; nationality (Brazilian, foreign) organized by sex; birth status (legitimate, illegitimate, legitimated, and foundling); religion (Catholic: Roman Orthodox; Protestant: evangelical, Presbyterian, other; Islamic; Positivist; and without religion); and literacy, organized by nationality (Brazilian or foreigners) and sex. Tables are not cross-tabulated.

120. Brazil. Ministério da Indústria, Viação e Obras Públicas. Diretoria Geral de Estatistica. *Synopse do recenseamento de 31 de dezembro de 1890*. Rio de Janeiro: Officina da Estatística, 1898. 133 p.

Initial table presents population of states of the Republic and the Distrito Federal. Subsequent tables present information on individual states and the Distrito Federal broken down by *munícipio, districto*, and *parochia*. Population of *parochias* organized by sex. Preface to the volume discusses conditions under which census was conducted and alludes to difficulties encountered.

121. Brazil. Ministry of Labour, Industry and Commerce. *Brazil of Today. Natural Wealth, Economic Forces, Progress*. Rio de Janeiro, 1931. 214 p.

Created with the goal of attracting foreign investment, includes information on contemporary Brazil including maps, statistics and narrative reports on topics such as crop production and exportation, wages of rural workforce, population, migration, climate, mining, and other aspects of the Brazilian economy.

122. Brazil. Serviço de Inspecção e Defesa Agrícolas. *Questionários sobre as condições da agricultura dos 173 municípios do Estado de S. Paulo. Inspectoria Agrícola do 140 Districto. De Abril de 1910 a Janeiro de 1912*. Rio de Janeiro: Typ. do Serviço de Estatística , 1913. 550 p.

Between 1910 and 1912 the personnel of the newly-created Inspetorias Agrícolas visited each of the 173 municipalities of the state of São Paulo, interviewing local agriculturalists and observing conditions. The results of the questionnaire are reported for each municipality in approximately alphabetical order. Questions cover climate, terrain, levels of production for specific crops and livestock, agricultural techniques, land prices, prices of commonly purchased goods, factories, transportation, public health, schools, diet, residents' most frequent complaints, and "hardworkingness of population." Of particular interest are entries under "nuclei of colonists" (describing presence or absence, size, and nationality); "system of work of agricultural personnel" (listing which labor systems are in use in the municipality, such as salary, contract, *empreitada*, etc.); and "salaries" (specifying average earnings for rural workers, *colonos, fazenda* administrators, carpenters, cooks, washerwomen, etc.).

123. Rio Grande do Sul. Secretaria de Coordenação e Planejamento.
Fundação de Economia e Estatística. *De Província de São Pedro a*
Estado do Rio Grande do Sul. Censos do RS: 1803–1950. Porto Alegre:
Fundação de Economia e Estatística, 1981. 330 p.

Includes a variety of population statistics extracted from censuses and
organized by *município*, as well as some statistics on literacy, agricultural
production, and the slave population before 1863. Also includes useful
summary information and maps relating to the frequently subdivided
municípios of Rio Grande do Sul and their *distritos*.

SECONDARY SOURCES

124. Abreu, Martha. *O império do divino: festas religiosas e cultura popular*
no Rio de Janeiro, 1830–1900. Rio de Janeiro: Nova Fronteira, 1999.
406 p.

Study of popular celebrations in Rio de Janeiro, principally the festival
of the Divino Espírito Santo. Analyzes the role of celebrations in the
construction of racial categories and other forms of difference as well
their role in urban struggles over labor, sex, the body, and political
power. Includes discussion of debates over the proper role of religion in
the lives of former slaves. Based on diverse records located mainly in the
Arquivo Geral da Cidade do Rio de Janeiro and the Arquivo Nacional as
well as published accounts by travelers, folklorists, and popular historians.

125. Aguiar, Adonias Filho. *Sul da Bahia: chão de cacau, uma civilização*
regional. 2d ed. Rio de Janeiro: Editora Civilização Brasileira, 1978.
113 p.

A short sketch of the historical formation of southern Bahian culture,
emphasizing the influence of cacao. Relies on secondary sources and
travelers' accounts to sketch the history of region that has served as the
setting for the author's many novels. Passing reference to free blacks who
were explorers and cacao planters. Some discussion of the relative absence of slavery in the zone and the minimal effects of abolition there.
Author suggests that the absence of slave labor in the region was crucial to the development of its "democratic" character, as well as its relative prosperity after abolition.

126. Almada, Vilma Paraíso Ferreira de. *Escravismo e transição: o Espírito Santo (1850/1888).* Rio de Janeiro: Edições Graal, 1984. 221 p.

Study of slavery and its demise in a coffee-producing region, Espírito Santo. Draws on primary data to document economic development. Briefly examines consequences of abolition for the development of the work force, emphasizing continuing importance of "national" as opposed to immigrant workers.

127. Almeida, Maria da Glória Santana de. "Uma unidade açucareira em Sergipe: O Engenho Pedras." *Anais do VIII Simpósio Nacional dos Professores Universitários de História* 8 (1976): 511–49.

Study of the evolution of the Engenho Pedras in the Cotinguiba region of Sergipe from the early nineteenth century until the 1970s. Author uses inventories, wills, and interviews to explore the engenho as it passed through economic crises and initiated the transition to *usina* in 1910. Shortage of documents makes a complete history impossible, though there is fairly detailed information about the consolidation of property as the Usina Pedras expanded, as well as a brief description of the terms of contracts between the factory and those furnishing cane. Includes information from an 1866 inventory regarding the composition of the slave population—approximately half men and half women.

128. Amaral, Luís. *História geral da agricultura brasileira no tríplice aspecto político-social-econômico.* 2d ed., 2 vols. São Paulo: Companhia Editora Nacional, 1958.

Wide-ranging history of Brazilian agriculture that covers nearly four centuries and relies on travelers' accounts, provincial and state government reports, institutional publications, and secondary historical sources. Divided into five parts according to theme, most of which cover the entire chronological span. Of greatest interest for postemancipation period are descriptions of rural life and work; the appraisal of the rural labor laws of the first decades of the twentieth century; the discussion of agricultural organizations and institutes; and the various sections which explore political, social, and economic factors by crop, which comprise over half of the text. Sections on sugar and coffee receive the greatest attention, but see also discussions of manioc, cotton, cereal crops, tobacco, cacao, fruit crops, and livestock. Statistics regarding prices and exports appear in most of these discussions, and the author attempts to provide a state-by-state portrait of production of many of the crops.

129. Andrade, Manoel Correia de. *Escravidão e trabalho 'livre' no nordeste açucareiro.* Recife: Editora ASA Pernambuco, 1985. 73 p.

Comprises two articles, "Transição do trabalho escravo para o trabalho 'livre' no nordeste açucareiro—1850/1888," which gives a general overview of the process of transition to free labor; and "Milet e a crise agrícola na segunda metade do século XIX, no nordeste," which provides biographical and bibliographical background on one of the most important observers of the late-nineteenth-century Northeast, the French émigré Henrique Augusto Milet. Also discusses labor systems in the Northeast.

130. Andrade, Manuel Correia de. *A abolição e reforma agrária*. São Paulo: Atica, 1987. 86 p.

Overview of the process of slave emancipation and land reform in rural Brazil from Brazilian independence to the present. Based on secondary sources. Includes a glossary of terms and small annotated bibliography of major works on slavery and abolition.

131. Andrade, Manuel Correia de. *A terra e o homem no nordeste*. 4th ed. São Paulo: Livraria Editora Ciências Humanas, 1980. 278 p.

Classic study of economic geography of Brazilian Northeast. Discusses the process of settlement by Europeans and Africans, history of land use, changes in labor relations (including transition from slave to wage labor) and contemporary struggles over land and other resources in four subregions: 1) the "Zona da Mata" and eastern littoral, where sugar production has historically been concentrated, 2) the "Agreste," 3) the "Sertão" and northern littoral, and 4) the zone between the Northeast and Amazônia, including Maranhão and Piauí. Includes information on class structure, transformation of sugar industry, wage levels, and survival strategies of rural peoples. Available in English translation as *The Land and People of Northeast Brazil* (Albuquerque: University of New Mexico Press, 1980).

132. Andrews, George Reid. *Blacks and Whites in São Paulo, Brazil, 1888–1988*. Madison: University of Wisconsin Press, 1991. 369 p.

Addresses topics including process of emancipation, European immigration, experience of black and white workers in rural and urban work, ideology of racial democracy, and black political movements. Discussion of racial discrimination in industrial work in the city of São Paulo focuses on years between 1920 and 1960 and is based on personnel records of Jafet textile factory and São Paulo Tramway, Light, and Power.

133. Azevedo, Celia Maria Marinho de. *Onda negra, medo branco: o negro no imaginário das elites—século xix*. Rio de Janeiro: Paz e Terra, 1987. 267 p.

Discusses ideology of white abolitionists and 'immigrationists' in nineteenth-century Brazil, emphasizing their fear of Afro-Brazilians. Examines racism as a specific social construct used to justify immigration and to disparage capacities of the majority of Brazilians. Includes chapter on slave crime and resistance. Uses abolitionist writings, immigration projects, legislative debates, police records, and newspaper articles.

134. Azevedo, Celia Maria Marinho de. *Abolitionism in the United States and Brazil: A Comparative Perspective.* New York: Garland, 1995. 200 p.

Discusses how abolitionist movements in the United States and Brazil influenced one another and how movements in both countries participated in the construction of an image of Brazil as a racial paradise.

135. Azevedo, Elciene. *Orfeu de Carapinha: a trajetória de Luiz Gama na imperial cidade de São Paulo.* Campinas: Editora da Unicamp, 1999. 280 p.

Biography of Afro-Brazilian abolitionist Luiz Gama (1832–82). Discusses Gama's work as a legal advocate for slaves, a journalist, public official, and Republican activist in the city of São Paulo.

136. Azevedo, Fernando de. *Canaviais e engenhos na vida política do Brasil: ensaio sociológico sobre o elemento político na civilização do açucar.* Rio de Janeiro: Instituto do Açucar e do Álcool, 1948. 243 p.

Discusses sugar and politics from the sixteenth century to the twentieth century, including politics within the sugar industry and the place of sugar in national politics. Includes background on ecological, geographic, economic, and demographic aspects of sugar production in Brazil. Discusses kinship and patrimonial politics as well as abolitionism. Based on published primary and secondary sources.

137. Azevedo, Thales de. *Povoamento da cidade do Salvador.* 3d ed. Bahia: Editora Itapuã, 1969. 427 p.

Wide-ranging study by anthropologist of the settlement and history of the city of Salvador and, to a lesser extent, of the surrounding townships of the Bahian Recôncavo. Employs both archival and secondary sources and provides a discussion of census data from the colonial era through most of the twentieth century. Divides the discussion equally between the colonial and postcolonial periods. Provides commentary on race relations, religion, vagabondage, and the presumed unsuitability of free Brazilian labor. First published in 1949.

138. Bacelar, Jeferson. *Galegos no paraíso racial*. Bahia: Ianamá, 1994. 188 p.

Study of Galician immigrants in Bahia in the first half of the twentieth century. *Galegos* occupied an intermediate position both economically (as small-scale retailers) and socially (between the small local elite and the poor, mainly Afro-Brazilian majority). Emphasizing the hostility between *galegos* and Afro-Brazilians, Bacelar analyzes racial ideology as it was recreated by immigrants who were themselves marginalized because of their ethnicity. Primary sources include commercial records of import firms, newspapers, testaments, and the archives of Galician voluntary associations.

139. Bahia. Secretaria do Planejamento, Ciência e Tecnologia. *A inserção da Bahia na evolução nacional, 2a. etapa: 1890–1930*. Salvador: Estado da Bahia, 1980.

Situates the state of Bahia within the context of the expansion of capitalism and the international division of labor in the 1890 to 1930 period. Contains numerous tables on exports, the internal market, land use, foreign investment, and the expanding railroads. Includes detailed information on the cacao sector of Southern Bahia.

140. Baiocchi, Mari de Nasaré. *Negros de cedro: estudo antropológico de um bairro rural de negros em Goiás*. São Paulo: Ática, 1983. 201 p.

Ethnography of community of Afro-Brazilians in rural Goiás. Focuses is contemporary, addressing issues including economic activities of community members, family structure, medical practices, religion, and leisure activities. Brief discussion of foundation of community by freedpeople in late nineteenth century is based on oral history and property records.

141. Bakos, Margaret Marchiori. "Repensando o processo abolicionista sul-rio-grandense." *Estudos Ibero-Americanos* 14 (December 1988): 117–38.

Discussion of the role of slave resistance in the abolition of slavery in Rio Grande do Sul. Focuses on escapes from slavery, the formation of *quilombos*, and revolt. Based primarily on secondary literature.

142. Bakos, Margaret Marchiori. RS: *Escravismo e abolição*. Porto Alegre: Mercado Aberto, 1982. 165 p.

On abolitionism and abolition in Rio Grande do Sul, emphasizing debates about slavery and abolition in the provincial legislature (Assembléia Provincial Rio-Grandense) and, especially, in newspapers of the 1870s and 1880s.

143. Baptista Filho, Olavo. *A fazenda de café em São Paulo*. Documentário da Vida Rural no. 2. Rio de Janeiro: Ministério da Agricultura, 1952. 32 p.

Basic introduction to the coffee farm of São Paulo. Describes in thirty-two pages the expansion of the crop throughout the state; techniques for growing, harvesting, and processing; early experiments with European labor; work and social lives of the *colonos*; and the physical settings where they and their descendants have lived. Emphasis on first decades of the twentieth century.

144. Barickman, B. J. *A Bahian Counterpoint: Sugar, Tobacco, Cassava, and Slavery in the Recôncavo, 1780–1860*. Stanford: Stanford University Press, 1998. 276 p.

Discusses the use of slave labor in agricultural production for export and local consumption in the Recôncavo region of Bahia during a period when the export economy experienced significant growth. Based on archival sources including postmortem inventories of planters, manuscript censuses, property surveys, and correspondence.

145. Barickman, B. J. "Persistence and Decline: Slave Labour and Sugar Production in the Bahian Recôncavo, 1850–1888." *Journal of Latin American Studies* 28 (1996): 581–633.

Study of slave labor and sugar production that contrasts the Recôncavo with other sugar-producing areas of northeastern Brazil.

146. Baronov, David Mayer. "The Process of Working-Class Formation: The Abolition of Slavery in 19th-Century Brazil in World-Historical Perspective." Ph.D. diss., State University of New York at Binghamton, 1995.

147. Bastide, Roger. *Le candomblé de Bahia (Rite Nagô)*. Paris: Mouton, 1958. 260 p.

Classic work on *Candomblé*. Also see Roger Bastide, *African Religions of Brazil: Toward a Sociology of the Interpenetration of Civilizations* (Baltimore: Johns Hopkins University Press, 1978).

148. Beiguelman, Paula. *A formação do povo no complexo cafeeiro*. São Paulo: Pioneira, 1978. 152 p.

Analysis of political and social context that gave rise to (and also resulted from) the São Paulo coffee boom of the late nineteenth and early twentieth centuries. Explores political changes (chiefly the destruction of slavery) that led to the widespread importation of foreign labor. Provides detailed discussion of elite views of national workers as unsatisfactory for the coffee sector due to supposed indolence and unreliability. Links this elite vision to the secondary role played by Brazilian laborers (both ex-slaves and those never enslaved) in coffee and in the industrial labor market of São Paulo.

149. Bell, Stephen Andrew. "Ranching in the Campanha of Rio Grande do Sul, Brazil, 1850–1920: An Historical Geography of Uneven Development." Ph.D. diss., University of Toronto, 1991.

150. Braga, Julio Santana. *Sociedade Protetora dos Desvalidos: uma irmandade de cor.* Salvador: Ianamá, 1987. 94 p.

History of Afro-Brazilian religious brotherhood and mutual aid society established in 1832 and still active today. Describes the Sociedade as a mechanism of both acculturation and autonomy, concluding that it served as a source of prestige and social mobility for nineteenth-century blacks. Quotes extensively from the minutes of the Sociedade. Compares statutes of 1874 and 1956 at length.

151. Brazil, Étienne Ignace. "O fetichismo dos negros do Brazil." *Revista do Instituto Histórico e Geográphico Brazileiro* 74 (1911): 193–260.

Discussion of African-Brazilian religion by a Catholic priest who treats it as backward, fanatical and superstitious. He maintains that syncretism between inferior African 'fetishism' and superior Catholicism will destroy the former in Brazil. The article provides some ethnography based on personal observations in Bahia. Describes gods, their names, position in the African pantheon, food taboos, images, symbols, and ceremonies (including an initiation rite); types and purpose of amulets; the hierarchy and function of cult members; temple, altar, musical instruments, and so on.

152. Brazil, Étienne Ignace. "Os malês." *Revista do Instituto Histórico e Geográphico do Brasil* 72, pt. 2 (1909): 67–126.

Unsympathetic view of African Muslims (malês) in Brazil by a Catholic priest. Discusses the 1835 rebellion. Of importance to postemancipation period is his description of Muslim practices at the turn of the century, often based on first hand observation.

153. Brazil. Associação Nacional dos Professores Universitários de História. *Terra e poder.* Special issue of *Revista Brasileira de História* 6 (March–August, 1986). São Paulo: Editora Marco Zero, 1986.

Includes following articles with relevance to postemancipation studies: Ana Lúcia Duarte Lanna, in "O café e o trabalho 'livre' em Minas Gerais—1870/1920," discusses free labor in coffee regions of Minas

Gerais and emphasizes importance of "national" laborers, in contrast to employment of immigrants in São Paulo. Drawing on debates in agricultural congresses, examines sharecropping, wage labor, and seasonal migration. Ademir Gebara, in "Escravos: fugas e fugas," discusses slave flights in the last years of slavery, noting that instead of fleeing to form runaway communities in the countryside, slaves now fled toward a free labor market in the cities. Maria Lúcia Lamounier, in "O trabalho sob contrato: a Lei de 1870," discusses implications of labor law in São Paulo. João Luís Ribeiro Fragoso, in "A roça e as propostas de modernização na agricultura fluminense do século XIX," discusses continuities and proposals for change in agricultural techniques in the town of Paraíba do Sul, Rio de Janeiro, between 1830 and 1885, using travelers' accounts, agricultural journals, probate records. Vera Lúcia de Amaral Ferlini, in "A subordinação dos lavradores de cana aos senhores de engenho," discusses cane farmers in Brazilian Northeast during the colonial period and in nineteenth century. Uses travelers' accounts, legal rulings, and estate records. Also provides useful definitions. Discussion of cane cultivation is relevant to postemancipation tenantry in sugar regions not only in Brazil but elsewhere.

154. Brazil. Departamento Nacional do Café. *O café no segundo centenário de sua introdução no Brasil.* 2 vols. Rio de Janeiro, 1934.

Over two hundred essays ranging from technical treatises to travelogues; from statistical summaries of production, export, and consumption to interviews with the great and eccentric personalities of Brazilian coffee; from polemics over processing methods to a celebratory ode to coffee. Separate essays cover coffee in São Paulo, Ceará, Rio de Janeiro, Mato Grosso, Paraíba, Paraíba do Sul, Minas Gerais, Bahia, Espírito Santo, Algoas, Goiás, and Amazonas. Other entries of interest include "O trabalhador nacional na lavoura de S. Paulo," "Um viveiro morto da mão de obra negra para o cafezal," and "A influência da imigração branca sobre a lavoura de café no Espírito Santo." Most helpful is the lengthy bibliography (pp. 670–88) of Brazilian and foreign publications on coffee in Brazil.

155. Bresciani, Maria Stella Martins. "Suprimento de mão-de-obra para a agricultura: um dos aspectos do fenômeno histórico da abolição." *Revista de História* 106 (April–June 1976): 333–53.

Analysis of elite opinion regarding the transition from slavery to free labor in São Paulo based on reports of the presidents of the province of São Paulo from 1885 to 1889.

156. Burns, E. Bradford. "Manuel Querino's Interpretation of the African Contribution to Brazil." *Journal of Negro History* 59 (January 1974): 78–86.

A bibliographical essay that explores the life and writings of the Bahian artist, abolitionist, and labor organizer, Manuel Querino (1851–1923). Querino was the first Brazilian of color to study and write about the history of Afro-Brazilians, and his books and essays detail the cultural and artistic contributions by Africans and their descendants. Author confines bibliographic notes to the footnotes of the article while devoting the body of the piece to a description of Querino's life.

157. Butler, Kim D. *Freedoms Given, Freedoms Won: Afro-Brazilians in Post-Abolition São Paulo and Salvador.* New Brunswick: Rutgers University Press, 1998. 285 p.

Comparative study of postemancipation society in the cities of São Paulo and Salvador da Bahia from abolition to 1930.

158. Campos, João da Silva. "Ligeiras notas sobre a vida íntima, costumes e religião dos africanos na Bahia." *Anais do Arquivo do Estado da Bahia* 29 (1943): 289–309.

Brief overview of the cultural and work lives of free Africans living in the city of Salvador in the last decades of the nineteenth century and the first part of the twentieth century. Although the emphasis is on urban life, the author's description of such things as marital practices, religious ceremonies, the street life of vendors and carriers, and ethnic differences among Africans is useful for the scholar of rural Northeastern Brazil in the postemancipation period.

159. Cardoso, Ciro Flamarion, org. *Escravidão e abolição no Brasil: novas perspectivas.* Rio de Janeiro: Jorge Zahar Editor, 1988. 112 p.

Two essays on historiography of slavery and abolition. First essay is by multiple authors and addresses models of the slave economy (by João Luís Ribeiro Fragoso), slaveholding outside the export-oriented plantation economy (by Hebe Maria Mattos), and slavery, ideology, and society (by Ronaldo Vainfas), with concluding remarks by the essay's organizer, Ciro Flamarion Cardoso. Second essay by Cardoso reviews historiography of emancipation since 1960, discussing abolitionism, class conflict, immigration, the theme of representation in the "new history," and socioeconomic structures.

160. Cardoso, Ciro Flamarion S. *Escravo ou camponês? O protocampesinato negro nas Américas.* São Paulo: Editora Brasiliense, 1987. 125 p.

Examines "peasant breach" in the slave system, or the use of provision grounds and the development of a protopeasantry within slavery. Draws on evidence from the United States, the Caribbean, and Brazil. Uses travelers' accounts and documentary evidence from recent theses. Theoretical in orientation.

161. Cardoso, Fernando Henrique. *Capitalismo e escravidão no Brasil meridional: o negro na sociedade escravocrata do Rio Grande do Sul.* 3rd ed. Rio de Janeiro: Paz e Terra, 1977. 303 p.

Fourth edition of classic early (first published in 1962) analysis of slavery in the *charqueadas* (jerked-beef establishments) and ranches of Rio Grande do Sul. Includes discussion of the myth of gaúcho democracy, as well as chapters on abolitionism, the disintegration of slavery, and the situation of blacks in Rio Grande do Sul after abolition. Based largely on printed primary sources such as travelers' accounts and reports by provincial presidents.

162. Carneiro, Edison. *Candomblés da Bahia.* 7th ed. Rio de Janeiro: Civilização Brasileira, 1986. 145 p.

Classic study of Afro-Brazilian belief system in province of Bahia. Explores origins, diffusion, location, practices, and terminology of *Candomblés.* Approach is relatively ahistorical; does not focus specifically on transformations after slavery.

163. Carvalho, José Murilo de. *Os bestializados. O Rio de Janeiro e a República que não foi.* 2d ed. São Paulo: Companhia das Letras, 1987. 196 p.

Study of urban politics and practice of citizenship in Rio de Janeiro during transition from Empire to First Republic. Addresses issues such as the suppression of *capoeiras* after the fall of the monarchy, voter participation in the early republic, and the Revolta da Vacina of 1904. Based on printed sources, including newspapers and government documentation from the period, as well as research in archives including the Arquivo Geral da Cidade do Rio de Janeiro, the Public Records Office in the United Kingdom, and the Archive Diplomatique of the Ministère des Affaires Etrangères in France.

164. Castan. *Scenas da abolição e scenas várias. Horrores da escravidão no Brasil.* 2nd ed. São Paulo: Imp. Methodista, 1924. 212 p.

Brief, fictionalized sketches of slavery and abolition in rural areas of São Paulo and Santos. Provides vivid descriptions of last years of slavery, including discussions of cooperation between slaves and *caifazes,* or abolitionists, in pursuit of emancipation.

165. Castro, Jeanne Berrance de, and Júlia Maria Leonor Scarano. "A mão-de-obra escrava e estrangeira numa região de economia cafeeira (Uma experiência de pesquisa quantitativa na história rioclarense, 1875–1930)." *Anais do VI Simpósio Nacional dos Professores Universitários de História* 6 (1973): 717–38.

Authors describe an (apparently) ongoing study of an unusually complete collection of death certificates (*registros de óbitos*) from the important coffee *município* of Rio Claro in São Paulo. Focusing on 1,570 death records for the immigrant white laboring population, and on 2,170 records from the African-born and *crioulo* population (both enslaved and free), this article addresses the potential and means of constructing a data base from these documents rather than offering conclusions about the research itself. These records provide invaluable information regarding the age at death and morbidity of the laboring population as well as information regarding professions, rates of indigence, civil status, family ties, and the location of residences and workplaces. Authors note that when used in tandem with census records, death certificates provide an excellent portrait of the historical demography of Rio Claro.

166. *Cativeiro e liberdade.* (Seminário do Instituto de Filosofia e Ciências Humanas da Universidade do Estado do Rio de Janeiro). Rio de Janeiro: Universidade do Estado do Rio de Janeiro, 1989. 268 p.

Proceedings of a conference at the University of Rio de Janeiro during the one hundredth anniversary of abolition in 1988. Among the papers relevant to postemancipation period are: Francisco C. T. da Silva, "Terra e política no Rio de Janeiro na época da abolição," which discusses the position of Rio planters and lawmakers toward emancipation, their reaction to the original 1884 sexagenarian law project which envisioned the transformation of ex-slaves into small landholders, their lack of enthusiasm for European immigration, and their struggle for indemnization and for the maintenance of monopoly over land after abolition; Lucia P. Guimarães and Tânia Ferreira, "Os deserdados da abolição," which gives a summary of an ongoing project on perceptions of the other by elites and ex-slaves, giving a few examples of racism, persecution and denial of citizenship to blacks in law and the press in the aftermath of abolition in Rio de Janeiro; Hebe Mattos de Castro, "O estranho e o estrangeiro," which presents a historiographical discussion arguing for the validity of the concept of peasantry (in both the economic and cultural sense) in the analysis of small landholders in both pre- and postemancipation southern coffee regions; Márcia M. M. Motta, "Os 'Sem-Terra' e os minifundistas em face à crise do trabalho escravo (1850–

88)," which reports on research in progress about landless producers and small landholders (both slaveowners) and the impact of abolition on them; Lená M. de Menezes, "Trabalho e liberdade no Brasil: ensaio sobre a questão das permanências," which discusses how, after abolition, manual labor continued to be despised and coerced by society and state; Luitgarde O. C. Barros, "Abolicionismo-ideologias em debate num Ceará precursor," discusses abolition in Ceará, a northeastern province where slaves were emancipated four years before global emancipation, and examines social groups with different approaches to abolition.

167. Chalhoub, Sidney. *Cidade febril: cortiços e epidemias na Corte imperial.* São Paulo: Companhia das Letras, 1996. 250 p.

Investigates struggles over living space and epidemics in the city of Rio de Janeiro and their importance for debates over race and slavery in Brazil from the 1850s through the Revolta da Vacina in 1904. Based mainly on research in the Arquivo Nacional do Rio de Janeiro and the Arquivo Geral da Cidade do Rio de Janeiro.

168. Chalhoub, Sidney. "Medo branco de almas negras: escravos, libertos e republicanos na cidade do Rio." *Revista Brasileira de História* 8 (March/August 1988): 83–105.

Discusses antagonism of Rio de Janeiro's black population to government following the proclamation of the Republic in 1889, one year after the abolition of slavery. Notes that black opposition was rooted in cultural assertiveness linked to a long and complex struggle against slavery.

169. Chalhoub, Sidney. "Slaves, Freedmen and the Politics of Freedom in Brazil: The Experience of Blacks in the City of Rio." *Slavery and Abolition* 10 (December 1989): 64–84.

Focuses on manumission in the 1860s through the 1880s. Makes innovative use of legal sources.

170. Chalhoub, Sidney. *Visões da liberdade: uma história das últimas décadas da escravidão na corte.* São Paulo: Companhia das Letras, 1990. 287 p.

Discusses attitudes of masters, lawyers, judges, lawmakers and especially slaves toward liberty in the last decades of slavery in the city of Rio de Janeiro. Analysis of how slaves reacted against what they considered to be unfair practices, such as being sold against their will, and how they used the law to obtain freedom or to protect already acquired manumision. Based on primary data, especially court records. For a study of the black urban population in a later period by the author, see *Trabalho, lar e botequim: o cotidiano dos trabalhadores no Rio de Janeiro da Belle Époque* (São Paulo: Brasiliense, 1986).

171. Conrad, Robert. *The Destruction of Brazilian Slavery, 1850–1888.* Berkeley: University of California Press, 1972. 344 p.

Based on archival research as well as printed primary sources and synthesis of other secondary accounts. Includes extensive bibliography of printed primary sources and twenty-six tables presenting information on demography of slavery during the second half of the nineteenth century.

172. Costa Filho, Miguel. "Engenhos centrais e usinas." *Revista do Livro* 5 (September 1960): 83–91.

 Reviews the legislation of the 1870s and 1880s that set the conditions of government concessions for *engenhos centrais. Engenhos centrais* were restricted to processing the harvests of many small producers, while *usinas* combined both agricultural production and processing. Discusses how the democratic and cooperativist character of the *engenhos centrais* led to their replacement by the *usinas,* which enjoyed the support of the economically dominant classes.

173. Costa, Emília Viotti da. *Da senzala à colônia.* São Paulo: Difusão Européia do Livro, 1962. 497 p.

Influential early study of the transition from slave to free labor with a focus on the coffee zones of southeastern Brazil.

174. Costa, Emilia Viotti da. *The Brazilian Empire: Myths and Histories.* Chicago: The University of Chicago Press, 1985. 287 p.

A collection of essays, several of which are directly relevant to the formation of Brazilian society after slavery: "Land Policies: The Land Law, 1850, and the Homestead Act"; "Masters and Slaves: From Slave Labor to Free Labor"; and "The Myth of Racial Democracy: A Legacy of the Empire."

175. Costa, Iraci del Nero da, ed. *Brasil: História econômica e demográfica.* São Paulo: Instituto de Pesquisas Econômicas, 1986. 322 p.

Collection of essays by prominent scholars. Maria Luiza Marcílio, "A população do Brasil em perspectiva histórica," discusses census data and general and regional population estimates from the colonial era through 1970. Includes tables of population totals and birth, death, migration, and growth rates. Robert Slenes, "Grandeza ou decadência? O mercado de escravos e a economia cafeeira da província do Rio de Janeiro, 1850–

1888," challenges the idea that the Paraíba Valley coffee economy was in decline in the second half of the nineteenth century. Explores the local slave market through census data, slave registration records, provincial presidents' reports, and other sources. Concludes that demand remained high throughout the period.

176. Costa, Lena Castello Branco Ferreira. *Arraial e coronel: dois estudos de história social.* São Paulo: Editora Cultrix, 1978. 206 p.

Half of this volume provides a study of the rural life of a *coronel* (local notable) in Maranhão and Piauí based on the diaries, notarial records, correspondence, and family oral histories of Domingos Pacífico Castello Branco (1877–1932). Reflects observations made between 1918 and 1932 on the Fazenda Santa Cruz in Maranhão (though the *coronel* based his personal wealth and political power on property ownership in both states). Describes the varied economic strategies and social milieu that characterized life in the "backlands" of northern and northeastern states. Provides a detailed description of labor relations between the *coronel* and the *agregados* and day laborers who worked in the fields and in the production of sugar and cane liquor on the *fazenda.* Appends a copy of the *coronel*'s "Normas para os agregados," which spelled out his expectations of his dependents. Includes discussion of the rise of *coronelismo* during the First Republic.

177. Cowell, Bainbridge, Jr. "Cityward Migration in the Nineteenth Century: The Case of Recife, Brazil." *Journal of Interamerican Studies and World Affairs* 17 (February 1975): 43–63.

Based primarily on parish registers in Recife. Analyzes different factors in rural-urban migration, including changes in the organization of sugar production in the late nineteenth century. Author states that in contrast to southern Brazil, the final abolition of slavery did not lead to a significant cityward migration of freedpeople in Pernambuco.

178. Cunha, Manuela Carneiro da. "Silences of the Law : Customary Law and Positive Law on the Manumission of Slaves in 19th Century Brazil." *History and Anthropology* 1, part 2 (February 1985): 427–43.

Discusses the customary practice of freeing slaves who paid their price and debates about writing this practice into law, which did not occur until the 1871 "law of the free womb." Covers the entire nineteenth century up to emancipation. Includes information on relations between exslaves and their former masters. Useful background to the emancipation process and postemancipation dependency relations. Based largely on contemporary accounts, laws, and debates in legislative bodies.

179. Cunha, Manuela Carneiro da. *Negros, estrangeiros: os escravos libertos e sua volta à África*. São Paulo: Editora Brasiliense, 1985. 231 p.

Study by anthropologist of return to Africa of former slaves, with a focus on the construction of ethnicity among Afro-Brazilians in Lagos, Nigeria. Contains some statistical estimates of total volume of migration. Uses missionary records, newspapers, and governors' reports. Contributes to an understanding of an important, if infrequent, response to emancipation: emigration to Africa.

180. Dalla Vecchia, Agostinho Mário. *Os filhos da escravidão: memórias de descendentes de escravos da região meridional do Rio Grande do Sul*. Pelotas: Editora Universitária/Universidade Federal de Pelotas, 1993. 297 p.

Discussion of slavery, abolition, and postemancipation society in Rio Grande do Sul based largely on interviews conducted by the author with thirty-two descendants of slaves. Includes brief discussions of different aspects of former slaves' lives, including work, migration to urban areas, race relations, political organization, family, religion, and leisure. Section on *filhos-* and *filhas-de-criação*, or children of former slaves, orphans, and others who were given to wealthier families to be raised and employed as household servants. Includes photographs and sketches of artifacts and places related to slaves and their descendants, as well as an extensive bibliography on slavery in Rio Grande do Sul. Full transcripts of interviews appear in two companion volumes compiled by author entitled *Vozes do silêncio: depoimentos de descendentes de escravos do Meridião Gaúcho.* (See separate listing in section on primary sources.)

181. Dantas, Beatriz Góis. *Vovó Nagô e Papai Branco: usos e abusos da África no Brasil*. Rio de Janeiro: Graal, 1988. 262 p.

Interpretation of the Afro-Brazilian belief system of *Candomblé*. Based on field research in several cult houses in the state of Sergipe and in-depth analysis of one of them. Of interest for postemancipation era are passages presenting oral history of a house as told by its priestess, discussion of repression of *Candomblé* in the first decades of the twentieth century, and treatment of anthropological works of the same period.

182. Dean, Warren. *Rio Claro: A Brazilian Plantation System, 1820–1920*. Stanford: Stanford University Press, 1976. 234 p.

Examination of a municipality in the province and later state of São Paulo, covering labor in the period of slave emancipation.

183. Deffontaines, Pierre. *Geografia humana do Brasil*. Rio de Janeiro: Instituto Brasileiro de Geografia e Estatística, 1940. 116 p.

Overview of Brazilian geography, focusing on interaction of humans with different natural regions. Discusses regional distribution of economic activities and racial groups, emphasizing importance of what is portrayed as the whitening or *branqueamento* of the Brazilian population over time.

184. Degler, Carl. *Neither Black nor White: Slavery and Race Relations in Brazil and the United States.* New York: Macmillan Publishing, 1971. 302 p.

Important early English-language synthesis and overview.

185. Diégues Jr., Manuel. *O banguê nas Alagoas: traços da influência do sistema econômico do engenho de açúcar na vida e na cultura regional.* Rio de Janeiro: Instituto de Açúcar e do Alcool, 1949.

An enlarged version of his *O engenho de açúcar no nordeste* with much greater emphasis on the regional history and bibliography linked to sugar in Alagoas. Includes a bibliography of "fundamental sources" on Alagoas which that primary and secondary sources. Deals primarily with the pre-1888 period. Useful discussion of the transition from *banguê* to *usina*, the early-twentieth-century crises in agriculture, the formation and discussions of the first agricultural associations, and the cultural and folkloric traditions surrounding the sugar mill. Also discusses individual *engenhos* in the nineteenth and twentieth centuries and families who owned them.

186. Diégues Jr., Manuel. *O engenho de açúcar no nordeste.* Rio de Janeiro: Ministério da Agricultura, 1952. 68 p.

Author uses personal observations, travelers' accounts, and an interview with a former *engenho* owner to provide a brief portrait of the technical, social, and economic features associated with the northeastern sugar mill in the nineteenth and twentieth centuries. Includes short descriptions of the physical plant of the mill and the different types of mills; the means of planting and processing cane; and the festivals and folklore associated with mill life. Contains useful information regarding labor (mill owners, cane "furnishers," and rural workers) as well as information regarding the changes in conditions of rural laborers in the twentieth century. Includes a two-page abstract in English.

187. Diégues Jr., Manuel. *População e açúcar no nordeste do Brasil.* Rio de Janeiro: Comissão Nacional de Alimentação, 1954. 236 p.

History of sugar cultivation in northeastern Brazil from its introduction to the 1950s. Discussion of postemancipation period includes analyses of transformation of work and labor relations after slavery, as well as migration patterns of rural workers, diet, and struggles for land. Based primarily on printed documents, including government reports and travel accounts.

188. Donald, Cleveland, Jr. "Slave Resistance and Abolition in Brazil: The Campista Case, 1879–1888." *Luso-Brazilian Review* 13, 2 (winter 1976): 182–93.

189. Duque-Estrada, Osorio. *A Abolição. Esboço histórico, 1831–1888.* Rio de Janeiro: Leite Ribeiro e Maurillo, 1918. 328 p.

Historical account of the demise of the slave trade and slavery, focusing on parliamentary politics and activities of well-known abolitionists such as Joaquim Nabuco, Rui Barbosa, and André Rebouças. Includes introduction by Rui Barbosa.

190. Eisenberg, Peter. *Homens esquecidos: escravos e trabalhadores livres no Brasil, séculos XVIII e XIX.* Campinas: UNICAMP, 1989. 394 p.

Posthumous collection of articles and other writings by major historian that address topics including changes in the sugar industry of Pernambuco between 1840 and 1910; the transition from slavery to free labor in Brazil; the working lives of the free, freedpeople, and slaves in the nineteenth century; and the history of sugar production in São Paulo.

191. Eisenberg, Peter L. *The Sugar Industry in Pernambuco, 1840–1910: Modernization without Change.* Berkeley: University of California Press, 1974. 289 p.

History of the sugar economy in Pernambuco from 1840 to 1910, including attempts at modernization and the transition from slavery to free labor.

192. Ellis Junior, Alfredo. *O café e a Paulistânia.* São Paulo: Universidade de São Paulo/Faculdade de Filosofia, Ciência e Letras, 1951. 699 p.

History of coffee cultivation in São Paulo based primarily on published information including government reports and work of Affonso d'Escrangolle Taunay. Addresses issues such as internal migration, foreign immigration, and regional shifts in coffee production. Brief account of emancipation criticizes abolition of slavery in 1888 as premature and prejudicial to interests of freedpeople and Brazilian economy. Includes statistics on coffee production and exportation for São Paulo and Brazil as a whole.

193. *Estudos Afro-Asiáticos: Seminário "O Negro no Rio de Janeiro"* 15 (June 1988).

Proceedings of a conference at the time of the 100th anniversary of abolition. The following papers are particularly relevant to postemancipation studies: Francisco de Assis Barbosa, "A missão de Lima Barreto," inaugural talk of the conference, discusses the work of Lima Barreto, socially and racially conscious black writer of the early twentieth century; José Murilo de Carvalho, "As batalhas da abolição," discusses recent historiography of slavery and emancipation, which maintains that political pressures (including from slaves) were as important in ending slavery as socioeconomic processes, and compares Brazilian and U.S. emancipation; Lana L. da G. Lima and Renato P. Venâncio, "Os orfãos da lei: o abandono de crianças negras no Rio de Janeiro após 1871," based on Santa Casa da Misericórdia records, discusses the increase in numbers of black children abandoned by masters who then hired out their slave mothers as nurses in Rio de Janeiro after the 1871 "Free Womb Law"; Nancy P. S. Naro, "Limites do comportamento aceitável e mecanismos de dominação social no meio rural brasileiro: 1850–1890," based on court records, discusses the use of the law by slaves to free themselves or keep already acquired freedom, the actions of freemen who helped slaves to resist, land conflict between large and small landholders in a rural area of Rio de Janeiro in the second half of the nineteenth century; Joel Rufino dos Santos, "O negro no Rio pós-abolição: marginalização e patrimônio cultural," briefly touches on several different themes of postemancipation Rio, such as the idea that blacks were not prepared to compete in the labor market and the relation of a black culture of "festa" to this idea, black resistance in early republican era (the Revolta da Vacina, for instance), and the creation of black organizations such as carnival groups, soccer teams, and clubs; Yvonne Maggie, "Religiões mediúnicas e a cor de seus participantes," based on police records, discusses authorities' conflicting opinions on repression/tolerance of spiritist cults and shows racial profile of persons accused of spiritist practices in Rio between 1912 and 1945, finding that the majority were white, and more than a quarter of them European immigrants; Roberto Moura, "No Rio depois da Aurea," briefly touches on many themes of black life and culture as well as race relations and state control in Rio between emancipation and the 1970s.

194. *Estudos Econômicos*. Special issue: *Economia escravista brasileira* 13 (1983). 287 p.

Special issue on slavery. Of relevance to postemancipation studies are several articles which discuss the crisis of slavery and the transition from slave to free labor before abolition, including Peter Eisenberg, "Escravo e proletário na história do Brasil," a historiographical discussion of the similarity and differences between slave labor and wage labor based on Brazilian secondary literature and some travel accounts; and Manuel Correia de Andrade, "Transição do trabalho escravo para o trabalho livre no Nordeste açucareiro: 1850–1888," which discusses the limits of slave labor in the Brazilian Northeast.

195. *Estudos Ibero-Americanos.* Special Issue: *I Simpósio Gaúcho Sobre a Escravidão Negra* 16 (July–December 1990). 344 p.

Papers presented at a conference at the Pontifícia Universidade Católica do Rio Grande do Sul. Several concern primary sources available in Rio Grande do Sul, particularly in Porto Alegre. While most of the papers focus on slavery, the following are relevant to postemancipation studies: Jorge Euzébio Assumpção, "Idade, sexo, ocupação e nacionalidade dos escravos charqueadores (1780–1888)," which is based on *inventários*; Vera Lúcia Maciel Barroso, "Novas fontes para a história da escravidão negra no RS/USCPM (1850–1900)," on death certificates of slaves and free blacks who were buried in the cemetery of the Santa Casa de Misericórdia de Porto Alegre; Marília Conforto, "Breves considerações sobre a criminalidade escrava segundo o 'Livro de sentenciados' da Casa de Correção de Porto Alegre (1874–1900)"; Dora Isabel Paiva da Costa, "O mercado de escravos na comarca de Bananeiras, Província da Paraíba: 1860–1888"; Rita Gattiboni, "Cartas de alforria em Rio Grande (1874–9/1884–9)"; Ieda Gutfreind, "O negro no Rio Grande do Sul: O vazio historiográfico"; Paulo Roberto S. Moreira, "Os contratados: Uma forma de escravidão disfarçada," based on newspapers and police records; Maria Lúcia de Souza Rangel Ricci, "A Guarda-Negra no contexto brasileiro de final do Século XIX," on a monarchist black militia in Rio de Janeiro, based mainly on newspapers; Liana Maria Reis, "Escravos e abolicionismo na imprensa mineira (1850–1888)"; and Agostinho Maria dalla Vecchia, "Memórias do cativeiro e transição," based on interviews with children and grandchildren of slaves in the southern region of Rio Grande do Sul.

196. Fausto, Bóris. *Trabalho urbano e conflito social.* São Paulo: Difel, 1976. 283 p.

History of Brazilian labor movement in the late nineteenth and early twentieth century, including a discussion of the general strike in São Paulo in 1917.

197. Ferlini, Vera Lúcia do Amaral. "A subordinação dos lavradores de cana aos senhores de engenho." *Revista Brasileira de História* 6 (March–August 1986): 151–67.

Discusses cane farmers in Brazilian Northeast, in colonial period and in nineteenth century, using travelers' accounts, legal rulings, and estate records. *Lavradores* were renters who supplied cane to mills and occupied an ambiguous position within white slaveholding class. The organization of cane farming is relevant to postemancipation tenantry in sugar regions not only in Brazil but elsewhere; essay provides useful definitions and background.

198. Fernandes, Aníbal. *Um senhor de engenho pernambucano.* Rio de Janeiro: Edições o Cruzeiro, 1959. 152 p.

An admiring biography of Antonio da Costa Azevêdo (1882–1950), who rented or owned a variety of *engenhos* in the municipalities of Nazaré and Catende (both in Pernambuco) over the course of his life. Describes politics in Recife and Nazaré in the first decades of the century. Includes occasional anecdotes regarding Costa Azevêdo's harmonious relations with his workers.

199. Fernandes, Hamilton. *Açúcar e álcool ontem e hoje.* Rio de Janeiro: Instituto do Açúcar e do Álcool, 1971. 165 p.

A guide on sugar and alcohol with brief historical information and abundant technical data. Lavishly illustrated with drawings on the evolution of sugar and alcohol making.

200. Flores, Moacyr, org. *Cultura Afro-Brasileira.* Porto Alegre: Escola Superior de Teologia São Lourenço de Brindes, 1980. 64 p.

Brief essays on Afro-Brazilians in Rio Grande do Sul, including the following of interest for postemancipation studies: Dante de Laytano, "O negro no Rio Grande do Sul"; Moacyr Flores, "O Partenon Literário e abolição da escravatura em Porto Alegre"; Pe. Rubens Neis, "A igreja e a abolição da escravatura"; Hélio Moro Mariante, "O negro e o folclore do Rio Grande do Sul."

201. Flory, Thomas. "Race and Social Control in Independent Brazil." *Journal of Latin American Studies* 9 (November 1977): 199–224.

202. Fraga Filho, Walter. *Mendigos, moleques e vadios na Bahia do século XIX.* São Paulo/Salvador: Editora Hucitec/EDUFBA, 1996. 188 p.

While this work focuses on urban life, the final chapter, "A vadiagem reconsiderada," makes suggestions regarding links between rural emancipation and urban migration.

203. Fundação Casa de Rui Barbosa. *O abolicionista Rui Barbosa*. Rio de Janeiro: Fundação Casa de Rui Barbosa, 1988. 112 p.

Collection of six essays on different aspects of abolitionist activity of Rui Barbosa and a chronologically organized bibliography of his published writings on abolition. Essays include Mozart Monteiro, "Rui, Abolicionista"; Homero Pires, "Rui Barbosa e a Abolição dos Escravos"; Brício Filho, "Rui Barbosa e o Abolicionismo"; Antônio Constantino, "Dois Momentos na Vida do Estudante Abolicionista Rui Barbosa"; Américo Jacobina Lacombe, "Rui e a Abolição"; Rejane Mendes Moreira de Almeida Magalhães, "As Idéias Abolicionistas de Rui"; and Eni Valentim Torres, "Roteiro da Atividade Abolicionista de Rui Barbosa."

204. Galvão, Helio. *O mutirão no Nordeste*. Documentário da Vida Rural no. 15. Rio de Janeiro: Ministério da Agricultura, 1959. 75 p.

Study of a form of voluntary, cooperative work usually performed in return for a party thrown for the participants by the person or people who benefit from their work. Associated with labor-intensive projects such as the clearing of fields and the roofing of houses. Book is anecdotal and based largely on printed secondary sources. Focuses on *mutirão* in the Northeast of Brazil but documents the existence of similar practices in other parts of Brazil and the rest of the world. Discusses slavery only to dispute a theory of the African origins of the practice in the Northeast, finding its explanation in human instinct.

205. Gama, Ruy. *Engenho e tecnologia*. São Paulo: Duas Cidades, 1983. 359 p.

Large format, illustrated history of sugar plantation technology, in Brazil and elsewhere, with focus on evolution of the division of labor and of labor productivity. Although the primary focus is on the colonial period and the early nineteenth century, the book contains some photographs of the central mills whose introduction followed emancipation.

206. Garcia Junior, Afrânio Raul. *Terra de trabalho: trabalho familiar de pequenos produtores*. Rio de Janeiro: Paz e Terra, 1983. 236 p.

Volume 8 of the series "Estudos sobre o nordeste," though not necessarily catalogued as such, this anthropological study explores the lives of contemporary peasants at the margins of sugar production in Pernambuco. Uses a mixture of ethnographic and theoretical approaches to explore the links between surplus production, the division of family labor, and household consumption. Provides historical discussion of relationship between large landowners and dependents (*moradores*) as well as somewhat less dependent peasants. Bases historical analysis both on the established secondary literature and on accounts of lesser known local historians.

207. Garcia Junior, Afrânio Raul. *Libres et assujettis: Marché du travail et modes de domination au Nordeste.* Paris: Editions de la Maison des Sciences de l'Homme, 1989. 174 p.

An analysis of the results of anthropological field studies carried out in the 1970s and early 1980s in the sugar region and its periphery in the state of Paraíba in the Brazilian Northeast, particularly the communities of Areia and Remigio. Of particular interest to historians is the analysis of conceptions of freedom among the informants, including the opposition of "free" (*liberto*) and "subjugated" (*sujeito*). The author also signals the social importance of residence within or outside the domain of the plantation, and the impact on agricultural labor relations of the rise of industrial labor markets.

208. Gebara, Ademir. *O mercado de trabalho livre no Brasil (1871–1888).* São Paulo: Editora Brasiliense, 1986. 221 p.

History of the formulation and implementation of law regarding the organization of slavery and the free labor market from the 1871 Law of the Free Womb through final abolition in 1888. Examines legislation on the level of the nation, the province of São Paulo, and the *município* of Campinas. Combines analysis of printed primary and secondary sources with archival research in Great Britain and Brazil, including investigation of the papers of national political figures such as Rio Branco and the records of the Fazenda São Pedro in Campinas.

209. Gomes, Flávio dos Santos. *Histórias de quilombolas: mocambos e comunidades de senzalas no Rio de Janeiro, século XIX.* Rio de Janeiro: Arquivo Nacional, 1995. 431 p.

History of *quilombos* (communities of runaway slaves) in nineteenth-century Rio de Janeiro based on sources including police records, postmortem inventories of property, and records from the Ministério da Justiça and Ministério da Guerra. First two chapters focus on Iguaçu and Vassouras, respectively, treating issues such as the constitution of *quilombos*, their social and economic organization, and relations between *quilombos* and different facets of slave society. Third chapter stresses how lives of *quilombolas* (residents of *quilombos*) and slaves on rural *fazendas* were intertwined, examining the importance of their cooperation in bringing about the end of slavery during the decades leading up to final abolition.

210. Gomes, Núbia Pereira de Magalhães. *Negras raízes mineiras: os Arturos: cem anos da abolição, 1888–1988.* Juiz de Fora: Ministério da Cultura/Editora da Universidade Federal de Juiz de Fora, 1988. 531 p.

Ethnography of a community founded by freedpeople and their descendants in Contagem, Minas Gerais. Focus is primarily contemporary. Includes analysis of religious beliefs and rituals, dances, festivals, and songs, including a commemoration of emancipation by community members. Briefly discusses foundation of the community following abolition of slavery and aspects of nineteenth-century slave society, including lay brotherhoods and music. Contains photographs, song lyrics, diagrams of dances, glossary, and extensive bibliography.

211. Gouvea, Fernando da Cruz. *Abolição: a liberdade veio do norte.* Recife: Fundação Joaquim Nabuco/Editora Massangana, 1988. 292 p.

Political history of abolition based largely on contemporary newspaper accounts.

212. Graden, Dale Thurston. "From Slavery to Freedom in Bahia, Brazil, 1791–1900." Ph.D. diss., University of Connecticut, 1991.

213. Grinberg, Keila. *Liberata: a lei da ambigüidade. As ações de liberdade da Corte de Apelação do Rio de Janeiro, século XIX.* Rio de Janeiro: Relume-Dumará, 1994. 122 p.

Study of attempts by slaves to win their freedom through the courts in the nineteenth century. Based on analysis of 380 suits for the liberty of slaves, or *ações de liberdade,* filed in the Court of Appeals of Rio de Janeiro between 1806 and 1888. Interprets changes in law and legal practice related to emancipation during the nineteenth century, focusing on tensions between slavery and liberalism.

214. Hasenbalg, Carlos Alfredo. *Discriminação e desigualdades raciais no Brasil.* Translated by Patrick Burglin. Rio de Janeiro: Edições Graal, 1979. 302 p.

Portuguese translation of the author's doctoral dissertation from the University of California, titled "Race Relations in Post-Abolition Brazil: The Smooth Preservation of Racial Inequalities." Includes a chapter on the social consequences of abolition and one on racial inequality after abolition.

215. Heredia, Beatriz Maria Alásia de. *A morada da vida: trabalho familiar de pequenos produtores do Nordeste do Brasil.* Rio de Janeiro: Editora Paz e Terra, 1979. 164 p.

Vol. 7 of the series, "Estudos sobre o nordeste," though libraries do not necessarily catalogue it as such. As do other parts of the series, this anthropological study explores a community (Boa Vista) of the *zona da mata* of Pernambuco. Based on participant observation and interviews carried out in 1971. Focuses on the division of family labor among peasant producers who are renters and owners of small holdings in or at the margins of a former sugar estate. Author explores the relationship stemming from the need to produce both for family consumption and for sale in the local market. Some historical discussion of the transition from *moradores* to wage laborers.

216. Holloway, Thomas H. *Immigrants on the Land: Coffee and Society in São Paulo, 1886–1934.* Chapel Hill: University of North Carolina Press, 1980. 218 p.

    History of workers in the coffee economy of São Paulo, with a focus on immigrants.

217. Holloway, Thomas H. *Policing Rio de Janeiro: Repression and Resistance in a 19th-Century City.* Stanford: Stanford University Press, 1993. 369 p.

    History of the police of the city of Rio de Janeiro from 1808 to 1889, including a discussion of the transformation of police work in relation to the abolition of slavery.

218. Huggins, Martha Knisely. *From Slavery to Vagrancy in Brazil: Crime and Social Control in the Third World.* New Brunswick, N.J.: Rutgers University Press, 1985. 183 p.

    Concentrates on Recife, Pernambuco, between the 1850s and 1920s.

219. Hutchinson, Harry William. *Village and Plantation Life in Northeastern Brazil.* Seattle: University of Washington Press, 1957. 199 p.

    Community study of the town of São Francisco do Conde (the name of which author changes to "Vila Recôncavo") in Bahia. Based on anthropological research carried out from 1950 to 1951, the volume explores the differences in labor relations and daily life on a privately owned "plantation" and a corporate *usina*, with some information on occupational hierarchies and wage structures. Provides separate chapters on town and family life, religion, and the correlations between race and class in rural society.

220. Kliemann, Luiza H. Schmitz. *RS: terra e poder, história da questão agrária.* Porto Alegre: Mercado Aberto, 1986. 173 p.

History of conflict over land in Rio Grande do Sul, covering the years between 1850 and 1930. Focuses on the role of European immigrants. Based on a variety of primary sources. Notable for its use of German-language newspapers.

221. Kossoy, Boris, and Maria Luiza Tucci Carneiro. *O olhar europeu: o negro na iconografia brasileira do século XIX*. São Paulo: Editora da Universidade de São Paulo, 1994. 235 p.

Collection of paintings, sketches, and photographs of black people in Brazil by Europeans who visited the country in the nineteenth century. Includes reproductions of the work of Jean-Baptiste Debret, Victor Frond, Paul Harro-Harring, and Johann Moritz Regendas. Book is divided into sections with themes such as categories of identity among slaves (physical marks denoting ethnicity, clothing styles, etc.), different kinds of slave work, urban slavery, and slave markets. Section entitled "The Photographic Portrait" includes a photograph of a freedwoman and portraits of others whom the editors suggest may have been ex-slaves. Book begins and concludes with brief essays by the editors on the European representation of blacks in Brazil in the nineteenth and early twentieth centuries. List of sources includes thorough documentation for each of the images that appears in the book.

222. Kowarick, Lúcio. *Trabalho e vadiagem: a origem do trabalho livre no Brasil*. 2d ed. Rio de Janeiro: Paz e Terra, 1994. 124 p.

Sociological essay on the formation of the free working population in the late nineteenth and early twentieth centuries, including both national and immigrant workers. Based largely on secondary sources.

223. Kraay, Hendrik, ed. *Afro-Brazilian Culture and Politics. Bahia, 1790s to 1990s*. Armonk, N.Y.: M. E. Sharpe, 1998. 208 p.

Essays of special interest for postemancipation studies in this collection include Hendrik Kraay's study of the black militia during the independence period, Mary Ann Mahony's study of postemancipation struggles over land on the "cacao frontier," and Kim Butler's afterword on patterns of Afro-Bahian politics.

224. Lago, Luiz Aranha Corrêa do. "O surgimento da escravidão e a transição para o trabalho livre no Brasil: um modelo teórico simples e uma visão de longo prazo." *Revista Brasileira de Economia* 42, 4 (October–December 1988): 317–69.

225. Lanna, Ana Lúcia Duarte. "O café e o trabalho 'livre' em Minas Gerais—1870/1920." *Revista brasileira de história* 6 (March/August 1986): 73–88.

Discusses free labor in coffee regions of Minas Gerais, emphasizes importance of 'national' laborers and contrasts with use of immigrants in São Paulo. Analyzes debates in agricultural congresses. Examines sharecropping, wage labor, and seasonal migration.

226. Lanna, Ana Lúcia Duarte. *A transformação do trabalho*. Campinas: Editora da UNICAMP, 1988. 124 p.

Discusses transition from slave to free labor in *zona da mata* coffee region of Minas Gerais, between 1870s and the turn of the century. Compares Minas Gerais with São Paulo, where immigrant labor was used on a scale unknown in the former. In Minas Gerais sharecroppers, temporary wage laborers, seasonal migrants, and a reduced number of immigrant *colonos* formed the postemancipation labor force. Author notes that government reports and other official sources do not identify ex-slaves as a distinct group, but she argues that most sharecroppers *(parceiros)* were ex-slaves, based on a selective look at police and court records between 1891 and 1899, in which color is mentioned. Based mainly on presidential reports and other government reports, as well as primary published works.

227. Lessa, Renato. *A invenção republicana: Campos Sales, as bases e a decadência da Primeira República brasileira*. São Paulo: Vértice/Rio de Janeiro: Instituto de Pesquisas do Rio de Janeiro, 1988. 173 p.

History of the formation of the Brazilian state during the First Republic with a focus on the career of Manoel Ferraz de Campos Sales. Discusses relations between the national and state governments, the construction of citizenship, and changing concepts of political order.

228. Levine, Robert M. *Vale of Tears: Revisiting the Canudos Massacre in Northeastern Brazil, 1893–1897*. Berkeley: University of California Press, 1992. 353 p.

History of the millenarian settlement of Canudos, located in the backlands *(sertão)* of Bahia, and its destruction by Brazilian military forces in 1897.

229. Libby, Douglas Cole. *Transformação e trabalho em uma economia escravista: Minas Gerais no século xix*. São Paulo: Editora Brasiliense, 1988. 404 p.

Study focused on the period between 1830 and 1889, emphasizing the importance of slavery in the economy of Minas Gerais up to 1880. Discusses inefficacy of efforts to reduce access by rural population to open lands and limited character of proletarianization. Major focus is on economic and demographic history, with emphasis on mining, metalworking, and "domestic textile industry," as well as agriculture. Uses archival data to develop wage series and a comprehensive demographic analysis. Contains statistical appendices, extensive bibliography.

230. Lima, Lana Lage da Gama. *Rebeldia negra e abolicionismo*. Rio de Janeiro: Achiamé, 1981. 165 p.

History of the relationship between slave resistance and abolitionism with a focus on the municipality of Campos, in the province of Rio de Janeiro. Based mainly on manuscript sources located in the Biblioteca Pública de Niterói.

231. Linhares, Maria Yedda Leite. *Terra prometida: uma história da questão agrária no Brasil*. Rio de Janeiro: Editora Campus, 1999. 211 p.

232. Lobo, Luiza. "A pioneira maranhense Maria Firmina dos Reis." *Estudos Afro-Asiáticos* 16 (1989): 91–100.

Discusses the work of mulatto romantic author Maria F. Reis (1825–1917), considered the first female abolitionist writer of fiction. She spent most of her adult life as a teacher in the village of Guimarães, in Maranhão, where she taught the sons of local farmers and ranchers. She wrote an intimate, melancholic diary written dating from 1853 to 1903 in which the themes of religious self-denial, death, and suicide recur.

233. Lopes, José Sérgio Leite. *O vapor do diabo: o trabalho dos operários do açúcar*. 2d ed. Rio de Janeiro: Paz e Terra, 1978. 220 p.

A study of sugar mill workers in Pernambuco in the early 1970s. Includes much information on everyday work life, different categories of workers, and the attitudes of workers. Based primarily on interviews with workers and union officers. Although the data are contemporary, the work is useful for historical purposes, both for the precise discussion of categories of work, and for its analysis of class relations.

234. Luna, Luiz. *O negro na luta contra a escravidão*. Rio de Janeiro: Leitura, 1968. 237 p.

Collection of synthetic essays on the history of slavery and slave resistance, including a brief discussion of the economic and social situation of former slaves after abolition.

235. Machado, Maria Helena. *O plano e o pânico: os movimentos sociais na década da abolição*. Rio de Janeiro: Editora Universidade Federal do Rio de Janeiro/São Paulo: Editora da Universidade de São Paulo, 1994. 259 p.

History of connections between slave revolts in rural areas and urban abolitionism in the provinces of São Paulo and Rio de Janeiro in the

1880s. Investigates politics, religious practice, and economic aspirations of rural slaves and *libertos*, including former slaves' rejection of supervised gang labor, their efforts to acquire access to land, and their preference for growing crops for local consumption. Discusses collaboration between slaves and abolitionists based in cities, especially in Santos, whose ranks included *libertos*, free people of color, and radical immigrants. Analyzes reforms advocated by antislavery activists, whose political vision was largely thwarted upon the establishment of the Republic. Makes extensive use of police records.

236. Machado, Maria Helena. *Crime e escravidão. Trabalho, luta e resistência nas lavouras paulistas, 1830–1888*. São Paulo: Brasiliense, 1987. 134 p.

Study of criminal records involving slaves in São Paulo, focusing on Campinas and Taubaté. Discusses masters' strategies of domination and slave resistance as well as slaves' conceptions of justice and rights during final years of slavery.

237. Maciel, Cleber da Silva. *Discriminações raciais: negros em Campinas (1888–1921)*. Campinas: Editora da UNICAMP, 1987. 209 p.

Studies racism in postemancipation period (1888–1926) in coffee-producing township of Campinas, São Paulo. Explores outcome of policies which, since the earliest "threats" of abolition, had excluded people of color in the search for a suitable substitute labor force. Notes employers' overwhelming preference for European immigrants in all occupations, including those in which slaves had been the mainstay. Discusses demographic decline of population of color as well as socioeconomic milieu in which nonwhite population lived. Relies heavily on newspapers, especially on the black and mulatto press.

238. Mahony, Mary Ann. "The World Cacao Made: Society, Politics, and History in Southern Bahia, Brazil, 1822–1919." Ph.D. diss., Yale University, 1996.

239. Mahony, Mary Ann. "Afro-Brazilians, Land Reform, and the Question of Social Mobility in Southern Bahia, 1880–1920." *Luso-Brazilian Review* 34 (winter 1997): 59–79.

Study of the implications of 1897 land law in Bahia for Afro-Brazilians involved in cacao cultivation, with a focus on the Bahian *município* of Ilhéus.

240. Maia, Eduardo Santos. *O banditismo na Bahia (contos da minha terra). Trechos de história e geographia e o relato verídico de lendas, factos e tradições regionaes*, 1928. 258 p.

Twenty-one impressionistic essays on Bahia focusing on the city of Belmonte and rural areas. Describes different aspects of popular culture, including the celebration of Christmas, *sambas*, and burial practices. Critiques rural agricultural techniques and portrays the working lives of *canoeiros*, or boatmen, on the Jequitinhonha River. Discussion of bandits draws on contemporary theories of race and criminality in recounting the exploits of local strongmen, or *coroneis*, and their followers.

241. Maia, Nayala de Souza Ferreira. *Açúcar e transição para o trabalho livre em Pernambuco, 1874–1902.* Recife: Fundação Antonio dos Santos Abranches-FASA, 1985.

Case study of the Colônia Agrícola Industrial Orfanológica Isabel, founded in 1874 in Pernambuco. The government-sponsored colony, which lasted thirty years, was initially aimed at caring for orphans and creating a skilled free labor force for the sugar industry. Colony is particularly interesting for its effort to organize sugar production by first establishing *lavradores* and then transforming them into *fornecedores de cana* for a model sugar central. Based on governors' reports and archival materials. Contains appendix of the 1904 discussion of the experiment in the local press.

242. Martins, José de Souza. *O cativeiro da terra.* São Paulo: Editora Hucitec, 1986. 157 p.

Examines São Paulo coffee plantations after abolition and use of nonwage *colono* labor. Analyzes forms of labor relations on large farms, in particular the *colonato* system of family labor. Based on secondary and published primary sources.

243. Martins, José de Souza. *A imigração e a crise do Brasil agrário.* São Paulo: Pioneira, 1973. 222 p.

Study of European immigration to São Paulo in the late nineteenth and early twentieth centuries. Based on archival research in governmental and landholding records in São Paulo as well as secondary sources. Discusses the implications of emancipation for state immigration policy. Based on a case study of São Caetano, a community of Italian immigrants or *colonos* founded on the outskirts of the city of São Paulo in 1877. Argues that while *colonos* sometimes became important producers of foodstuffs for local consumption, they were mostly frustrated in their aspirations to independent land proprietorship, becoming dependent instead on employment by large planters or in the growing industrial sector of São Paulo.

244. Mattos, Hebe Maria. *Ao sul da história: lavradores pobres na crise do trabalho escravo*. São Paulo: Brasiliense, 1987. 190 p.

Study of the coexistence of slave-based agriculture with a free population of poor, small-scale cultivators in the municipality of Capivary, in rural Rio de Janeiro, from the demise of the slave trade in the 1850s to the final abolition of slavery in 1888. Documentation consulted includes property registries, censuses, and wills. Final chapter uses censuses and oral history to discuss landholding practices, labor relations, and migration patterns from abolition into the early twentieth century.

245. Mattos, Hebe Maria. *Das cores do silêncio: os significados da liberdade no sudeste escravista, Brasil Século XIX*. Rio de Janeiro: Nova Fronteira, 1998. 379 p.

History of abolition and postemancipation society in the rural Southeast, including regions of Minas Gerais, Rio de Janeiro, and São Paulo where slavery remained economically important until final abolition. Based on sources including the testimony of slaves in criminal records, suits for the liberty of individual slaves (*ações de liberdade*), postmortem inventories of property, and records related to conflict over land. Part I discusses slave society in the second half of the nineteenth century, analyzing physical mobility among slaves, familial ties between slaves and free people, and deployment of color categories in official records. Part II discusses slavery on large *fazendas* during the last decade of slavery. Part III investigates masters' attempts to control the process of emancipation through selective manumission and the frustration of those efforts by slaves. Part IV examines postemancipation struggles between former masters, ex-slaves, immigrants, and previously free native workers with a geographical focus on the north of the state of Rio de Janeiro. Notes importance of former slaves' labor in agricultural production through the 1890s and investigates how former slaves understood citizenship and sought to improve working conditions. A brief summary of Mattos's findings is available in Spanish in "El color inexistente. Relaciones raciales y trabajo rural en Rio de Janeiro tras la abolición de la esclavitud," *Historia Social* 22 (1995): 83–100. (Note: works by Mattos, formerly Mattos de Castro, are sometimes alphabetized under Castro.)

246. Mattos, Hebe Maria. *Escravidão e cidadania no Brasil monárquico*. Rio de Janeiro: Jorge Zahar, 2000. 74 p.

Synthetic overview of the history of concepts of citizenship and race in Brazil from the promulgation of the Constitution of 1824 to the demise of the Empire in 1889.

247. Mattoso, Kátia M. de Queirós. *Família e sociedade na Bahia do século XIX*. São Paulo: Editora Corrupio, 1988. 212 p.

Discusses white, *mestiço*, and black family structures and family life. Sees the family as the basic and the most dynamic mechanism of collective solidarity and of interclass control, based on extremely flexible laws and values.

248. Mattoso, Kátia M. de Queirós. *Testamentos de escravos libertos na Bahia no século XIX: uma fonte para o estudo de mentalidades*. Salvador: Centro de Estudos Baianos da Universidade Federal da Bahia, 1979. 53 p.

Based on wills of former slaves.

249. Mattoso, Kátia M. de Queirós. *Bahia: a cidade de Salvador e seu mercado no século XIX*. São Paulo: Editora HUCITEC/Salvador: Departamento de Assuntos Culturais, Secretaria Municipal de Educação e Cultura, 1978. 387 p.

Classic work of urban history.

250. Mattoso, Katia M. de Queirós. *Bahia, século XIX: uma província no Império*. Rio de Janeiro: Editora Nova Fronteira, 1992. 747 p.

Comprehensive history of Bahia in the nineteenth century with focus on years before the foundation of the Republic in 1889. Divided into seven parts devoted to different aspects of the region's history, including geography, demography, family, the state, church, everyday life, and the economy. Of particular interest to scholars of postemancipation society are discussions of family structure of slaves and *libertos* before final emancipation (based on *cartas de alforria*, wills, and postmortem inventories of property), pre-emancipation marriage strategies of *libertos*, the church's position regarding emancipation and provision of charity to former slaves, and religious practice among slaves and free blacks. Analysis of labor market (chapter 28) notes landowners' opposition to landholding by immigrants and descendants of slaves, workers' aversion to agricultural fieldwork (especially in sugar), and changes in organization of labor after final abolition.

251. Mendonça, Joseli Maria Nunes. *Entre a mão e os anéis: a lei dos sexagenários e os caminhos da abolição no Brasil*. Campinas: Editora da Unicamp, 1999. 417 p.

History of struggles over the creation and implementation of the "Lei dos Sexagenários," the 1885 law that granted conditional freedom to slaves over sixty years of age. With a focus on the region of Campinas, illustrates how legal measures intended to slow abolition, such as the right of masters to indemnization, could be used by opponents of slavery, including slaves themselves, to further emancipation through the courts. Based primarily on the records of the Brazilian parliament and the Tribunal Judiciário de Campinas. Covers the period between 1871 and 1888, with a focus on the 1880s.

252. Mello, Evaldo Cabral de. *O Norte agrário e o Império, 1871–1889.* Rio de Janeiro: Editora Nova Fronteira, 1984. 298 p.

Concerns relations between the sugar- and cotton-producing regions of northern Brazil and the national government during the last two decades of the empire. Focuses especially on policies of the national government regarding credit, tariffs, modernization of sugar mills, transportation infrastructure, and changes in labor regimes. Includes a chapter on the controversy about interprovincial slave traffic and another chapter on the relationship of the North to immigration policy. The main sources used are annals of the Câmara and Senate and the *relatórios* of cabinet ministers.

253. Mendes, J. E. Teixeira and José de Castro Mendes. *Lavoura cafeeira paulista. Velhas fazendas do município de Campinas.* São Paulo: Departamento Estadual de Informações, 1947.

Collection of fifty-four black-and-white reproductions of watercolors by José de Castro Mendes of coffee *fazendas* in Campinas. No date given for the paintings but a brief introduction by J. E. Texeira Mendes states that pictures represent *fazendas* in their contemporary state, around 1947. Included are numerous paintings of *senzalas, casas grandes* or *sedes*, and outbuildings. Accompanying titles identify the subject of each picture and the *fazenda* where painted. Focus is on architecture, not buildings' inhabitants, although one picture portrays an unnamed 105-year-old woman who was once a slave.

254. Meyer, Doris Rinaldi. *A terra do santo e o mundo dos engenhos: estudo de uma comunidade rural nordestina.* Rio de Janeiro: Editora Paz e Terra, 1979. 186 p.

Anthropological study of a contemporary rural village in Pernambuco located on the land of an *engenho*. The author is particularly interested in relations between villagers and the owner of the *engenho* and in relations between the village and small farms in the surrounding area worked by villagers. Includes some discussion of the historical origins of the small farms and of the village itself. The book, including historical interpretation, is based primarily on participant-observation and interviews with village residents.

255. Milliet, Sérgio. *Roteiro do café e outros ensaios*. São Paulo: Coleção Departamento de Cultura, 1939. 186 p.

Collection of historical essays on São Paulo addressing topics such as coffee cultivation, landholding practices, and the making of censuses. Contains numerous maps and tables including information on coffee production and population.

256. Mitchell, Simon, ed. *The Logic of Poverty: The Case of the Brazilian Northeast*. London: Routledge and Kegan Paul, 1981. 189 p.

Collection of eight essays on poverty in the Northeast in the twentieth century. Contributors focus primarily on the contemporary Northeast with the exception of Jaime Reis, whose "Hunger in the Northeast: Some Historical Aspects" combines secondary and primary sources (including census materials, newspapers, and travelers' accounts) to document a decline in the nutritional value of the diet of unskilled laborers in the sugar zone of Pernambuco between 1870 and 1920.

257. Monbeig, Pierre. *Pionniers et planteurs de São Paulo*. Paris: Librairie Armand Colin, 1952. 376 p.

Focus is the spread of coffee and the attendant settlement and labor patterns in São Paulo as seen through an "Annales school" approach. Explores the "marche pionnière" (or the westward advance of coffee) in stages: the period between 1900 and 1905; the crisis of 1929; and the post-1929 period. Contains a chapter about the health conditions of the rural sector.

258. Monteiro, Anita de Queiróz. *Castainho: etnografia de um bairro rural de negros*. Recife: Fundação Joaquim Nabuco, Editora Massangana, 1985. 94 p.

259. Monteiro, Hamilton de Mattos. *Nordeste insurgente, 1850–1890*. 2nd ed. São Paulo: Editora Brasiliense, 1981. 99 p.

260. Morel, Edmar. *Vendaval da liberdade: a luta do povo pela abolição*. 3rd ed. São Paulo: Global, 1988. 231 p.

History of the abolitionist movement focusing on life of Francisco José do Nascimento. Based on secondary and printed primary sources.

261. Mott, Maria Lúcia de Barros. *Submissão e resistência: a mulher na luta contra a escravidão*. São Paulo: Editora Contexto, 1991. 86 p.

Discussion of the role of women in struggles against slavery.

262. Motta Sobrinho, Alves. *A civilização do café (1820–1920)*. São Paulo: Editora Brasiliense, 1968. 184 p.

History of the coffee industry in the Paraíba Valley in Rio de Janeiro from the early nineteenth century through the industry's decline in the late nineteenth and early twentieth centuries. Based largely on printed primary and secondary sources and papers of Moreira Lima family, who were among the most important landowners in the valley in the second half of the nineteenth century. Includes brief accounts of a violent conflict between ex-slaves and slaveowners in the village of Cruzeiro in 1875, the abolitionist activities of Antônio Bento, the labor shortage faced by planters after final abolition in 1888, and subsequent attempts to attract European immigrants to the valley. Presents a listing of the number of slaves in the Paraíba Valley in 1884 organized by *município*. Concludes with transcriptions of selected letters and documents from the business correspondence of the Moreira Lima family from 1862 and 1896 as well as the 1879 will of Joaquim José Moreira Lima.

263. Motta, Márcia. *Nas fronteiras do poder: conflitos de terras e direito agrário no Brasil de meados do século XIX*. Rio de Janeiro: Vício de Leitura, 1998. 247 p.

264. Motta, Roberto, coord. *Os afro-brasileiros: anais do III Congresso Afro-Brasileiro*. Recife: Fundação Joaquim Nabuco/ Editora Massangana, 1985. 159 p.

Edited proceedings of the third Afro-Brazilian Congress, held in Recife, Pernambuco, in 1982. Contains brief scholarly essays, without footnotes, on various topics in the history of slavery and Afro-Brazilians. Includes transcript of discussion of "Estudos Afro-Negros no Brasil" by historian Thales de Azevedo, sociologist Carlos Hasenbalg, and others. Useful as an overview of changing scholarly interpretations of Afro-Brazilian history and culture in the early 1980s.

265. Moura, Clóvis. "O negro após a abolição." *Revista de História e Arte* 10 (1977): 45–64.

Compares the situation of Afro-Brazilians before and after abolition and discusses the continuing role of racial discrimination in Brazilian society.

266. Moura, Clóvis. *Os quilombos e a rebelião negra*. 3rd ed. São Paulo: Editora Brasiliense, 1983. 100 p.

Synthetic history of *quilombos* (communities of runaway slaves) in Brazil, with a brief discussion of the role of *quilombos* in the abolition of slavery.

267. Moura, Margarida Maria. *Os deserdados da terra. A lógica costumeira e judicial dos processos de expulsão e invasão da terra camponesa no sertão de Minas Gerais.* Rio de Janeiro: Bertrand Brasil, 1988. 250 p.

Anthropological study of contemporary conflicts over land, relations of dependence, customary law, and the judicial system in the Valley of Jequitinhonha, a region of Minas Gerais characterized by cattle ranching. Potentially useful for interpreting prior struggles over parallel issues.

268. Moura, Margarida Maria. "The Customary Relationship of Agregação on Brazilian Fazendas." *Journal of Legal Pluralism and Unofficial Law* 23 (1985): 129–51.

Focuses mainly on contemporary changes in *agregação* and efforts of *agregados* to prevent eviction in the Jequitinhonha Valley of Minas Gerais. Description of customary relations between *agregados* and *fazendeiros* and of notions of right and entitlement held by *agregados* could be useful for studies of the early twentieth century. Also includes information on the kinds of work done by the wives and children of male *agregados*. Based on interviews and union and court documents.

269. Naro, Nancy Priscilla Smith. "Customary Rightholders and Legal Claimants to Land in Rio de Janeiro, Brazil, 1870–1890." *The Americas* 48 (April 1992): 485–517.

Study of the role of struggles over land in the transition from slavery to free labor in rural Rio de Janeiro, with a focus on the *municípios* of Vassouras and Rio Bonito.

270. *Negras imagens: ensaios sobre cultura e escravidão no Brasil.* São Paulo: Estação Ciência, Universidade de São Paulo, 1996. 236 p.

271. Nequete, Lenine. *O escravo na jurisprudência brasileira: magistratura e ideologia no segundo reinado.* Porto Alegre: Centenário da Abolição, 1988. 352 p.

Discusses different aspects of Brazilian law related to slavery from 1850 to 1888, including the legal avenues for emancipation available to slaves, such as self-purchase and *ações de liberdade*. Based mainly on printed primary sources, including compilations of laws and legal journals.

272. Nishida, Mieko. "Manumission and Ethnicity in Urban Slavery: Salvador, Brazil, 1808–1888." *Hispanic American Historical Review* 73, 3 (August 1993): 361–91.

Draws on author's doctoral dissertation on Salvador, Bahia.

273. Nogueira, Oracy. *Tanto preto quanto branco: estudos de relações raciais.* São Paulo: T. A. Queiroz, 1985. 133 p.

Republishes the essay "Preconceito racial de marca e preconceito racial de origem" (originally presented in a 1954 congress) by one of Brazil's pioneers in the field of race relations. The twenty-seven page piece provides a comparative exploration both of the literature and the author's conclusions (based on participant observation) of race relations in the United States and Brazil. Volume includes introductory essay written by author in 1979 that places the essay in a more recent intellectual context as well as a second essay on racist hiring practices in domestic sector in São Paulo in the early 1940s.

274. Nonato, Raimundo. *História social da abolição em Mossoró.* Rio Grande do Norte: Edição do Centenário/Coleção Mossoroense, 1983. 305 p.

Celebratory account of abolition of slavery in 1883 in Mossoró, a *município* of Rio Grande do Norte. Based largely on secondary sources, newspapers, and other printed primary sources. Focuses on activities of Sociedade Libertadora Mossoroense.

275. Novais, Fernando, Coord. *História da vida privada no Brasil.* Vol. 2. *Império e a modernidade nacional.* Edited by Luiz Felipe de Alencastro. São Paulo: Companhia das Letras, 1997. 523 p.

Second of a collection of volumes on the history of private life in Brazil. Of special interest in this volume, which covers the period from independence through the end of the Empire, are João José Reis, "O cotidiano da morte no Brasil oitocentista," which includes a discussion of slave burial customs in the nineteenth century; Katia M. de Queirós Mattoso, "A opulência da Bahia," which includes a short discussion of the relations between slaves and *libertos* in nineteenth-century Bahia; Ana Maria Mauad, "Imagem e auto-imagen do Segundo Reinado," which briefly addresses changes in portrait photography after abolition; Robert W. Slenes, "Senhores e subalternos no oeste paulista," which analyzes power relations between planters, slaves, and immigrant workers in the west of São Paulo province mainly in the second half of the nineteenth century; and Hebe M. Mattos de Castro, "Laços de família e direitos no final da escravidão," which addresses topics including the role of family ties between the enslaved and free in manumissions, struggles between former masters and former slaves, and relations between *libertos* and freeborn citizens after abolition.

276. Olinto, Antônio. *Brasileiros na África*. 2d edition. São Paulo: Edições GRD, 1980. 324 p.

Discusses author's visit to Nigeria and contemporary links between Brazil and Africa. Includes extensive information on persons of Brazilian descent living in Nigeria, some of them descendants of former slaves. Contains some interviews, genealogical information. Author has written a thesis and a novel on subject of Brazilian slaves who returned to Africa.

277. Oliveira, Francisco de. *O elo perdido: classe e identidade de classe*. São Paulo: Brasiliense, 1987. 134 p.

An economist discusses ethnic and class identity in Bahia since abolition. Argues that ethnic identity, constructed primarily around religion, inhibited class solidarity and social conflict. Largely based on secondary sources.

278. Oliveira, Maria Inês Côrtes de. *O liberto: seu mundo e os outros*. São Paulo: Corrupio, 1988. 111 p.

A study of freedpeople in Salvador, Bahia, from the beginning of the nineteenth century to general emancipation in 1888. Covers process of individual manumissions, freedpersons' family patterns, property, religious life, and attitudes toward death. Based on ex-slaves' wills.

279. Olszewski Filha, Sofia. *A fotografia e o negro na cidade do Salvador, 1840–1914*. Salvador: Empresa Gráfica da Bahia and Fundação Cultural do Estado da Bahia, 1988. 131 p.

A study of how people of color were seen through studio cameras of the period. Contains twenty-nine photographs.

280. Orico, Oswaldo. *O tigre da abolição*. Rio de Janeiro: Civilização Brasileira, 1977. 308 p.

Biography of abolitionist José do Patrocínio.

281. Passos Subrinho, Josué Modesto dos. "Desagregação do escravismo e transição para o trabalho livre na província de Sergipe." *Estudos Econômicos* 24 (September–December 1994): 465–93.

Study of the transition from slave to free labor in the province of Sergipe. Based mainly on secondary sources, with a focus on access to land and labor supply.

282. Pedro, Joana Maria, Ligia de Oliveira Czesnat, Luiz Felipe Falcão, Orivalda Lima e Silva, Paulino Francisco de Jesus Cardoso, Rosângela Miranda Cherem. *Negro em terra de branco: escravidão e preconceito em*

Santa Catarina no século XIX. Porto Alegre: Mercado Aberto, 1988. 64 p.

Short book about antiblack prejudice among whites in Santa Catarina during the final decades of slavery. Includes a chapter on abolition. Based mainly on newspapers and municipal records.

283. Perruci, Gadiel. *A república das usinas: um estudo de história social e econômica do Nordeste: 1889–1930.* Rio de Janeiro: Editora Paz e Terra, 1978. 246 p.

An economic history concentrating on the production and commercialization of sugar and other agricultural products in Northeastern Brazil, especially Pernambuco, during the first republic. Includes much quantitative data on prices, exports, population, investment (domestic and foreign, especially French), industrial production, and so on. Primary sources used include Pernambuco newspapers, government publications, and documents found in the archives of the French foreign ministry.

284. Perruci, Gadiel. "Estrutura e conjuntura da economia açucareira no nordeste do Brasil, 1889–1930." *Anais do VIII Simpósio Nacional dos Professores Universitários de História* 8 (1976): 107–44.

Analyzes sugar production in the Brazilian Northeast during the First Republic (1889–1930) in order to point to structural problems that contributed to the underdevelopment of the region. Uses primary and secondary sources to explore the contradictions first of the central mill system and then of the *usinas.*

285. Pesavento, Sandra Jatahy. *Emergência dos subalternos: trabalho livre e ordem burguesa.* Porto Alegre: Editora da Universidade Federal do Rio Grande do Sul and FAPERGS, 1989. 84 p.

On search by elites for new forms of domination over workers after slave emancipation in Rio Grande do Sul. Concentrates on debates about emancipation and ex-slaves found in newspapers.

286. Pinho, José Wanderley de Araújo. *História de um engenho do Recôncavo: Matoim, Novo Caboto, Freguesia: 1552–1944.* 2d. ed. São Paulo: Companhia Editora Nacional, 1982. 601 p.

Lengthy historical study of the Engenho Freguesia in Matoim, Bahia. This is as much a history of one portion of the Recôncavo as it is of one *engenho.* Emphasis is on the pre-emancipation period though author used rare daybook records from the last years of the nineteenth century to trace the demise of the plantation's milling operations and the eventual rental of its lands to farmers growing cane for central *usinas.* Scattered information regarding sugar prices and wages.

287. Pinto, Maria Inez Machado Borges. *Cotidiano e sobrevivência: a vida do trabalhador pobre na cidade de São Paulo, 1890–1914.* São Paulo: Universidade de São Paulo, 1994. 260 p.

History of poor working population in the city of São Paulo from 1890 to World War I. Based largely on contemporary newspapers, addresses questions such as immigration policy, the creation of a casual labor force, and the working conditions and leisure practices of the urban poor. Discussion of emancipation is brief, with focus mainly on the experiences of European immigrants.

288. Pinto, Regina Pahim. "Movimento negro e etnicidade." *Estudos Afro-Asiáticos* 19 (1990): 109–24.

Analysis of São Paulo's black press and the formation of the Brazilian Negro Front between c. 1900 and 1937. Black Paulista press, in author's view, condemned or was silent about aspects of "black culture" such as Afro-Brazilian religion and encouraged readers to adopt mainstream Brazilian values.

289. Porto Alegre, Sylvia. "'Fome de braços': questão nacional. Notas sobre o trabalho livre no Nordeste no século XIX." *Revista de Ciências Sociais* 16/17 (1985–1986): 105–42.

Overview of the decline of slavery in the Northeast, struggles over plantation labor supply, and out-migration from the Northeast to São Paulo, Rio de Janeiro, and Amazônia, focusing primarily on the period between 1830 and 1940. Gathers statistics related to slavery, the export economy, free labor, and internal migration from a variety of printed primary and secondary sources. (See below for citation to second part of the article.)

290. Porto Alegre, Sylvia. "'Fome de braços': questão nacional; notas sobre o trabalho livre no Nordeste do século XIX." *Cadernos C.E.R.U.* 2 (1988): 67–91.

Second part of article cited above.

291. Proença Filho, Domício. "A participação da literatura no processo abolicionista." *Revista Tempo Brasileiro* 92/93 (January/June 1988): 9–32.

Author discusses how both romantic and realistic nineteenth-century Brazilian abolitionist fiction saw slaves as unprotected, humble, sometimes noble and loyal, but always dehumanized. Abolitionist writers emphasized the role of slaves as victims who did not react, transferring the agency of the struggle against slavery to free people. Discusses novelists and poets such as Gonçalves Dias, José de Alencar, Joaquim Manuel de Macedo, Trajano Galvão de Carvalho, Francisco Leite Bittencourt

Sampaio, Fagundes Varela, Castro Alves, Luís Gama, José do Patrocínio, Bernardo Guimarães, Aluísio de Azevedo, Machado de Assis, Cruz e Souza. Critique is useful if one wishes to use fictional materials as a historical source.

292. Queiroz, Renato S. *Caipiras negros no Vale do Ribeira: um estudo de antropologia econômica*. São Paulo: Faculdade de Filosofia, Letras e Ciências Humanas/Universidade de São Paulo, 1983. 166 p.

Ethnography of a rural community of people of African descent located in the Vale do Ribeira, on the southern coast of the state of São Paulo. While focus is contemporary, book includes a discussion of changes in agricultural practices, ritual celebrations, family organization, and the phenomenon of *mutirão* (a system of mutual aid among community members based on unpaid, cooperative labor) in the nineteenth century and the first half of the twentieth century. Based primarily on interviews with community members.

293. Queiroz, Suely Robles Reis de. *A abolição da escravidão*. São Paulo: Brasiliense, 1981. 97 p.

Synthetic overview of the history of slavery and abolition in the nineteenth century.

294. Ramos, Arthur. *O folclore negro do Brasil: demopsicologia e psicanálise*. Rio de Janeiro: Casa do Estudante do Brasil, 1954. 264 p.

Psychoanalytical and anthropological interpretations of the Afro-Brazilian "collective unconscious" through the study of religion, dance, music, popular feasts and short stories. Based on primary observations and secondary sources. Seeks to identify diverse African origins of these cultural phenomena. Originally published in 1935, the material, although usually undated, reflects on Afro-Brazilian culture after emancipation.

295. Ramos, Arthur. *O negro brasileiro*. São Paulo: Companhia Editora Nacional, 1940. 434 p.

A study of Afro-Brazilian religion in the first decades of the twentieth century as well as historical background and African origins. Discusses pantheon of gods, rituals, hierarchy, dance, music, and syncretism. Presents what the author calls a "psychoanalytic exegesis" of that religion.

296. Reis, J. J., and E. Silva. *Negociação e conflito. A resistência negra no Brasil escravista*. São Paulo: Companhia das Letras, 1989. 151 p.

Collection of archive-based articles related to the history of slave resistance and negotiation. Focused mainly on Bahia in the first half of the nineteenth century.

297. Reis, Jaime. "Abolition and the Economics of Slaveholding in North East Brazil." *Boletín de Estudios Latino-Americanos y del Caribe* 17 (1983): 3–20.

298. Reis, João José, and Flávio dos Santos Gomes, org. *Liberdade por um fio*. São Paulo: Companhia das Letras, 1996. 509 p.

Collection of eighteen major essays, most based on primary sources, concerning *quilombos* (communities of runaway slaves) located in various parts of Brazil. Includes discussions of small and medium-sized settlements near cities or plantations as well as classic examples of more isolated fortified communities. The majority of the case studies are from the colonial period, although Matthias Röhrig Assunção and Euripedes Funes discuss *quilombos* in Maranhão and the lower Amazon valley up to the eve of final abolition. The authors' approaches to linkages between runaways and surrounding society are relevant to settlements that persisted beyond emancipation.

299. Reis, João José, ed. *Escravidão e invenção da liberdade: estudos sobre o negro no Brasil*. São Paulo: Editora Brasiliense, 1988. 323 p.

Collection of essays on slavery, emancipation, and Afro-Brazilian culture, primarily in Bahia. Part I treats life under slavery, and includes essays on punishment, godparenthood, manumission, and slave rebellions. Part II treats oppression, resistance, and the "invention of liberty," and includes essays on carnival, candomblé, and Afro-Brazilian social movements. Particularly relevant to postemancipation society are the essay by Renato da Silveira, on Bahian culture, and the essay by Peter Fry, Sérgio Carrara and Ana Luiza Martins-Costa entitled "Negros e brancos no Carnaval da Velha República."

300. Reis, Liana Maria. "Escravos e abolicionismo na imprensa mineira, 1850–1888." *Estudos Ibero-Americanos* 16, 1–2 (July–December 1990): 287–98.

301. Reis, Liana Maria. "Fugas de escravos e formação do mercado de trabalho livre na província mineira, 1850–1881." *Revista Brasileira de Estudos Políticos* 73 (July 1991): 203–17.

302. *Revista do Instituto de Estudos Brasileiros: edição comemorativa do centenário da abolição da escravatura* 28 (1988). 188 p.

In this commemorative issue of the one hundredth anniversary of abolition, several of the articles are directly relevant to postemancipation studies. Beatriz W. de C. Leite, in "Abolição e política: o debate parlamentar," considers the parliamentary debates on emancipation between

1871 and 1888, and discusses how economic transformations favored abolition. Maria Isaura P. de Queiroz, in "Viajantes, século XIX: negras escravas e livres no Rio de Janeiro," discusses information about slave and free, black and mulatto women in Rio de Janeiro in the nineteenth century until abolition in 1888, as seen through the eyes of foreign travellers. Maria de L. M. Janotti and Suely R. R. de Queiroz, in "Memória da escravidão em famílias negras de São Paulo (projeto de pesquisa)," present an oral history research project that aims to record memories of slavery and postemancipation society. Octavio Ianni, in "Literatura e consciência," discusses how turn-of-the-century black writers are now properly recognized as Afro-Brazilians not only in terms of skin color but also in terms of literary problematics. Teófilo de Queiroz Júnior, in "Abolicionismo, um processo em questão," considers how abolition came as a result of socioeconomic transformations at the national as well as international levels. Yone Soares de Lima, in "A presença do negro na coleção de artes visuais Mário de Andrade," reproduces pieces of art representing blacks, some of which were made before 1930, from the Mario de Andrade Collection at the Instituto de Estudos Brasileiros, São Paulo.

303. Sallum Júnior, Brasilio. *Capitalismo e cafeicultura: Oeste paulista: 1888–1930*. São Paulo: Duas Cidades, 1982. 258 p.

Sociological study of the abolition of slavery and the rise of the *colonato* in the western part of the state of São Paulo. Based on secondary and printed primary sources.

304. Santos Filho, Lycurgo. *Uma comunidade rural do Brasil antigo (Aspectos da vida patriarchal no sertão da Bahia nos séculos XVIII e XIX)*. São Paulo: Companhia Editora Nacional, 1956. 447 p.

Detailed study of rural life in the dry cattle-raising region of Bahia. Based on an extensive collection of family papers, which includes account books, wills, property inventories, and personal memoirs, the study spans 150 years and four generations of ownership of the Fazenda "Campo Sêco." Main emphasis is on the eighteenth century and first half of the nineteenth century. Nevertheless, the author provides glimpses of a later period, as the last male head of household died in 1900. Chapters consider both the social relations (control of "dependents," acquisition of military titles, etc.) and mixed-agricultural endeavors (livestock, cotton, sugar, manioc, etc.) upon which local patriarchs based their influence. Provides additional discussion of the commercial activities which linked the outerlying *sertão* with the important sugar region of the Bahian Recôncavo.

305. Santos, Ana Maria dos and Sonia Regina de Mendonça. "Representações sobre o trabalho livre na crise do escravismo fluminense, 1870–1903." *Revista Brasileira de História* 6 (Sept. 1985/Feb. 1986): 85–98.

Analyzes the "discourse of decadence" employed in discussions of emancipation and labor systems by representatives from Rio, who, before abolition, sometimes supported radical economic reforms such as division of large landed property and creation of a landed immigrant working class. As abolition approached, this solution to agricultural crisis slowly gave way to conservative proposals, such as formation of rural police and laws against vagrancy. Author uses proceedings of the provincial assembly and debates in agricultural congresses.

306. Santos, Corcino Medeiros dos. "O trabalho nas frentes pioneiras." *Anais do VI Simpósio Nacional dos Professores Universitários de História* 6 (1973): 787–819.

Relies on secondary sources to trace the settlement of the far western frontier of São Paulo in the late nineteenth and early twentieth centuries. Traces three waves of settlers: an initial group from Minas Gerais who arrived before coffee production was feasible in distant areas; a second group of European and Japanese immigrants, many of whom went to the frontier; and a final wave of immigrants from the Brazilian Northeast. Author notes that the last group served as day laborers—often in clearing the forest or in the cotton harvest—while Europeans (deemed healthier and better trained) served as coffee *colonos*. Concludes with historical sketch of the life of a Japanese farm family who settled in the frontier in 1917 and moved from subsistence farming to coffee production, eventually hiring contract workers of their own.

307. Santos, Ronaldo Marcos dos. *Resistência e superação do escravismo na Província de São Paulo*. São Paulo: Instituto de Pesquisas Econômicas, 1980. 142 p.

History of the final abolition of slavery in São Paulo with a focus on the changing character of slave resistance. Based mainly on newspapers and police records located in the Arquivo do Estado de São Paulo.

308. Santos, Sydney M. G. dos. *André Rebouças e seu tempo*. Rio de Janeiro, 1985. 580 p.

Biography of black abolitionist André Rebouças from his birth in 1838 to his death in 1898. Compares Rebouças's writings on the role of former slaves in postemancipation society to the writings of Joaquim Nabuco and Louis Couty on the same subject.

309. Schwarcz, Lilia Moritz. *Retrato em branco e negro: jornais, escravos e cidadãos em São Paulo no final do século XIX*. São Paulo: Companhia das Letras, 1987. 284 p.

A study of representations of Afro-Brazilians in the press before and after emancipation in nineteenth-century São Paulo. Discusses news on slave crimes and flights as well as abolitionist propaganda and literary pieces. Analyzes racial stereotypes and how they changed over time.

310. Schwarcz, Lilia Moritz. *O espetáculo das raças: cientistas, instituções e questão racial no Brasil, 1870–1930*. São Paulo: Companhia das Letras, 1993. 287 p.

History of racial ideology explores how Brazilian intellectuals, working within specific institutional contexts, developed the ideas of Social Darwinism and evolutionism into new notions of race. Schwarcz examines the racial discourses generated in ethnographic museums, institutes of history and geography, and faculties of law and of medicine, drawing on institutional archives and publications. Published in English as Lilia Moritz Schwarcz, *The Spectacle of the Races: Scientists, Institutions, and the Race Question in Brazil, 1870–1930* (New York: Hill and Wang, 1999).

311. Scott, Rebecca J. "Defining the Boundaries of Freedom in the World of Cane: Cuba, Brazil, and Louisiana after Emancipation." *The American Historical Review* 99 (February 1994): 70–102.

Section on Brazil focuses on the Northeast, emphasizing the incompleteness of the transition to wage labor and the importance of choices made by former slaves and other rural workers.

312. Scott, Rebecca J., Seymour Drescher, Hebe Maria Mattos de Castro, George Reid Andrews, Robert M. Levine, contributors. *The Abolition of Slavery and the Aftermath of Emancipation in Brazil*. Durham: Duke University Press, 1988. 173 p.

A collection of essays originally published in vol. 68 (August 1988) of the *Hispanic American Historical Review*. Includes Scott, "Exploring the Meaning of Freedom: Postemancipation Societies in Comparative Perspective," which provides theoretical overview and comments on other essays; Drescher, "Brazilian Abolition in Comparative Perspective," which places Brazil in context of Anglo-American and continental patterns of abolition; Mattos, "Beyond Masters and Slaves: Subsistence Agriculture as Survival Strategy in Brazil during the Second Half of the Nineteenth Century," which uses notarial records to develop portrait of municipality in province of Rio; Andrews, "Black and White Workers: São Paulo, Brazil, 1888–1928," which examines patterns of Afro-Brazilian incorporation in the urban work force; and Levine, "'Mud-Hut Jerusalem': Canudos Revisited," which examines perceptions and reality of movement in Northeastern Brazil led by Antônio Conselheiro.

313. Silva, Katia Maria de Carvalho. *O Diário da Bahia e o século xix*. Rio de Janeiro: Edições Tempo Brasileiro, 1979. 258 p.

History of the Bahian newspaper from 1856 to 1899. Chapter 4, which details the newspaper's evolving content, is helpful both as a source of brief citations and as a guide to further research in the *Diário*. Sections cited include editorials, news articles, readers' letters (which were published for a fee), and advertisements. From 1868 to 1899 the paper served as the organ of the Partido Liberal, vigorously advocating electoral reform and abolition. Coverage from 1889 to 1899 centered on political conflict, upheaval in the Sertão, and Canudos. Also appearing in the 1890s are notices of Afro-Brazilian religious festivals and debates over public health issues.

314. Silva, Leonardo Dantas, ed. *A abolição em Pernambuco*. Recife: Fundação Joaquim Nabuco, Editora Massangana, 1988. 131 p.

Reprints articles and documents related to abolition in Pernambuco including F. A. Pereira da Costa, "A idéia abolicionista em Pernambuco," an intellectual history of abolitionism originally published in 1891 in the *Revista do Instituto Arqueológico Histórico e Geográfico Pernambucano*, and from the same issue, "Documentos relativos à prioridade de Pernambuco na questão da emancipação dos escravos," a collection of three documents related to manumission and abolition of slave trade from the early nineteenth century. Also reprints historical essay by Coriolano de Medeiros entitled "O movimento da abolição no Nordeste," originally published in *O livro do Nordeste* in 1925. Concludes with a reprint, facsimile edition of a catalog for a 1938 exhibition of artifacts, official documents, photographs, and correspondence related to abolition in Pernambuco entitled "Cinqüentenário da abolição em Pernambuco. Catálogo da exposição realizada no Teatro de Santa Isabel de 13 a 31 de maio de 1938."

315. Skidmore, Thomas. *Black into White: Race and Nationality in Brazilian Thought*. New York: Oxford University Press, 1974. 299 p.

Classic early work on nationalism and racial ideology.

316. Slenes, Robert W. "The Demography and Economics of Brazilian Slavery, 1850–1888." Ph.D. Diss., Stanford University, 1976. 728 p.

Includes a study of internal slave trade in Brazil and makes important revisions to commonly-accepted population statistics.

317. Slenes, Robert W. *Na senzala, uma flor: esperanças e recordações na formação da família escrava, Brasil Sudeste, século XIX*. Rio de Janeiro: Nova Fronteira, 1999. 299 p.

Collection of essays on the slave family, focusing mainly on the Southeast and Campinas. Topics include the demography of the slave family, African cultural influences, and architecture. Sources include baptismal records, postmortem inventories, and travelers' accounts.

318. Soares, Carlos Eugênio Líbano. *A negregada instituição: os capoeiras no Rio de Janeiro*. Rio de Janeiro: Secretaria Municipal de Cultura, Departamento Geral de Documentação e Informação Cultural, 1994. 335 p.

History of *capoeira*—an Afro-Brazilian ritual martial art—in the city of Rio de Janeiro in the nineteenth century. Based on records including governmental reports, judicial and police records, newspapers, and records of the Casa de Detenção da Corte. Discusses organization of *capoeiras* into groups or *maltas*, the division of the city into areas dominated by different *maltas*, the ritualization of conflict, and changes in the social composition of *maltas*, whose ranks included slaves, free people, and immigrants. Analyzes role of *capoeiras* in political events of the second half of nineteenth century, including passage of the Free Womb Law, struggles over abolition in the 1880s, and party politics. Examines governmental attempts at suppression, especially during the early Republic.

319. Souza Barros. *A década 20 em Pernambuco*. 2nd ed. Recife: Fundação de Cultura/Cidade do Recife, 1985. 318 p.

Political and economic history of Pernambuco in the 1920s by Manuel de Souza Barros, a writer and political activist who participated in many of the events described. Topics addressed include the history of the sugar industry in the late nineteenth and early twentieth centuries, workers' movements, the political activity of Gilberto Freyre, the Prestes Column, and the "Cleto Campelo" movement.

320. Spiller Pena, Eduardo. *Pajens da Casa Imperial: jurisconsultos, escravidão e a lei de 1871*. Campinas: Editora de Unicamp/Centro de Pesquisa em História Social de Cultura, 2001. 393 p.

Focuses on lawyers, jurisprudence, and the role of the Instituto dos Advogados Brasileiros in the unfolding of abolition in Brazil. Author's close reading of the texts and ideology underlying plans for gradual emancipation make this a useful background study for inquiries into slaves' use of various laws, including appeals for the freedom of their children.

321. Spindel, Cheiwa R. *Homens e máquinas na transição de uma economia cafeeira. Formação e uso da força de trabalho no estado de São Paulo.* Rio de Janeiro: Paz e Terra, 1979. 184 p.

Sociological study of labor and relations of production in São Paulo between 1850 and 1930, including the transition from slavery to free labor, the use of immigrant labor, and the creation of a population of urban, industrial workers. Based principally on secondary sources.

322. Stein, Stanley J. *Vassouras: A Brazilian Coffee County, 1850–1890.* New York: Atheneum, 1976. 315 p.

Classic study of slavery and abolition in Vassouras, a coffee-producing municipality in the Parahyba Valley of south-central Brazil. Uses notarial records, inventories, testaments and other municipal records, as well as oral interviews and documentary photographs.

323. Stolcke, Verena. *Coffee Planters, Workers and Wives: Class Conflict and Gender Relations on São Paulo Plantations, 1850–1980.* Houndmills (England): Macmillan Press in association with St Antony's College, Oxford, 1988. 344 p.

Historical ethnography of labor and gender among immigrant workers on coffee plantations in São Paulo.

324. Stolcke, Verena and Michael M. Hall. "The Introduction of Free Labor on São Paulo Coffee Plantations." *The Journal of Peasant Studies* 10 (January/April 1983): 170–200.

325. Sussekind, Flora, and Roberto Ventura. *História e dependência: cultura e sociedade em Manuel Bonfim.* Rio de Janeiro: Moderna, 1984. 248 p.

Interpretive essay on the work of the early twentieth-century Brazilian writer, Manuel Bonfim, and a number of excerpts from his work. Authors assess Bomfim's contribution to Brazilian literature, suggesting that his relative obscurity stems from far-reaching ideas that separated him both from the proponents of scientific racism and those (such as Nina Rodrigues) who took a more anthropological approach to Afro-Brazilian contributions. Contains excerpts from *A América Latina* (1905), *O Brasil na América* (1929), *O Brasil na História* (1930), and *O Brasil nação* (1931).

326. Taunay, Affonso d'Escragnolle. *Pequena história do café no Brasil (1727–1937).* Rio de Janeiro: Departamento Nacional do Café, 1945. 558 p.

Detailed narrative history of two centuries of coffee production in Brazil. Describes planter opulence and life on *fazenda* in last decades of the empire. Chapter 12 addresses the transition from slavery in terms of low productivity of slave labor, a "crisis" occasioned by abolition, and abandonment of the *fazendas* by *libertos.* Chapters on postemancipation decades focus on market fluctuations and planter/government efforts to support prices. Throughout book author cites, and frequently criticizes, other Brazilian and foreign authors' writings on Brazilian coffee.

327. *O Negro e a abolição.* Special issue of *Tempo Brasileiro* 92/93 (January–June 1988). Rio de Janeiro: Tempo Brasileiro, 1988. 194 p.

Issue commemorating centennial of abolition, dedicated to Afro-Brazilian studies. Of importance to postemancipation period are: Domício Proença Filho, "A participação da literatura no processo abolicionista," which discusses how both romantic and realist nineteenth-century abolitionist fiction and poetry saw slaves as unprotected, humble, sometimes noble and loyal, but always dehumanized; Edilberto Coutinho, "Futebol cheio de raça," which discusses the evolution of soccer through the prism of black participation, noting the elitist and racist soccer environment from its introduction in 1895 until at least the 1930's, when professional clubs were created; Paulo Pereira, "Cruz e Souza e a linha de cor," which discusses turn-of-the-century black symbolist poet Cruz e Souza and the issue of African influences in his works. Other items in this issue refer tangentially to postemancipation period.

328. Toplin, Robert Brent. *The Abolition of Slavery in Brazil.* New York: Atheneum, 1972. 291 p.

Political history of abolitionism.

329. *Trabalhos apresentados ao 2° Congresso Afro-Brasileiro (Bahia): o negro no Brasil.* Rio de Janeiro: Civilização Brasileira, 1940.

Proceedings of the second Afro-Brazilian Conference in Bahia, 1937. Among the authors are Melville Herskovits, Edison Carneiro, Jorge Amado, Arthur Ramos and Donald Pierson. The majority of the twenty-three usually short papers discuss different aspects of Afro-Brazilian religion and culture in different regions of Brazil, including an essay on the status of Afro-Brazilian religion in law. There are also papers on race relations in Bahia and on various aspects of preemancipation history. Like the two volumes of proceedings of the first such congress, this volume reflects views about Afro-Brazilians in the 1930's, and includes information on the first decades after emancipation.

330. Trochim, Michael R. "The Brazilian Black Guard: Racial Conflict in Post-Abolition Brazil." *The Americas* 44 (January 1988): 285–300.

History of the "Black Guard," an Afro-Brazilian political organization, focusing on the late 1880s.

331. Turner, Lorenzo D. "Some Contacts of Brazilian Ex-Slaves with Nigeria, West Africa." *Journal of Negro History* 27 (January 1942): 55–67.

Discusses the survival of the Yoruba language, African religious practices, and other cultural phenomena in Bahia made possible by the flow of Afro-Brazilians back and forth between Nigeria and Bahia. Based on interviews author conducted in 1940–41 with ex-slaves and the children of ex-slaves then making their homes in Bahia. Argues that many Bahian families spoke fluent Yoruba well into the twentieth century.

332. Verger, Pierre. *Flux et reflux de la traite des nègres entre le Golfe de Benin et Bahia de Todos os Santos.* Paris: Mouton, 1968. 720 p.

Voluminous history of economic and cultural exchanges between the Bight of Benin in West Africa and Bahia. Emphasizes slave trade and slave traders on both sides of the ocean. Of relevance to the postemancipation period is his discussion of African ex-slaves who returned to Africa in the nineteenth and early twentieth centuries, before and after abolition, and carried with them many aspects of Brazilian culture, including Catholicism, popular feasts, and so on. Based on extensive research in Brazilian and European archives, and author's observations in Africa and Brazil.

333. Vianna, Luiz, Filho. *O negro na Bahia.* Rio de Janeiro: José Olympio, 1946. 167 p.

Classic early study of Afro-Brazilian culture based on extensive research in the city archives of Salvador da Bahia. First half deals with the slave trade, tracing the different ethnic origins of those imported, with special emphasis on the Bantus and Sudanese. Second half describes the cultural adaptations of black people in the city of Salvador and the estates of the Recôncavo. Specific examples drawn from period of slavery alternate with generalizations about contemporary (1940s) Brazilian society. Lauds the mulatto as both symbol and agent of racial integration.

334. Vogt, Carlos, and Peter Fry, with the collaboration of Robert Slenes. *Cafundó: a África no Brasil, linguagem e sociedade*. São Paulo: Editora Schwarcz, 1996. 373 p.

Ethnography of a rural community in São Paulo founded by former slaves. The bulk of the book focuses on the survival and transformation of African linguistic forms among community members. The second chapter, coauthored by Robert Slenes, combines oral history and archival research to reconstruct the relationship between grants of land and grants of freedom to slaves in the final years of slavery and follows the history of land-related struggles in the community through the 1970s. The conclusion reviews the history of the community up to the present. Includes a glossary of words of African origin and their Portuguese equivalents.

335. Weimer, Günter. *O trabalho escravo no Rio Grande do Sul*. Porto Alegre: Editora da Universidade Federal do Rio Grande do Sul and Editora Sagra, 1991. 100 p.

Quantitative study of slave population and occupational structure of slavery in Rio Grande do Sul. Consists mainly of statistics on slave occupations compiled from advertisements for sale, rent, and purchase of slaves published in various newspapers. Much of the information dates from the 1870s and 1880s. Concludes with two appendices. The first reprints three abolitionist texts by Carl von Koseritz. The second concerns the celebration of abolition by white elites in Porto Alegre.

336. Wimberly, Fayette Darcell. "The African *Liberto* and the Bahian Lower Class: Social Integration in Nineteenth-Century Bahia, Brazil, 1870–1900." Ph.D. diss., University of California at Berkeley, 1988.

Examines the integration of freedpeople into Bahian society, with particular attention to the role of religious organizations. Draws on archival evidence from the state and religious archives of Bahia, local archives in the town of Cachoeira, and oral interviews with contemporary leaders of Afro-Brazilian *Candomblés*. Focuses in particular on two towns of the Bahian Recôncavo, Cachoeira and São Felix.